THE LONG SIXTIES

FROM 1960 TO BARACK OBAMA

BY

TOM HAYDEN

PARADIGM PUBLISHERS
Boulder & London

Chapters 22 and 23 are reprinted with permission from *The Nation* (March 24, 2008, and April 23, 2008, respectively).

Published in the United States by Paradigm Publishers, 3360 Mitchell Lane Suite *E*, Boulder, CO 80301 USA.

Paradigm Publishers is the trade name of Birkenkamp & Company, LLC, Dean Birkenkamp, President and Publisher.

Library of Congress Cataloging-in-Publication Data

Hayden, Tom.
  The long sixties : from 1960 to Barack Obama / Tom Hayden.
    p. cm.
  Includes bibliographical references and index.
  ISBN 978-1-59451-739-6 (hardcover : alk. paper)   1. United States—History—1961–1969.   2. United States—History—1969– .   3. United States—Social conditions—1960–1980.   4. United States—Social conditions—1980– .   5. United States—Civilization—20th century.   6. Social movements—United States—History—20th century.   7. Social change—United States—History—20th century.   I. Title.
  E839.H39 2010
  973.92—dc22

                                                                        200902687

Printed and bound in the United States of America on acid-free paper that meets the standards of the American National Standard for Permanence of Paper for Printed Library Materials.

Designed and Typeset by Straight Creek Bookmakers.

13 12 11 10 09   1 2 3 4 5

Contents

7029

Acknowledgments

*A*s we arrive at the fiftieth anniversary of everything that happened in the sixties, I want to thank my research assistant, Emily Walker, for her talent and focus in working on the dateline included in this book, as well as doing research on several chapters. She was preceded by an able graduate student, Rachel DiFranco, who began the effort several years ago. I apologize and take responsibility for any omissions. My intention is to battle amnesia with remembrance as the decades pass. Many of the fiftieth-year milestones will be reported by the media, but the question is, Whose stories will be remembered? Memory is the final battlefield.

I also want to thank Dean Birkenkamp and the good folk at Paradigm Publishers for embracing this book and its companion, *Movements against Machiavellians,* a longer look at our history, to be published by 2011.

As always, I live in the present, with my sweet artist wife, Barbara, and our nine-year-old, Liam. I research, write, teach, and advocate for better policies toward Iraq, Afghanistan, Pakistan, the Middle East, Venezuela, Cuba, and Latin America; toward inner-city youth here at home; and toward our wounded environment. But there is no escaping the sixties for me, and so I feel a permanent responsibility to tell the stories and legacies, not in order to live in the past, but to preserve the living past against the vultures of history.

The sixties were a time of dreaming like no other, when the very contemplating of someone like Barack Obama was a criminal desire in many states and places. His triumph is one of the postsixties generation, but the postsixties grow out of the sixties, not out of thin air. Without the civil rights reforms, without the opening of the Democratic Party after Chicago, without the spirit and tools of participatory democracy, without the experience of the Vietnam generation, there likely would have been no Obama presidency.

When Obama won the Iowa Democratic primary, my thirty-four-year-old son, Troy, had to remind me of something:

> It amazes me that the DNC [types are] supporting Hillaryites' claims that the Iowa caucus is "severely flawed," that too many people's jobs prevented them from attending, blah blah blah. Never mind the fact that record numbers turned out, almost doubling the last election's total. It amazes me that all these talking heads cannot even fathom the idea that perhaps Barack is simply a better, more qualified, more in touch candidate. Why can't they celebrate Barack's definitive victory? Why can't they celebrate the fact that a monumental shift in our nation's identity is occurring? Why can't they celebrate that for the first time in a generation young people stood

up to be heard? I wish, that for one moment, these baby boomers would turn off the arrogant noise in their searching heads and listen. Look and listen to the changing fabric of this country. In the midst of dark times an incredibly beautiful spirit is awakening. A spirit that we were told about by you, our parents. A spirit that so many fought for. It was a dream for you, an idea that you almost attained before it was violently taken away. That dream has matured, it has come full circle, it walks with your children. In fact, this is no longer a dream but an actual happening. I hope you see your self in this new spirit.

He was right. My generational experience, I realized, weighted me with so many memories of death, assassination, and betrayal that I no longer carried the pure spirit of my early twenties, and it would take that spirit once again—including an inevitable dose of naïveté—to achieve the unexpected miracle of Obama's election. It is not that my worries about Obama—that he favored an escalated war in Afghanistan and Pakistan, that he would surround himself with the very people responsible for Wall Street deregulation and military quagmires—were misplaced. But the appearance of a new social movement with the determination to usher in the Obama age surprised and overwhelmed me. Whatever the outcome of his presidency, the Obama generation will be the cradle of social activism in America for the next thirty years.

When Obama won, hundreds of thousands of people rallied joyously in Grant Park, the scene of the bloody confrontation between antiwar forces and the Chicago police forty years before. I sat at home wondering if anyone remembered. A few days later, a letter came from a friend passing along a message from David Axelrod, Obama's campaign manager. It quoted Axelrod as saying it was a "conscious decision" to hold the rally in Grant Park, because they "wanted to do something that would symbolically overcome the damage that had been done to American idealism forty years before—there, in Memphis, and in Los Angeles."

The new president was immediately faced with an economic crisis, one that hardly existed in political debate when his campaign began in 2007, and yet one that made his victory possible. Once in office, he was confronted with two dangers to his tenure: first, the obstinate refusal of the economic oligarchy to accept deep economic and energy reform through government intervention, and second, the lurking possibility of a right-wing populist revolt if his neo-Keynesian approaches failed. As in the thirties, the new president would need a popular movement on the Left to achieve such reforms as the reregulation of Wall Street, universal health care, or bottom-up economic development. No sooner had a social movement elected him than it was time for a new social movement to bring about a new New Deal. Lest his domestic initiatives sink in the quagmires of Iraq, Afghanistan, and Pakistan, a new peace movement must rise as well.

Will that social movement arrive in time? Who can say? In the meantime, what is apparent is that the legacies of the radical thirties will have to be joined with those of the sixties to back a movement for democratic renewal by the Obama generation. We of the sixties are the bridge to the other side, where the future is rising.

Tom Hayden
Los Angeles
February 12, 2009

PART I

The First Sixties, 1955–1965

Movements against Machiavellians

What is important is that the action took place, at a time when everyone judged it to be unthinkable. If it took place, it can happen again.
—Jean-Paul Sartre, 1968[1]

Employers are going to love this generation.... They are going to be easy to handle. There aren't going to be any riots.
—Clark Kerr, president, University of California, 1963[2]

There is a time when the operation of the machine becomes so odious, makes you so sick at heart, that you can't take part; you can't even passively take part, and you've got to put your bodies upon the gears and upon the wheels, upon the levers, upon all the apparatus and you've got to make it stop. And you've got to indicate to the people who run it, to the people who own it, that unless you're free the machine will be prevented from working at all.
—Mario Savio, Berkeley Free Speech Movement, December 2, 1964[3]

I've always felt a curious relationship to the sixties. In a sense, I'm a pure product of that era.
—Barack Obama[4]

*T*HE SIXTIES SHAPED MY CHARACTER PERMANENTLY. It remains a decade that still reverberates in America and around the world. No less an authority than Bill Clinton, a Vietnam draft resister who became president, has written that "if you look back on the sixties and, on balance, you think there was more good than harm, then you're probably a Democrat. If you think there was more harm than good, you're probably a Republican."[5] Our new president, Barack Obama, writes of himself as a "pure product" of the time, though repeatedly asserting a new agenda of the postsixties generation. The truth, this book will argue, is that Obama was created in a classic sixties rebellious act of interracial love; shaped by black theologians from the sixties like Reverend Jeremiah Wright; benefited from the openings to the mainstream created by the sixties; gave his first speech at a student rally against South African apartheid; and was prepared by the sixties to enter a postsixties elite, thereby becoming the first African American president, the first community organizer president, the first to be elected on an antiwar platform, and the first to cite social movements from the bottom up as a primary force in making America a better place. Of course, he is equally postsixties, his very character embodying the era of globalization. How he finesses the contradictions between movements and Machiavellians—his story encompasses both—will shape his presidency and perceptions of the sixties and beyond.

I chose the title *The Long Sixties* to recognize the length of this era over our lives. The term "the long sixties" has floated into academic discourse in the past decade, its origins obscure.[6] The concept is useful in two ways. First, it lengthens the period by locating its proximate origins in the civil rights movement and beat generation of the fifties and its ending with America's defeat in Vietnam and the Watergate scandal that drove President Richard Nixon from office. And second, the concept recognizes that the sixties are with us still, as demonstrated most recently in the personal narratives of the major 2008 presidential candidates. John McCain was a navy pilot who bombed North Vietnam two dozen times before being shot down and imprisoned in Hanoi. Hillary Clinton was an early feminist who shared the values of the 1962 Port Huron Statement (PHS). Barack Obama, born at the time of the 1963 March on Washington, sought validation from a preacher of black liberation theology and was accused during the campaign of "palling" with a former Weathermen founder, William Ayers. As the fiftieth commemoration of everything that occurred in the sixties will be upon us in 2010, it is appropriate that a historic timeline be published as well, for the use of students, historians, and participants in what I call the coming "battle over memory."

This book is a reflection on the sixties told through my experiences looking forward as a participant and later looking backward across the decades. And I will argue that events seemingly long behind us can reverberate in the present as a prologue to the future. For example, as I write these lines in 2008, the wars in Iraq, Afghanistan, and Pakistan contain echoes of Vietnam, Cambodia, and Laos in the sixties. After the first Persian Gulf War, then-president George H. W. Bush exclaimed that America finally had defeated "the Vietnam syndrome." This was a president comparing antiwar sentiment to a mental health condition, fearing that norms of the sixties—against more Vietnams, against policing the world, against an imperial presidency—would become impediments to future wars unless vanquished by a quick and successful battlefield triumph. Few today, however, look back on the long wars in Iraq and beyond with any triumphalism. Instead, the desert wars remind us of the jungle wars before, with superpower occupation fiercely resisted by nationalism and culture, with Lyndon Johnson's passing to Richard Nixon a paranoid syndrome of secrecy, plumbers in the White House, conspiracy indictments, and Phoenix programs, those in turn foreshadowing George Bush's warrantless wiretaps, secret renditions, Guantánamo gulag, and media manipulation by planted military commentators. Including Central America in the toxic mix, we have been suffering from hot wars to secret wars against conspiratorial bogeymen since the ominous showdown between John Kennedy and Fidel Castro at the Bay of Pigs. In coming full circle, we are even reviving the Vietnam era's discredited "Phoenix" assassination program in the long war that began with Iraq.[7]

"But where are the protesters, hippies, blood-soaked radicals?" many will ask. "Aren't those shocking sixties radicals long gone, replaced by a sleek geek generation, the 'microserfs' of Douglas Coupland's novels?" Actually, the evolution of the two generations is more consistent than it appears. The participatory sixties broke the institutional doors open with the vote for eighteen-year-olds, the suspension of the military draft, and the far greater inclusion of people of color and women than ever before. The Internet revolution—participatory democracy on an unprecedented scale—subverted from below many control mechanisms. The "indymedia" explosion was a quantum leap beyond the early reach of the *Berkeley Barb,* the Black Panther newspaper, or the *Village Voice.* MoveOn.org generated $180 million in contributions for liberal peace candidates in 2003–2004 alone, breaking the special-interest money barriers and amassing a budget greater than those of all the peace groups in the past century combined. Michael Moore's *Fahrenheit 9/11* eclipsed all box office records for documentaries. The old counterculture was merging and surging into the contemporary mainstream. A majority of Americans came to feel that Iraq was a "mistake" more rapidly than had the majority during Vietnam, although American casualties had been twenty times greater in the earlier conflict.

Then came Barack Obama, who famously dismissed the sixties as a tiring replay of "old politics," as "the psychodrama of the Baby Boom generation—a tale rooted in old grudges and revenge plots hatched on a handful of college campuses long ago."[8] He added in 2007 that the culture wars that followed the sixties were "so '90s."[9] He then declared the arrival of a new day. In a literal sense, Obama was right. He was five years old in the middle of the sixties. But when he sought civil rights validity, there he was, arm in arm with the old civil rights leaders on the Selma, Alabama, bridge. He sought to position himself as a new centrist between the old extremes of cold war senator Henry "Scoop" Jackson and the "Tom Hayden Democrats,"[10] but legions of sixties people voted and sent checks because of his 2002 speech against the Iraq War. Obama could not shake off the sixties, and the Republicans would not allow him to, especially when his pastor of twenty years, Reverend Jeremiah Wright, was revealed to be a vintage-sixties black liberation theology proponent.

So how do we make sense of the sixties? Though some argue that no single narrative line is possible, and others see only chaos and the melting down of old ways, the sixties already are remembered as an *era* with a distinctive heart and ethos, whether revered or hated. What is therefore necessary, I think, is to define and explain an essence that is intuitively felt by many. This can be done on two levels: the macro (or overview) level of the era as a whole and the micro level through concrete case studies of specific movements.

A Model of Social Change

The story of the sixties I propose to tell is within a larger framework of "movements against Machiavellians," a model I have tried to apply to American history as a whole. In its simplest terms, I can describe the concept in stages. First, a few definitions, beginning with the letter M; thus the M/M model of social change.

(Though gimmicky, I find the repetitive M approach is grasped most widely and easily among my students.)

- *Movements* are mass gatherings of people outside society's institutional structures who assemble for the purpose of righting a moral injury that those institutions refuse or fail to address. Examples of such movements include those for civil rights, women's rights, gay/lesbian rights, the rights of unorganized workers, disabled people, peace movements, and environmental movements. The sixties overall were an expression of the commonalities of all these movements and countercultures. The sixties were a period of more movements than at any time in American history.[11] The 2007–2008 campaign for Barack Obama was a social movement in electoral form, a renewal of sixties energies inside a political system and culture broken open under sixties pressures.
- *Machiavellians* are power technicians, often from corporate legal firms and national security agencies, who represent the institutional hierarchies of business, government, the military, the intelligence agencies, the media, and organized religion.[12] They will differ according to interests, political affiliations, and degrees of enlightenment, but their core objective is to maintain incumbent power by whatever means are available. The Machiavellian code excludes values such as honesty, decency, and democratic accountability where they conflict with the primary ethos of preserving and expanding power. According to archconservative (and passionate opponent of the radical sixties) Harvard professor Harvey Mansfield, Niccolò Machiavelli's *The Prince* is "the first and the best book to argue that politics has and should have its own rules and should not accept rules of any kind or from any source where the object is not to win or prevail over others."[13]

  Read in their entirety, Machiavelli's works are more complex than the axioms associated with his name. The notion that the means justify the end is explained more fully: If the prince wins battles and improves the reputation of the state, his means will be judged honorable because, "in the action of all men, and especially of princes, where there is no court to appeal to, *one looks to the end.*"[14] For another example, the belief attributed to Machiavelli that statesmen should avoid truth and charity because neither quality is the way of the world is formulated more subtly: "A prince, and especially a new prince, cannot observe all those things for which men are held good, since he is often under a necessity, to maintain his state.... He needs to have a spirit disposed to change as the winds of fortune and variations of things command him, and as I said above, not depart from good, when possible, but know how to enter into evil, when forced by necessity."[15] In the hands of Mansfield (or Karl Rove, who passed around copies of *The Prince* to White House staff), a rather rough and robust set of lessons is drawn: "A new morality consistent with the necessity of conquest must be found" or

"The haves of this world cannot quietly inherit what is coming to them; lest they be treated now as they once treated others, they must keep an eye on the have-nots."[16]

- *Machiavellian interest groups* in the sixties period would be typified in the Johnson and Nixon administrations by the military-industrial complex that Dwight Eisenhower had warned about and by the "wise men" who counseled Johnson to disengage from Vietnam. Perhaps the most stunning example of the Machiavellian preoccupation with reputation was contained in an internal Pentagon memo advising that 70 percent of the rationale for Vietnam was "to avoid a humiliating U.S. defeat."[17] Throughout the cold war, the most potent charge in American politics was that a party or candidate "lost" (China, Korea, Vietnam, etc.) and thus weakened the American superpower reputation. Later, the Machiavellians would be represented by the neoconservative faction who largely captured the Bush administration, together with Dick Cheney, and fabricated a pretext for war to a gullible public.

- The overarching and bipartisan consensus on Machiavelli's relevence is summarized in a 2009 book, *Power Rules,* by Leslie Gelb, a longtime eminence of the Council on Foreign Relations. The jacket of Gelb's book reads: "Inspired by Machiavelli's classic *The Prince,* Gelb offers illuminating guidelines on how American power actually works and should be wielded in today's Machiavellian world. Power is still, as in the days of Machiavelli, about pressure and coercion, carrots and sticks.... Reason, values, and understanding are foreplay but not the real thing." (Leslie Gelb, *Power Rules,* New York: HarperCollins, 2009, cover notes)

- Movement and Machiavellian conflicts can be both external and internal, may occur in all arenas, and may coalesce around single issues as well as broader campaigns. In the early sixties, for example, the civil rights movement tried to exploit differences between southern (segregationist) power structures and more liberal national elites. The Kennedys and J. Edgar Hoover both belonged to the Machiavellian caste, but the differences between them ultimately came close to an internal civil war.[18] Nixon believed that he was brought low by conspiratorial eastern elites; as a consequence of this paranoid thinking, he sent campaign operatives to illegally break into the rival Democratic Party's 1972 headquarters, an act that set in motion his own impeachment.

The sixties were dominated by an overarching Machiavellian cold war competition between American and Soviet establishments, a conflict that drove power relationships, budget priorities, and resource allocations on both sides. In the view of the American cold warriors, it was necessary to create clandestine spying, covert military operations, and unsavory alliances with virtually any nation-states or leaders who were anticommunist. In the words of the dean of cold war historians, John

Lewis Gaddis, "*The Cold War transformed American leaders into Machiavellians.*"[19] The newly created CIA was tasked with the powers to undertake "propaganda; economic warfare; preventive direct action, including sabotage, antisabotage, demolition and evacuation measures; subversion against hostile states, including assistance to underground resistance movements, guerrillas and refugee liberation movements, and support of indigenous anticommunist elements in threatened countries of the free world."[20]

According to a National Security Council memorandum at the start of the cold war, these actions were designed so "that if uncovered the U.S. government can plausibly disclaim any responsibility for them."[21] As Gaddis shows, the number of CIA covert operatives rocketed from 302 in 1949 to 2,812 in 1952, with another 3,142 contractors at forty-seven hidden locations overseas.[22] By 2008, the cumulative intelligence budget for the U.S. government was $30–40 billion.

Outside the two cold war power centers, the rest of the world was united by a common threat of nuclear annihilation that could be triggered at any moment by remote, secret, and largely uncontrollable elites. The rest of the world also was unified, and perversely so, by secondary status and dependencies on one camp or the other. *The cold war thus would globalize the sixties experience* and set the stage for prodemocracy, human rights, peace, independence, and spiritual movements that were fundamentally similar across the world despite their national differences.

Did the Media Cause the Sixties?

Another school of thought attributes the global character of the sixties to the new technology and information revolution: "The whole world was watching." The networks vastly accelerated communications and images around the world, enabling a locally based solidarity without significant organizational linkages. The images—particularly that of Earth from the moon—also gave visual focus to a rising global consciousness of interconnectedness. But these media networks were one of the means, not the ends, of the multiple movements across the planet. And they were not transparent networks. Instead of an even playing field, or the interactive relationship favored by Bertolt Brecht in the early days of radio, there were news biases that favored the ownership of the media and a bombardment of advertising that channeled desire into consumption. The great fallacy of Marshall McLuhan's axiom that "the medium is the message," which was embraced especially by the counterculture, was the corollary belief that meaningful images and information could be transmitted without distortion to an audience waiting to be radicalized. It would take the independent media, beginning with the underground press, to redress the balance. The corporate media never saw the sixties coming, and when the sixties arrived, the media, with a few honorable exceptions, transmitted a message of uninviting, unattractive bedlam.[23]

Were There Leftist Conspiracies behind the Sixties?

There were others who advanced conspiracy theories to explain the sudden unrest of the time. Though it seems archaic now, Johnson and Vice President Hubert Humphrey were convinced that the sixties movements were coordinated by Moscow. The CIA junked the conspiracy model in a top-secret 233-page report, "Restless Youth," requested in 1968 by the Johnson White House.[24] The CIA's global survey concluded that "there is no convincing evidence of control, manipulation, sponsorship of student dissidents by any Communist authority.... The dissidents are contemptuous of the neanderthal leaderships entrenched in most national communist parties, including the CP/USA." That was not quite true. For a time, the Cuban, Vietnamese, and Chinese communist parties held a revolutionary allure for the global New Left, but this was more a horizontal affinity between movements rooted in their own indigenous conditions, not a top-down conspiracy directed or funded from a distant center.

The Movement Model

Machiavelli was confounded by one exception to his rules: the figure of Moses, the iconic symbol of many social movements in the West. Moses defied the pharaohs and was credited with leading the slaves out of Egypt, with parting the waters, and with guiding these slaves to the promised land. Moses became an icon for social movements in the sixties for civil rights and farm labor. The problem for Machiavelli was how to account for a movement from the bottom up. But his attempt to categorize the Moses figure as an exception, belonging to another dimension of existence, was tortured and implausible. Thus did social movements enter Machiavellian theory as the critical threat to the prince.

The social movement model begins as mysteriously as Moses; that is, without the forecast of pundits, professors, or even the initial activists themselves. The social movement comes out of "nowhere," as the future no one expected, the child in the bulrushes.[25] Before the dawn, the Machiavellians experience the comfort of complete hegemony over thought, culture, and institutional structures, either through coercion, manipulation, or safety valves of partial participation, or some combination. This was the general perception of conditions in January 1960 from the vantage point of the elites, despite the existence of racial and cultural fissures. Western society was described by sociologists as in a state of "equilibrium" (Talcott Parsons). It was "the end of ideology" (Daniel Bell). The power elite had tranquilized the new middle classes (C. Wright Mills). We lived in a one-dimensional society (Herbert Marcuse).[26] The critical imagination was dead (Mills again). As the leading exponent of "people's history," Howard Zinn, summed up his own experience: "I have gone through, in my life, a number of social movements and I have seen how at the very beginning of these social movements or just before

8

these social movements develop, there didn't seem to be any hope."[27] Or analytic prediction.

New movements arise from prophetic minorities at the margins, culturally, economically, and politically. No one quite knows why four African American students held a sit-in at a segregated lunch counter in a small North Carolina town on February 1, 1960, much less why thousands of our generation soon joined them. Occasional sit-ins, even freedom rides, had been attempted in the decades before, ending in oblivion. No one knows either why an unknown young poet named Allen Ginsberg broke the icy silence with "Howl" or why young Bob Zimmerman decided to hitchhike from Minnesota to New York in search of Woody Guthrie and then, as Bob Dylan, linked the past and present of folk music.

New movements are based not simply on narrow interests or abstract visions, but on moral injuries that compel a moral response. The argument is a complicated one. A "moral injury" is deeply personal enough to elicit resistance from large numbers of people who share an experience of being violated. But it is concrete enough to be actionable. The Gandhian movement in colonial India, like the American Revolution on this continent, began with salt, tea, and taxes. The civil rights movement began at lunch counters and bus stops. The antiwar movement began with draft notices. The farmworker movement began with short-handled hoes. The Free Speech Movement (FSM) began with the right to leaflet. The larger goals of independence or liberation evolved in the consciousness-raising process of a popular struggle.

The original grievances arose from everyday life, allowing the resistance to be carried out by millions of people in their personal milieus. The grievances were not simply the material kind, which could be resolved by slight adjustments to the status quo. To desegregate one lunch counter would begin a tipping process toward the desegregation of larger institutions; to permit student leafleting would legitimize a student voice in decisions; to prohibit the short-handled hoe meant accepting workplace safety regulations. All of these reforms meant recognizing the dignity of the excluded. Deeper than concrete demands was a hunger for human dignity requiring more than hamburgers to fill, a wound that a bandage could not heal. The concrete held the embryo of the deep.

Where do these sentiments come from in the human personality? Perhaps it is a threat to the uniqueness that each of us feels about her- or himself. Perhaps there is an ego dignity that resists annihilation or shaming. Undoubtedly, there are moral legacies that inform us. In my own case, it has been a combination. As the Port Huron Statement declared in 1962, our generation was troubled by the contradiction between ideals we were taught and realities we experienced. We felt these contradictions, or paradoxes, in the form of *insults*—status rankings, bullying, belittling, snubbing, threats, punishments, sheer unfairness—that we either accepted and internalized or questioned, resisted, and, ultimately, defied. I came to think that the well-known Machiavellian concept of divide and conquer began with an insidious division of the self that attempted to make each of us accept inferiority and become too embarrassed to question. Later as organizers, we encountered the same feelings in those we attempted to draw into action, particularly the apathy that arose from feelings of being "unqualified" to participate on equal levels with official authorities. Participatory democracy, then, contained a psychic liberatory dimension, not simply blueprints for citizen action.

New movements at first are met with indifference or hostility by the Machiavellians; these movements are never welcomed. As they gather popular interest, though still at the margins, these *movements pass through transformative moments of crisis* that can trigger either expansion or decline. The first freedom rides through the Deep South were a literal trial by fire. The fierce liberal and media opposition to the first Students for a Democratic Society (SDS) anti-Vietnam demonstration in April 1965 was another example. Both the freedom rides and the 1965 antiwar demonstration were attacked for "aiding America's enemies" in the cold war, yet resonated with enough people to become new poles of attraction.

These transformative moments are sometimes described as "thresholds," when a given body changes from one state to another. Some use complexity theory to describe them as occasions of nonlinear transformation, as when a singular event sets off a dynamic trajectory.[28] In my experience, successful passage across the threshold requires that the action resonate with the sympathies of a sufficiently large public and that the action of the Machiavellians be repugnant to that same audience. A classic example is when police are seen as carrying out overkill against demonstrators for a reasonable cause and the moment leads to increased public support for the cause.

New movements, if they are to grow, must awaken and resonate with histori-cal memories in the wider population. The "newness," as the Transcendentalists labeled their new consciousness, must be related to a shared history or collective unconsciousness in others. The rise of the nineteenth-century women's rights movement, for example, rested on the same Declaration of Independence from which women were excluded. Malcolm X drew applause when he demanded to know when the Declaration of Independence and right to bear arms would apply to African Americans. The liberation theology movement resurrected the historical Jesus as a social activist against the Roman Empire. The environmental movement awakened an intuitive bond with nature, felt by young John Muir, through the Earth First movement of the twentieth century; that bond echoed the "oceanic feeling" that had so troubled Sigmund Freud.[29] The modern immigrant rights movement similarly appeals to the immigrant memories of other Americans.

New movements develop communities of meaning to enrich their lives during the ups and downs of the long journey. These communities of meaning are countermainstream in nature, resting on narrative stories, legends, folk music, art, writing, religious or spiritual groupings, organic and communal living experiments, even alternative insti-tutions such as credit unions (the United Farm Workers, or UFW, 1965) or freedom schools (Mississippi Summer, 1964), to provide services denied by the oppressive system. Movement activists declare and embody new assertions of identity in phrases such as "Sisterhood is powerful" or "Black is beautiful" or in events such as gay pride parades. In these varied ways, members of movements find it possible to begin *living* what they believe and improving their lives in the here and now.

New movements eventually enter the mainstream when they reach a range of about 25 percent support for their core goals from the general population. At this point, the *Machiavellians are beginning to divide between their own militants and the moderates,* those who still insist on blocking and discrediting the new movement as a threat to the nation (including sponsors of counterintelligence operations) versus those who believe their interests lie in gradual accommodation to core movement demands largely to calm the people, prevent further radicalization, and stabilize the social and economic order.

Some would argue that there are sharp "material" differences within the ruling strata that align certain elites with the movement, differences that the movement in turn should exploit. For example, differences between Northern manufacturers and Southern planters are said to have underlain the conflict that became the Civil War, or the rise of the information-based economy led to a new working class of knowledge workers different in its interests from the old. But the consciousness of social movements is not directly or mechanically caused by these intraclass rivalries. The demand for more leisure time was put forward by early humanistic "Marxists" (including Karl Marx) under conditions of severe industrial capitalism and by "new age" prophets of postindustrial conditions one century later. Social movements have a self-generating, self-determining character. They do not arise and take shape in any mechanical way. As movements turn into institutional parties or interest groups, as the agrarian populists of the nineteenth century did, they can and will articulate sectoral demands, but movement activism is driven by a thirst for such universals as dignity and participation. The recent demands for "green jobs" or a "green economy" are demands that reflect a transition point in the economy, but they are driven by social movements such as environmentalism.

In a parallel process to the Machiavellians, *the movement divides between militants and moderates,* between the pragmatists who hope to reform the worst abuses of the system and the more radicalized elements who have come to believe that the larger system must be confronted or even overthrown. The militant tendency usually subdivides along two paths: The refusal by the Machiavellians to concede on seemingly small and reasonable demands breeds a frustration that ignites a search for deeper answers, or the use of wanton institutional force breeds a rage that becomes violent or tolerant of violence even among otherwise nonviolent persons.

The matter is complex. But generally speaking, when sufficient rage and frustration lead to a perception that all peaceful, legal means have been exhausted, a rise of moral urgency leads to action outside the boundaries of conventional discourse, action that may include peaceful civil disobedience, street fighting, self-defense, deliberate property damage, arson or bombing of symbolic targets, or violence intended to inflict a significant cost. The rule is that when the power of logic fails, the logic of power is the option that remains. Costs are forced on the Machiavellians: costs in symbolic damage, costs in stability, costs in public confidence, costs to their reputation of invincibility, costs if they choose repression, costs if they negotiate with the adversaries with whom they refused to negotiate in the beginning, and so on. But those who engage in militant tactics and rhetoric, especially threats to public order, property damage, or assaults on the powerful, may gain in their leverage (or threat level) but endanger the public support they vitally need. These dynamics account for the frequent pattern in which the cause is carried to completion by the moderates while the revolutionaries who lit the flame become the ash.

When an armed movement retains significant public support, it has passed beyond the stages of a social movement or resistance movement and has become an actual guerrilla movement. The African National Congress (ANC), for example, was launched with a political platform but was soon driven underground, where an armed wing was consolidated. The guerrilla cadre survived decades of warfare, torture, repression, and mass incarceration to enter negotiations and the reorganization of the ANC as an electoral party, resulting in the successful 1994 election of Nelson Mandela.

The moderate and militant tendencies often interact in complementary ways, with the pragmatic bloc enhanced because of elite fear of the more radical elements. Martin Luther King was strengthened in negotiations because of the elite's fear of Malcolm X. At the same time, the radicals often benefit from the broader reach of the moderates within the institutions and among the wavering or uncommitted public. Revolutionaries like the Panthers often found themselves defended by attorneys skilled in making constitutional appeals.

The growth of ideological rigidity, sectarianism, and factions is an inevitable and problematic stage for social movements. As the stakes and personal risks increase, more people crave systemic answers to the question, What am I sacrificing so much of my life for? Ideologies emerge in response, like religious worldviews providing catechisms of complete answers. An ideology purports to name the governing system, describe the contradictions in the system, identify the agents of change that will arise, and even point to the stance and location an individual should take up in order to become an integral part of the revolutionary model. The larger social movement becomes a host for small factions purporting to have these answers. Typically, these factions will fight over the body of the social movement to become the vanguards of their revolution, killing the autonomy and spontaneity of the movement in the process.

But history has demonstrated the failure of many scientific and ideological claims.

Communist revolution was supposed to occur in Germany, not Russia, but then the Soviet Union was supposed to be the center of a world revolution, like the Vatican in relation to Catholicism. According to this model, communism was not to break out in Cuba, but it happened anyway. From any Marxist viewpoint, students in an advanced capitalist country like America could not be considered a class, but only a supporting appendage of the working class. African Americans were supposed to see themselves as a black colony, a nation within an imperial mother country, not claimants to equal rights under the American Constitution. Anarchism claimed that the working class could take power without taking power, that the state would become smoke from the barricades. Marxists claimed that the working class could take power only through a vanguard party that then would assist the state in withering away. The lesson is not that these traditions always were wrong, but that their lessons from experience ossified into dogma. The writings of Marx became Marxism. The anarchist experiments became the dogma of anarchism. Like the splits in great religions, the *isms caused schisms.* Social movements, by their nature organic, experimental, and ad hoc, become weakened by these fights among tight-knit ideologically driven sects. Police and intelligence agencies become skilled at manipulating and fueling these internal divisions.

Social change occurs when the short-term interests of the movements and those of moderate Machiavellians coincide. Examples from the sixties include most prominently (1) the 1965 Selma, Alabama, civil rights march creating conditions for Congress to pass and President Johnson to sign a voting rights bill and declare, "We shall overcome"; and (2) the resignations of Johnson (1968) and Nixon (1973) in the face of unprecedented antiwar fury and the advice of leading establishment figures to disengage and step down in order to restore an establishment-driven order. As Henry Kissinger, perhaps the leading modern Machiavellian, noted, "There was a foreign policy consensus then [during the cold war], and its disintegration during Vietnam is one of the great disasters of our history. *You need an establishment.* Society needs it. You can't have all these constant assaults on national policy so that every time you change presidents you end up changing direction."[30]

The same process of convergence among the moderates was evident on the international level. The 1980s policies of détente were designed by the West Germans, the Soviets, and Kissinger partly to stabilize their internal status quos by a domestic version of containment, this time against the threat of radical reformers opposed to their own cold war establishments. The secret 1968 CIA memo on "Restless Youth" pointed out the global character of protests in both power blocs. By 1966, even China was destabilized by the youthful Red Guard phenomenon. Unexpectedly, at least for analysts of totalitarianism, peaceful democratic change would eventually sweep through the Soviet bloc thirty years later, while the more flexible Western powers were able to ride out their domestic challenges more effectively.

Social movements eventually achieve a popular majority consensus favoring the achievement of their original core goals. These moments may take a century, as in the case of women's suffrage, or a shorter time frame, as in the example of Vietnam. Victory for the social movement means a radical reform, not a complete overthrow, of the status quo. Definitions may differ, but I would argue that a reform is "radical" when it eliminates an arrangement of power and privilege long thought to be permanent and necessary for the perpetuation of the state. The key signs that a reform is meaningful, not simply pacifying, are (1) whether an opening is created for an excluded group or class, (2) whether greater power-sharing is a result, (3) whether there are concrete material benefits realized by the protesting movement, and (4) whether lasting and enforceable norms, laws, and regulations are instituted.

As the previously radical reform becomes a norm incorporated into the laws and regulations of the new status quo, however, the popular base of the activist movement declines, leaving the radicals isolated and creating a new professionalized caste of organizers, advocates, and representatives to defend the reform against the rising storm of a countermovement. The primary cause of this decline, according to Richard Flacks, is that most people want to return to their everyday lives enriched by the reform. "Liberation movements begin to lose their intensity as members of the movement find daily space more livable and as the movement achieves some legislative and policy gains in the public arena.... This disposition is what frustrates conscious leftists."[31] From this perspective, Flacks concludes, "movements are part of endlessly repeating historical cycles—mass involvement alternating with mass withdrawal—that reflect the 'system's' ongoing capacity to maintain or restore its equilibrium."[32] This is not, however, a demonstration of the maxim that the more things change, the more they stay the same. The difference is the enlargement of democratic opportunities and benefits to millions of persons who previously lacked them.

The success of the reform relaxes the movement's base while inflaming a countermovement among those recalcitrant Machiavellians who feel displaced by the change. The countermovement may rage dangerously against the reform but generally adopts new Orwellian strategies and tactics to contain and hollow out the reform from within. The long debate over science-based evolution versus Christian creationism in the schools is one example, with the creationists lately demanding "equal treatment" in the schools for both approaches. The battle against abortion rights since *Roe v. Wade* (1973) until recently has focused on defunding clinics, threatening doctors and nurses, and chipping away at the scope of *Roe*. Similarly, sixties-era voting rights laws are subject to continuing cries for "state's rights" against Justice Department monitoring, campaigns to strike felons from the voting rolls, restrictions on voter registration by date and place, and limitations on ballot access around high-propensity Democratic precincts. The steady transformation of New Deal labor laws from their original proworker goals to regulations and procedures favoring employers is another well-known example. In such cases the original purpose of the radical reform is left unchallenged as the countermovement frames its new assaults. The ballot initiatives rescinding affirmative action in state universities, for example, are labeled as "civil rights" measures. The antiunion statutes are called "right-to-work" laws. Measures restricting women's right to choose an abortion are explained as "prolife." When and if these countermeasures threaten the essence of the original reform, the movement can be reignited against the threat, with a broader stratum of support from people who thought the matter was settled.

The rest is a battle over memory, monuments, and museums. Instead of the streets or ballot box, the battle over memory is carried out in the media, in the schools, in public debates over museums, monuments, and memorials. This is the primary battlefield for the sixties generation as we approach the fiftieth anniversary. This is far more than a struggle to retain forgotten facts, arguments, and events. This is not the lost-and-found. Above all, it must be remembered that "forgetting is a key element of the system.... It is a factor of power."[33]

Promoting Amnesia

There are those who, never favoring social movements or reforms in the first place, wish to banish the memories of social movements altogether or discredit them with a false triumphalism. The general approach is to reduce the whole sixties to a blurred story of violence, sex, drugs, and rock-and-roll signifying nothing. This requires a difficult removal of the civil rights, feminist, and farmworker movements from that history, leaving a dismembered sixties remembered as burning buildings and overdosed hippie freaks, a reframing of the decade as turned off, tuned out, and dropped dead.

Indeed, the conservative effort to wrap Vietnam in triumphalism has met with some success. By any measure, the actual Vietnam War was lost in 1975. There arose a public consensus that the whole venture was doomed, a mistake, with lessons for the future extremely challenging to the national security apparatus. Public majorities, for example, began rejecting the imperial notion that America should act as policeman of the world. Many in the military and the conservative/neoconservative political establishment set out to exterminate what they called "the Vietnam syndrome," a medical model denoting weakness. Ronald Reagan deemed Vietnam a "noble cause." *Rambo* movies popularized the idea that the backstabbing press, the Democratic liberals, and the antiwar movement were to blame. Books and articles in military journals began claiming that the 1968 Tet Offensive, which caught the entire American government by surprise, was actually a military victory for the United States.[34] These analyses claimed that Vietnam was a winnable war, that Congress cut off funding before the communists could be defeated, and so on.

It is our internalized myth of superpower status that makes defeat impossible for many Americans to imagine.

So far, however, the conservative/neoconservative revisionists have failed to revive the McCarthy-era repression induced by the fable that China was "lost" because of subversives in the State Department, a staple of right-wing Republican politics for decades.[35] Juries in multiple antiwar conspiracy trials during the sixties rejected the government's case, and the revelations of the Watergate conspiracy simply turned more Americans against the Nixon-Agnew administration.

Managing Memory to Serve the Institutions

Certain journalists, historians, and politicians manage the meaning of history to suit their ends, marginalizing the role of social movements. In this narrative, those who once were scorned for dangerous radicalism become symbols of America's resilient progressive character. Malcolm X becomes a postage stamp. Martin Luther King becomes a hero of conservative moral standards for his words extolling the content of one's character. César Chávez, like King, becomes an example of nonviolence for inner-city youth. Rosa Parks becomes a better angel of our character. Their inclusion in our evolving pantheon of Great Americans is said to be a testimony to our progressive nature, not to the force of social movements that brought them to public notice in the first place. In this version of managed memory, it is the Machiavellians who are credited for great reforms, never the radicals who created the climate making those reforms necessary. In this narrative of history from the top, Abraham Lincoln abolished slavery, Woodrow Wilson passed the suffrage amendment, Franklin Roosevelt caused the New Deal, Dwight Eisenhower and John Kennedy ended Jim Crow, and Lyndon Johnson declared that we would overcome. It is true that enlightened Machiavellians played crucial roles in achieving these reforms under the pressure of movements, but this version of memory becomes a Mount Rushmore sculpturing.

Memory as Movement Legacy

There is another version of history that attempts to transform memory into a legacy for future generations. The paradox is that what is won in real history can be lost in the later telling. When that happens, history is turned upside down. The role of social movements disappears, and reform is credited to the inherent liberalism and exceptionalism of the American political system. Activist generations are born, as I was, in a culture with no memory of progressive forces in history. It is no accident that the fight over memory began with challenges to the dominant curriculum in the schools and colleges in the sixties and continued as the so-called culture wars up to the present, more than forty years later.

The importance of the struggle over memory can be illustrated by the endurance, until the sixties, of the creation myth of the United States itself. All countries promote founding narratives meant to cement long-term loyalties to the nation across time and internal differences. But the American myth has been exceptional in its distorting effects for hundreds of years.[36] The basic story is that brave explorers like Christopher Columbus were the discoverers of the continent, introduced civilization to a savage world, and opened the earliest chapter of progressive globalization. Two hundred years later, our Pilgrim fathers, fleeing persecution and monarchy, created a City on the Hill, fought a revolution against British colonizers, and created a democratic republic as a model for the world.

The grains of truth in this account have been sufficient to feed the hopes of millions, often in social movements, who have aspired to inclusion in the unfolding promises of the Declaration of Independence. What is dangerous is the historic failure to notice that our democracy was created out of a genocide against native people who long before had "discovered" and inhabited the continent. Even today, the term "genocide" is testily disputed by many scholars, teachers, and politicians because of the threat it represents to national legitimacy. If their only concern was sincerely seeking an empirical model of what constitutes genocide—as opposed to terms like "massacres," "ethnic cleansing," or "intentional versus unintentional outcome"—the debate might be worthy of pursuit. But the result is to buttress the creation myth of America as unblemished by anything greater than an "unfortunate chapter" or two (slavery usually is added). That the infant America was born in the blood of rape is too difficult for many Americans to process. Even today it is likely that a majority of (white) Americans harbor a belief that the Indians (and for that matter the African slaves and indigenous Mexicans, Cubans, Puerto Ricans, Filipinos, Hawaiians, and others) are better off having been incorporated into American society.

The sixties were about a fundamental assault on this national creation story and its replacement by a more honest one. Massive pressure, including street riots, was necessary to open the universities and schools to a diversity of long-ignored works by and about women, African Americans, Asian Americans, Latino/as, and gay/lesbian people. Works by environmentalists such as Rachel Carson and Aldo Leopold added the subject of biological diversity to that of cultural diversity. Divinity schools began including women's spirituality, black liberation theology, Native American spirituality, and ecospiritualities in their offerings. It was a profound reshaping of American assumptions and thought, including a crippling blow to the creation myth itself.[37] Deep educational reforms were achieved, along with a wave of new hires of women and minority faculty. (As early as 1974, for example, there were women's studies programs at seventy-eight institutions and two thousand courses on women at five hundred campuses.[38])

Central to these revisions was a new importance for the role of social movements in the "people's history" of America, the title of Howard Zinn's enormously popular book written in the eighties. There was a place in this new hybrid story for *both* native resistance to the occupation of the continent *and* the universal language of the Declaration despite its glaring omissions. The original sin of America was a fact that required recognition and redemption, not cover-up and denial.

In response, a furious countermovement attacked what it described as "political correctness," an inverted argument claiming that the Left was imposing dogmas based on political ideology. Somehow all previous standards were said to be based on timeless and objective definitions of "quality," a test that resulted in an all-white, all-Western canon. The cultural countermovement still continues, despite its failures. Right-wing foundations pump millions into campus programs whose goal is to "restore … the teaching of western culture and a triumphal version of American history."[39]

It should come as no surprise, then, that the history of the sixties is muddled from many directions. A thoughtful centrist such as Tom Brokaw titles the narrative of his interesting book *Boom!*;[40] he thereby reduces the sixties generation to the demeaning demographic terminology of baby boomers. Although it may not have been his intention, *Boom* makes a subliminal association with bombs. The implication is that our generation, having exploded into the world, blew itself up in the end. A *New York Times* article on Obama was titled "Shushing the Baby Boomers."[41] Other attacks on the sixties have been more scurrilous:

- The late Harvard professor Samuel Huntington, who wrote of a "clash of civilizations," warned that the sixties represented an excess of democracy, a "distemper" that threatened national security.[42]
- National security adviser and Columbia professor Zbigniew Brzezinski called 1968 "the death rattle of the historical irrelevants."
- Conservative icon Robert Bork called the PHS "a document of ominous mood and aspiration."
- Journalist Christopher Hitchens compared the Port Huron vision to that of the Unabomber.[43]
- A 2005 controversy at Harvard University included accusations that its president, Lawrence Summers, "meant [to] eradicat[e] the influence of the 1960s."[44] Summers was replaced after he made comments suggesting that women were biologically inferior in the sciences. In 2009, Obama named him a top economic adviser.
- Countless Republican political campaigns, commentators, and authors have blamed the sixties for sexual permissiveness, drug addiction and overdoses, the Vietnam defeat, the rise of gang violence, even support for al-Qaeda.
- Ronald Reagan rose to power, like Richard Nixon had, by attacking the "filthy speech movement" and "radical professors" at Berkeley, with covert assistance from both the CIA and FBI.

Many of these attacks appear to be personally motivated. David Horowitz, for example, was a Trotskyist and Black Panther supporter before seeing the light and joining the Reagan Revolution. Years later he visited me with a promise that my political career would reach the highest levels if I was willing to renounce my sixties past. Dick Cheney and his wife, Lynne Cheney, were graduate students at Madison stepping over the bodies of antiwar protesters. Karl Rove was a campus Young Republicans leader denouncing me, SDS, and the Weathermen. William Bennett, who claims to have dated Janis Joplin, became a leading opponent of political correctness in the Reagan years. William Kristol, Bennett's former chief of staff and editor of the *American Spectator* and the *Weekly Standard,* was a Harvard student in 1972 hailing Nixon's B-52 bombing of Hanoi as "one of the great moments in American history."[45] A full sociogram of antisixties neoconservatives would take many pages, but the point is clear enough: Along with thirties achievements such as social security and labor laws, the sixties are the focus of unrelenting conservative attacks because of the radical reforms of power and privilege generated from below by that decade's social movements.

The list of those achievements is quite striking when we consider the fog of amnesia and distortion that infects most memories of the era. These achievements include the following:

- Voting rights for southern black people and eighteen- to twenty-one-year-olds, a total of 26 million Americans
- The end of the Indochina wars in which at least 2 million people, including fifty-eight thousand Americans, were killed
- The end of the compulsory military draft
- The fall of two presidents
- Added congressional checks on the imperial presidency, the CIA, and the FBI
- Amnesty for fifty thousand draft evaders in Canada
- Normalized relations with Vietnam
- The Freedom of Information Act
- The Media Fairness Doctrine
- The 1973 *Roe v. Wade* decision
- Tougher environmental, consumer, and health and safety laws than any passed since
- Reform of presidential primary and delegate selection rules
- Union rights for public-sector employees
- The first collective bargaining rights for farmworkers
- Fundamental reform of school and university curricula
- Freedom of sexual desire and a decline of censorship
- Expanded participatory rights for many marginalized minorities, from college students to disabled Americans

Time wears on reform, especially after four decades of pounding by the rejectionists. The tendency to forget is an accomplice of the countermovement. So is the complacency of former radicals and reformers now in their twilight period. Reforms themselves do not stand simply like trees in the wind; they need constant amendment and perfecting.

On the whole, the sixties reforms seem all the more impressive given the wear and tear. The prospect of losing these gains would be disturbing to many nonpolitical Americans, given the deep planting of these gains in the patterns of everyday life. That life is constructed to an invisible degree on the sacrifices and achievements of radicals long departed.

It is also a heavy truth that these reforms were not enough to stop the momentum of repression still contained in a system that seeks pervasive control over lives and resources. Fifty years after the Summer of Love, for example, our authorities arrested nearly nine hundred thousand Americans in 2008 for marijuana violations. The American standard of living has little improved since 1973, with more family members working longer hours for less share of the pie. Abroad, the wars in Iraq, Afghanistan, Pakistan, Colombia, and the Philippines continue unabated, with others on the near horizon. In fact, top military strategists write of a long war that will require military commanders "not just to dominate land operations, but to change entire societies."[46] Those "entire societies" lie in the poorer regions of the globe, where U.S. foreign aid in 2008 was significantly less than in 1960.

America thus remains deeply divided over the meaning of events long ago. The difference is the existence of the living legacy of the sixties as a stubborn obstacle to turning back. But what appears as progress from the standard of 1960 seems at best to be nostalgia-filled compromise to many of those growing up in more recent decades. The Long Sixties are not over at fifty.

I

Dawn

It is the great weakness of revolutionaries brought up in any of the versions derived from classical Marxism that they tend to think of revolutions as occurring under conditions that can be specified in advance, as things which can be, at least in outline, foreseen, planned and organized. But in practice this is not so.... Most of the great revolutions ... have begun as "happenings" rather than as planned productions.[1]
—Eric Hobsbawm

MACHIAVELLIANS CAUSE MOVEMENTS. The power ripens the seed of the other. For example, by the eve of the American Revolution, the British had "lost the opportunity to prevent or abort insurgency by failing to engage in pre-emptive reforms or other actions which would have reinforced their legitimacy while undercutting that of the dissidents."[2]

So it was for a complacent American establishment in January 1960. There were few signs of coming revolution in those winter days. A presidential campaign lay ahead. The governor of Georgia promised to cut off funding for any college that integrated its student body. A handful of students in Ann Arbor met to discuss forming a group called Students for a Democratic Society. Something was coming, but no one could see what it was.

Four black students at North Carolina A&T, in Greensboro—David Richmond, Ezell Blair, Franklin McCain, and Joseph McNeil—sat in their rooms discussing what to do about a racism that foreclosed their future possibilities.[3] They wondered why the older generation—their parents, professors, and preachers—had settled for decades of second-class existence. One of them had heard the term "sit-in" from a relative, and driven by a youthful urge to do something, the four began to consider "sitting in" at the segregated Woolworth's lunch counter downtown, across the railroad tracks. They had no idea they were launching the sixties.

The beginning of a social movement is virtually impossible to predict or discern. Memories and legacies play a part. There is never really one isolated moment. As Charles Payne points out, decades of unpublicized protests, community organizing, and storytelling preceded and fertilized the birth of the decade.[4] In the words of Jacquelyn Dowd Hall, "the long civil rights movement" came before.[5] Indeed, there were many precursors, tremors of the sixties, just outside the mainstream. In retrospect, however, it was hard to understand how so many missed the simmering fifties:

- The cold war division of the world was breaking up, despite successful U.S. coups in Guatemala and Iran. The Vietminh defeated the French empire at Dien Bien Phu on May 7, 1954; the Algerian revolution broke out in November of the same year; and shortly after, in April 1955, thirty-four Asian and African nations met in Bandung to form a nonaligned bloc.
- Twenty-four African nations became independent through revolution or decolonization, seventeen of them in 1960 alone.
- Partly in response to cold war pressure, the U.S. Supreme Court issued unprecedented desegregation orders. On May 3, 1954, in *Hernandez v. Texas,* the Court desegregated an all-white jury system, extending constitutional protections to Mexican Americans for the first time.[6] On May 17, the Court ordered school desegregation in *Brown v. Board of Education.* The forcible desegregation of the Little Rock, Arkansas, schools was accomplished in September 1957 by order of President Dwight Eisenhower, who sent the 101st Airborne to make his wishes clear.
- Fourteen-year-old Emmett Till was beaten, shot, and drowned in Mississippi's Tallahatchie River with a seventy-five-pound cotton gin fan tied to his neck on August 28, 1955, after allegedly making overtures to a white woman in a country store. Although hundreds of black men had been lynched and drowned during previous decades, the Till case sparked a worldwide campaign for justice.
- Rosa Parks ignited a three-year bus boycott in Montgomery, Alabama, on December 1, 1955, by being arrested for refusing to give up her seat to a white passenger. The young Reverend Dr. Martin Luther King, a recent arrival in Montgomery, was chosen to lead the boycott.
- The beat generation was born when poet Allen Ginsberg, on peyote, imagining the Francis Drake Hotel as the Phoenician god Moloch, a demon who destroys human souls, wrote *Howl,* which was published (and censored)

in 1955. Norman Mailer wrote his essay extolling "The White Negro" in 1957. Bearded Cuban revolutionaries arrived in Havana in 1959.

On the other side of the color line, I was living in the isolated whiteness of the first suburbs north of Detroit. Third World revolution and southern school desegregation were far away, but there were cracks appearing. The contradictions were hard to miss. To our adolescent minds, it was completely absurd that crawling under a school desk could protect against an atomic bomb. We read Albert Camus on existential resistance and devoured comic books when they were banned in Detroit by the Committee for Decent Literature. We created a high school underground newspaper called *The Daily Smirker*, inspired by *Mad* magazine (which called itself a magazine to avoid the comic book censor). J. Edgar Hoover was calling us the most lost of the many "lost generations" he had been surveilling. We began to wonder why our town was all white, suspecting secret racial covenants (we were correct).[7] In this atmosphere of apparent nothingness, the beat generation exploded, with *Howl* in 1955, James Dean's *Rebel without a Cause* in 1955, Elvis Presley's "Heartbreak Hotel" in 1956, and Jack Kerouac's *On the Road* in 1957, my senior year in high school. For many of us, the search for a way out, for a meaningful life, would find release in the book stores, coffee shops, and bars where blues and jazz were heard, and soon there appeared role models among young people in the South.

Looking at the Greensboro sit-in years later, Pulitzer Prize–winning historian Taylor Branch wrote of this first "spontaneous and open-ended" sit-in:

> *No one had time to wonder why the Greensboro sit-in was so different.* In the previous three years, similar demonstrations had occurred in at least sixteen other cities. Few of them had made the news, all faded quickly from public notice, and none had the slightest catalytic effect anywhere else. By contrast, Greensboro helped define the new decade. Almost certainly, the lack of planning helped create *the initial euphoria.* Because the four students at Woolworth's *had no plan,* they began with no self-imposed limitations. They defined no tactical goals. They did not train or drill in preparation. They did not dwell on the many forces that might be used against them.... The *surprise* discovery of defensiveness within the segregated white world turned their fear into elation.[8]

Branch's key insights are emphasized: *No one had time ... the initial euphoria ... had no plan ... surprise.* These phrases are signs of the mystery and spontaneity that accompany the birth of social movements.

If one searched the forums of public opinion on the eve of February 1, 1960, there was not the slightest hint of what the next day would bring. On February 2, after the four were arrested, "no word of the sit-in had appeared in the public media."[9] On February 3, there were *eighty* protesting at Greensboro lunch counters, then *four hundred* by the weekend. In a month, thousands were being arrested and jailed in forty southern cities. An Atlanta student named Julian

Bond—a descendant of distinguished educators and, until recently, the national chairman of the National Association for the Advancement of Colored People (NAACP)—circulated a call to action, and in April students from nine states formed the Student Non-Violent Coordinating Committee (SNCC), a catalytic coordinating body of the spreading revolt. In Ann Arbor, I noticed picket lines for the first time, a student boycott of Woolworth's launched by those who soon became Students for a Democratic Society. SNCC, like SDS, would be a bottom-up, catalytic organization based on direct action. It would continue through the life of the student civil rights movement.

This was a spontaneous beginning, but one informed by legacy. The sit-in required a definite leap into the unknown, but it was known that others had gone before. A sit-in had taken place in nearby Durham in 1957; as long before as 1947, Bayard Rustin had been among those arrested in Chapel Hill for refusing to sit in the back of the bus. But as Charles Cobb writes in his indispensable *On the Road to Freedom*, "You simply cannot tell when a spark will light a fire."[10] There was no reason to expect success in Greensboro on that February day, but the four simply refused to settle for the past as their future. Millions in their generation had little idea they felt the same way until the example was set. Soon the sit-ins flowed into freedom rides, challenging not only "liberal" southern cities like Chapel Hill and Nashville, but also the citadels of the Deep South. The bonds formed in southern jails were among the foundations of the new social movement. As Charles Sherrod of SNCC learned in jail: "You get ideas in jail. You talk with other young people you have never seen. Right away we recognize each other. People like yourself, getting out of the past. We're up all night, sharing creativity, planning action. You learn the truth in prison, you learn wholeness. You find out the difference between being dead and alive."[11]

At about the same moment, on March 21, 1960, South African police shot and killed sixty-nine black people peacefully protesting apartheid and interned thirteen thousand more. African National Congress leaders Nelson Mandela, Walter Sisulu, Chief Albert Luthuli, and Duma Nokwe burned their race-based pass cards, and an underground movement was born.[12] Revolutions from Cuba to Vietnam were reshaping the cold war struggle in the global south, and Africa was on fire with independence movements.[13] A pan-African dimension, or spirit, was threaded into the early foundations of the civil rights movement. When the charismatic and democratically elected leader of the former Belgian Congo, Patrice Lumumba, was overthrown and murdered with U.S. and Belgian complicity, demands rose from activists in places such as Harlem for the United States to withdraw from its imperial ventures.[14]

As described in the model in the Introduction, the new movement survived its early moments of trial—the sit-ins and jails, the Alabama and Mississippi freedom rides—and penetrated the national mainstream, starting with a great debate among the parents of the larger black community, who gradually decided to be on the side of their children. A frightened and violent countermovement swept through much of the threatened white community. Northern white liberals became sympathetic, although mainly from a distance. By the summer of 1960, the movement even was becoming a political issue in the contest between John Kennedy and Richard Nixon.

And while thinking we were subjects of history, we were becoming objects of suspicion. I remember attending a National Student Association (NSA) convention in Madison in August 1961 and being thrilled to actually meet the leaders of SNCC, who were flown up to the event as our contemporary heroes. Those contacts changed my life, drawing me from crusading student journalism and toward the crusade itself. At the same conference, the shadowy leadership behind the NSA gathering drew my questioning. Why were the top NSA leaders in the national office older than thirty? Where did they get their funding? It was not yet revealed that the association, a gathering of thousands of young leaders, was funded and controlled in large part by the CIA. The purpose was to cultivate a fresh new generation of reliable anticommunists to compete with Moscow for world opinion. Covert funding came through a CIA conduit, the Foundation for Youth and Student Affairs. According to a CIA memo, "The penetration we have made" even included a secret draft deferment for Allard Lowenstein, a key liberal figure for several decades.[15] At the 1961 convention, I came across a yellow pad left on an officer's desk with a chart of forces arrayed at the convention. On the right was a box identified as "YAF," the Young Americans for Freedom, promoted by ex–CIA official and author William F. Buckley, whose leaders would go on to exercise considerable influence over the Republican Party in subsequent decades. On the left of the page was a box labeled "Haber-Hayden" and perhaps "SDS," I don't recall, which meant the radical activist forces on the campuses. At the top of the chart was a box with the words "control group," referring to a group of NSA operatives managing the convention. Some of them were CIA funded and directed. Years later I confirmed my memory with an e-mail from Mark Furstenberg, one of those student leaders:

> The control group: I was part of it. My most vivid memory of it was one late night meeting (we always met late at night) when a bat flew into the room, and all of us— including the tough guys who later turned out to be CIA agents—ducking under the table to continue our meeting. It's a pity you didn't see that.

> But you were the lefty then, you and Haber. Howard Phillips and Tom Huston on the other side. And we virtuous ones were in the middle, liberal cold warriors, very secure, some of us witting, some not.[16]

The Port Huron Vision of SDS

With rebellion, awareness is born.

—Albert Camus[1]

*T*HE MOVEMENT COORDINATED BY SNCC breathed life into a national student movement for the first time. Although centered on a few campuses—most notably Berkeley—the movement spread through student governments, campus newspapers, and the emerging bohemian subcultures in every campus town. Some efforts directly mirrored SNCC, like the Northern Student Movement, which mobilized students to become active in tutorial programs in the ghettos next to their campuses. The largest of these groups was Students for a Democratic Society, which blossomed in Ann Arbor.

The history of SDS has been a subject of many books, including several of my own. Without repeating those works, I want to describe the role of SDS in the process of social movements. The organization at first was a derivative of the League for Industrial Democracy (LID), a distinctive creature of the older Left, one that had seen more vibrant days. Organized as an advocacy group of the anticommunist labor-Left, the LID once included such influential luminaries as John Dewey, whose writings on education and democracy, summarized in the phrase "learning by doing," were of huge importance to the thinking of the New Left. The concept of participatory democracy, passed on by University of Michigan professor Arnold Kaufman, originated in the works of Dewey. Though Dewey's thought was consistent with democratic socialism as well as populism, his central orientation was that of "progressive pragmatism," a term that was ultimately discredited by its association with the politics of compromise. In its earlier philosophical sense, however, pragmatism contained the seeds of the kind of grassroots community organizing techniques common to the earliest New Left (the same tradition that attracted Barack Obama to Chicago years later).

As 1960 began, the Student League for Industrial Democracy was a handful of students, many of whose parents came from the parent organization's social democratic tradition, the children of organizers in the needle trades, the auto workers, and the New Deal labor reform era. As young people they were excited by the possibilities of the new student activism exploding across the South. Many of them quickly became the backbone of the Woolworth and Kresge boycotts in northern campus towns. They boldly decided to rename, and eventually rebirth, themselves as SDS. In doing so, they were recognizing—without telling the elders—that the notion of a factory-based "industrial democracy" could not be a beacon for middle-class students in Ann Arbor, much less for the young black militants attracted to SNCC. Students for a Democratic Society suggested a broader coming together than simply workers in the manufacturing sector.

Such questions required a heavy rethinking of Left orthodoxies. Was the industrial working class still central to the prospects of socialism? What was the role of organized labor? The Democratic Party? Students as an agency of social change? These were enough questions to endanger this small circle of Ann Arbor students with stagnation. What saved SDS from this fate back then was "the urgency of now," the compelling example of direct action by the southern students. The region was not that distant. As a university senior, I drove with several friends and a carload of food to Fayette County, Tennessee, to aid black sharecroppers who had been driven off their land for trying to vote. In a single weekend, we accomplished our mission, were confronted by an intimidating white sheriff, and were forced out of town by a mob of whites carrying chains and other weapons. Such radicalizing encounters were common, and SNCC speakers on northern campuses told even more vivid stories. We could not think and debate our way out of this crisis; we felt a need to act. And perhaps only by committing ourselves would our thinking be sharpened and crystallized. An insight arose: Experience was the teacher.

But awareness led back to other questions. What was the goal of direct action? If people were risking everything to vote, what was there to vote for? And so in May 1961, SDS sponsored a workshop in North Carolina with SNCC's direct action leaders about the relationship between our new movement and politics. The SNCC people were suspicious, and rightly so, of the tendency of SDS—and northern sympathizers in general—to indulge in theorizing while others braved the front lines. But it became clear over those several days that a national movement would have to drive the Dixiecrats out of the Democratic Party. In fact, it was an inevitability if the black voter registration drives continued to deepen their presence. The questions forced on the movement were extremely practical ones: Who were the northern allies the movement needed in order to succeed? In addition to civil rights and voting rights, what other barriers stood in the way of the full liberation people were seeking?

The dilemmas raised at that North Carolina meeting evolved into the agenda for the founding convention at Port Huron one year later. Sometime between Chapel Hill and Port Huron, the SDS national council asked me to draft a vision and strategy document for the SDS convention. I began drafting notes for the manifesto while briefly in jail in December 1961 for participating in a freedom ride in Albany, Georgia. That it was first drafted in a letter from a cell illustrated, I think, how our ideas were shaped by direct experience rather than the other way around.

The idea of participatory democracy, for example, reflected our newfound sense that history could be shaped from the bottom up and that people risking their lives, jobs, and reputations were entitled to a voice in decisions. We found inspiration in Henry David Thoreau's description of voting as just one form of direct action ("Cast your whole vote, not a strip of paper merely, but your whole influence. [2]") Representative democracy had been tried and found wanting. Only a participatory democracy could hold representatives accountable or replace them at will. We aspired, so to speak, to participation in all things, including our universities, not simply in a brief few minutes in a voting booth.

Besides institutionalized racism, we identified cold war institutions as the main barriers to change. The Dixiecrats not only oppressed southern blacks but also were leading the anticommunist crusade with huge spending for nuclear weapons. As the Port Huron Statement said: "First, the permeating and victimizing fact of human degradation, symbolized by the southern struggle against southern bigotry, compelled most of us from silence to activism. Second, the enclosing fact of the Cold War, symbolized by the presence of the Bomb, brought awareness that we ourselves, and our friends, and millions of abstract 'others' we knew more directly because of our common peril, might die at any time."[3]

The key notion, also elaborated the following year in SDS's "America and the New Era," was that independent social movements would galvanize civil rights and peace activists, a new labor movement, and new liberal political activists into a coalition that would change the Democratic Party.[4] *The pressure of new domestic priorities would force an end to the cold war preoccupation.* In this quest we were heartened by Dwight Eisenhower's farewell warning about the military-industrial complex and John Kennedy's growing opposition to the cold war after the near-catastrophe of the Cuban missile crisis in 1961. We were guided by best sellers such as Michael Harrington's *The Other America* and John Kenneth Galbraith's *The Affluent Society.*[5]

Thus, even though the Port Huron Statement was utopian in aspiration, it was eminently practical on matters of strategy and tactics. Its goals were a range of *radical reforms* midway between a revolution (of some sort) and a mere tinkering with institutions. Future parallels between the cold war and the later global war on terrorism, between anticommunism and antiterrorism, were far beyond the future we could imagine.

⌒ 3 ⌒

New Left versus New Frontier

THE MACHIAVELLIAN STATUS QUO was being pushed toward a sharp realignment in response to the movement. The diehard elements were anchored in the South, where for generations they had enjoyed material privileges and power as the Dixiecrat wing of the Democratic Party. Northern liberal Democrats were being challenged to break the historic compromise with white racism that had lasted since 1877, when Congress made Rutherford B. Hayes president in exchange for the end of Reconstruction. Enlightened pragmatists like the Kennedys tried to woo the southern black vote without antagonizing their white southern allies, a balancing act that would be unsustainable in a few short years. *The fledgling social movement was forcing the political parties to realign and choose new allies.* John Kennedy placed a sympathetic call to the wife of Dr. King late in the election campaign, perhaps attracting sufficient black votes to win the popular majority against Nixon. But that was only the beginning. Strategically, the Democrats began aligning themselves with the political aspirations of the civil rights movement from 1960 through 1965, channeling foundation funding and other resources to black voter registration campaigns and away from militant direct action, calculating that millions of new black voters would make up for defections by traditional white Democrats.[1]

The raging countermovement among whites in the South, however, blocked any dream of a peaceful transition. Again and again, black organizers and activists were arrested, beaten, bombed, lynched, shot, and killed in the first years of the sixties. By credible estimates, seventy black churches were burned to the ground. The result was greater militancy and radicalization within the movement. The Kennedys were threatened by the loss of their control over events at the hands of an independent movement. During the freedom rides, Bobby Kennedy was angered by the freedom riders' impatience and called for a cooling-off period. "This is too much," he said, adding that they were creating "good propaganda for America's enemies"; he even questioned "whether they have the best interest of their country at heart" and noted to a deputy that one of the riders was against the atom bomb.[2] Early in his administration, JFK muttered on private White House tapes about SNCC being "real radicals" and "real sons of bitches."[3] He even initially opposed the concept of the 1963 March on Washington for fear it would antagonize white moderates and conservatives. The Kennedys counted on moderate black leaders to contain the young militants, to little avail. SNCC representative John Lewis, now a congressional insider, was angry enough to ask the 1963 marchers, "Where is *our* party?"—an attack on the national Democrats' integration with the Dixiecrats. James Baldwin was prevented from even speaking at the March.

These attitudes would disappear as the Kennedys were drawn closer to the freedom movement, especially in comparison with the odious southern Democratic diehards. Kennedy officials were beaten up trying to help James Meredith integrate the University of Mississippi in 1962. Kennedy went on national television in 1963 with a moral appeal for civil rights. His original idea for what became the War on Poverty was a moderate version of the designs of SNCC and SDS: "empowering the poor to agitate against the local political structure for institutional reform," according to a biography of the president's brother-in-law, Sargent Shriver.[4] As for the cold war, Kennedy gave an April 10, 1963, speech that tended toward the aspirations of the Port Huron Statement, the writings of peace advocate Norman Cousins, or the activists of Women's Strike for Peace:

> Total war makes no sense in an age when great powers can maintain large and relatively invulnerable nuclear forces and refuse to surrender without resort to those

forces. It makes no sense in an age when a single nuclear weapon contains almost ten times the explosive force delivered by all the allied air forces in the Second World War. It makes no sense in an age when the deadly poisons produced by a nuclear exchange would be carried by wind and water and soil and seed to the far corners of the globe or to generations yet unborn.[5]

I make no claim that JFK was influenced directly by our writings and appeals. He came to these views out of his own experiences with civil rights, Cuba, the Soviet missile crisis, and the extreme hawkishness of his own security advisers. But in those early days there were few walls between the movement, the Kennedy administration, and its liberal allies, such as Walter Reuther. SNCC workers and Dr. King were on the phone to the Justice Department and White House all the time, usually expressing frustration but also requesting direct intervention in local crises.

Here are several small examples of the porousness:

- In October 1960, I helped draft a one-page appeal to Kennedy and his opponent Richard Nixon urging them to explore options in regard to the cold war nuclear arms race. One of the ten points was a proposal for alternatives to military service. As it happened, Kennedy was campaigning in Ann Arbor on October 10 and a member of our tiny group, Dave McCloud, simply approached him in a hallway as he prepared to speak. Kennedy read the letter, placed it in his pocket, and said, "I'll speak to one of your points tonight." An hour later, as I took notes beside him on the Michigan Union steps, Kennedy proposed the Peace Corps. His advisers were mystified. They called Ann Arbor a few days later asking for more details on the proposal.[6] The Peace Corps was one of Kennedy's lasting innovations, even if it became institutionalized in cold war rivalries.
- In mid-1962, Al Haber and I, full of youthful exuberance, met at the White House with Arthur Schlesinger to brief him on the Port Huron Statement and leave a copy for the president. Nothing came of the encounter, but Kennedy was definitely reading the Harrington book on poverty, listening to Galbraith and Cousins on the cold war, and warming to the relationship with King and the civil rights movement.
- These converging paths reached a peak with the August 28 March on Washington for Jobs and Justice. As noted, JFK originally opposed the protest, fearing it would antagonize the Dixiecrats further. In the end, however, the president offered coffee, conversation, and congratulations to the leadership, while two hundred fifty thousand people assembled at the Lincoln memorial. I came joyously from Harlem on a bus crowded with black people. We felt represented at the rally by the radical (for those times) speech by John Lewis. It seemed certain on that magical day that our combined movements—SNCC, SDS, the unions, the traditional civil rights movement, linked somehow to the Kennedy administration—would

unite against racism, poverty, unemployment, and the deadly weight of the arms race. At the time, many in SDS were planning to launch community organizing drives around poverty issues in northern cities, to foster what we (naively) hoped could be an "interracial movement of the poor."

☞ 4 ☜

From the Washington March to the Assassination of JFK

I T IS IMPORTANT TO RECALL THIS CONVERGENCE toward a new majority in America. Movements and Machiavellians had fought their way to common ground. No one could stop us. I was almost twenty-three years old.

But the same crescendo of progress set off a furious backlash. On September 15, two weeks after the Washington march, bombers blew up a Birmingham church, killing four African American children: Addie Mae Collins, Denise Mc-Nair, Carole Robertson, and Cynthia Wesley. On November 22, John Kennedy was murdered in Dallas, and the plates beneath us began to shift. Who killed him and why? The evidence may remain blurred forever—even today, mountains of documents remain classified—but there is a street wisdom that continues to shadow my empirical and objective sorting of the evidence. Street or folk wisdom is a way of telling "stories" that define the orientation of social movements. The stories of Moses and the slaves is one such story, the crucifixion of Jesus another. The stories can mislead people into unprovable theorizing, but the stories also describe something authentic. The stories contain characters who become larger than life, leaders of slave insurrections, martyrs for justice, figures like pharaohs and gods on Olympus.

The murder of John Kennedy became one of those stories. As for the facts, it may always be impossible to reach consensus, despite the overwhelming evidence of a Warren Commission cover-up. There is reasonable doubt that Lee Harvey Oswald was the lone assassin who fired that single bullet. But the street knowledge, shared in part apparently by his grieving brother Robert, contained a suspicion of conspiracy.[1] And because of the sequence of events—Kennedy's growing relationship with the civil rights movement and disaffection from the cold war in the months leading to his death—the impression was cemented that he was killed for what he was coming to believe, for what *we* as a whole already believed.

Social movement theories include little space for political assassinations, much less for lone assassins. In general, these theories pay attention to the flow of contradictions between classes, races, social forces, or in this version, movements against Machiavellians. The interruption of this flow by an assassin(s) is deeply problematic. Can the course of history be altered by the death of a single leader? If assassinations are isolated events like "acts of nature," how is history predictable at all? I suspected, then and now, that two possibilities had to be held open against the competing psychic need for closure. One is that isolated cases of murder can in fact matter, requiring that a sense of tragedy, the absurd, and pure chance be incorporated into explanatory models. Another is that the question of *who benefited* from the assassination has to be explored where the actual empirical evidence is fragmentary. In street wisdom, the question of who benefited often leads to an unsustainable equation: If "they" benefited, "they" must have done it. But if we simply evaluated who gained and who lost from a given assassination, there may be another key to how history works.

The theory would be that social movements, if perceived as threatening enough to take power, set in motion an *atmosphere* that is intense, hysterical, and frequently violent, in which all sorts of countermovements are hatched. In this way, it becomes inevitable that potential assassins will emerge even if there is no organized intelligence unit pulling their strings. If there was enough fear in Dallas that Kennedy was a "nigger lover," that Kennedy was "procommunist," that Kennedy was going after the generals, the oil barons, and the mobsters, such panic could bring forth any number of deranged individuals with guns, needing only a bit of help or luck. Or in the case of Abraham Lincoln's murder, the hate- and violence-filled atmosphere surrounding him could spawn a conspiracy by a group of *some* Confederates who, sensing military defeat, wanted to block the march to Reconstruction by elevating the more conservative Andrew Johnson to the presidency. In the jargon of the intelligence world, then, Lee Harvey Oswald or John Wilkes Booth could be assets of parties unknown, with the origins of their deeds forever obscured.

In the case of John Kennedy, the subsequent murders of Martin Luther King and Robert Kennedy—I would include Malcolm X as well—would inflict a permanent lesson, in the street sense, on the sixties as a whole: *Any real possibility of radical reform, a peaceful transition of power, will be blocked by assassins, whether directed by conspiracy or by reactionary rage.* The project of ending the cold war and addressing poverty and racism through a reformed government was a real possibility save for the unpredictable factor of violent backlash.

For the moment, however, Lyndon Johnson positioned himself as an extension of Kennedy's policies at home and abroad. Perhaps the movement never quite processed Kennedy's death.[2] The movement mainly continued its work, forced to assume that nothing much had changed in the transition. We know now that everything had changed; the war in Vietnam would eclipse the War on Poverty.

⌒ 5 ⌒

The Mississippi Freedom
Democrats' Challenge

*T*HE INHERENT TENSIONS BETWEEN the social movements and the Machiavellians came to a boil in 1964–1965, at first over Mississippi and then over Vietnam. The southern voter registration campaigns led to a unique movement perspective on electoral politics. Consistent with the blend of direct action and community organizing, the civil rights workers conceived of a plan to pressure northern Democratic liberals to phase out their immoral coalition with the Dixiecrats or lose the emerging black vote. First, SNCC and the Congress of Federated Organizations recruited hundreds of northern white students to join Mississippi Summer,[1] deploying them as organizers in Black Belt communities such as McComb, Ruleville, Itta Bena—something like five hundred Daniels in the lion's den.[2] The premise was that the risks being taken by the volunteers would cause greater engagement by their families, the media, and many other northern liberals. Almost immediately, three volunteers—Andy Goodman, James Chaney, and Mickey Schwerner—were kidnapped from their car in Neshoba County, tortured, shot, and buried in a swamp.[3] J. Edgar Hoover joined the Mississippi establishment in scoffing at the disappearances ("These three might have gotten rather fresh," he strangely remarked).[4] But the Mississippi Freedom Summer project went forward, and many northern liberals were galvanized to defend the right to vote, with their own children on the front lines.

These new ripples in the mainstream would support a second strategy: to build a Mississippi Freedom Democratic Party (MFDP) as the political arm of the voter registration drives. Poring over the details of state and national party rules, the local organizers succeeded in creating a grassroots party consistent with the integrationist principles of the national Democratic Party and sharply different from the all-white Mississippi delegation to the party's national convention. The idea was to build a movement from below, starting with challenging the seating of the racists at the upcoming Democratic National Convention. The outside-inside MFDP project may have been the most brilliant organizational achievement of the sixties movement. If successful, it could have realigned the national party at a moment in 1964 when Lyndon Johnson was still capable of winning a November election against Barry Goldwater. Within two years the moment was lost, the movement was hopelessly fragmented, and the Vietnam War began.

The MFDP was a singular innovation in the long history of how party reformers and independent third parties related to the two-party system. Unlike most other Western democracies, the American political system is inhospitable to third parties. The two-party system as a whole works as a shock absorber against insurgencies of all kinds. Those I have called the moderate Machiavellians seek to channel reforms through the two-party system. Party rules and voting laws also channel voter discontent toward the better of two choices ("the lesser evil"), leaving third parties open to the charge of "spoiling" the outcome, as happened to Ralph Nader in 2000. Therefore, many social movement activists choose the pragmatic path of advocacy, lobbying, and support for the most progressive candidates in the Democratic primaries, paying a certain price in the radicalism of their vision and independence of their movements.

Meanwhile, third-party advocates experience long periods of isolation interspersed with moments of brief success wherever the two-party system defaults on a great issue. The nonpartisan nature of most local elections often is advantageous to independent progressive parties, at least briefly. The most significant examples in American history were the populist, socialist, and progressive parties that grew out of the small-farmer, labor, and urban reform movements of 1890–1911. They created lasting impacts on public policy—the direct election of the U.S. Senate being only one—before being absorbed back into the two-party system. The threat of radical third parties, and radical insurgencies within the Democratic Party, had a major influence in shaping the New Deal in the 1930s.[5] In 1967–1968, both Robert Kennedy and Eugene McCarthy would speak of opening channels inside the two-party system when explaining the reasons for their presidential campaigns.

The birth of the MFDP came at a unique moment before the country became polarized over war and race in the late 1960s.[6] The white Democratic Party of Mississippi flaunted its anti–Democratic Party politics with impunity, calling for the "separation of the races in all phases of our society" and demanding that the United States pull out of the United Nations and that the U.S. Supreme Court be purged of liberals.[7] The MFDP, by contrast, rallied twenty-five hundred grassroots people for its August 6 statewide convention in Jackson, hearing from its legal counsel, the national liberal leader Joseph Rauh, that many northern party delegations were pledged to seat the MFDP at the Atlantic City convention. Sympathy for the Mississippi civil rights fighters increased dramatically as the mangled bodies of Chaney, Goodman, and Schwerner were dredged out of an earthen dam in Neshoba County two days earlier, on August 4.

Documents released years later showed that the Johnson White House secretly geared up to prevent the MFDP challenge from reaching the convention floor, where White House officials believed it would pass on northern delegation votes. Johnson was threatened by the prospect of expelling the white Mississippians, claiming that the South would be lost to the (white) Democrats for decades. The Democratic majority first created during the New Deal, and built on a northern alliance with southern segregationists, would collapse before the MFDP challenge. This was all about preserving the institutional status quo, because most analysts believed that Johnson would defeat the extremist Republican Goldwater, at least in that presidential year. As long as the racial crisis was perceived as white supremacists beating pious black people in *southern* towns, the American center-liberal majority would vote for Johnson.

The secret Johnson strategy was two-pronged. First, he recruited leading liberal Democrats such as United Auto Workers (UAW) president Walter Reuther and Hubert Humphrey (both of whom were working for Humphrey to become Johnson's successor, starting with the vice presidency) to pressure and cajole the party liberals into a token compromise, the core of which was to promise two seats to the MFDP, "welcome" delegation members as "honored guests," and create a party commission to integrate all state delegations by the 1968 convention. The compromise fell far short of meeting the demands of the Mississippi movement, which, in the words of Fannie Lou Hamer of Ruleville, Mississippi, "didn't come all this way for no two seats."[8] Hamer, a heroine to all in the movement, became a national icon with her televised testimony in front of the credential committee on the eve of the convention. Whether a more progressive compromise might have been achieved is lost in history. The MFDP position was simply to meet the Machiavellians on their own terms: to seat all members of the rival Mississippi delegations willing to sign a loyalty oath to the national Democratic Party, a proposal put forward by Oregon representative Edith Green. This sent the Machiavellians, driven by Johnson, into overdrive and overreaction.

On the one hand, Johnson was consumed by his vanities, personally ordering summer slacks with longer pockets, complaining that "the crotch, down where your nuts hang, is always a little too tight."[9] On the other hand, he was coping with an enormous matter of state secrecy: how to cover up the American role in instigating the Tonkin Gulf incident, which he used to justify the bombing of North Vietnam and win congressional passage of a resolution authorizing war. Claiming that "we seek no wider war," Johnson was going crazy over a statement by Humphrey that "we have been carrying on some operations in that area" (LBJ: "And that is what we have been doing! ... The damned fool just ought to keep his goddamned big mouth shut on foreign affairs, at least until the election is over").[10]

Simultaneously, he was given news of the killings in Mississippi, a crisis sure to intensify the movement demand for seating of the MFDP.[11] Johnson could have used this case of murder and cover-up to justify the suspension of the (white) Mississippi Democratic Party and its replacement by the MFDP. Instead, he plotted to turn the screws on the civil rights delegation, acting on the advice of a southern senator who told him, "We just cannot take any more civil rights advocates now."[12]

Johnson personally threatened individual Democratic delegates with retribution, demanded that Humphrey and Reuther get their northern Democratic friends in line, and avoid at all costs a roll-call vote, in which Johnson believed the northern states would prevail: "New York and Pennsylvania and California and Ohio and Michigan cannot afford to have it said that they are for the governor of Mississippi ... against the Negroes in their own town, where they've got 20 percent Negroes."[13] This would drive a lasting wedge of bitterness between liberals of an earlier generation, who were abandoning the MFDP and supporting the war in Vietnam, and the new social movements that stood for exactly the reverse priorities.[14]

The White House also infiltrated the MFDP in Atlantic City with thirty FBI agents, using undercover informants, gaining NBC's cooperation in allowing agents to pose as interviewers, and wiretapping Dr. King and the Atlantic City offices of SNCC and the Congress of Racial Equality (CORE). Johnson's operatives included his press secretary at the time, Bill Moyers, whose FBI code name was "Bishop."[15] This was the same FBI whose southern agents enjoyed close relationships with southern law enforcement and whose director scoffed at the disappearance of Chaney, Schwerner, and Goodman; believed Dr. King was under communist influence; and shared LBJ's hostility toward the Kennedys. It was not difficult for SNCC to suspect that in a showdown many of its northern liberal friends would be in coalition with the FBI to preserve existing power arrangements.

The MFDP demobilized and gradually dwindled after its rejection at the 1964 convention, although certain goals of desegregating the Mississippi party, registering the unregistered, electing black representatives, and, of underlying greatest importance, breaking the atmosphere of fear and violence that was so pervasive in Mississippi were achieved very gradually in the following decades. What *might* have happened in 1964 would have been extraordinary, a sudden and radical realignment of the Democratic Party and the national political process from below. What might have occurred without Vietnam would have been nothing less than a second effort at Reconstruction, with flourishing schools, a real War on Poverty, economic development from below, a surge of equal rights for women and minorities. What might have happened would have been a nationwide poor people's movement for empowerment, sparked by Mississippi. (I went to the Atlantic City convention as a community organizer from Newark, one of thirteen northern and Appalachian projects modeled after the SNCC approach.)

What *did* happen was a splintering of the social movements and a rise of the Vietnam shadow. SNCC and SDS would fall apart in three years, sundered by factions and counterintelligence programs. Beginning at the same time, there was a gradual opening of formerly racist police states to peaceful reform. By 1968, two hundred fifty thousand black people were registered to vote in Mississippi, 60 percent of those eligible. A stalwart in the Black Belt, Unita Blackwell became mayor of her town, Mayersville. By the 1990s, there were 825 black elected officials in Mississippi, including 42 in the legislature, more than in any other state. Bennie Thompson, a Jackson MFDP activist in 1964, became a county supervisor, then a member of Congress who now chairs the House Subcommittee on Homeland Security. Nevertheless, the decade of Vietnam casualties and costs, coupled with black rebellions in northern cities, left southern black communities poor and frustrated, while fueling the massive white and Republican backlash that Johnson feared.

Two final points should be clear in looking back. First, the movement, whether beginning in Montgomery in 1955 or Greensboro in 1960, was multiclass in nature, with its center of gravity among the black poor and working classes. It is not fully accurate to argue, as William Julius Williams does, that "low income blacks had little involvement in civil rights politics up to the mid-1960s," which passes over the 1964 MFDP challenge.[16]

Second, in arguing that social movements begin in spontaneity, I do not mean to understate the prior role of community organizing, training workshops, or acts of rebellion that may have been precursors or signs of things to come. Rosa Parks was an organizer. The Montgomery boycott was well organized. But no one could predict when and how the chain of events might begin or where it would lead or the sudden surge of popular determination.

Seeds from the Early Sixties Movements

There were offshoots of the creative energy of the early civil rights movement. By a process of *transference,* like seeds blowing in the wind, other movements branched out. Women from SNCC (and SDS) were instrumental in women's consciousness-raising circles, which led rapidly to the women's liberation movement. Other SNCC organizers were instrumental in the early farmworkers' campaigns and the emergence of the Chicano/a movement in the Southwest. Returnees from Mississippi Summer were in the leadership of the Berkeley Free Speech Movement. The first 1965 national demonstrations against the Vietnam War were chaired and led by activists directly out of Mississippi. When the Black Panther Party (BPP) was formed in 1967, it took its symbol from the Lowndes County, Alabama, political movement organized by SNCC. Within three years, the gay liberation movement was born in the Christopher Street riots; its "gay manifesto," written in the spirit of Port Huron, was authored by a veteran of the civil rights and antipoverty movements, Carl Wittman. These erupting nodes of energy represented the process by which social movements were able to cross-fertilize through networks from below, though lacking an institutional umbrella that might hold such diverse forces together. The core ideas of consciousness-raising, community-based organizing, and participatory democracy were the only glue holding these forces together in the absence of a Democratic Party that instead was marching off to war at just the moment a new governing majority was genuinely possible.

6

The Berkeley Free Speech Movement, 1964–1965

*T*HE PORT HURON STATEMENT, drafted in late 1961, reflected a stirring among students about radical reform of our universities. "The significance," we wrote, "is in the fact that the students are breaking the crust of apathy and overcoming the inner alienation that remain the defining characteristics of American college life."[1]

The Port Huron vision of students causing radical democratic reform of their universities took active form two years later at the University of California (UC) in a huge protest that occurred at the turning point between domestic reform and the war in Vietnam. The Free Speech Movement (FSM) helped sparked a global student movement, led in time to significant campus reform, and deepened the crisis among Democratic liberals, which gave an opening to the Right after the defeat of Goldwater in 1964.

Berkeley students formed the first campus political party, Slate, in 1958, in response to university conditions that were becoming intolerable. Slate translated some of the absurdity of campus life into political terms. None of us could vote. Student life was governed by the in loco parentis doctrine, which meant university monitors served as substitute parents over our personal lives.[2] Student governments could not take stands on "off-campus" political issues like disarmament or segregation. By the time of the sit-ins, student organizations were prohibited from advocating positions or protests that might result in misdemeanors. Hundreds of southern black students were being expelled from high schools and colleges under a version of this doctrine. At Berkeley and other universities, it would mean a prohibition on advocacy of civil rights activism that might include civil disobedience.

In early 1960, Bay Area students, many holding left-wing memories, protested a House Un-American Activities Committee hearing in San Francisco and were clubbed, dragged, and hosed down the building's ornate steps. In the small world of student activism, this was a campus equivalent of Greensboro. J. Edgar Hoover issued a report on an alleged "communist plot" to take over campuses and targeted UC Berkeley as the central hotbed of "pro-Communist" faculty. The university itself was deeply polarized over "loyalty oaths," which had been required of all faculty members since the height of the cold war in 1949.

I hitchhiked from Ann Arbor to Berkeley that summer, a young editor exploring the beginnings of the student movement. After thanking the final driver, who carried me from Salt Lake City to Berkeley's Telegraph Avenue, I had coffee at the Mediterranean, already a famous hangout, and began looking for a place to stay. It happened that a young woman was leafleting at Telegraph and Bancroft, and I stopped to introduce myself as a wandering student editor from Michigan looking for a summer apartment. She quickly responded, introduced me to some friends, and before the day was over I was living in an apartment of student radicals on Hillegass Street. All I remember of the next weeks was a swirl of nonstop meetings, discussions, more meetings, and picket lines. At summer's end I covered the Democratic National Convention in Los Angeles for *The Daily*, then returned to my first meetings with SNCC activists at the NSA convention in Wisconsin. I wrote lengthy pieces for *The Daily* on the "new student movement" I was seeing around me, articles that a University of Michigan vice president, James A. Lewis, found to be incendiary. Calling me into his office, he warned that such incitement could prompt the rise of another Adolf Hitler or Joseph Stalin. At the time, I had not even crossed the line from advocacy to activism. Interviewing Martin Luther King on a picket line at the LA convention did make me question what I was doing with my life, but I was not yet an activist crusader.

By 1964, the campus climate was different, especially in Berkeley. Strong feelings about the civil rights movement, the awakening farmworkers' struggle, and the university's role in developing nuclear weapons raised questions about the purpose of the university itself. A controversy arose when Berkeley students, including a twenty-one-year-old Mario Savio, joined sit-ins against discriminatory hiring at San Francisco's Sheraton Palace Hotel. As a result, the hotel owners agreed to hire more black people in higher-status jobs not only at the Sheraton but also across San Francisco as a whole. In response, many business owners and Republicans started calling for an administrative crackdown on protests launched from the Berkeley campus, in effect advocating prior restraint on free speech.[3] When Savio and others returned from a radicalizing 1964 experience with SNCC's Mississippi Summer Project, the stage was set for confrontation. Pressured by businessmen and the Republican publisher of the *Oakland Tribune*, William Knowland, UC administrators shut down the Bancroft Strip, a campus entrance where student organizations of all sorts handed out leaflets on a regular basis (this was the area where I was leafleted in the summer of 1960). This was both a concrete blow and a moral injury to students' rising expectations at the time. The Free Speech Movement was born.

Two years before, the PHS condemned "social and physical scientists [for] neglecting the liberating heritage of higher learning [to] develop 'human relations' or 'morale-producing' techniques for the corporate economy, while others exercise their intellectual skills to accelerate the arms race."[4] By 1964–1965, the FSM was taking its analysis to a higher level, comparing student life to the software agreement on an IBM punch card, "Do not fold, bend, or mutilate." In the dawning age of the computer, we were programmed to become technicians in the information economy, "microserfs" in the later phrase of Douglas Coupland. Berkeley graduate students sang Beethoven's Ninth Symphony with new words:

> From the tip of San Diego
> To the top of Berkeley's hills
> We have built a mighty factory
> To impart our social skills.
> Social engineering triumph
> Managers of all kinds
> Let us all with drills and homework
> Manufacture human minds.
> Keep the students safe for knowledge
> Keep them loyal, keep them clean
> This is why we have a college
> Hail to the IBM machine![5]

Secretary of Defense Robert McNamara applied this mentality to war games and body counts; Clark Kerr applied it to the new "multiversity." Both liberal Democrats, the two seemed to think that number-crunching and problem-solving were identical, that ideological conflicts could be replaced by scientific management, that politics was nothing more than administration. Students were objects who received their educational inputs and went forth to staff the new bureaucracies, including the Pentagon. Kerr wrote of the university "merg[ing] its activities with industry as never before ... [and of] the professor taking on the characteristic of an entrepreneur.... The two worlds are merging physically and psychologically."[6] This was a modern form of Machiavellianism, the soft variety. Kerr even acknowledged and defended as inevitable one of the primary grievances of all undergraduates: the massive lecture classes in which individual students felt lost and invisible.[7] In this mood, Kerr made his astonishing observation in 1963 about students being "easy to handle."

Suddenly, a united front of student groups protested the arbitrary removal of their tables and literature and began a sit-in on September 30 at Sproul Hall, singing, "We shall overcome." In the three-day confrontation that ensued, hundreds—sometimes thousands—of students surrounded a police car on Sproul Plaza after the arrest of a CORE activist named Jack Weinberg. As politely as possible, often removing their shoes, the students turned the roof of the police car into a speaker's platform for an extended rally. Savio would remember all this as a magical moment.

The California governor at the time was Edmund G. "Pat" Brown, father of future governor Jerry Brown and a strong liberal in the New Deal tradition, first elected in 1958. At Atlantic City that summer, he had helped Lyndon Johnson with pressure tactics to keep the delegates from seating the MFDP.[8] He exemplified the politics of growth, building universities and highways, and was a strong supporter of the Vietnam War. He appointed and protected Clark Kerr with a slight majority of appointees on the UC Board of Regents. Brown's broad coalition included Republicans in the liberal tradition of former governor Earl Warren, as against the fanatic countermovement of the "China Lobby," the John Birch Society, and *Oakland Tribune* publisher William Knowland. Over his shoulder, Brown also worried about the rabid right-wing state superintendent of schools, Max Rafferty; the rising presence of actor Ronald Reagan on the Republican scene; and the constant menace of Richard Nixon, whom Brown had defeated in the 1962 governor's race by two hundred fifty thousand out of 6 million votes. Brown calculated that the most extreme days of the "red scare" were over and that Californians and Americans were comfortably liberal. If he attended to his career properly, Brown thought he might be in line for the presidency.

Now, however, Republicans were pounding the Regents' table for the restoration of law and order in Berkeley and demanding the head of Clark Kerr. So Brown felt obliged to order nine hundred state police to the steps of Sproul Hall. Coercion failed to work, however, and the conflict grew for months, stoking demands for law and order statewide. Polling showed 74 percent public disapproval of the FSM.[9]

After a November occupation of Sproul Hall, and Savio's legendary speech on December 2, the authorities carried out "the largest preventive arrest in the history of the United States," including beating, kicking, and dragging away many bodies of nonviolent student protesters.[10] Twenty thousand students and faculty attended a December 7 convocation in Berkeley's Greek amphitheater, called by Kerr, at which Savio was grabbed by campus police as he attempted to speak. As the weeks progressed, Kerr attempted again and again to break the moderate FSM leaders (some connected to the Democratic Party) from the militants he associated with Savio, but he faced internal differences between the administration and the majority of faculty as well. As a professional mediator, Kerr perceived himself caught between the FSM and the growing conservative countermovement in Sacramento calling for a crackdown. But he also represented that generation of American intellectuals, many of them liberal, who believed in the cold war, supported the Vietnam invasion in 1965, and did not comprehend or identify with their own students. Kerr at one point even compared the FSM to the Ku Klux Klan and white supremacists in the South.[11] He rejected the recommendations of a faculty committee he himself had appointed, because it suggested a more lenient approach to disciplining the student leaders, including Savio.[12]

Nearly eight hundred FSM activists were tried for trespassing and disorderly conduct in a six-week courtroom drama in April 1965, the same month as tens of thousands of American troops were flowing into Vietnam and the first anti-Vietnam protest was occurring in Washington, DC. By then the free speech issue was flowing into a common tributary with Vietnam. Issues of student empowerment and opposition to the draft and war were joined. Serving as a foil against these new student radicals was an Alameda County district attorney, Edwin Meese, who became an intimate of Ronald Reagan, who later appointed Meese attorney general of the United States in 1985. (Another future Reagan official was Alex Sherriffs, a Berkeley vice chancellor who argued vociferously to shut down the Bancroft Strip. Sherriffs became Reagan's education adviser.) The main plank of Reagan's 1966 gubernatorial campaign was to restore law and order at Berkeley against "the beatniks, radicals, and filthy speech advocates."[13] The head of his campaign advisory committee was none other than top Machiavellian John McCone, who left the CIA after four years in April 1965 to join the Reagan team in August 1966.[14] McCone was an ardent cold warrior who came from the air force and defense bureaucracies to chair the Atomic Energy Commission, where he was closely tied to the UC nuclear labs. This leading "wise man" apparently believed it was more important to combat the social movements domestically than to conduct the Vietnam War and secret operations around the world. Teamed with Hoover, the two conspired to block the evolution of the new radicalism that they accused the university of coddling.

Hoover was the earliest to see the opportunity in an alliance with Reagan. A seventeen-year lawsuit by the *San Francisco Chronicle*, settled only in 2002, revealed that Reagan had a "longtime secret relationship with the Bureau" and that Hoover conspired with McCone, then the head of the CIA, to "harass" UC faculty and student protesters. According to the counsel of the legislature's Un-American Activities Committee, Kerr was a communist sympathizer who should be "neutralized in his present job or even removed." As for those suspicious UC faculty and students, seventy-two were listed on a secret FBI "security index" and, in the event of a national emergency, would be rounded up without warrants and held on Angel Island. A close examination showed that twenty-two UC professors were identified by the FBI for having engaged in "illicit love affairs, homosexuality, sexual perversion, excessive drinking or other instances of conduct reflecting mental instability."[15]

When Reagan was elected governor in 1966 as the symbol of the countermovement, Hoover wrote a memorandum saying: "Reagan is obviously determined to take appropriate action to quell the unrest on the Berkeley campus. This presents the Bureau with an opportunity to take positive steps to thwart the ever increasing agitation by subversive elements on the campuses. *Agitators on other campuses take their lead from activities that occur at Berkeley. If agitational activity at Berkeley can be effectively curtailed, this could set up a chain reaction that will result in the curtailment of such activities on other campuses throughout the United States.*"[16]

Like Vietnam on a far bloodier scale, the question about the Berkeley FSM always has been why this had to happen in the first place. Why did the Johnson Democrats choose to bomb North Vietnam and refuse to seat the civil rights delegation from Mississippi in 1964? That fateful decision was followed in Berkeley by the provocation of shutting down the student tables, as if leafleting could be swept off the campus. What did that UC administrator have in mind when he shut down those student organizations? Were such decisions simply inevitable? Were they made because the chill of McCarthyism still hung heavily on the university and country as a whole? Or was it that those like Sherriffs, Knowland, and Hoover were initiating a confrontation that wiser heads could have averted? Was it McCone who saw the importance of crushing campus dissent so that Vietnam and the cold war could proceed uninterrupted?

Who can say? In the chain reaction that followed, no one was able to back down and agree that the Berkeley students plainly were right, that they were being denied liberties that would be protected from prior restraint if they were American citizens living off the campus. Historian Robert Cohen, in describing how the moderates failed to undermine the FSM, correctly writes that the history "underscores how idealism rather than Machiavellianism guided the FSM's founding."[17] At one point, Kerr "was willing to give in, but didn't want to give in to Mario, because that would cause him to lose too much face," according to a faculty ally of the president's.[18] That would have been like serving coffee and hamburgers to the Greensboro students at the lunch counter. To do so would display loss of control and risk sending the countermovement to an incendiary level. The void of liberal leadership, increasing after Kennedy's assassination, seemed to intertwine with the countermovement to plunge the campuses and the country into conflicts that, in hindsight, never were necessary. Seating the MFDP. Avoiding escalation in Vietnam. Launching an antipoverty program at home. Opening space for the blacks, Chicanos, women, and students who were demanding their rights from the streets. These would have been difficult reforms for many Machiavellians to accommodate, but they would have been nothing compared to the storms that ripped through American society after the countermovement led by Reagan stepped into the leadership vacuum.

The Free Speech Movement won its core demand, then lost its energy and declined. The UC faculty voted on December 8, by 824–115, to endorse the FSM demand "that the content of speech or advocacy should not be restricted by the University." The Regents, too, decided eventually to redraw their regulations on speech consistent with "the purview of the First and Fifteenth amendments to the U.S. Constitution." When learning of the academic senate's decision, thousands of students (and faculty, too) wept and danced over their victory, but also over the larger rebuke of the fifties era of witch hunts and Big Brother.

The FSM (and the radical antiwar groups that followed its trail) succeeded in changing cultural norms and institutional practices on the campuses and beyond. Upon succeeding, however, the FSM faded, fragmented, or rechanneled its bountiful energy into other causes. Pragmatists and militants fought for position. Indeed, the newly won freedom sometimes descended into ravings, and the beautiful community into subcultures of burnout and addiction. But the rights to assemble and protest, even to commit civil disobedience, on the Berkeley campus were secured for decades. Campuses across the country dropped most of their restrictions on free speech. Student governments could opine at will on issues beyond the campus, could even pay sizable honoraria to radical speakers. In loco parentis was replaced by a new tolerance for student freedoms, the old faculty dinosaurs replaced by new scholars touched by social movements. Programs in African American, Latino, and Asian American studies were accepted. UC even designed "alternative" campuses, such as Santa Cruz, to purposely channel the student desire for smaller classes and new disciplines, such as women's studies and environmentalism. Angela Davis, once fired for her revolutionary associations, became a tenured author, lecturer, and professor in the UC system.

The vision and program of university reform as proposed in the Port Huron Statement were achieved to a considerable extent. Those who remained restless under these programs of liberal tolerance perhaps were expecting a revolution that was never possible. Even with the backlash and "culture wars" of later decades, these university reforms mostly remain in place. Few wish to go back to the universities in the time before the Free Speech Movement. It would be impossible without provoking another storm.

In 1997, shortly after Mario Savio's early death from heart failure, the university renamed the steps at Sproul Hall, from which FSM rallies had been launched, the Mario Savio steps. A new chancellor, Chang-Lin Tien, sent Savio's widow, Lynn (Hollander), a letter describing him as "a gifted leader whose passionate conviction and eloquence inspired a generation of students across America. His name is forever linked with one of our nation's most cherished freedoms—the right to freedom of expression. We are proud that he was part of the community at the University of California."[19]

Savio was prevented from returning to graduate work at UC, instead teaching as an untenured lecturer at Sonoma State until his death. Meanwhile, the Reagan and Nixon presidencies had risen on a platform of culture wars and law and order that required decades, and a twenty-first-century economic depression, to reverse.

Today, the University of California still allows only one student on its twenty-six-member Board of Regents, the vast majority of whom are Republican contributors. The university still fights to retain control over the nuclear weapons laboratories in Berkeley and Los Alamos. The multiversity's goal of academic capitalism is thriving, with knowledge protected through university patents and administrators negotiating equity deals for the licensing of university technology. The largest organization on the Berkeley campus in 2008 was the student Republican club. UC officials recently spent two years clearing students from the upper reaches of a grove of redwoods it was cutting down for an athletic facility. The students voted for Barack Obama in November 2008.

The Counterculture, 1964–1965

BETWEEN THE 1964 MFDP REJECTION and the 1965 invasion of Vietnam came a breaking point in the decade. The possibilities of reform grew dimmer, the meaning of life more absurd. Those in power, with the acquiescence of an older generation, began to rebuff, dismiss, and alienate the new generation. For us, a generational lifespan could be defined as the difference between 1963's hopeful "Blowing in the Wind" and 1968's "Sympathy for the Devil." In SDS only five years separated the Port Huron generation from the resistance generation. The shift from SNCC to the Black Panther Party, the Brown Berets, the Young Lords, and the Third World Liberation Front at San Francisco State all spanned the same brief period of time.

It is no accident that the so-called counterculture began mushrooming as the space for political opportunities shriveled, appearing to be a mirage. If our elders were clueless, not listening, did not know what was happening, what was the point of meeting them halfway with reasonable demands they would inevitably reject? The distancing became somatic, a revulsion felt in our bodies. Young men's hair grew longer overnight. Bras fell off. The clothing one wore became a badge of separation. Widening the generation gap was the arrival of a drug culture, turning a majority of young people into criminal outlaws in the eyes of the authorities. Marijuana use seemed universal. Then came acid, spiraling out of CIA laboratories and promoted by renowned artists and intellectuals.[1] Along came the other psychedelics: peyote, mescaline, and mushrooms. Presumably by accident, LSD exploded on the streets in early 1965, just as the Vietnam escalation unfolded.

I am not arguing that the CIA dosed the younger generation as a counterinsurgency tool, but there is substantial evidence that LSD was developed and used in CIA covert operations and mind-control programs like MK-ULTRA and that places such as Haight-Ashbury were monitored by the CIA as if it were experimenting with human guinea pigs. It was estimated that 4 million Americans were trying acid by 1965, on average once every three or four months. Counterculture ghettos arose from the Haight to the East Village. Perhaps bohemias are inevitable under any circumstances, and great art is always oppositional, but there was a definite link between the closed rigidity of the dominant culture and the forming of the counterculture. Cultural revolution overtook, competed with, and, it could be argued, weakened the idea of radical political reform.

The counterculture fit the model of movements erupting from the margins to become mainstream a few years later. *Hair* was on Broadway by 1967, the same year that "All You Need Is Love" was reaching a satellite audience of 700 million. Soon professors were predicting the "greening" of all America. Buddhism crossed the ocean. A new spirituality insisted that psychedelics were the gateway to transcendence of the ego. The revolution, some thought, would be blissful evolution, flower children wielding flower power. These feelings were widespread, whether a person was dropping out in the Haight, gardening naked on a commune, escaping the draft by fleeing to Canada, or marching on the Pentagon. The commingling was reflected in the defendants in the Chicago conspiracy trial, where the government chose to prosecute the New Left, the Yippies (Youth International Party), and the Black Panthers all at once and where the defense introduced into evidence an "om" from Allen Ginsberg. Among the high points were the Human Be-In in Golden Gate Park (1966); the Monterey Pop Festival, which replaced progressive folk music with acid rock (1967); and the three-day Woodstock Festival (August 15–18, 1969), where three hundred thousand young people celebrated the rude birth of a new nation. To many, it seemed that the Woodstock Nation would overcome.

This was an acid dream. The counterculture was most robust among a vast cross section of young white people who were isolated from the black, Chicano, and Native American communities they revered at a distance. Although hating Vietnam and joining the occasional mass march, the counterculture was inherently uninterested in door-to-door community organizing or electoral campaigns. This was also a generational fight, pitting the young against their parents. To the extent that it could be said to be revolutionary, the counterculture was in the great tradition of antibourgeois artists and bohemians who defined themselves by flaunting mainstream ways. Its very nature fueled the backlash among "clueless" Americans who could be recruited to calls for law and order. Although the passing of years gave the counterculture more acceptance, even co-optation into consumer culture, the critical period between 1965 and 1972 was one of conservative advantage, with lasting political consequences.

At the height of the counterculture concerts, be-ins, and festivals, a later declassified CIA report optimistically viewed the mass spectacles as "a new political force that would be an alternative to street action for young people."[2] In retrospect, the counterculture definitely depoliticized the movement while escalating the backlash. The new drugs were reminiscent of the distribution of alcohol for Americans Indians, gin for the "gin mills" of Irish and British workers, and Britain's introduction of opium into China. Tolerance of cultural "revolutions" and various forms of spiritual escapism was an old imperial tactic employed to siphon energy away from threatening political movements.[3] The counterculture could be channeled either into counterproductive purposes or into a limited revolution of style, a youth market rather than a youth nation. Although Timothy Leary, encouraged by Marshall McLuhan to advertise "a new and improved accelerated brain," was advising millions of young people to merely turn on, tune in, and drop out, police were cracking down on and infiltrating longhairs everywhere, and politicians such as Ronald Reagan and Richard Nixon, advised by J. Edgar Hoover, were exploiting white middle-class anxieties to win offices from Sacramento to the White House. It was a strategy for a conservative political realignment as drafted by Kevin Phillips, senior adviser to Nixon beginning in 1967.[4]

Whereas the reactionary countermovement had been confined to the racist South in the first years of the sixties, now the backlash came from parents and working-class people in the Democratic suburbs coast to coast. To many in the counterculture, however, the backlash did not matter very much at all, in fact was an outcome that might be desired if the point was to be a prankster, to freak out "straight" society. So Ken Kesey's brilliant 1962 novel *One Flew over the Cuckoo's Nest*, like J. D. Salinger's *Catcher in the Rye*, Paul Goodman's *Growing Up Absurd*, and R. D. Laing's radical critique of psychiatry, virtually turned psychosis into a revolutionary stance, the only rational response to an insane society. Where Rosa Parks had ridden a bus to defy segregation, Kesey, Neal Cassady, and friends painted a bus in psychedelic colors, dubbed it "Furthur," and drove it across America as a "happening." Next came Kool-Aid Acid Tests in public parks, acid-driven celebrations of psychedelic consciousness, and constant "pranking" of mainstream consciousness.[5]

Because the elders had failed us, it seemed, all that was left was for us to fail them. Since politics and persuasion were hopeless, it was time to break on through "the doors of perception" to the other side. Instead of patience, the young flew on acid, then on speed. At the extreme, as brilliant an observer as Norman Mailer would describe a book about Andy Warhol and Edie Sedgwick as "the book of the Sixties that we have been waiting for."[6] Warhol was an avant-garde artist who eschewed politics and Sedgwick a model who died of numerous addictions. She was not alone. The toll of artists dead from overdoses included Brian Epstein (1967), Frankie Lymon (1968), Brian Jones (1969), Janis Joplin (1970), Jimi Hendrix (1970), Alan "Blind Owl" Wilson (1970), Jim Morrison (1971), Billy Murcia (1972), Danny Whitten (1972), Gram Parsons (1973), Nick Drake (1974), Tim Buckley (1975), Phil Ochs (1976), and Keith Moon (1978). My friend and co-conspirator Abbie Hoffman overdosed and died on April 12, 1989. My friend and co-conspirator Rennie Davis, the greatest organizer I ever knew, went to India in 1972 at the height of the Vietnam War and came back transformed into a devout follower of a fourteen-year-old boy-god. As my friend Gary Snyder told me years later, the mixture of drugs with Western individualism and materialism was a destructive brew.[7]

Things would become worse. On August 9, 1969, the Charles Manson commune, with roots in both the Haight and the Southern California dropout scene, massacred the pregnant actress Sharon Tate and four others in her Hollywood Hills home. Both Jerry Rubin and Bernardine Dohrn separately made statements interpreted as sympathetic to Manson. Then on December 6, 1969, the Hells Angels, long courted by many in the counterculture, beat to death a black man, Meredith Hunter, in full view of the Rolling Stones and their fans at an Altamont concert. "If you were forced to select an event that 'ended' the optimistic promise of the Haight-Ashbury era, Altamont would be as good as any," wrote Digger communard Peter Coyote in his autobiography.[8]

I cannot be completely judgmental about those crazy years, however. There was nothing wrong with smoking marijuana in a society of tobacco smokers and alcoholics. There was nothing wrong with sex out of marriage or monogamy, or communal living, or gay/lesbian sex for consenting partners. There was nothing wrong with obscenity. There was nothing wrong with hitchhiking or dropping out, and who in their right mind could complain about heretical poetry? The extremes of destruction do not render the behavior illegitimate. The counterculture was ahead of its time, an extreme response to extremes of conformity. The response to it was a systemic overreaction, sometimes spontaneous and understandable but too often deliberate and political, on the part of society and its Machiavellians. The entire youth revolt was in response to a failure of the elders. It was the elders, after all, who insisted on the straitjacket conformity, the delay and denial of blatant inequalities, the suffocating repression and waning of hope that drove so many of their own children into an alienated search for new identities. The elders' promotion of extreme self-interested individualism, extolled in the novels of Ayn Rand, prompted an opposing quest to drop out and destroy the ego altogether, to be gratefully dead instead of gratefully pacified.

Moreover, it was the government, including both parties, that broke the hearts of the early student movement and went on to traumatize nearly an entire generation with the military draft for an unnecessary and deceitful war that left fifty-eight thousand young Americans dead and millions of Vietnamese, Cambodians, and Laotians dead, wounded, or displaced. It was the establishment that turned away from racial integration, triggering the rise of black power, brown power, separatisms of many sorts, and armed self-defense against out-of-control police and vigilantes. If the Machiavellians of the early sixties had chosen to listen to and act on the pleadings of the young, things would have turned out far differently. But that would have meant tolerating diversity, sharing power with the young from dinner tables to schoolrooms, and with southern blacks, Latino/as, Asians, women, and gays. It would have meant sharing power with an independent Vietnam. All this power-sharing seemed too much, too threatening, out of the question for too many at the time. And so began the radical defiance of the rejected. The New Left turned to resistance, Black Panthers took up the gun, the feminists raged, the counterculture migrated into acid dreams, and the second sixties of "uncivil wars" began.[9]

When the second sixties were winding down in the midseventies, the visible counterculture became a grotesque debacle of its former self. Tim Leary, imprisoned on drug charges in February 1970, escaped a California prison with support from the Weathermen and an underground network called the Brotherhood of Eternal Love, mainly acid distributors out of Orange County. Leary fled to Algeria, where he briefly bonded with the exiled Eldridge Cleaver and a dissident Panther faction, proclaiming a new center of the world revolution. But Cleaver soon turned against Leary, announcing to the counterculture that "your god is dead." Leary split Algeria for Switzerland, where he was relatively safe, before allowing himself to enter Afghanistan, at the time considered a haven for hashish and hippies, where he was captured by federal agents. Back in prison, the FBI pressured Leary to turn evidence against the Weathermen, the agency's prime target. Leary did turn state's evidence against a number of people, including his lawyer Michael Kennedy, whom Leary deemed the "mastermind" of his escape. But the charge against Kennedy came to nothing because prosecutors could never describe Leary as both an acid king and a reliable witness; worse, they would have to reveal the government undercover techniques that were developed by Tom Charles Huston, G. Gordon Liddy, E. Howard Hunt, Charles Colson, and Richard Nixon's plumbers.

Jerry Rubin, Abbie Hoffman, Richard Alpert (later Ram Dass), and a (reluctant) Allen Ginsberg denounced Leary as an informant at a September 18, 1974, press conference. In exchange for cooperating, Leary saw twelve years shaved from his sentence for escape and possession; after serving two years, eight months, he finally was released.

Cleaver returned from exile in Algeria claiming to be a born-again Christian and a patriotic American. Jerry Rubin announced he was a "yuppie" and toured campuses debating Abbie Hoffman. Leary spoke in Berkeley in 1977, announcing his new three-point platform: space migration, a longer life span, and higher intelligence. Cleaver joined him onstage, where Leary declared that "the successful hippies of the last decade are now taking over the country."[10] He may have been an ego-centered madman, but his prophecies were not all wrong. The Clinton era of "successful hippies" would soon begin.

47

Movements and Machiavellians: The Case of Feminism

Just what was this problem that has no name? Sometimes a
woman would say, "I feel empty somehow ... incomplete."
Or she would say, "I feel as if I don't exist."
—Betty Friedan, *The Feminine Mystique* (1963)[11]

By the early 1960s, women were active in protests against strontium 90 hazards in mother's milk, forming Women's Strike for Peace in November 1961 and organizing fifty thousand demonstrators in sixty American cities. In 1962, Rachel Carson's best-selling *Silent Spring* exposed pesticides as a threat to human life and the ecosystem. She was attacked as "hysterical" by producers of DDT and the chemical industry.

By the time Betty Friedan's book became a best seller in 1963, large numbers of women had flooded into the southern civil rights movement and nascent student movement, where they discovered internal barriers based on gender. This would lead to explorations, discussion, defiance, and separations within SNCC and SDS in the years to follow.[12]

By 1964, the newly passed Civil Rights Act included a prohibition on sex discrimination, although the act was mainly intended to address the racial crisis. Furthermore, the Equal Employment Opportunity Commission (EEOC) was created to enforce protections against sex discrimination in hiring, training, and promotion.

The National Organization for Women (NOW) was founded in 1965 at a convention of three hundred women, issuing a bill of rights whose first demand was an equal rights amendment (ERA) to the U.S. Constitution. The other demands were the enforcement of the ban on job discrimination, maternity leave rights, a tax deduction for child care and other home expenses, the creation of child day care centers, equal and "unsegregated" education, equality in job training, and "the right of women to control their reproductive lives."

At the same time, consciousness-raising groups were springing up everywhere among women as a vast, decentralized, networking base of the feminist movement. Designed exclusively for women, these groups liberated women from dependency and transformed "personal" problems into "political" ones. A powerful new identity politics was being claimed.

The split between moderate and more militant directions gained power in the latter half of the sixties, though it was usually defined as the advent of gender and identity politics. Refusing to be objectified in sexual terms, women led by Robin Morgan, the former child star of the TV series *I Remember Mama*, protested the 1968 Miss America Pageant in Atlantic City, an event described as "bra-burning" (although none were). Media-centered techniques designed to shock grew in popularity. The deepening feminist critique defined patriarchy as an oppression similar to racism or capitalism. Soon NOW was being criticized for being only a reformist, not a liberation, movement. More militant groups, such as the New York Radical Women (1967), Redstockings (1969), and WITCH

(Women's International Terrorist Conspiracy from Hell, 1969), took center stage. Lesbians came out of the closet, too, with gay and lesbian groups growing from fifty in 1969 to eight hundred by 1972.[13]

Policy successes came swiftly, despite these divisions.[14] Abortion laws were liberalized in Colorado, North Carolina, and California in 1967. Richard Nixon's Labor Department adopted affirmative action guidelines by 1970. Shirley Chisholm (1968) and Bella Abzug (1971) were elected to Congress. The designation "Ms.," originally the idea of civil rights activist Sheila Michaels, came into use. The ERA was endorsed in both party platforms, passed the Senate in March 1972, and was ratified by twenty-eight states by 1973, one short of the necessary three-fourths, when it stalled. Ms. magazine was launched by Gloria Steinem and others in 1972. The U.S. Supreme Court delivered its decision on Roe v. Wade in January 1973. A community of meaning was flourishing, with feminist bookstores, feminist music, feminist counseling centers all declaring that "sisterhood is powerful." By 1974, there were seventy-eight new women's studies programs and two thousand classes on women, almost none of which had existed ten years before, taught at five hundred universities.[15]

At the 1972 convention, the Democrats adopted rules requiring "affirmative steps" toward greater representation of women, but suddenly encountered deep internal divisions unleashed by the George McGovern campaign. Mostly these were over the Vietnam War and the displacement of the Democrats' old guard, but feminist politics was a core point of contention. From inside and outside the party, a "potent backlash" had begun.[16] From the rightist fringe of the Republican Party came figures such as Phyllis Schlafly claiming that the ERA threatened what she called "family values," including marriage, the nuclear family, contraception, and male privileges generally.[17] By now, J. Edgar Hoover's FBI was conducting heavy surveillance of feminists, with the director himself issuing a memo instructing that "it is absolutely essential that we conduct sufficient investigation to clearly establish the subversive ramifications of the WLM [women's liberation movement] and to develop the potential for violence presented by the various groups connected with this movement as well as any possible threat they represent to the internal security of the United States."[18] The hard-core base of this countermovement was the Deep South, the stronghold of other countermovements for a century.

As early as a Harper's article in 1976, a "requiem for the women's movement" has been repeatedly invoked.[19] The truth was that the feminist movement, like many other social movements, may have been weakened by divisions within and a fierce backlash without, but it demobilized in the wake of successful reform. The benefits may have been distributed unevenly according to racial, class, and geographic divisions. Women continued to be underrepresented in politics and especially in the corporate hierarchy. But the victories proved to be lasting ones, opening space for an unpredictable new feminist wave in the future.

César Chávez and the Chicano Movement

The labor reforms of the New Deal excluded agricultural workers, mainly Mexican immigrants, from the union protections of the 1935 National Labor Relations Act. The exclusion reflected a compromise between northern industrial Democrats and the traditional South, but also a common belief that rural migrants were difficult to organize in comparison with factory workers.

Thirty years later, amid the birth of sixties idealism, the National Farm Workers Association (NFWA), soon to be the United Farm Workers union, was born under the leadership of César Chávez, Dolores Huerta, and Gilbert Padilla. Chávez, whose parents were farmworkers in Arizona and California, became a paid organizer for the Community Services Organization (CSO), a branch of the Industrial Areas Foundation, a network of door-to-door organizers founded by Saul Alinsky.

"I'd never been in a group before, and I didn't know a thing. We were just a bunch of pachucos—you know, long hair and pegged pants."[20]

Chávez later broke from the CSO over the priority of concentrating on farm-workers and began the NFWA with a dozen friends and organizing colleagues. This was a singular case of a social movement being *organized into existence*. They registered twenty-five thousand farmworkers in a house meeting drive, collected dues of $3.50 per month, and began creating services such as death benefits and a credit union. But the workers in the fields were ahead of the organization, and on September 8, 1965, Filipino workers launched a grape strike. Chávez was "momentarily caught off guard," but his NFWA decided to join the strike with only $70 in its account and no backing from organized labor.

Perhaps the most useful of the analyses of the farmworkers' movement is by Marshall Ganz, originally from Bakersfield, a Harvard dropout, participant in SNCC's Mississippi Summer Project, and for two decades a principal UFW organizer.[21] In 2008, Ganz transmitted his extensive organizing experiences to Barack Obama's training camps for volunteers. Concentrating on the historic march from Delano to Sacramento in 1966, Ganz notes the "power of story" in empowering what became a movement even more than a union.

The story of the black civil rights movement was a central element, as well as the wind of liberation theology then blowing through the Catholic church. The long history of Mexican farmworkers and revolutionaries was a third. Friday night meetings were like "revivals," with *corridos* and *actos* (songs and guerrilla theater) performed by the Teatro Campesino. In different ways, according to Ganz, the power of story taught the participants how to become agents of history, rather than expendable objects, a key insight into the seemingly spontaneous formation of social movements from inner resources rather than top-down organizations. A new slogan was heard: *Sí, se puede!*

The 1966 strikers marched for three weeks, camped like Moses' people across the Sacramento River from the "promised land," and to their surprise immediately won the first union contract in California history.[22] Some called it "a miracle."[23] From that point, one of the largest and longest-lasting boycotts in American history began, connecting the UFW with a vast new network of religious, student, and labor activists across the country.

The UFW would suffer through violent countermovements from growers and their political allies, as well as Teamsters Union goons. Chávez personally undertook hunger strikes. In so doing, he attracted personal visits by Robert Kennedy, then running for president in the California Democratic primary. By 1970, Coachella Valley growers appeared to relent and signed contracts representing "the most significant victory in the long history of farm-worker organizing."[24] But it was not over. More than three thousand striking lettuce workers were arrested in California while Richard Nixon, who ate grapes to mock the UFW, became president. In 1973, the growers launched a ballot initiative, Proposition 22, to criminalize secondary boycotts, but California voters supported the UFW by more than 1 million votes, 4.3 million to 3 million.

It was not until the 1974 election of Governor Jerry Brown that the UFW's long struggle appeared to climax. In 1975, led by Brown and his emissary Elizabeth "Rose" Bird, California adopted the first meaningful protections of farmworkers since the exclusion in 1935.

With success came reversals. The new law did not legitimize secondary boycotts, and when Brown was replaced by Republican George Deukmejian as governor in 1982, he loaded the Agricultural Relations Board with conservative appointees who stopped its gears (for example, by allowing years to pass before elections won by the UFW were certified). It was not until 2002, after another march on Sacramento, that California required outside mediation in farm labor disputes and safe vehicles for transporting farmworkers to their jobs. In addition, internal divisions broke out within the UFW as its struggle lost momentum. The union was never broken, but neither did it regain the dynamism and power of the 1965–1974 years.

Chávez and the UFW played a catalytic role, though far from a controlling one, in the surge of the greater Chicano movement during the same years. One force that went beyond labor organizing was the rise of *chicanismo*, a new nationalism. Chávez was never a nationalist himself but became a nationalist icon in later representations. As blacks and other people of color redefined their identities in the late sixties, so did Mexican Americans. One inspiration was the concept of *Aztlán*, a homeland both imaginary and rooted in the realities of dispossession in the American Southwest. In New Mexico, an *allianza* led by Reies López Tijerina attacked a courthouse and attempted to seize lands that they asserted belonged to them under the 1848 Treaty of Guadalupe Hidalgo.[25] At one time, four hundred fifty New Mexico National Guardsmen conducted operations in New Mexico's wilderness looking for Tijerina's cadre. In Colorado, cultural nationalism became the cause of the Crusade for Justice, led by a former boxer and poet, Rodolfo "Corky" Gonzáles. On the campuses and in certain barrios, an armed self-defense group formed, calling itself the Brown Berets. In March 1968, fifteen thousand Chicano/a high school students staged walkouts ("blowouts") in "the birth of Brown Power."[26] A student organization was created in 1969 that continues to this day—El Movimiento Estudiantil Chicano de Aztlan, or MECHA. Three Chicano Moratoriums against

Vietnam were organized by MECHA, with two thousand marchers in December 1969, five thousand in February 1970, and a massive thirty thousand on August 29, 1969, when the protesters were attacked by sheriffs' deputies and three people were killed, including *Los Angeles Times* reporter Ruben Salazar.[27] Not long after came the Raza Unida Party, a third-party organization based in Texas that had a profound effect on Chicano politics in the next decade.

There is no question that the FBI and undercover police were involved in operations against the Chicano movement. Certain that communists were infiltrating the UFW, the FBI launched a probe (which can be accessed at http://foia.fbi.gov/chavez.htm). Several FBI memos were forwarded to U.S. Army intelligence, including one that monitored a march of thirty persons "attempting to gain recognition for California grape pickers."[28] Another complained that the UFW's legal office had been "most difficult to deal with to date," a view that echoed the bureau's response to civil rights workers trying to draw attention to violence in the South.[29] More lethal were the undercover operations of local and federal police, who ordered an infiltrator, Frank Martinez, to "cause confusion ... to provoke incidents in order 'to eliminate' the Brown Berets and the NCMC [National Chicano Moratorium Committee]."[30]

Though he remained principally a farmworker union organizer, César Chávez was a huge influence in the rise of all these events. He became a movement icon who evoked enormous pride throughout the Mexican American community. He contributed to the training of more organizers than any single leader of the sixties movements. Even when the militants disagreed with his nonviolence or his loyalty to the Democratic Party, they were moved by the passion of his hunger strikes and his modest concreteness when he offered advice. The elevation of his persona to the status of a virtual saint, however, undermined the bottom-up strategies of rank-and-file ranch committees proposed by many UFW organizers. The social movement he inspired never fully succeeded, though it was never defeated either. Its legacy was more powerful than law.

In 1993, he died suddenly of a heart attack in his sleep, in Arizona. I was one of hundreds who carried his coffin, in turns, to his grave in Delano. Although to observers of the surface, Chávez and the farmworkers seemed to have faded into oblivion, suddenly, spontaneously, there were thirty thousand of us marching again. Each of us had been touched by the experience in ways we never could forget. César, for example, gave me the blueprint for how farmworker organizing techniques could be applied to modern electoral campaigns, how a new kind of political machine could arise from house meetings.

The vast cultural impact triggered by the UFW has been embodied, for example, in the work of Luis Valdez, who in 1965, at age twenty-five, was inspired as a young playwright and actor. For two years, he fostered a theatrical version of participatory democracy, improvising countless *carpas*, or Mexican tent shows, from flatbed trucks in the fields. This Teatro Campesino elicited feelings and stories from the farmworkers themselves, then invited them to act those stories out directly or perform them as ballads (*corridos*).

Valdez left the UFW staff eventually to carry his writing, acting, and directing to the world. It is safe to say he became the foremost Mexican American playwright/director of the era. He delved deeply into his Mayan roots, the history of nineteenth-century "banditos" such as Tiburcio Vasquez, the pachuco past in *Zoot Suit* (1992), the Richie Valens story in *La Bamba* (1987), and *Corridos* with Linda Ronstadt on PBS (1987).[31] When Jerry Brown became governor in 1975, Valdez was a prominent speaker at the inauguration. He writes and speaks today from his Teatro Campesino compound in San Juan Bautista. When I voted to establish California's César Chávez Day as a state holiday in 2000, Valdez was there to speak, embrace the new Latinos on the Senate floor, and shake hands with the politicians from grower constituencies, all of whom, I seem to recall, voted for the bill. In 2003, the U.S. government issued an official César Chávez thirty-seven-cent commemorative postage stamp.

After losing the 2008 New Hampshire primary, and before heading for the Latino-rich states of Arizona, New Mexico, Colorado, California, and Texas, Barack Obama began introducing a new campaign chant: "Yes, we can." Every Spanish speaker in the nation knew instantly it was a sign. Obama was channeling César Chávez: *Sí, se puede.*

The Environmental Movement:
New Consciousness, Old System

Earth Day—April 22, 1970—was by far the largest public gathering of the sixties generation. Its advent was met by the swiftest package of policy reforms achieved by the sixties generation as well, many of them delivered by the Nixon administration. The question is why.

There were plenty of precursors. The earliest clean air laws were passed in 1955 and 1960, as thousands of people choked and even died on the newly recognized threat of "smog."[32] Adlai Stevenson spoke of a fragile "spaceship Earth" and criticized nuclear fallout in his losing 1956 presidential campaign. Rachel Carson's 1960 *New Yorker* articles on the cover-up of pesticide poisoning, published as *Silent Spring* in 1962, warned of an ecocide caused by Strontium 90 from nuclear testing and toxic sprays like DDT; her work contributed to antitesting protests and the 1963 nuclear test ban treaty. The 1964 Wilderness Act drew more congressional support mail "than any other piece of legislation" that year, though preserving only 9 million of an available 60 million acres of public lands and containing loopholes for mining, dams, and power plants.[33] At the time, the social movements about civil rights and Vietnam were dominating public attention, and the environmental issue was more the domain of traditional outdoor groups like the Sierra Club, Audubon Society, Nature Conservancy, and the newer World Wildlife Fund (formed in 1961). But the public was becoming conscious.

The issue detonated toward the end of the sixties. A passionate 1967 campaign by the Sierra Club to prevent the U.S. Bureau of Reclamation from damming 150 miles of the Colorado River in the Grand Canyon was surprisingly successful, earning club director David Brower the label "archdruid" in a *New Yorker* article. The dam controversies provoked more than polite petitions as chronicled in Edward Abbey's classic *The Monkey Wrench Gang* (1975) and the eco-anarchist movement symbolized by Earth First!

In 1968, Paul Erlich published an apocalyptic book on overpopulation.[34] In the same year, Ralph Nader established his Center for Study of Responsive Law and recruited "Nader's Raiders" to go after corporate polluters. In 1969, Cleveland's Cuyuhoga River burst into chemical flames and Lake Erie was pronounced biologically dead. In January of the same year, a Union Oil well blew up in the Santa Barbara channel, causing an 800-mile oil slick, the death of thousands of birds, and miles of heavy tar to cover popular beaches. More than the Grand Canyon campaign, the anti-oil campaign (named GOO, or Get Oil Out) sent political shock waves across the media as oil executives arrogantly dismissed the incident as "Mother Nature letting some oil come out."[35]

The Santa Barbara oil spill was followed by the localized People's Park campaign in Berkeley, when ecology-minded radicals planted organic gardens and play areas on an abandoned lot owned by the university. The battle over the park continued for weeks, resulting in one killing and hundreds of woundings and arrests by police and troopers. That 30,000 Berkeley residents would march demanding "take back the park" after Nixon's reelection and the height of the Vietnam War was a sign that the environmental issues were woven into a larger social movement. People's Park was not an isolated project; the *New York Times* estimated there were 2,000 communes in America, a number that is considered far too low.[36]

The movement to protect deserts, old-growth forests, and oceans gave rise to a new global embrace of ecology and a proliferation of direct action organizations like Greenpeace. Perhaps most of all, it was the July 16–20, 1969, Apollo moon landing that triggered a global change of perception, including a spiritual dimension, in humanity's consciousness of our place in the universe. The images from space were displayed on banners and walls across the world. The long-held assumptions of humans as at the center of the universe, of humans as God's custodians of nature, was humbled and reversed by a sense of creation itself as somehow holy. Environmentalism was no longer a secondary "issue" but fundamental to the very meaning of things, an attitude that marked the sixties generation as different than those who came before.

The escalation to Earth Day in 1970 was unexpected, in keeping with the model of social movements offered here. Drawing on the Vietnam teach-in experience, a handful of environmentalists, including Senators Gaylord Nelson and Edmund Muskie, proposed in late 1969 that there be a "national teach-in on the crisis of the environment" aimed for the following April. A March 1970 kickoff teach-in in Ann Arbor drew a surprising 15,000. When April 22 came, according to *Time* magazine, there were 20 million Americans involved in decentralized public events.[37]

Earth Day reversed some key dynamics of the late sixties by vaulting the movement moderates into leadership along with Machiavellians like Richard Nixon and even a corporate establishment worried about "a broad attack on the entire industrial system."[38] Movement radicals in this period were more preoccupied with Vietnam, the Panthers, conspiracy trials, and the like. While certain environmental issues like napalm and defoliants had captured the anger of the antiwar movement, the space and opportunity now existed for environmentalism to be cast as a less polarizing issue. The organizers of Earth Day were explicit in not wanting to antagonize the middle class, nor even the state and corporate sectors. While leaders like Denis Hayes condemned "corporate irresponsibility" and Earth Day activists booed the interior secretary off a campus stage, the events as a whole had the quality of flower power in full blossom. Dow Chemical helped fund Earth Day at the University of Michigan, Chicago's Commonwealth Edison sent 175 speakers to Earth Day events, and Dow Chemical scrubbed its napalm image with advertisements for pollution control technologies.

Nixon leaped ahead of the parade by signing the 1969 National Environmental Policy Act in January and devoting major emphasis to the environment in his January State of the Union address just before Earth Day. The *New York Times* headlines reported that "Nixon, Stressing Quality of Life, Asks in State of Union Message for Battle to Save the Environment."[39] There was a direct political motive for Nixon's co-optation; he sought to undermine the front-running Muskie's presidential campaign by pre-empting a major Muskie platform plank. Nixon simultaneously sought to win many of the eighteen- to twenty-one-year-olds who would be voting for the first time in 1972. More deeply, Nixon was trying to preventively contain the environmental issue from fanning the flames of a greater radicalism in the country. Instead of a radical restructuring of America's values of growth and its exploitation of natural resources, Nixon sought to channel and institutionalize environmentalism toward technical fixes and new management systems. His strategy toward the younger generation became "Out of the streets, into the system."

Nixon signed a raft of environmental laws and institutions. The Environmental Protection Agency (1970). The Council for Environmental Quality (1970). Clean Air Act amendments (1970). The Water Quality Control Act (1970). The Occupational Safety and Health Act (1970). The Water Pollution Control Act (1972). The Marine Mammal Protection Act (1972). The Pesticide Control Act (1972). The Coastal Zone Management Act (1972). The Endangered Species Act (1973).

This speed and substance of the Nixon reforms were breathtaking, considering the negligent record of past administrations. Nothing like the Nixon agenda passed again until the environmental initiatives of the Obama administration in 2009. Like all serious reform, it was important for Nixon to deliver—and indeed, measurable progress would occur, enough to keep environmental groups engaged and the general public expectant. For example, the domestic use of DDT was banned one decade after Carson's outcry. But in the years ahead, it would become clear that the abatements were completely inadequate to prevent, say, global warming, and the sense would grow among many environmentalists that "progress" was measured by slowing the rate of decline.

What Nixon had accomplished was the construction of a bureaucratic puzzle zoo, incentivizing a pathway for environmental organizations to become bureaucratic, legalistic, and skilled at institutionalized bargaining within forums distant from the urgency of the everyday crisis. For example, years could pass in setting standards for criteria pollutants while thousands of new chemicals entered the marketplace. Years could pass while Superfund sites were studied prior to cleanup, if they ever were cleaned up at all. Years could pass as biologists fought with industry scientists over whether to list salmon species as "threatened" or "endangered." Environmental impact reports required public hearings and testimony but little more; developers were not required to testify under oath and they routinely padded their project proposals before making faux concessions on matters such as traffic density. A whole industry of environmental professionals grew up to enter an elaborate system of courtroom and regulatory hearings or sat in workshops to plot out "win-win" scenarios with former adversaries.

This new environmental leadership, in the judgment of early SDS leader and leading historian Robert Gottlieb, "never became linked to the possibility of creating a new kind of social movement."[40] Between 1960 and 1990, says historian Roderick Nash, environmentalism changed "from a religion to a profession.... The blue-jean-and-granola style of conservation evident at the time of the first Earth Day in 1970 gave way two decades later to pin-striped suits and briefcases full of sophisticated data."[41] There would, however, be a postage stamp for Rachel Carson in 1981.

Ralph Nader, who spawned much of the new advocacy, knew the stakes. In 1970, he wrote that pollution control standards were out of date, that sanctions against polluters were feeble, that disclosure requirements were flouted routinely, and that only "the force of public awareness" could possibly extract real change from the new environmental apparatus of decision-making.[42] But the possibility of "the force of public awareness" was mainly limited to channeling through the judiciary (for example, through new groups like the Environmental Defense Fund, formed in 1967, and the Natural Resources Defense Council, formed in 1970) or intervention in electoral campaigns on behalf of the better of traditional politicians (through the League of Conservation Voters, formed in 1970).

This pool of environmentalists succeeded three decades after the sixties in making possible the vice presidency and eventual presidential campaign of Al Gore. Interestingly, Vice President Gore found it necessary to retreat from his environmental stance when faced with the power of the auto-industrial complex. Had he become the first environmental president in 2000, a real test of the interaction between movements and Machiavellians would have ensued.

There always were more radical or militant approaches rising at the margins, as reflected in the writings of Edward Abbey, E. F. Schumacher, Thomas Berry, and "deep ecologists" like Arne Naess and Aldo Leopold. An environmental spirituality would take root from the traditions of Native America, Thoreau, and Muir. The direct action campaigns of Greenpeace and the antinuclear civil disobedience of the Clamshell Alliance and Earth First! would evolve into a more radical social movement in the decade ahead. The countermovement would erupt starting in the Reagan era, symbolized by Interior Secretary James Watt representing a complex of mining, oil, gas, nuclear, gun, and real estate development interests.

But for Nixon, it seemed enough to keep the seventies from becoming an extension of the sixties. He succeeded, but only by helping legitimize antipollution policies and setting the stage for future environmental reforms.

PART II

The Second Sixties, 1965–1975

~ 8 ~

America Invading Vietnam, Vietnam Invading America

*T*HERE WAS ANOTHER MAJOR FACTOR IN THE DEMOCRATIC LEADERSHIP'S rejection of the MFDP in August 1964. In that same month, at the highest levels, some Democratic leaders already knew they were going to escalate the war in Vietnam.[1] Given that the Dixiecrats were not only racist but also hawkish,[2] could the Democrats have gone to war abroad if the party was turning toward civil rights and antipoverty efforts at home? At the very least, the road to war would have been more complicated.

The Tonkin Gulf "incident," which triggered the first U.S. bombing raids on North Vietnam, took place on the day of the Mississippi funeral for James Chaney, Andrew Goodman, and Michael Schwerner. Bob Moses noted that day that the United States was bombing and killing Vietnamese people while it was not protecting civil rights workers in Neshoba County.

Vietnam was virtually unmentioned in the June 1962 Port Huron Statement except for making the list of dictators being supported by the United States around the world. We believed, as later evidence tended to show, that John Kennedy might have kept America out of an expanded ground war.[3] We were shaken when Lyndon Johnson sent the bombers and obtained a declaration of war from a supplicant Congress over the Tonkin Gulf incident. Denial, like dreams, dies hard.

A similar pattern emerged in the 2008 election of Barack Obama. A huge out-pouring of voters wanted to reject the Bush era and place their hopes in Obama and a Democratic bloc that pledged to end the war in Iraq. But Obama, consistent with the 2007 bipartisan Baker-Hamilton Study Group report, proposed to withdraw combat troops, leaving behind at least twenty-five to fifty thousand counterterrorism, special operations, training, advising, and backup forces. But the national security elites, apparently seeking a face-saving redeployment of American troops, managed to negotiate a pact between the Iraqi regime and the outgoing Bush administration, calling for a phased withdrawal of all troops by 2011, a course that Obama then announced on February 27, 2009, at Camp Lejeune. At the same time, the new president escalated the Afghanistan war by dispatching seventeen thousand troops and escalated the secret war in Pakistan, including numbers of drone attacks and presence of special ops, further roiling anti-American sentiment in the region. It appeared to be Vietnam in 1963 all over again, this time with the American economy in tatters and no possibility of sending five hundred thousand troops—unless another September 11 suddenly came to pass.

Fall 1964 then resembled 2007–2008 in the sense that a presidential candidate seemed to promise an end to war while the dynamic of escalation was obscured from view. Late in 1964, the SDS national council met in New York and decided to follow two antiwar tracks: first, to plan what would be the first national demonstration against the Vietnam War the following April and second, to endorse Johnson against Barry Goldwater on a slogan of "part of the way with LBJ." We were deeply invested in our community and campus organizing projects, after all, and the concept of a military draft for a war with Vietnam despite presidential promises to the contrary was a shocking adjustment the organization was not fully prepared to make.

According to Daniel Ellsberg, who was then in the Pentagon, the president set up an interagency task force *the day before the November 3 election* to escalate the war as soon as the voters went home: "It hadn't started a week earlier because its focus might have leaked to the voters.... Moreover, we didn't start the work a day or week later, after the votes were cast, because there was no time to waste.... It didn't matter that much to us what the public thought."[4] Johnson himself ordered his top aides in early December to keep the secret because he feared public opinion: "I consider it a matter of the highest importance that the substance of this position should not become public except as I explicitly direct."[5]

This was not the first suspicious step in the escalation process. Two days before his murder, John Kennedy announced a plan to withdraw between one thousand and thirteen hundred American troops from South Vietnam. Two days after his murder, on November 24, a covert plan was adopted in National Security Memorandum 273 that authorized secret military operations, "graduated in intensity," against the North.[6] One of those intensified operations was aggressive probes in North Vietnamese waters by U.S. naval vessels. At the other end of the spectrum, some generals were advocating latitude to use nuclear weapons if U.S. escalation led to an invasion of Vietnam from China.[7] After the Tonkin Gulf incident, top Pentagon official John McNaughton authored a plan "to provoke a military DRV [Democratic Republic of Vietnam] response and be in a good position to seize on that response." Overt escalation was held back until the November election was over, but by March 1965 the eight-year bombing and ground war had begun. Some one hundred fifty thousand American ground troops were on their way by the date of the SDS March on Washington.

There is no easy explanation as to why the Machiavellians chose to go to war in 1964. Although some like Noam Chomsky and historian Stanley Karnow disagree, claiming that LBJ was following JFK's Vietnam policy, I believe, with Peter Dale Scott, Gareth Porter, and Daniel Ellsberg, that John Kennedy might not have escalated the ground war in Vietnam and that official U.S. policies were changed immediately following his death. My own theory is that the Kennedys became *reforming* Machiavellians partly because they were younger leaders in a time of change—John and Robert Kennedy were younger than Barack Obama when they were elected and when they died, at ages forty-six and forty-two, respectively. Unlike remote and unaccountable members of the elite, the Kennedy identities were forged largely in democratic elections where they had to listen and seek popular support at a time of rising social movements, which turned them into reformers. According to Robert Kennedy's later account, his brother wanted to concentrate on domestic issues such as civil rights and unemployment in his second term.[8] The key reservation shared by the Kennedys (and echoed in Johnson's 1964 campaign rhetoric) was not primarily a moral one but was rather a strategic concern that a U.S. ground war against a Vietnam backed by China could represent another looming quagmire like Korea, at a time of rising aspirations for change at home.

With John Kennedy gone, however, any possibility of reexamining the cold war premises disappeared as well. What remained intact was the false premise that South Vietnam was essentially a "domino," or proxy, in a cold war power rivalry over populations, resources, and territory. The long history of Vietnamese nationalism, demonstrated against the Chinese, the French, the Japanese, and the British, was discounted by cold warriors beginning in the 1950s. As the cold war set in, a key State Department official wrote of the "unpleasant fact that Communist Ho Chi Minh is the strongest and perhaps ablest figure in Indochina and any suggested solution which excludes him is an expedient of uncertain outcome."[9] The possibilities of cooperation with Ho were replaced by another model. Ignored, for example, were such incongruous facts as the initial support of the French Communist Party— presumably agents of the Soviet Union in the cold war model—*for* funding and troops to fight France's colonial war *against* the Vietnamese communists from 1946 to 1954.[10] Despite these irregularities in the cold war model—Ho's independent nationalism, French communists opposing the Vietnamese—the United States embarked on the path of intervention. In addition to the domino theory, nearly all the Machiavellians further assumed an easy military victory once the United States threw its forces against tiny Vietnam. Once committed, they were wedded to the reputational agenda of all Machiavellians: to appear never to lose. As expressed by top Pentagon official John McNaughton in a confidential memo, the American goals were mostly to avoid a humiliating defeat to the U.S. reputation as a guarantor, and then to "keep South Vietnam (and the adjacent territory) from Chinese hands" and, last, "permit the people of South Vietnam to enjoy a better, freer life."[11] As early as 1964, even before the invasion, McNaughton wrote a memo advising that "if worst comes and Saigon disintegrates or their behavior becomes abominable[, we should] 'disown' South Vietnam, hopefully leaving the image of 'a patient who died despite extraordinary efforts of a good doctor.'"[12]

The men of power most concerned about protecting America's reputation as a guarantor of South Vietnam were the "special advisory group" of corporate lawyers, bankers, diplomats, and retired military men who came to be dubbed "the wise men" in Johnson's time. Living prototypes of C. Wright Mills's theory of the power elite, these were self-appointed custodians of the nation's interests who occasionally sat down for private dinners with the president. Founded by such men as Averill Harriman, Robert Lovett, Dean Acheson, John McCloy, George

Kennan, Charles Bohlen, and Clark Clifford, the group comprised the architects of cold war policy, who, above all, cared for the stability of the economic system as a whole, one that protected American privileges in the world. Given America's control of so much of the world's wealth, Kennan had written in a secret memo early in the cold war, "we cannot fail to be the object of envy and resentment." He went on to offer a manifesto for all Machiavellians: "Our real task in this coming period is to devise a pattern of relationships which will permit us to *maintain this pattern of disparity* without positive detriment to our national security. To do so, we will have to *dispense with all sentimentality*. We should cease to talk about vague and unreal objectives such as human rights, the raising of living standards and democratization. The day is not far off when we are going to have to deal in *straight power concepts*."[13]

The goal of the wise men in the sixties was the stabilization of the global status quo they viewed as threatened by the domino of Vietnam, and so from the earliest stage they supported Johnson's war. When they eventually changed their minds in 1968, because the war was both unwinnable and tearing the country apart, Johnson swiftly resigned, complaining that "the establishment bastards have bailed out."[14] Had he lived, Robert Kennedy most likely would have been the standard-bearer of both the "wise men" and the radicals in the streets.

But that was not to be. So war it was, born in deceit both at home and abroad. The CIA's initial counterinsurgency campaign would be led by Edward Lansdale, who "aspired to be a modern Machiavelli," according to a former State Department official who knew him well.[15] Going to war meant opposing the aspirations of many at home, as a State Department memo warned in 1967: "A serious concern of U.S. foreign policy [is that] the policy priorities of youth may run counter to the requirements imposed on the U.S. by its role as a world power."[16]

In Rick Perlstein's indispensable 2008 epic, *Nixonland*, the author frames the sixties as a Shakespearean conflict between the resentful and paranoid lower-middle class (the Orthogonians), represented by Richard Nixon, and the more liberal professionals (the Franklins), who he claims gave rise to the New Left (thereby leaving out the origins of the sixties in the black experience).[17] Perlstein's choice also ignores the equally dominating shadow of Lyndon Johnson over the decade and is written largely from a top-down view of history. He wants to assert that Nixon's troubled, resentful, almost psychotic persona reflected the repressed nature of American culture as a whole. Perlstein also underplays the secret figure of J. Edgar Hoover, who shadowed both presidencies, Democrat and Republican. Hoover, more than anyone, symbolized tenacious opposition to any changes in the cold war status quo, and he influenced events as disparate as the rise of Ronald Reagan, the killings of Black Panthers, and the Chicago conspiracy trial.

Historians often speak of the year 1968 as a turning point, and they are not wrong. Escalating social movements, combined with an establishment accustomed to deploying blind force, spun American society out of balance. As the moderate center collapsed, the question was whether movements of the center-Left or countermovements of the Right would prevail and be able to constitute a new center. Only today, in the Obama era, do the broad sentiments and agenda of the sixties era seem to be surfacing again.

The year 1968 began with the shock of the Tet Offensive in Vietnam, an event that is smothered in revisionist controversy even today. What I know from direct sources and later documents is that the Pentagon disregarded evidence that a general offensive was being prepared for the New Year.[18] The surprise attacks took place in virtually every South Vietnamese city and town, including the grounds of the U.S. Embassy in Saigon. The offensive finally was repulsed and thereby failed to overthrow the Saigon regime. A Machiavellian military legend then grew that claimed that Tet was an American "victory," reinforcing the propaganda claim that the war was being lost on the battlefield of the media and public opinion in America. In this attempt to rewrite the meaning of Tet, the stunning surprise of coordinated countrywide uprisings in zones long believed to be pacified under five hundred thousand American troops was ignored. The North Vietnamese and Vietcong were everywhere, including the American Embassy and the presidential grounds, before falling back. It was a strategic victory against the U.S. occupation, leading Walter Cronkite—the reassuring voice of the moderate Machiavellians—to pronounce the war a "stalemate" in which no victory was possible. With Cronkite's defection, Johnson knew the war was lost. In a matter of weeks, the wise men were gathering at the White House to recommend disengagement, followed by Eugene McCarthy's New Hampshire upset and Johnson's statement of resignation. These were signal outcomes for the social movements in the decade. They had destabilized the social order, forced a formidable president out of office, and presented an electoral challenge powerful enough to force the Machiavellians toward a new strategy.

In retrospect, McCarthy and Kennedy promised nothing more, and perhaps less, than Barack Obama did when he pledged to end the Iraq war. Running on anti-Vietnam, anti-Johnson sentiment among the voters, McCarthy and Kennedy essentially pledged a negotiated peace. It was enough to ignite a progressive passion that would not be seen again until 2008. The assassinations of Martin Luther King in April and Bobby Kennedy in June, however, ended the possibility of the sixties culminating in a new progressive presidency and governing majority. The space was opened for the backlash buoying the Wallace and Nixon campaigns based on law and order (against hippies, radicals, and black nationalists), the southern strategy (to realign the Republican Party to incorporate defecting Democrats), and the continued effort to hide, divide, and control Vietnam (described as "Vietnamization").

Leaderless, traumatized, and fragmented, our movements lacked the capacity for strategic direction. The Chicago Democratic National Convention appeared, at least to some of us, as one last chance to fling ourselves against the war-making state in the hope that the Democrats would understand that their interest as a party lay in peace. LBJ actually feared "that the antiwar movement would drive him out of the White House," according to authoritative histories and records of the period.[19]

⌒ 9 ⌒

Toppling the Ivory Tower: The Student Strikes at Columbia and San Francisco State, 1968–1969

*T*HE ASSASSINATION OF CHE GUEVARA IN OCTOBER 1967, the huge Pentagon march in November, the Tet Offensive in January 1968, McCarthy's March challenge to Johnson in New Hampshire, Bobby Kennedy's entry into the presidential race that same month, the murder of Dr. King in Memphis in April and Kennedy in June—all these cumulative shocks demonstrated that the Machiavellian order was out of control. It was a time of rebellion on every continent (see this book's Timeline).

The road to the Chicago convention, already lacking any map, turned into a roller coaster as campuses around the world exploded with spontaneous and uncoordinated student occupation of campus buildings, the only method by which students might obtain leverage against their uncaring administrations. The revolt made the Port Huron Statement seem moderate. This was the lunch counter sit-in extended to the liberal North and the Free Speech Movement gone global, exposing the complicity of universities within the larger system, birthing a generation still known to many as the 68ers.

I have written before about my experiences during the Columbia student revolt, and the subject has been covered in numerous histories.[1] There are certain crucial points that need to be emphasized in the context of this book, however.

First, SDS had reached a militant and revolutionary position in response to the escalation of Vietnam, the urban "disorders," and the assassination of leaders such as Dr. Martin Luther King, not simply through the exhortation of its new generation of leaders. That said, those SDS leaders were escalating their rhetoric and analysis to apocalyptic levels as they sought a theory and practice of revolution. Many were influenced heavily by the examples of Che Guevara and black revolutionaries inside the United States. They rejected as ineffective the reformist ideas and experiences of the earlier generation of SDS leaders, including myself, and treated movement moderates (supporters of Eugene McCarthy, university reformers, Democratic activists) as enemies leading students into the snares of co-optation. Instead of participatory democracy, or "letting the people decide," they were moving into heated debates over varieties of Marxism-Leninism as they sought answers to the crisis. In short, they were on the extreme end of the social movement spectrum in theory and practice, though sharing a spirit of the times with the majority of other students. At one point, SDSer Mark Rudd wrote a letter to the university president ending with a line by LeRoi Jones: "Up against the wall, motherfucker, this is a stickup!" It also was the name of a Lower East Side anarcho-revolutionary affinity group that helped occupy Columbia's buildings.

Second, while SDS was factionalizing and dismissing reformism as reactionary, the base for a more pragmatic radical approach was growing by leaps and bounds among students everywhere. The causes were twofold: the conditions of draft, war, and racial divide and the natural tendency of newly awakened activists to choose incremental reforms over wholesale revolution. In practice, this would mean a chronic division between the SDS leaders, who wished to transform Columbia into a springboard for revolution, and the students, who wanted to empower themselves in a more democratized university system. To their credit, the revolutionaries produced a brilliant analysis of Columbia's ties to the war machine and commercial developers in a tightly researched pamphlet called "Who Rules Columbia?"[2] In addition, the student strike commanded massive and unified student support for many weeks. The split between the two tendencies was never resolved, but suffice it to say the institution weathered the storm, in a somewhat reformed state.

Third, as with so many social movements, events developed beyond the control of any organizational conspiracies. In his memoir, Rudd recalls the following scene: "I got up on an overturned trashcan, intending once again to specify the options to the crowd. But before I could say anything, someone yelled, 'To the gym site!' From the trashcan, I watched three hundred people stream off toward Morningside Park.... I had never been to the gym site before, but all I had to do was follow the running crowd and the noise of the police sirens."[3] When confronted by an SDS member who told him, "Your demonstration's out of control," Rudd replied, "I know, I don't know what to do." And so on it went.

Fourth, what made Columbia the "Lexington" of the student revolution was its strategic location in New York City, the media and financial capital of America and, at that time, of the world. The university president, Grayson Kirk, gave a national speech in April saying that "disturbing numbers" of young people were taking "refuge in a turbulent and inchoate nihilism whose sole objectives are destructive." Columbia's approving white male trustees included some with links to Lockheed, Consolidated Edison, IBM, and such luminaries as William Paley of CBS and the publisher of the *New York Times*, Arthur Sulzberger, himself a Columbia graduate. Instead of taking a moderate or supportive approach to the students' substantive and negotiable grievances,[4] the *Times* set the tone in demonizing the students as "hoodlums," while the trustees chose a polarizing strategy of sending in the New York police in an early morning raid, resulting in widespread beatings of students and 720 arrests, myself included.[5] As one example of the university's institutional arrogance, an administrator replied to a question about student voice in decisionmaking by saying, "Whether students vote yes or no on an issue is like telling me they like strawberries." The diffident paternalist remark became the title of a best-selling book by a Columbia sophomore and a Hollywood film as well.

Forty years later, it is difficult not to appraise Columbia as another case of the same cold war liberal default already seen over Vietnam, Mississippi, and Berkeley, a default that temporarily unified the academic, military, business, and political establishments around inflexible law-and-order positions usually associated with right-wing Republicans. Drowned in the pandemonium were any proposals for radical reform, beginning with ending the war itself, ending ties with war contractors, or developing a more equal relationship with the Harlem community. The moderates were in retreat in all directions.

Columbia was the most noted student uprising of the year, but there were thousands of others across the country and the world, the beginning of a wave that largely immobilized higher education by 1972. (Combined with desertions, defections, and defiance in the armed forces, this meant that the younger generation had rendered two key pillars of the status quo dysfunctional.) Perhaps the most important, and less remembered, of the 1968–1969 student strikes took place at San Francisco (SF) State College. It was the longest strike in the history of higher education, lasting nearly five months from November 6, 1968, until March 21, 1969. In addition, it was a genuinely Third World strike, led primarily by the Black Student Union, but equally including the Latino American Students Organization, the Mexican American Student Confederation, the Intercollegiate Chinese for Social Action, the Philippine American Collegiate Endeavor, the Asian American Political Alliance, and the campus American Indian organization grouped in a common front, the Third World Liberation Front (TWLF). Future leaders such as actor Danny Glover were involved directly. This rainbow reflected the state of higher education outside the elite institutions like Columbia, had the characteristics of an actual strike, and was inseparable from the uprisings in Third World countries against neocolonial rule.[6] The main demand was for a self-determining school of ethnic studies, increased enrollment of nonwhite students, and the creation of a financial aid program that became known as the Educational Opportunity Program (EOP). Although the strike, if not all its tactics, enjoyed vast support in San Francisco, the countermovement in response lifted an obscure semanticist, S. I. Hayakawa, to a national prominence comparable to that of Ronald Reagan, Richard Nixon, and Spiro Agnew and finally to a U.S. Senate seat.

The roots of this movement were in the southern SNCC experience, transported to northern cities by young organizers such as Jimmy Garrett, whose purpose in enrolling at SF State was, in his own words, "to organize."[7] These young student organizers formed ghetto tutorial projects and explored avenues to break the admission barriers to colleges and universities in the Bay Area. The concept of black power suggested the need for black and ethnic studies programs in institutions that could fairly be said to serve a white power structure. Meanwhile, the government's own War on Poverty programs, though minimal in funding, served to co-opt and empower many young activists into their first experiences in organizing, including the TWLF's first chair, Ron Quidachay, and, in Oakland, Bobby Seale. SF State, in response to rising student demands, also created an experimental college that allowed students to design their own courses and that became an incubator for ethnic studies.

Meanwhile, Machiavellian power was centralized in Sacramento through an appointed board of twenty-one trustees, including one African American, that governed the system's nineteen separate campuses. The state powers chose and controlled the SF State president, leaving the academic senate and student body organizations under the system of remote control, lacking significant grievance mechanisms. At the center of the power grid was Governor Ronald Reagan, having ridden to office on a promise to crush campus radicalism.[8]

Although 50 percent of San Francisco residents were nonwhite in 1968–1969, the enrollment at taxpayer-subsidized SF State was 75.9 percent white, 5.3 percent black, 2.3 percent Mexican, 7.9 percent "Oriental," 1 percent Filipino, 0.5 percent Native American, and 7 percent "other."[9] The faculty, although progressive on political and labor issues, was overwhelmingly white as well.

Racial friction was intense. In late 1967, several black students attacked a campus editor for articles they considered racist and demeaning. The blacks were placed on interim suspension, provoking a protest by hundreds of black students and a one-day closing of the campus. Reagan and the trustees then issued new orders placing control of the campus in the hands of police in the event of future disturbances. Most faculty, administrators, and students were opposed. President John Summerskill resigned in frustration shortly after.

Summerskill's letter of resignation was prophetic. In addition to charging that the educational institutions were being "taken over by people running for office," he warned that "discipline isn't going to solve the problem that 80 percent of our students are opposed to the Vietnam war.... I do not think we will see peace on our campus until we see peace in our cities, peace in Vietnam."[10] In a late 1968 report to faculty, he had sounded similar themes, proposing to

- make education relevant to issues of the day—peace, poverty, discrimination, social progress, etc.
- make all of higher education accessible to a larger portion of citizens.
- make effective the sharing of decisionmaking more broadly through democratic processes with those affected by the decisions—especially students and faculty.[11]

Summerskill's list of critical problems included only one directed at campus militants: "Preventing the manipulation of academic institutions by willful minorities for private or nihilistic ends."[12] An August 1968 Chancellor's Office report made a similar diagnosis, listing the causes of campus unrest as "(1) war protest, (2) racial discrimination, (3) desire to use the colleges and universities as vehicles for social change, (4) curricular irrelevance, (5) institutional inertia and resistance to change.... So closely have large universities, for example, become interwoven with the federal government in military programs and defense research (e.g., IDA [Institute for Defense Analysis]) that higher education in its major centers ... appears to have committed itself so fully to the political and financial world outside the cloister that this association seems unlikely to be reversed."[13] This was a vindication of the analysis of universities begun in the Port Huron Statement, deepened by the Free Speech Movement, and repeated in the "Who Rules Columbia?" pamphlet, now echoed by the president of a large statewide university.

At the time, Jimmy Garrett called Summerskill "a good man but living in the wrong century.... He could have reformed us right out of existence. But it wasn't him. He did not have the confidence of the faculty, or those administrators. So we got hung up in committees, stuff like that."[14] In the absence of rapid reform, the most radical student perspective gained ascendancy. Not only had several Black Student Union members physically struck a white campus editor, but also a Black Panther minister of education, George Murray, was hired to teach general education classes in September 1968. Murray was a former teaching assistant and active in tutorial programs. There never were complaints about Murray's classroom performance, but he rattled the establishment with militant speeches outside the classroom. On October 24, speaking of delays in funding the black studies program, he was quoted as saying, "We are all slaves and the only way to become free is to kill all the slavemasters."[15] This was certainly protected speech, but it sent the trustees into a frenzy, and Murray was quickly suspended by SF State's new president, Robert Smith. On another matter of great interest to students, the trustees rejected the building of a new $6.8 million student union even though it would be funded by student fees. The strike was now inevitable, and it began on November 6.

This was unlike the spontaneous Columbia strike or other campus strikes in protest of a particular indignity. This was not about the temporary occupation of buildings. The SF State strike was an attempt to blend the tactics of labor strikes and consumer boycotts to force a significant transformation of the college's funding priorities and decisionmaking practices. On most days 40–50 percent of classes were shut down. Picket lines were thrown up at the entrances to buildings. Strike representatives demanded time in classes to urge students to walk out. Low-level vandalism and fires broke out. Faculty began mobilizing to join the strike. Police tactical units tried to occupy the campus on November 13, causing Vice President of Student Affairs Dan Garrity to say: "They blew it right there. [It was] a flat out mistake."[16] Nevertheless, the inflamed student militants seriously misread the balance of forces, thinking they could "seize power" on behalf of "non-negotiable" demands.

President Smith shut down the campus temporarily on November 13 in an attempt to calm the waters, but his moderate hands-on approach was not enough for the trustees. The state's bipartisan political elite, led by Republican governor Reagan and Democratic speaker "Jess" Unruh (another pro-Humphrey, pro-Johnson, prowar liberal Democrat), declared the closure an act of "capitulation" to radicals. Unruh added that it was a "triumph for anarchy."[17] In that atmosphere, a new voice of the countermovement was heard, that of sixty-two-year-old semanticist S. I. Hayakawa, a perfect instrument for Nixon's silent majority.

Rising at a faculty meeting two days after the campus was shut down, Hayakawa said, "I wish to comment on the slovenly habit, now popular among whites as well as blacks, of denouncing as racist those who oppose or are critical of any Negro tactic or demand." As a Japanese American, Hayakawa was the first significant person of color to become the spokesperson against other minorities in the changing sixties (Hayakawa justified the internment of Japanese Americans during World War II).[18] In the mad confusion of the next few days, as the politicians and trustees pressured President Smith to "immediately" retake the campus from the strikers, against Smith's plea for a brief period of informal convocations with faculty and students, Smith abruptly resigned on November 26. On the same day, the trustees named Hayakawa as acting president.

Hayakawa's stated belief was precisely what the rising countermovement wanted to hear: that students were alienated not for "the usual neurotic reasons" but because "they are taught this alienation by professors," especially in the liberal arts and humanities where the famed semanticist detected a "cult of alienation among intellectuals ... such as you find in the *New York Review of Books* or *Partisan Review*."[19] Hayakawa explicitly declared that the purpose of the college was to pass on the existing culture, even if that culture itself was the subject of sweeping reexamination. The liberal arts departments were becoming "centers of sedition and destruction," he added.[20] It did not seem to matter that this assertion was false or at least exaggerated in the extreme. This was about political theater, building an off-campus constituency for a president with little on-campus support.

Reagan soon would say of San Francisco State, "Those who want to get an education, those who want to teach, should be protected in that, at the point of bayonets if necessary."[21] In Nixon's Washington, the State Department transmitted to the White House a packet of documents to be "kept on hand at all times," draft proclamations to declare martial law "with blanks to fill in the date and the name of the city."[22] The Bay Area surely was high on the list.

Under Acting President Hayakawa, a state of emergency was declared on November 30, and the campus reopened on December 2. Given to wearing a photogenic Tam o' Shanter and holding a steady stream of press conferences, the new acting president on that day mounted a flatbed truck that the striking students were using for a rally on the edge of campus. He ripped the wires from the speakers, waved them to television cameras, and, in his own description, became "a folk hero." On the next day, when nine were injured and thirty-one arrested, Hayakawa called it "the most exciting day of my life since my tenth birthday, when I rode a roller-coaster for the very first time."[23] On that same day, Bay Area black community leaders for the first time came to the campus to support the students; they included Assemblyman Willie Brown, who later became speaker, and Berkeley councilman Ron Dellums, who served later in Congress and as Oakland mayor.

Hayakawa's real situation only worsened in the next weeks. He ordered the campus closed one week early for Christmas, an action that would have been rebuked under the previous president. When the campus reopened on January 6, 1969, it was engulfed by a new strike, this time by the American Federation of Teachers (AFT) local. Six weeks later the AFT announced a settlement, and on March 20 the TWLF declared the strike over. Under Hayakawa, the first College of Ethnic Studies was established, including a black studies department. One hundred twenty-eight new slots were opened for EOP students. Looking back, a dean of undergraduate studies, Joseph White, who was African American, reflected that "the machinery of the college is not set up to deal with black demands, it is set up to deal with white reality. We will never return to normal. More education has gone on since the strike started than the six years I went to school here."[24]

The fissures would continue to deepen between the vast cultural changes rising from below to challenge the status quo of campus power and curriculum and the politicians and elites, cold war liberals and conservatives, who benefited from acting as champions of law and order even as they lost control of the younger generation. The militants, for their part, could not "seize power" or prevent the decline of support from more pragmatic students who desired reform without Red Books or guns. But there is no doubt that the rudeness of the revolutionaries forced what reform did occur on campuses such as SF State: The experimental college, the tutorial and outreach programs, EOP, minority admissions, and Third World studies came gradually and, unfortunately for academia, more in response to the logic of force than to the force of logic.

⌒ 10 ⌒

The Chicago Conspiracy

CENTRAL TO THE COLD WAR PARADIGM was the targeting of domestic "conspiracies" of alleged communists and other subversives. The template of fifties McCarthyism was imposed on the sixties in the form of several conspiracy trials, the most well-known being that of the Chicago 8. Eight individuals, myself included, were indicted as a cross section of symbols of the New Left. Rennie Davis, Dave Dellinger, and I were symbols of the antiwar movement and SDS; Abbie Hoffman and Jerry Rubin, the counterculture and Yippies; Bobby Seale, the Black

Panther Party; and John Froines and Lee Weiner, university antiwar leaders. Each of us was indicted on two counts carrying five-year sentences: first, having committed a conspiracy to cross state lines to incite a riot, and second, having engaged in an overt act said to be in furtherance of that conspiracy. A conspiracy could be alleged as a "state of mind" regardless of whether the conspirators knew each other at the time. (For example, Jerry Rubin could be indicted as a conspirator for crossing state lines in spring 1968 and throwing a sweater at a police officer in August, an act that he did commit. Though Bobby Seale was the only conspirator really accountable to an organization, we were tried as symbols of larger social movements that, by their nature, did not fit any cold war hierarchal organizational category and therefore could not be suppressed from above.

Stories of the 1968 street demonstrations and the 1969–1970 Chicago conspiracy trial have been told in several books and films and will not be repeated here except as they illustrate the themes of this book. Several of us were targeted for "neutralization" in an FBI counterintelligence program; according to a May 14, 1968, J. Edgar Hoover memorandum, written months before the 1968 convention: "One of your prime objectives should be to *neutralize* [Hayden] in the new left movement.... The purpose of this program is to *expose, disrupt, and otherwise neutralize the activities of various new left organizations, their leadership and their adherents.* ... We must frustrate every effort of these groups and individuals to consolidate their forces or recruit new and youthful adherents.... *No opportunity should be missed to capitalize on organizational or personal conflicts of their leadership.*"[1] Two months before, on March 4, Hoover had written a related and more menacing memo on preventing the rise of a "coalition of black nationalist groups" or a "messiah" who could unify such a coalition.[2] Dr. King was shot and killed one month later, and the black community was radicalized along with the vast majority of all activists at the time. The divide between militants and movement moderates was deepened by the force of events. The growth of law-and-order politics was becoming a bridge between liberals, moderates, and the Republican Right.

As the conspiracy trial began, Hoover expanded his counterintelligence, or COINTEL, efforts. His forces had been instrumental in provoking the events of 1968 when they delivered false and inflammatory intelligence about the coming protests in Chicago to city officials and the White House. These FBI fantasies ranged from a black uprising on the South Side to the Yippies dosing the Lake Michigan water supply with LSD. His agents had infiltrated the demonstrations and wiretapped the defendants individually, the conspiracy defense office, and meetings of the legal team. When the trial began in 1969, Hoover boasted in a classified memo that "a successful prosecution of this type would be a unique achievement of the Bureau and should seriously disrupt and curtail the activities of the New Left."[3]

Conservative forces were becoming more extreme in general, especially through the campaign of former Alabama governor George Wallace, who received 13 percent of the national vote in 1968, including a majority of the white South.[4] Wallace first emerged in 1963 as a fierce defender of segregation, then added northern white working-class support around issues such as school busing. In choosing General Curtis LeMay as his running mate, Wallace—whose Alabama was described as a "police state" in *Time* magazine[5]—secured the loyalty of the most ardent police and military interests. He was too extreme for most voters, but Wallace could influence the direction of the Republican Party and national discourse. Nixon strategists such as Kevin Phillips had their own "southern strategy" to rechannel white southern Democrats to change party loyalties. In five short years, we who thought the white South could be defeated by the liberal North instead began to see the national majority become more like the white South itself.

Riding this law-and-order countermovement, Richard Nixon won the presidency in November and immediately encouraged the then-dormant prosecution of the Chicago 8 through his attorney general, John Mitchell. This was based on the case built by Hoover, who had been denied an indictment by the outgoing Democratic attorney general, Ramsey Clark.

Even with this law-and-order manipulation, Nixon also resorted to high Machiavellian intrigue to thwart Lyndon Johnson—and the moderate establishment—over Vietnam. In what arguably was treason, Nixon conspired with the Thieu regime in Saigon to delay the opening of peace talks, an event that would have enormously benefited Humphrey, who ultimately lost by 0.7 percent, 43.4–42.7.[6] The divided Democrats offered too little, too late, and the countermovement triumphed.

Now Nixon, in complicity with Hoover, risked a fundamental Machiavellian error of going well beyond the consensus of public support and constitutional law. Although the public favored law and order in general, there was surprise, even shock, at subsequent unfolding revelations of Nixon's enemies' lists, clandestine spying, wiretapping, raiding of bank accounts, fabrication of feuds between movement organizations, or the presence of undercover agents present during assassinations. By moving to the hard Right, the Republicans were risking the center. The range of Nixon's targets constituted an enemies' list of the moderate establishment: "I refer not simply to press and TV but the University community, religious organizations, finance, Eastern Establishment, the major Senate/House/Gubernatorial/Party leaders on the other side, and the special interest groups like Labor and Minorities."[7]

To remake the status quo in a radically conservative direction would require the adoption of secret and extreme methods that, when discovered, would fatally damage the Nixon coalition and threaten the stability of the FBI and CIA. At the end of the sixties, Nixon was pursuing not only a secret and illegal war abroad but also another illegal one against dissent at home. This inherent tendency to overreach agreed norms and legal boundaries activated a vigorous progressive response from the center more than the Left—on both popular and Machiavellian levels—that resulted in the Senate Watergate hearings, eventual defunding of the war by 1975, and, in 1976, congressional reforms of the secret programs of the intelligence community. In a pattern that would repeat, Democrats would gain power because Republicans had gone too far.

Meanwhile, in late 1969, the conspiracy trial defendants were moving with a radical tide that required new theories of resistance. The legal claim of innocence partly rested on an extrajudicial claim from the earliest American social movement, the Revolution itself. Our defense asserted a "right of resistance" in cases where government exceeded its legitimate authority. We argued that the government had no right in Chicago to deny permits for assemblies and marches or for people to sleep in public parks. The issuing of permits, we said, was an administrative function never to be utilized as a form of prior restraint on assembly. We felt we held the inalienable right to what Jesse Jackson testified was a "moral permit." Our historic example was the Boston Massacre of March 1770. The British were the occupying force in Boston, exercising arbitrary authority over the ordinary rights of the colonized people. Youngsters in those times began calling the British redcoats "lobsterbacks," an eighteenth-century version of "pigs," throwing chunks of ice at them. The British troops shot and killed five of the Bostonians. Historian Staughton Lynd testified further, "That's why acts of resistance, even though certainly far more than the customary speech and assembly, seemed appropriate to people like Sam Adams and Thomas Jefferson because they were responses to an oppressive situation which had gone far beyond those normal circumstances in which speech, assembly, free press and petition were adequate responses."

This argument for a level of resistance beyond petitioning or voting, but short of overthrowing the state, was part of an escalation that might not have happened if Robert Kennedy and Martin Luther King had lived. But by 1969, the more militant tendencies in the social movements were escalating in response to the continued war and Nixon's counterintelligence programs. It was Attorney General Mitchell, after all, who told a reporter that "this country is going so far to the right you are not even going to recognize it."[8] By 1969, the sides were moving toward a civil conflict that might have resulted in a prolonged breakdown of order, even perhaps a police state instead of the stable consensus so treasured by the Machiavellians. In response, the moderates in both camps began acting with greater urgency to stabilize the system by ending the war and enacting democratic concessions. Their first major initiative was the fall 1969 anti-Vietnam moratorium, in which antiwar liberal Democrats gained relative dominance over the radical, pacifist, and student wings of the antiwar movement for the first time. The lead organizers came from the McCarthy campaign, including such figures as Sam Brown, Curtis Ganz, and David Mixner. The supporters of the call for the moratorium even included such Machiavellians as Averill Harriman, one of Johnson's premier "wise men" and the president's emissary to the Paris peace talks. At the time, the Nixon hard-liners still maintained their advantage. Ending the war in 1969 was beyond the capacity of the moderates. But in less than three years, the Watergate scandal—a classic example of an excessive countermovement—would provoke a crisis of state and provide the new moderates their opportunity to bring down Nixon and, in the process, undermine the war and restore domestic stability.

In November 1972, the U.S. Seventh Circuit Court of Appeals threw out our Chicago convictions, citing misconduct by both judge and prosecutors. It was a stunning acquittal, implying that "the system worked" at a moment of near-complete despair and radicalization among many in the social movements. Equally significant were the jury acquittals in other conspiracy trials that the Nixon administration mounted against draft resisters (the Catonsville Nine), Vietnam veterans (the Gainesville Seven), and Black Panthers (the Panther Twenty-one) in the same period. These acquittals, combined with post-trial discovery that four of the Chicago jurors were convinced of our utter innocence, were strong hints that Middle America was shifting against the perceived excesses of the Nixon regime.

But in 1969–1970 it was difficult to see any hope for the new moderates. In December, Fred Hampton, a twenty-three-year-old Chicago Panthers leader and liaison to Bobby Seale, was murdered in his sleep in a fusillade of bullets by Chicago police. A second Panther, Mark Clark, was killed in the same assault. Immediately after, Los Angeles police laid siege to the barricaded Panthers office in south-central LA. The Chicago killings provided a final rationale for the newly formed Weathermen faction of SDS to go underground and prepare for armed attacks on the institutions of power. After the chaining and gagging of Bobby Seale and the Hampton-Clark assassinations, it was not a simple matter to wave off the Weathermen analysis. I still believed in the power of movements to force institutions to change and adapt, but I could easily imagine Nixon shifting the judiciary so far to the right that traditional appeals became irrelevant. There was talk in radical circles about death squads and detention centers down the road. The street protests continued to be emboldened; on the day of our jury verdict countless protests broke out across the country, and a Bank of America branch was burned in Isla Vista.

⁀ 11 ⁀

Cambodia, Yale, and Kent State

> Never underestimate the value of turning the student
> thing to our advantage, especially if they get rough. We
> have to go on the offensive against the peaceniks.
> —Richard Nixon to H. R. Haldeman[1]

*T*WO MONTHS AFTER THE CONSPIRACY TRIAL, on April 30, Nixon escalated the war by invading and bombing Cambodia. On the following day, May 1, there was a rally planned to "free Bobby" (Seale) on the Yale Green in New Haven, where he was on trial for conspiracy to murder (a charge of which he was later acquitted). Coming the day after the Cambodian "incursion" (as Nixon called it), the situation could not have been more volatile. The administration already was busy prosecuting 33,960 young men for draft resistance (compared to 380 five years before), not to mention some 16,000 arrests in recent black riots, and it now sought to extend the crackdown to protesting students as well.[2] A whole new generation of right-wing youth, trained in Nixon's culture of dirty tricks, were flooding into the Republican Party that year, including Karl Rove, who especially despised SDS, myself, and the Weathermen.[3] Others in the Nixon White House, such as Tom Huston, a founder of Young Americans for Freedom, were drafting plans for infiltrating movement organizations, tapping phones without authorization, opening private mail, and carrying out home and office break-ins ("black bag" jobs).

The vast majority of Yale students were outraged moderates, including the young law student Hillary Rodham. Yale officials were in the forefront of the moderate Machiavellians, including campus president Kingman Brewster and chair of the board Cyrus Vance, later a secretary of state under Jimmy Carter. Brewster already had expressed the startling view that a black revolutionary could not receive a fair trial in America. However, even though the Panthers wanted a disciplined peaceful protest, some radicals were stockpiling weapons in apartments and communes. In one crashpad I visited, skinny twentysomethings were carrying armloads of shotguns and M-1s. Outside, many storeowners boarded up their windows. Along with a few others, I met with Brewster and Vance, as I had with Governor Richard Hughes during the Newark riots three years before, trying to convince them to avoid provoking a confrontation. It was hard to realize that the military buildup in America, once aimed at seething ghettos, now was blanketing the prestigious New Haven Green. The gap between movements and Machiavellians seemed unbridgeable.

Violence somehow was kept to a minimum, for the moment. New Haven was not Chicago. At the rally on the Green, I was handed a note and instructed to read it to the twenty thousand people assembled. It affirmed that students from nearly one hundred campuses had decided on a nationwide student strike against the Cambodia invasion. As I came to the word "strike," the crowd took it up in a long chant. In the days ahead, an estimated 4 million students shut down eight hundred campuses, many of them for the rest of the school year, the greatest student strike in American history.[4] Within a week, more than one hundred thousand people assembled in Washington to protest at a White House encircled by tanks and armored vehicles. According to *New York Times* reporter Max Frankel, the protests "sent tremors of fear through the White House that revolt and repression might be nearer than anyone had dared to imagine," an analysis that ignored the simpler choice of ending an unpopular war.[5]

Shortly before the Cambodia invasion, Ronald Reagan declared to a growers' meeting in California: "*If the students want a bloodbath, let's get it over with. No more appeasement.*"[6] He meant what he said. Several months earlier, Reagan had authorized helicopter spraying of Sproul Plaza with CS gas and the use of lethal ammunition by state troopers, resulting in the killing of one young man, James Rector, and the blinding of another, Alan Blanchard, as they sat peacefully on a Telegraph Avenue rooftop. Innocents were dying in college towns as collateral damage, as they had in black and Latino communities for years. In May, my close friend Richard Flacks, another target of Hoover memoranda, was assailed in his University of Chicago professor's office by someone wielding a hammer, leaving his skull shattered and wrists cut. He survived. The official and unofficial violence already unleashed on black and Latino militants was spreading to zones of privilege.

Following Reagan's rhetoric, Ohio governor James Rhodes was issuing virulent comments of his own against the protesting students at Kent State, a traditionally quiet campus an hour's drive south of Cleveland. Protests had erupted there in sympathy with the conspiracy defendants and now in response to Nixon's invasion. The *New York Times* headline of May 2 reported that "Students Protest Nixon Move," mentioning even Ohio Young Republicans among the opponents of the invasion.[7] Rather than ending the war, which was the logical alternative, Nixon chose to escalate at home, claiming that if the war was ended, the "bums" would simply find another issue over which to "blow up campuses" and "burn books."[8] In a classic Machiavellian declaration, he accompanied the invasion by claiming on April 30 that a superpower reputation was at stake: "If when the chips are down, the world's most powerful nation, the United States of America, acts *like a pitiful helpless giant*, the forces of totalitarianism and anarchy will threaten … throughout the world."[9]

The notes of White House counselor H. R. Haldeman for May 1 revealed the spin of the day for the president: on Cambodia, "cold steel—no give … mainly stay strong—whole emphasis on 'back the boys'—sell the courage of the P."[10] Haldeman wrote a further directive from the president to his hard-line political consultant Murray Chotiner: "*Chot: Rhodes esp. ride this,*" which is precisely what the Ohio governor was doing.[11] On May 3, with five days to go in a rough Republican primary battle, Rhodes condemned the campus radicals as "*brown shirts*" who should be "*eradicated.*"[12]

SDS was the conspiratorial bogeyman looming behind events at Kent and beyond, even though the organization had closed its national offices in February due to irreconcilable factional differences. At Kent, where the small chapter had been a militant one, SDS was largely a spent force by 1970. The FBI's later investigation could find no SDS leaders to blame; they had been banned from campus and were smothered beneath past felony charges. One historian has written that "the truth, from both sides of the spectrum, was that the SDS had nothing to do with the confrontation at Kent State. Then why do so many still believe that it did?"[13] SDS was the spectral threat haunting the ruling class in 1970. Though no longer in formal existence, SDS was banned at Kent State and elsewhere; thirty-nine state legislatures drafted four hundred laws targeting student radicals in 1969 alone.

On May 4 at noon, hundreds of students milled around the grassy Kent Commons, protesting Cambodia but also the contingent of state troopers who had occupied the Kent campus for four days. Suddenly, a phalanx of those guardsmen whirled, knelt, and fired sixty-seven shots in thirteen seconds, killing four students and wounding thirteen others. Immediately, a spokesman suggested that a "sniper" provoked the incident, a claim that proved to be unfounded. Officials denied there was any order to fire on the students, though thirty-seven years later a tape was recovered on which the order was clearly heard: "Right here! Get set! Point! Fire!"[14] The nearest students shot were at least 70 feet away, the farthest 750 feet.[15] Only two were shot on their front sides, the rest in their backs. An official national commission—moderate Machiavellians led by Republican governor William Scranton of Pennsylvania—later found the shootings "unnecessary, unwarranted, inexcusable."[16]

Whether there was a prior shoot-to-kill order, there is little doubt that Nixon's secret invasion, combined with his rhetoric and that of Spiro Agnew, Ronald Reagan, and James Rhodes, provoked the crisis and precluded alternatives. Undercover agents were involved, and a cover-up of the Kent State murders may have occurred at the highest levels. There were motorcycle gangs "baiting" the police and "egging the students on trying to create a disturbance" on the first night of the Kent troubles, according to an FBI report.[17] But none of these "gang" members were detained or arrested, and none were ever questioned by the FBI (unless their statements were withheld). After the May 4 killings, county officials complied with an unusual—and seemingly illegal—request from the U.S. Justice Department to forward the names of anyone likely to be indicted. Washington then struck certain names from those lists—perhaps its own agents—before a grand jury indicted twenty-four students and one professor.[18]

Nixon's aide John Ehrlichman sent a November 1970 memo to Attorney General John Mitchell conveying Nixon's order that there be no grand jury investigation of Kent State. Congressional hearings were deferred or derailed. During the depths of Watergate, the acting attorney general, Robert Bork, announced on December 11, 1973, that a federal grand jury would finally look at Kent State, an action that served to prevent congressional subpoenas and hearings.[19]

A majority of Ohio residents supported the National Guard, with only 12 percent calling the killings unjustified. In October 1970, a grand jury exonerated the guardsmen while indicting twenty-five students for acts of disruption. A 1975 jury trial on wrongful death charges again supported the National Guard's claims of innocence, a verdict that was overturned by the federal circuit court. In 1975, the case brought by the victims' families was settled out of court, with the state paying $675,000 and offering a statement of "regret," not an apology.

Journalist Philip Caputo compares the Kent State killings to the Boston Massacre, just as Staughton Lynd testified about the Chicago conspiracy trial.[20] But Caputo echoes the common view that the killings were somehow a *shared* responsibility, a *common* tragedy, in which no one really was to blame because everyone was to blame. James Michener echoed the same thinking in the influential book *Kent State*.[21] There is a moral equivalency in these authors' views between a single student giving the finger to an armed guardsman seventy feet away and the guardsman shooting him in the stomach with a round of 30.06 ammunition. Such an incident did occur on May 4, though nearly all those killed and wounded were passively protesting, observing, or passing by. There was no threat to the National Guard ever established by any of the formal inquiries. The victims and their friends, it seemed to some, had only themselves to blame. Caputo even says that Allison Krause, who was walking toward her boyfriend when she was struck down, was part of a "collective, destructive tantrum" and thus "collaborated in the tragedy that would claim her life."[22] Others, although not going as far as Caputo, concluded that the Kent State killings served to terminate the sixties rebellion. Mitchell predicted a "much calmer" fall semester.[23] Milton Viorst wrote that "few were ready to die, and so the decade reached its end." They were wrong.

The year 1968 had begun with troopers killing three black students and wounding at least twenty-five at Orangeburg State, South Carolina, during a struggle over desegregating a bowling alley. The media nationally paid little attention. So it was no surprise that when Mississippi troopers shot and killed two black students at Jackson State University two weeks after Kent State, the deaths made little impact in comparison with the white student deaths at Kent State.[24]

The Nixon-appointed 1970 Scranton Commission became a platform for the moderate Machiavellians. Their scathing report began by declaring that "the crisis on American campuses has no parallel in the history of the nation … as deep as any since the Civil War."[25] Besides condemning the Kent State shootings as unjustified, the Scranton report sounded like a blend of the 1962 Port Huron Statement and the 1968 CIA's "Restless Youth" document. It was a firm call for significant reform, identifying with the students who "seek a community of companions and scholars, but find an impersonal multiversity" suffocating them instead.[26] Although denouncing student violence, Scranton's commission correctly identified four basic issues that needed attention: the crises of race, the war, university reform, and what it termed the "new cultural revolution in lifestyles." "Nothing is more important than an end to the war in Indochina."[27] Without addressing these issues, the report concluded, the *"survival of the nation will be threatened."*[28]

~ 12 ~

The Watergate Coup and the Antiwar Movement

ICHARD NIXON'S TENDENCY TOWARD EXTREME OVERREACTION, rooted in his earlier anticommunist, pro–cold war crusades, pushed continually by J. Edgar Hoover's private units, led to violations of democratic norms that awakened the suspicions of moderates and centrists at many levels. At the same time, the radical social movements divided, one faction testing the electoral process beginning in 1972, another growing ever more apocalyptic. The result was Watergate, which should be understood as a coup from above made necessary by the spreading threat of radical divisions to American stability, constitutional arrangements, and the potential alienation of the next generation. Those who claim Watergate as evidence of the democratic resiliency of the American system of checks and balances are glossing over the level of unnecessary bloodshed and unnoticed subversion of the democratic process that occurred before Nixon's fall.

"The campus is the battleground of the revolutionary protest movement," wrote Tom Charles Huston, a young right-wing White House staffer on May 15, 1970.[1] He was not wrong. Berkeley, where I lived when not on trial in Chicago, was the scene of military occupation, shootings, pepper spraying, and mass confrontations for most of the academic year. But rather than yield to demands for peace, racial justice, and university reform, the authorities, including Reagan and Hoover, deemed it essential to destroy the radical movement at its Berkeley roots. Other campuses were targeted as well, though Berkeley was identified by Hoover as the nerve center. So on July 14, 1970, Nixon's aide H. R. Haldeman approved Huston's recommendations, seeking to avoid turf conflict with Hoover in the process.

By that time, the faction of SDS known as the Weathermen was underground, beyond Huston's and Hoover's radar, embarking on a campaign to attack government, corporate, and military property and help revolutionary fugitives survive a long underground battle. The FBI was never able to apprehend them, a point of extreme embarrassment. But the Weatherpeople had destroyed themselves, as three key members died in a March 6, 1970, explosion in a New York townhouse they had converted into a temporary bomb-making factory. I knew the victims and had seen them evolve from campus activists, to political radicals, to volunteers in the underground, having given up on the moderates and their system—each revolutionized in the space of three or four years. The bomb that was being prepared that day was designed to kill American soldiers at a social event at Fort Dix. (I reflect on their story in Chapter 15.)

Then on June 13, 1971, the perceived threat widened dramatically with the *New York Times* decision to publish the classified *Pentagon Papers,* a multivolume history of Vietnam decisionmaking produced at the Rand Corporation that vindicated the critics' case against the war. The guilty parties were two former hawks, Daniel Ellsberg and Anthony Russo, who were radicalized by both the antiwar movement and the counterculture. The irony was that just as the Weathermen were giving up on the establishment, members of that very establishment were beginning to risk treason charges. Knowing that they shared secrets that could help end the war, admiring those who resisted the draft on the outside, Ellsberg and Russo decided to commit *civil disobedience inside the system itself* by copying and carrying off thousands of documents from the Rand Corporation's files. Ellsberg then engaged in a frantic underground search for someone who would make the papers public, either someone with congressional immunity or a publisher willing to risk a constitutional test. Howard Zinn, among others, helped with the clandestine process. New York Times reporter Neil Sheehan, formerly a correspondent in South Vietnam, participated in the transmission of the stolen documents. Eventually, Senator Mike Gravel released most of the documents on the Senate floor, which allowed him protection from prosecution.

At the same time, a political opening was being created in the Democratic Party. After the Democrats lost to Nixon in 1968, the contradictions seen in Chicago became a reform movement that would not be denied, eventually leading to George McGovern's 1972 nomination and the fundamental reform of party rules, including guaranteed representation for women and grassroots presidential primaries. The reform movement provoked sharp divisions around race, gender, and the Vietnam War, with the leadership of the American Federation of Labor–Congress of Industrial Organizations (AFL-CIO) eventually feeling driven to support Nixon over the McGovernites in 1972.

But it was an opening nonetheless, and some of us in the antiwar movement decided upon an *inside-outside strategy* to end the war, building grassroots pressure groups in key electoral states to demand that candidates commit to cut funding for bombing and combat operations, not unlike the surge of antiwar pressure in the 2006–2008 elections, which enabled Barack Obama to succeed as a presidential peace candidate.

The issues of Watergate and war were becoming interconnected in ways we could not anticipate. In May 1971, thousands of protesters carried out civil disobedience in Washington, ending in thirteen thousand being arrested and held in RFK stadium. That June, Nixon authorized the covert operation known as "the Plumbers" to plug all White House leaks, wiretap suspects in the *Pentagon Papers* scandal, neutralize Ellsberg, and break into his psychiatrist's Beverly Hills files. "We might be able to put this bastard into a helluva situation and discredit the New Left," speculated White House aide Charles Colson,[2] who also suggested firebombing the Brookings Institution before sending in White House operatives to steal files.[3]

79

Nixon deployed as his plumbers former CIA agent E. Howard Hunt, who had been a leader of the 1961 Bay of Pigs operation, and former FBI agent G. Gordon Liddy, whose previous escapades included a failed effort to spy on and prosecute Timothy Leary in Duchess County, New York, where Liddy once fired a gun through the ceiling in summing up a case. Liddy was known to show off techniques for assassinating people with sharpened pencils.[4] Later he would design Operation GEMSTONE, which included plans to abduct, kidnap, and "surgically relocate" antiwar protesters at the 1972 Republican convention, apparently including myself, and take us to Mexico.[5]

With this mentality armed and in power, Nixon was on a collision course with both moderation and democracy. On August 16, 1971, the "enemies' list" was completed, issued as a memo from John Dean to Haldeman and John Ehrlichman. Liddy was now counsel to the Committee to Re-elect the President. On May 21, 1972, James McCord and a team of Cuban exiles loyal to Hunt broke into Democratic National Headquarters at the Watergate complex, bugged the phones, and stole documents. On a second break-in on June 17, the Liddy team was snared and arrested when a security guard discovered tape on a door and called the DC police. Four Nixon officials ultimately pled guilty to cover-up, destruction and secretion of documents, obstruction of official investigations, subornation of perjury, and offers of money and executive clemency to secure silence.[6]

By 1972, Nixon had blown away George McGovern and the media were proclaiming a massive Republican triumph over the sixties. But it was not to be. Nixon had withdrawn American combat troops from Vietnam while escalating the air war, but the fighting and domestic protest continued with a life of their own. Immediately after his reelection, when he claimed peace was "at hand," Nixon launched unprecedented B-52 raids over Hanoi at Christmas and then accepted the Paris Peace Accords, which brought American POWs home while leaving North Vietnam a strategic advantage over Nixon's allies in Saigon. In a monumental Machiavellian deception, Henry Kissinger negotiated a face-saving "decent interval" before the collapse of Vietnam to communist-led forces.[7]

At home Jane Fonda and I were leading a coalition called the Indochina Peace Campaign, dedicated to the inside-outside approach. Many veterans of the sixties were burned out, while others (like myself) were trying to recover from the intense pressures, radicalism, militancy, and sectarianism that afflicted the movements in the late sixties. Though still on appeal from the Chicago trial, I realized that American public opinion had shifted in a decidedly welcoming direction. Jane and I spoke at many state fairs, chambers of commerce, and universities, helping distribute by hand 1 million antiwar pamphlets and summaries of the *Pentagon Papers*. This was long before the Internet, so we utilized slide shows to show the Vietnamese with a human face. The singer Holly Near and a former POW, George Smith, often accompanied us, as did a French citizen who had been held captive by the South Vietnamese government. We noted that, "while not forgetting the role of Congress in supporting this inhuman, immoral war for twenty years, antiwar sentiment in America and the present vulnerability of Congress to public pressure are important tools available to us to finally end the war."[8]

We did not know it, but we were on the cusp of victory after an interminable decade on the margins. A decisive factor was the GI movement, consisting of thousands of remarkable individuals mainly from the lower echelons of the armed forces, the grunts, whose new image seemed an exact blend of warrior and long-haired hippie, the separated twins of our generation. Nixon could do nothing about them as they gathered on April 18, 1971, to celebrate the anniversary of the American Revolution with another shot heard round the world. "Not since the Bonus March of 1932 had the city seen such a fiercely determined, actual army of men, military veterans, come before the nation's government with so earnest a cause."[9] Despite enormous strains, many provoked by the Nixon administration, they camped out in parks, threw combat medals over the White House fence, and dialogued with members of Congress. From their ranks rose a remarkable young navy veteran, John Kerry, who posed a question no one dared answer at a Senate hearing: Who wants to be the last to die for a mistake?

These "winter soldiers"—the phrase was coined by Thomas Paine during the hard days of the American Revolution—included many deeply influenced by the peace and civil rights movements, especially the Black Panther Party, which posed a growing threat of an army in mutinous militance. The overall GI movement, a classic paradigm of a social movement, provided a powerful pressure to end the war before the U.S. Army, the last resort of the Machiavellians, fell apart.[10] The GI movement helped broaden the antiwar movement into the mainstream, with antiwar sentiment nearing a majority in the wake of the sixties. In 1971, legislation by Senators Mark Hatfield and (future presidential candidate) George McGovern aimed at cutting off war funding failed. But it was a marker. In 1972, the Case-Church Amendment to ban all U.S. military operations in Indochina was withdrawn for lack of majority support. Lobbying within the system was gaining traction, but Nixon was unyielding. It was the unraveling of the imperial presidency, caused by the Watergate hearings in 1973, that finally yielded our opportunity.

In January of that year, the trial of Ellsberg and Russo commenced in a Los Angeles federal court. I worked on the defense with my attorney friend from Newark and Chicago, Leonard Weinglass, and two antiwar activists, Paul Ryder and Sam Hurst. Under the leadership of Stanley Sheinbaum, a huge support movement was organized. Nevertheless, the two defendants faced multiple lifetimes in prison if Nixon's hopes of reviving McCarthyism could be vindicated. But suddenly, the prosecution case collapsed on April 27 when it was disclosed that Liddy and Hunt had burglarized the files of Ellsberg's psychiatrist. In fact, Nixon had offered the FBI directorship to the judge presiding over the *Pentagon Papers* trial!

It began to feel as if the sixties were all over, though there were more years ahead. In May, shortly after the White House plumbers' exposure, the House of Representatives for the first time voted to end funding for combat in Vietnam. The weakened Nixon threatened a veto. In June, both houses voted to set a deadline to terminate direct and indirect funding of all American military operations, excluding funds for training the Saigon regime's troops. Kissinger, now representing the stricken Nixon, insisted that the White House would refuse to accept any deadlines as an infringement on executive power. An administration effort to weaken the measure was defeated on a 204–204 tie vote, earning the Congress a real "advise and consent" role in any future combat, a foreshadowing of the War Powers Act. Grassroots pressure was decisive, but still the war was not over. It would take until April 1975, when the North Vietnamese essentially won a military victory, before the most recalcitrant Machiavellians were forced to surrender. Even then, the evidence is that Nixon wanted to resume heavy bombing but was prevented from doing so because his own presidency had unraveled from Watergate. According to *Time* magazine's account, Nixon had approved the resumption of bombing but gave it up because he was "loath to deal with simultaneous severe criticism on two major fronts."[11] He resigned on August 9, 1974.

The long sixties now were beginning to end. Out of the almost-forgotten struggles that began in McComb, in Selma, in Ann Arbor, in Berkeley, a new progressive center—or set of norms in the absence of a leader like Kennedy or King—was solidifying. Civil rights. An end to poverty. An end to pollution. No more Vietnams. No more imperial presidency. No more policing the world. A new consensus was being instilled. Few remembered where it had come from or at what cost. And despite Nixon's fall, the countermovement remained potent.

It took one more year of sustained movement activism, bolstered by the Watergate opportunity, before the war was terminated in 1975, when President Gerald Ford chose not to resume B-52 bombing as Saigon fell to the Vietcong and North Vietnamese forces. It was a prudent Machiavellian decision. The new norms solidifying in civil society, contrary to the cold war norms, were a public rejection of the imperial presidency, the arrogant notion of policing the world, and any thought of sending American troops into future quagmires. Those norms would last for decades, surfacing again in the public's skepticism toward Iraq in 2003.

The sixties, at least when defined as an era dominated by Vietnam, could continue no further. The battle over memory would begin. It is worth noting briefly the close parallels between the ending of the Vietnam War and the apparent winding down of the Iraq war thirty years later. Contrary to media and public perception, there was a strong movement against the Iraq war beginning in 2003. The lack of media recognition was precisely caused by the blurring of lines between "inside" and "outside" the system in the decades between the eras. There were, by my research, at least eleven national street demonstrations of more than one hundred thousand people. A majority of Americans polled by the Gallup organization turned against Iraq as a "mistake" more rapidly than had occurred during Vietnam, an indicator of the Vietnam legacy at work. Michael Moore's *Fahrenheit 9/11* broke box-office records for documentaries. The Dixie Chicks survived the administration's attempt to chill opposition by artists. Cindy Sheehan's protest at the Bush ranch aroused global interest and solidarity. MoveOn.org raised an unheard-of $180 million for federal candidates in the 2004–2005 voter cycle, especially benefiting the insurgent anti-Iraq candidacy of Howard Dean. Voters turned out the Republican Congress in 2006, and pressure grew on Congress to set a deadline for troop withdrawals and war funding in 2007–2008. Along came Senator Barack Obama on an anti–Iraq War platform in 2008; he became the first presidential candidate to be elected on such a pledge.

But unlike South Vietnam, Iraq did not collapse under the pressure of a united insurgency. Instead, the unstable and unpopular regime was held together by the same combination of air war and counterinsurgency applied during the latter years of Vietnam. The "wise men" had aged, but found their replacement in the "study group" chaired by James Baker and Lee Hamilton in 2007, which recommended a phased withdrawal to stave off utter collapse. Finally, in late 2008, a secret pact was negotiated between Baghdad and the White House to phase out all remaining U.S. troops by 2011. This appeared to be another "decent interval" arrangement, but as of this writing, the future remains unknown. President Barack Obama finds himself in 2009 positioned between the empire's Machiavellians and the social movements that helped his historic candidacy succeed.[12]

In any event, the movement moderates from the sixties would move on to roles in government, business, labor, education, and the media. One key example among many was Hillary Rodham Clinton, a 1969 Wellesley College graduate. Originally a Goldwater supporter, Rodham was awakened by the student and civil rights movements around her. She was an eyewitness to three nights during the 1968 Democratic National Convention protests. She was "clean for Gene" in the New Hampshire campaign. She debated with her roommates whether a revolution might happen. As she confided in a letter, "God, I feel so divorced from Park Ridge, parents, home, the entire unreality of middle class America."[13] Her 1969 commencement speech cited the New Left and tapped into themes of the Port Huron Statement:

> If the experiment in human living doesn't work in this country, in this age, it's not going to work anywhere....
>
> But we also know that to be educated, the goal of it must be human liberation, a liberation enabling each of us to fulfill our capacity so as to be free to create within and around ourselves, [and] to be educated to freedom must be evidenced in action....
>
> We are all of us exploring a world that none of us even understands and attempting to create within that uncertainty. But there are some things we feel, feelings that our prevailing, acquisitive, and competitive corporate life, including tragically the universities, is not the way of life for us....
>
> We're searching for more immediate, ecstatic and penetrating modes of living.[14]

She remained pragmatic at her core, running successfully for student body president. Her honors thesis on community organizer Saul Alinsky explored whether it was possible to be "that rare specimen, the successful radical."[15]

At Yale Law school the following year, Rodham was wearing a black armband to observe the Vietnam Moratorium, working with law students on the Panther trial in New Haven, though still very much within the system. From there she joined a Bay Area law firm run by radical attorneys, where she researched and eventually wrote a law review article on the rights of children, a foundation for her later work at the Children's Defense Fund.[16]

As the long sixties ended, Rodham married Bill Clinton in 1975 and followed the long road to the White House in 1992. With radical pressures disappearing from American culture, she was perceived by conservatives as no longer a moderate, but on the radical edge of acceptability. Accordingly, she made adjustments that grew over her sixties roots, winning acceptability as First Lady and, eventually, as a presidential candidate in her own right. Along the way, she broke with some of her closest allies over welfare reform in the nineties and supported the North American Free Trade Agreement (NAFTA) and the wars in the Balkans and Iraq. The most progressive remaining dimension of her public persona was the fact that she might break the glass ceiling as president in 2008. It was as if the Machiavellian order would accept a woman only if she broke with her feminist past and acted on national security like a male militarist.[17] In the end, she fell painfully short, though breaking the prevalent cultural norms about a woman's readiness to be president.

Here was a classic demonstration of the system at work. Acceptance of a woman president, long a goal of the social movements, seemed to mean obeying the Machiavellian insistence that she become as masculine as possible. It was enough to mobilize millions of women and their allies to passionate campaigning against the culture of the glass ceiling, but not enough to win politically.

Although the impact of the movement pragmatists fell short, the legacy of the more militant activists of the sixties was far more ambiguous. As the sixties waned and the pragmatists surged, the sixties radicals returned to the invisible margins of everyday life. From their relative oblivion, they would watch as others reaped the benefit of the cultural changes their sacrifices had produced. If the past was disappearing, how would their legacy reappear in future generations?

13

Wounded Knee and the End of the Sixties

*F*OR MOST PEOPLE, THE SIXTIES ENDED WITH the fall of Richard Nixon, the end of the war, the decline of revolutionary violence, and the domestic thaw that permitted Jimmy Carter to become president in 1976.

But if Nixon's fall and Vietnam's triumph were defining markers of change, and if Timothy Leary's decline was a marker of endgame absurdity, the most poignant example of the unresolved sixties was perhaps the battle of the American Indian Movement (AIM) for independence, cultural identity, and land against a domestic counterinsurgency carried on by vigilantes, police, the FBI, and the full machinery of the federal government. This was the final war of the Nixon presidency, one waged at home as the president himself was being forced out of office for crimes less lethal than those inflicted on Indian activists in the Black Hills.

The resurgent movement for "red power" grew from the margins of Indian ghettos, local jails, returning military veterans, and students newly enrolled in ethnic studies classes on college campuses. AIM's first battles in 1968 were against police brutality in Minneapolis–St. Paul, modeled after the Black Panther street patrols in Oakland. In those ways, AIM was similar to the Panthers, the United Slaves (US), the Brown Berets, the Young Lords, the Third World Liberation Front, and similar organizations fighting for rights and resources in the sixties. The movement that later became AIM arose in the early sixties with civil rights struggles such as the "fish-ins" over native rights in the Northwest (1963) and the emergence of a new generation of student activists, Vine Deloria and Clyde Warrior among them, in traditional organizations such as the National Congress of American Indians. Following the example of the southern student sit-ins, a group of Indian activists, including twenty-six-year-old Russell Means, temporarily occupied and claimed Alcatraz Island in March 1964, sending momentary shock waves through Indian Country. Occupations took place as well amid the presidential monuments sculpted into Mount Rushmore and overlooking historic Indian lands. A dramatic escalation occurred in the late sixties when seventy-eight Indians, mainly students, took over the abandoned Alcatraz prison island in the heart of San Francisco Bay, starting on November 20, 1969. Their essential demand was *full title to the island,* which they compared to the transfer of Manhattan to the Dutch centuries before. From the island power base would emerge a network of educational, cultural, and spiritual institutions. Some compared the occupation's symbolic meaning to planting a flag on the moon. But the revolution was not to be. Nevertheless, Alcatraz generated global attention, spurred other occupations, engaged cabinet officials in the Nixon administration, and was not brought to an end for nineteen months, in June 1971.

AIM activists intervened, often physically, in specific cases of violent injustices against Indians in local communities, such as the death of Raymond Yellow Thunder in the tiny town of Gordon, Nebraska, near the Pine Ridge Reservation, in February 1972. In response, fourteen hundred Indians from eighty tribes protested, took over buildings, and fought police and vigilantes on snowy streets.[1] Then, after the California murder of Richard Oakes, a former student who had led the Alcatraz occupation, the commitment to a continental march to Washington, DC, the Trail of Broken Treaties Caravan, was crystallized. The point was to demand a new treaty-making relationship between the tribes and the federal government.

The caravan reached Washington on November 1 and, lacking permits, food, and places to sleep, almost spontaneously occupied the hated Bureau of Indian Affairs building and renamed it the Native American Embassy. The failure of negotiations resulted in the BIA building—six blocks from the White House—being sacked by some of the activists and the furious Indians forced to return to the Plains at government expense.

At this point, AIM was an organizational metaphor for the classic dynamic of a social movement on fire with passion and spontaneity, running ahead of organizational structures with a life of its own. In an insightful description by two scholars of the movement, "It had become *a kind of prairie hurricane,* wreaking havoc on one place until seemingly defeated and spent, only to inexplicably reappear weeks later somewhere else."[2]

The functional identity of AIM, and thousands of loosely associated Indian activists, was that of traditional *warriors* who would fight with any weapons at hand against local racists, police, and, most importantly, the alleged "goon squads" deployed by traditional reservation councils with support from local white ranchers and the BIA. The Pine Ridge Reservation, then the poorest jurisdiction in the United States, was dominated by a particularly hostile tribal chairman, Richard Wilson. Under Wilson, tribal elections were rigged, and scores of activists were routinely beaten, and sometimes shot, by Wilson's forces. Gradually the pieces of a U.S. counterinsurgency campaign against AIM were pulled together, stimulated by a secretive Pentagon operation dubbed "Garden Plot."[3] Under this "Civil Disturbance Plan 55-2," the U.S. Army would be authorized to deploy, out of uniform at first, against alleged revolutionaries on American soil; this would come to mean more than ten thousand FBI agents, BIA agents, U.S. marshals, and state National Guardsmen destined for deployment to Wounded Knee, perhaps the most sacred historical site for native people on the continent.

At the end of the sixties, I sat on a Berkeley floor poring over Dee Brown's *Bury My Heart at Wounded Knee.*[4] The book is a widely read classic today, but it was a stunning new revelation at the time. Few American Indian books were circulating in those days (Vine Deloria's *Custer Died for Your Sins: An American Indian Manifesto* was another[5]), which made Brown's history of wanton massacres, a ninety-year counterinsurgency against native people, and a litany of America's broken treaties a conclusive indictment of the American government at the very time I was questioning its legitimacy. Now I saw Vietnam as an extension of foundational conflicts that had originated in the settlement of America itself (and Ireland slightly before). I wrote a book about Vietnam in 1971 using an observation from Sitting Bull as the title: "The Love of Possession Is a Disease with Them."[6] It recounted the startling parallels between Vietnam and the Indian wars, down to the naming of America's weaponry after defeated tribes (both Sioux and Apache originally meant "enemy," just as the term "Vietcong," or communist enemy, was imposed on the Vietnamese); then the names were made to adorn helicopters (the Apache) and all sorts of weapons (Tomahawk missiles, for example).

I realized the key difference between the native people's struggles and all others. Native struggles were not about civil rights, though Indians were entitled to the same rights as anyone, perhaps more. Rather, they were about *tribal* rights and *national* rights that had been voided by force by the U.S. government. African slaves had been uprooted from distant lands, whereas *native people and their lands* had been captured, conquered, and subordinated on the very territory from which they came. This conquest intermingled with democracy raised the question of *sovereignty*, the cardinal principle of the Machiavellian order. AIM and its adherents wanted at least a form of dual citizenship in order to travel in dignity between their two worlds and recognition of their treaty rights as tribal nations negotiating with the U.S. government. This was not necessarily an insoluble question, because many countries struggle with binational identities, but opening up the issue threatened the stability, power, moral reputation, and national narrative of the unitary American state. To do so would reveal certain untenable premises of the American nation, including the bizarre legal claim to a God-given "right of discovery" to inhabited native lands.[7] In that sense, the issue of full native self-determination was not on the table, not a contradiction that could be accommodated by the Machiavellian forces. According to the *New York Times* then, "the whole reservation structure may crumble" if Indian nations were to achieve independent status. What was the difference between our client regime in Saigon and the "reservation structure" imposed at home? I began to wonder.

In 1972, the federal government was pumping thousands of dollars into support of Wilson's candidacy, along with its patronage and "goon squads," against AIM. Evidence of vote rigging was overwhelming. This indeed was like South Vietnam or Latin America. If these actions were fully revealed, the United States would have to acknowledge an internal colonialism in which Washington-supported clients were subsidized, deputized, and militarized against insurgent Indian activists. Treaties might have to be reopened. Worse, many of the reservations, once considered desolate, now sat over massive quantities of oil, coal, uranium, gold, and other resources defined as strategic to the American government, the military, and corporations such as Union Carbide and Chevron ($8 billion in uranium, in 1979 dollars, was buried in South Dakota, mostly beneath the Black Hills).[8] The Black Hills were slated to become "the nucleus of a vast multinational energy domain."[9] Another Wounded Knee uprising at the time of the 1973 energy crisis would drill too deeply into these American contradictions.

The Sioux had defeated the U.S. Army in war the century before and had signed the 1868 Treaty of Laramie guaranteeing Indian ownership of the Black Hills and other parts of South Dakota.[10] Some movement leaders, such as Crazy Horse, refused to negotiate any treaties at all, considering them violations of preexisting sovereignty. But the treaties, some 371 altogether, were signed amid promises, pomp, and ceremony and then were violated, considered only expedient instruments for the army and government until frontier expansion necessitated their being abrogated. In the case of the Black Hills, the Gold Rush was the pretext for ripping up the treaty of 1868. Army raids led to the most famous defeat in the annals of the American military, that of George Armstrong Custer and the U.S. Army's Seventh Cavalry at the Little Big Horn in June 1876, known to the tribes as Greasy Grass. So traumatic was Custer's defeat that Walt Whitman, America's famed democratic poet, wrote a "glad triumphal sonnet" about Custer that extolled "the splendid fever of thy deeds."[11] Here was the hard truth: Peaceful coexistence with the native people was seen by the power elites as incompatible with the expansionary ideal of democracy. It would be a century before the sixties generation would be forced to examine the question once again.

Thirteen years later, the same Seventh Cavalry took its revenge. Sitting Bull, the victor at Little Big Horn, had returned from sanctuary in Canada with the promise of a pardon. Instead, police at Standing Rock, fearing the renewal of ghost dancing, killed Sitting Bull and eight other warriors on December 15, 1890. Under the leadership of Big Foot, some 350 Sioux fled under cover of darkness on a 150-mile journey to Pine Ridge, where they sought sanctuary from Red Cloud. But they were stopped on December 28 by Custer's old regiment alongside the banks of Wounded Knee Creek. Four cannons already were emplaced above the frozen and captured band. After the Indians were disarmed, the Hotchkiss guns were unleashed, firing fifty two-pound shells per minute. At least 300 were killed or wounded and left frozen in the creek bed.[12] That same year historian Frederick Jackson Turner issued his famous thesis that the American frontier finally had reached its end. Wounded Knee was seen as the last battle in the formation of the American character.

But nothing was over. Out of nowhere, the sixties experienced the revival of the Indian spirit and what it actually revealed about America's character. For many people, non-Indian as well as Indian, the 1890 Wounded Knee photos of frozen corpses with outstretched hands were the most notorious of an American atrocity until those taken at My Lai village, South Vietnam, in 1969. Photos of the two massacres, with scores of civilian bodies piled in ditches, seemed eerily identical despite the eighty-year passage of time. The impression of Vietnam as an extension of the Indian wars was sealed in my mind, and many others of the sixties genera-tion, in the caked blood of genocide. Many in the anti–Vietnam War movement juxtaposed the two photos in antiwar materials, and the Indochina Peace Campaign adopted in 1972 a poster that featured a Vietnamese peasant in a conical hat and that called for "no more broken treaties." It was the same year that the Indians caravanned to Washington, just one year before the next Wounded Knee.

The second battle of Wounded Knee, from February 27 until May 8, 1973, took place as the Nixon administration was floundering in its Watergate debacle and was driven by these memories on all sides.[13] AIM, which had been launched by urban Indians distant from reservation roots, now sought counsel from the elders at Pine Ridge. After a long meeting, the elders asked the AIM warriors to take a life-or-death stand at Wounded Knee. It was a powerful generational fusion, for the elders were invoking the spirit of the ancestors for a new generation of activists whose identities, languages, rituals, and histories had almost completely been stripped from them in white society. After consulting with the AIM warriors, the elders sent a formal letter to the White House and Senate.[14] Asserting their position under the 1868 treaty, they called for Senate hearings on their treaty rights and a full investigation of abuses on Sioux reservations across South Dakota.

Armed AIM members occupied the site where the 1890 massacre had taken place, seized a small store, and held its proprietors hostage for a short time.[15] But the firepower arrayed against the band of some two hundred occupiers was something never seen in hundreds of sixties occupations. According to the *New York Times,* two army colonels, including the chief of the Eighty-second Airborne Division, were on-site in civilian disguise. The U.S. Army and National Guard supplied hundreds of marshals and FBI agents with fifteen armored personnel carriers equipped with .50-caliber machine guns, one hundred thousand rounds of M-16 ammunition, M-79 grenade launchers, a squadron of aerial reconnaissance planes from Vietnam, eleven hundred parachute flares, twenty sniper rifles, gas masks, bulletproof vests, C-rations, ponchos, and blankets.[16] The *Times* compared the U.S. Army's role to that of "U.S. advisers [who] took command in Vietnam." During the seventy-one days ahead, there were numerous twenty-four-hour periods of shooting, sometimes thousands of rounds being fired overnight by the federal forces, the Wilson police, vigilante ranchers, and the lightly armed AIM members.

Aware that considerable public opinion was on the side of armed Indians, the army leadership rejected an FBI request to overrun Wounded Knee with two thousand regular forces.[17] Instead, "the military strategy was to starve them out, in a classic siege operation." Two AIM members were shot and killed during the long siege, one of whose ancestors had been at Wounded Knee in 1890, but many more might have been massacred were it not for the force of public opinion.[18] Thousands of activists participated in vigils, protests, letter-writing campaigns, clandestine backpacking with food and supplies into Wounded Knee, and even an unauthorized airlift by several anti–Vietnam War activists. The National Council of Churches pledged to stand between the armed forces and the Indian occupiers. With 93 percent of Americans following the news from Wounded Knee, Marlon Brando refused to accept his Academy Award for *The Godfather* and instead asked an Apache actress to receive the award and speak about the siege. Notable, however, was the default of the moderate Machiavellian group; for example, South Dakota's liberal senator, George McGovern, an initial sympathizer, started calling for AIM's physical expulsion and declared that it was "ridiculous to talk about the Treaty of 1868 being carried out."[19]

The difference between 1890 and 1973 was not only public opinion, but also Machiavellian concern for the global image of the United States. "The name of the game is not to kill or injure the Indians," said one internal army memo.[20] The U.S. Information Agency stated that "if Indians are killed, we can surely expect sharp and widespread foreign condemnation.… It would come at a particularly unpropitious time, giving Arab governments an excuse to fog up the terrorist issue."[21] Nevertheless, the greater concern for state interest drove the government to set an absolute May 8 deadline for removal of the Indians. Since "unilateral withdrawal by U.S. forces probably would lead to expansion of the territory controlled by the AIM militants," said a Justice Department options memo, if negotiations collapsed on May 8, "the U.S. marshals and the FBI will be given permission to *terminate* the Indian occupation of Wounded Knee by *whatever force they deem necessary*."[22] As a final incentive, the Nixon administration guaranteed substantive negotiations that week. Those talks would break down when the Indians asked for reinstatement of treaty-making powers.

A second massacre was not deemed necessary, as the occupation ended on May 8, thus climaxing "the high tide of the most remarkable period of activism carried out by Indians in the twentieth century."[23] But the struggle in the Black Hills was by no means over. On October 18, 1973, key AIM leader Pedro Bissonnette was shot and killed by the BIA police. In June 1975, two FBI agents were shot and killed along with one Indian in a mysterious gun battle near Pine Ridge. A young AIM member, Leonard Peltier, was targeted, tried, convicted, and sentenced to life imprisonment in a case that prompted worldwide petitioning, press coverage, and notable books, one by Peter Matthiessen that was banned from many bookstores for nearly a decade, and films, including a documentary by Robert Redford.[24] Peltier, who was among several Indians who fired shots when the two agents drove onto Indian property, was convicted despite a lack of any evidence linking his weapon with shells found near the victims' bodies. Peltier today remains incarcerated at Fort Leavenworth, Kansas, federal prison, in the heart of the Plains culture and the nineteenth-century wars of Manifest Destiny.

In addition to Peltier, more than five hundred Indian people were indicted by the federal government in relation to the 1973 Wounded Knee occupation. Even though 92 percent of the AIM-related cases were ultimately won by the defendants, the organization began to collapse under the legal burdens, "with breathtaking suddenness."[25] In addition, it became known that the organization was riddled with FBI agents and informants from a massive counterintelligence program. They included Dennis Banks's director of security, Doug Durham,[26] and years later, Kamook, an AIM activist, his lover, and the mother of his children.[27]

It was a remarkable time. The Nixon government was being driven from office for crimes against the Constitution arising from a war that seemed to be an extension of the nineteenth-century Indian wars. Indians were rising across the United States to demand a rewriting of constitutional arrangements. As 1976, the two hundredth anniversary of the nation's founding approached, a new American revolution, or a revision of the first Revolution, seemed imaginable. This was the post-Watergate era, when the Machiavellian reputation was in tatters. Jerry Brown, elected California's governor at thirty-four years of age, was intending to run for president. He was officially harboring AIM fugitive Banks in California, refusing to extradite him to South Dakota. As one who was there, I thought this was the finale of the sixties, the brief period after the fall of Nixon, the fall of Vietnam, the sudden rise of new antinuclear and pro-solar energy movements, and the improbable appearance of American Indians once again. Beyond the powerful reforms of the previous fifteen years—for the rainbow of social movements—we finally seemed to be facing the nightmare that shadowed the American dream: the fact that our democracy was founded on a genocide that had to be acknowledged and repudiated. Before this, by blood and spirit, we had achieved a succession of important reforms on which the Machiavellians had been forced to yield. What these sixties reforms held in common was the unfolding promise of equal democratic rights to those denied them: the African slaves, those of no property, women, unrepresented workers, farmworkers, eighteen-year-olds, a scroll of the disfranchised.

But the native people were different. They sought *sovereign* rights, not civil rights alone, and proposed a new historical narrative that exposed the hypocrisy and contradicted the legitimizing foundations of the state itself. They were the defiant ones, still standing, asserting transcendent natural rights, given to them by the Creator, that required a rethinking and restructuring of everything. The Indians and their supporters had resumed their fight against oblivion and extinction. Though a handful compared to their former numbers, they had threatened the established order more than at any time in a century. And the Machiavellians, both moderate and militant, were not going to let them carry their claims any further. Not in 1976.

The moment came and went. The Jimmy Carter years became a twilight time for the sixties, not another interim before the next uprising. Then, in response, came the Reagan counterrevolution.

But the Indian struggles of the sixties had imparted lessons that were especially profound: that ghosts never die and dead men live, that Manifest Destiny was an imperial frenzy, that our longest war—our American original sin—was against the first inhabitants of the continent. The sixties generation had traveled many roads to reach this understanding. And now the sixties were slipping behind us.

I have long wondered why there has been so little attention to the Indian wars that took place in the final and climactic years of the sixties. A sampling of the indexes of many well-known histories of the sixties—Tom Brokaw's *Boom!* (2007), David Caute's *The Year of the Barricades* (1988), Estelle Freedman's *No Turning Back* (2002), Richard Flacks's *Making History* (1988), Todd Gitlin's *The Sixties* (1987), Mark Kurlansky's *1968* (2004), Harvey Matusow's *The Unraveling of America* (1984), James Miller's *Democracy Is in the Streets* (1987), Rick Perlstein's *Nixonland* (2008), Kirkpatrick Sale's *SDS* (1973), Thomas Powers's *The War at Home* (1973), Robert Stone's *Remembering the Sixties* (2007), and Jeremy Suri's *Power and Protest* (2003)—reveals *no mention of Alcatraz or Wounded Knee* in their indexes.

Why? There are numerous—though perhaps not numerous enough—histories of Indian culture, Indian spirituality, Indian history, and Indian social movements that have been published since 1968. There are books by Dennis Banks, Russell Means, Leonard Peltier. But it is as if these works stand on an Indian shelf of their own, outside the framing of the sixties.

One possible explanation is that the indigenous continue to exist on an internal reservation in the mind-set of many. A racial double standard is at work, if only subconsciously, that results in a separation of the Indian story from the sixties story and from America's story. Perhaps a clearer way to put the matter is that the indigenous question is difficult to integrate into our assumptions about the sixties, about democracy, and about America itself without disrupting certain unconscious premises. We are not a special nation, a light unto the world, a city upon the hill, a melting pot of *e pluribus unum,* unless we also confront the bloody colonialism hidden and completely intertwined with and choking the roots of our history.

PART III

The Sixties at Fifty

⌒ 14 ⌒

Che Guevara and the Sixties

It is the hour of the furnace, and the light is all that can be seen.
—José Martí, quoted by Fidel Castro[1]

*T*HE STORMS OF THE SIXTIES WERE BECOMING MORE ELECTRIC as the climactic year 1968 began. In October 1967, Che Guevara was captured and killed in Bolivia with CIA assistance. Weeks later, one hundred thousand protesters surrounded and threatened to storm the Pentagon. Senator Eugene McCarthy was enlisting college students for his primary challenge to the president. Plans were afoot for confronting war-makers at the Chicago Democratic National Convention the following August. Unimaginable shocks lay just ahead: the Tet Offensive, the murders of Martin Luther King and Robert Kennedy, urban riots, campus strikes, the Soviet invasion of Czechoslovakia, uprisings in countries around the world.

On a January night in Havana, I was meeting with Fidel Castro. I came to the island with a contingent of New Left participants in a conference with a cross section of revolutionaries from Latin America, Asia, and Africa. It was a dizzying time.

My purpose was specific, urgent, and odd. I was an acquaintance of Elizabeth Burgos, the Venezuelan wife of the French revolutionary and Castro confidant Regis Debray, who had been captured and imprisoned in Bolivia during a secret visit to Che. Elizabeth was allowed to visit Debray in his Bolivian jail and smuggled out information about Che's predicament. Because I had been involved in securing the release of three American POWs from Vietnam that previous year, Elizabeth then came to me with a startling request: lobby the Vietnamese to release three captured American pilots to the United States in exchange for Debray's freedom. Nothing came of this audacious proposal, but it brought me as an intermediary to Castro at a house near Varadero beach. With me were Dave Dellinger, fresh from the huge Pentagon demonstration of October, and Carl Davidson, an SDS officer famous for his 1967 slogan, "from protest to resistance." The discussion would be a long one lasting into the night.

The 1959 Cuban revolution played a pivotal role in the global sixties and on the American home front. The Cubans were a vivid example of a new force breaking the boundaries of the cold war. There was no question about Cuba's discomfort with its military and economic alliance with the Soviets. In the Fidel-Che view, the Soviets were more interested in maintaining good relationships with the Americans than in offering aid to revolutionaries in poor countries; to the

Soviets, the Cubans were impetuous "fire starters."[2] The more militant Chinese were hegemonic in their approach to small countries as well, having pressured the Vietnamese to accept the 1955 Geneva partition of their country as permanent. Hazy reports of Mao Zedong's Cultural Revolution suggested, however, that the Chinese might be throwing their considerable weight behind Third World revolutions. The Cultural Revolution reinforced a growing view that revolutions became ossified with bureaucracy, which overlapped the Cuban criticism of communist parties that were reluctant to commence armed struggle.[3] This view would prove profoundly mistaken.

In this context, the Cubans were expanding the existing notion of nonalignment into one of *tricontinental revolution,* advocating and supporting guerrilla warfare everywhere against authoritarian clients of the United States, especially across the Americas. Forming this new "international" was an open challenge from tiny Cuba to existing communist parties and states in the orbits of Moscow or Beijing.

Debray was a formidable icon. He first visited Cuba as a philosophy graduate student in 1961. Then in his twenties, the Frenchman befriended the Cuban leaders and authored a brilliant short text, *Revolution in the Revolution?* based on the Cuban leadership's new guerrilla doctrines. In brief summary, the Debray/Cuban thesis was that revolution could be catalyzed by small *focos* (focal points) of armed revolutionaries acting as vanguards. The theory turned upside down the traditional view, once shared by Che himself, that guerrilla war was impossible until all peaceful and legal means of struggle had been exhausted.[4] In the new doctrine, a guerrilla uprising itself could create mass revolutionary consciousness by example, foment an organized radical movement, and put the establishment on the defensive. "It is not necessary to wait until all conditions for making revolution exist; the insurrection can create them."[5] And as the Cubans constantly repeated, "The duty of a revolutionary is to make the revolution."

Gradualism, then, appeared in this view to be an excuse for failing to start the chain of events leading to revolution. The *foco* concept was drawn largely from the experience of the Cuban revolution itself. In that case, only twelve of Fidel's eighty-plus insurgents survived the initial battles after the landing of the *Granma* from Mexico. A defiant Fidel nonetheless declared that the death knell of the dictatorship had sounded.[6] All the guerrilla survivors were Cubans except for Che, who was an Argentine exile. The surprised Batista regime eventually disintegrated, and the dictator fled the country. With support from the countryside and underground support networks, the columns of the Twenty-sixth of July Movement advanced into Havana, creating a romantic revolutionary spectacle for the global sixties generation.

This was not an illusion. The Cuban revolution helped inspire at least twenty-four guerrilla movements in Argentina, Bolivia, Chile, Colombia, El Salvador, Guatemala, Honduras, Mexico, Nicaragua, Peru, Venezuela, and Uruguay. All of them failed militarily to overthrow the state with the exception of Nicaragua. At the same time, a revolutionary spirit was spreading throughout Latin America's

Catholic communities in the form of liberation theology, formally embraced by the Latin American bishops in 1968. These two phenomena—Cuban-inspired guerrilla movements and Catholic base communities—were shaking the Machiavellians of the continent with redistributionist demands.[7] In most places, the church was mobilizing a nonviolent but often complementary alternative to the Cubans' Marxist model. As early as 1961, the Kennedy administration responded with its alternative to the Cuba revolution, the Alliance for Progress, an attempt to induce the oligarchies toward reform from within. In a truly fateful encounter, Kennedy emissary Richard Goodwin held an impromptu three-hour discussion with Che during the Alliance meeting in Punta del Este, Uruguay. This was not long after the debacle at the Bay of Pigs, yet an accommodation was still possible. In essence, Che proposed a modus vivendi. The United States would cease its attempts at subversion and blockade. In return, Cuba would compensate for the seizure of American properties, avoid a military alliance with the Soviet Union, and, most importantly, limit assistance to guerrillas in other Latin American countries.[8]

There was no follow-up from the Kennedy administration to the exploratory Cuban initiative, although the president was the first to smoke a cigar that Goodwin had brought back from Che. The Alliance for Progress failed as Che had predicted. Kennedy was murdered less than two years later. Che, chafing in Cuba, his modus vivendi overture ignored, took up guerrilla war once again as the U.S. invasion of Vietnam escalated.

These complicated subtleties were unknown amid the passionate movements developing in the Americas, both North and South. By 1967, the message spreading to the New Left in North America was that militant action itself was the incubator of consciousness. Small nonviolent cadres of SNCC, despite being described as outside agitators, were awakening the consciousness of rural black people; brutal police behavior, when televised, awakened a wider audience of sympathizers across the world. C. Wright Mills took the example further in his 1961 manifesto, *Listen Yankee!* written in the voice of a Cuban revolutionary. "For us, with our problems, it was simple: in Cuba we had to take to our 'Rocky Mountains'—you couldn't do that, could you? Not yet, we suppose. We're joking—we suppose. But if in ten years, in five years, if things go as we think they might inside your country, then know this, Yankee: some of us will be with you. God almighty, those are great mountains!"[9]

I took this message from Mills as pure fantasy, however inspiring, when I first read it, but within five years there actually were armed Mexican American guerrillas in the mountains of New Mexico, armed Black Panthers monitoring the police in multiple ghettos, Brown Berets and Young Lords sprouting up from LA to Spanish Harlem, and, by 1969, an armed Weather Underground. It was everywhere becoming "the hour of the furnace." But let me return to the late-night discussion with Fidel in January 1968.

I do not know if there ever were differences between Fidel and Che, but I assumed there might be. Fidel was Cuban; Che was not. Fidel was head of state, party, and army; Che was leader of guerrilla bands. Fidel needed diplomatic support against the United States and its embargo; Che threatened the diplomatic status quo. I assumed that on some deep level they were like brothers. But their different roles might have strained them.

This is what I was thinking while sitting across from Fidel, his several aides, and interpreters that late night. We began by speaking of Stokely Carmichael, then chair of SNCC and formulator of its black power doctrine, now becoming an icon of militant revolution in the path of Malcolm X. Stokely was a recent visitor to the island, where he had spent hours in conversations with Fidel. The CIA was on Carmichael's trail.[10]

Fidel was clearly worried about Stokely's activities and the threats to his life. "I told him he must have a united front," Fidel said, with the concerned tone of an elder. Instead, at the time SNCC had divided over black power and adherence to nonviolence. Its prior chairman, John Lewis, had been driven out over these issues. Stokely, organizer of the Lowndes County, Alabama, political party that had adopted the symbol of a black panther, now was engaged in fractious, long-distance negotiations over a merger with the Oakland Black Panther Party, an effort that collapsed. Through informants and dirty tricks, the FBI was involved in disrupting these efforts. At the time, the militant call for black power had driven away white financial and political support for SNCC, leaving Stokely as a media symbol with a mass following but little or no organizational base.

His dilemmas would only worsen in the months ahead. His rhetoric called for "guerrilla warfare" against a backdrop of flaming ghettos, but in fact there was no arsenal of weapons, few cadre, and an almost complete lack of organized popular support outside of small pockets of the black community and a handful of white radicals. I had witnessed the spontaneous ease of looting, burning, and street fighting in the Newark riots of July 1967, and, indeed, it was not difficult for a fevered mind to imagine a well-prepared *foco* overrunning City Hall, a domestic Moncada. But there were no organized guerrillas in Newark, not even the snipers who initially were blamed. What would come after such a storming of the state was not clear to me. As I wrote in a review of Newark that was dissected by Special Forces trainers, "The conditions are slowly being created for an American form of guerrilla warfare based in the slums." But, I added, "violence can contribute to shattering the status quo, but only politics and organization can transform it."[11]

There was a clear sense in which Fidel was reflecting on the fate of Che just three months earlier and on the failed *foco* theory that was becoming a global mantra. Che's first initiative after the Cuban revolution had been in Congo, where the elected nationalist leader Patrice Lumumba was murdered by the U.S.-backed Belgian colonialists in 1960 and the United States was encouraging white mercenaries to aid the secessionist province of Katanga. Che, believing that Congo "is the hottest spot in the world right now," made several trips to confer with African nationalist leaders and one trip to Beijing to solicit the mood of the Chinese leaders. He then led a unit of one hundred Cuban fighters, virtually all black, to Lake Tanganyika in April 1965, intent on turning the area into a "detonator to set off revolution in all the African countries."[12] But the allies Che counted on were unreliable, and, most important, there was almost complete "incompetence and disorganization," and many "Congolese who were not prepared to fight."[13] Che had been warned by Egypt's Gamal Nasser not to become "another Tarzan, a white man among black men, leading them and protecting them," but he led the struggle anyway. Che and the survivors were finally evacuated after a humiliating campaign.

Despite candid and serious self-criticism in his African diaries, Che became trapped in similar problems in Latin America. In diaries, interviews, and books published since, it is not entirely clear that Bolivia was Che's target, a stepping-stone to Argentina or, like Congo, a potential "detonator" of surrounding Latin American countries. As early as 1960, Fidel himself had declared that Cuba's example would "convert the Andes into the Sierra Maestre of the American continent."[14] Jon Anderson actually quotes Che in the jungle, according to one of his comrades' notes, as saying, "Bolivia will be sacrificed for the cause of creating the conditions for revolutions in neighboring countries."[15]

The record indicates that Che's campaign was largely opposed by the Bolivian Communist Party, itself consumed with internal debates along Soviet-Chinese lines. This meant he relied heavily on sending in Cuban agents to sew together an urban underground and supply network. The number of Bolivian fighters was less than one-half his effective combat force of forty-two.[16] The travels of Debray; an Argentine comrade, Ciros Bustos; and an East German–born operative known as Tania to the guerrilla zone may have alerted the CIA to Che's presence there.[17] Most importantly, Che never succeeded in attracting support from Bolivia's indigenous majority, perhaps in part because the class analysis of Marxism assigned little importance to native people, most of whom were unemployed or working in informal, family-based economic sectors. He also may have overestimated the degree of unpopularity of the La Paz regime. "The inhabitants of the region are as impenetrable as rocks.... You talk to them, and in the depths of their eyes it can be seen that they don't believe."[18]

It may or may not have been indigenous farmers who passed the word on Che's presence that led to his capture and assassination. But it was the CIA that guided the shooters to their quarry. According to Anderson's definitive account, the Bolivian interior minister already was on the CIA payroll.[19] A Cuban American CIA agent was present during the interrogations of Debray and Bustos. The agency recruited Felix Rodriguez, another Cuban American who had been with the CIA since the Bay of Pigs. Along with Cuban American Gustavo Villoldo, Rodriguez was involved in the hunt at the field level.[20] When the wounded Che was captured, Rodriguez arrived by helicopter, interviewed Che, and had a photo taken with him. The formal order to execute Che came from the Bolivian command in La Paz, which Rodriguez says he decoded and read. He claims to have advised the Bolivians not to shoot Che, then gave the invalid guerrilla a final hug, walked away, and lit a cigarette until the shot was fired.

The United States was long the hegemon over Latin America. The Cuban revolution, however, was like a *foco* writ large over the whole continent, inspiring many kindred movements but also a fierce military repression, involving the United States in training Latin American armies in torture techniques at the School of the Americas and secret campaigns of assassination through Operation Condor, often with direct support from multinational corporations such as ITT in Chile.[21] In place after place, the clouds of dictatorship suppressed popular movements and, as Che predicted, washed away the reformist fantasies of the Alliance for Progress. I think of the assassination of Che Guevara as the peak moment in the CIA's violent countermovement.

For years to come, the memory of Che would become vastly more significant than his activities in Bolivia. Then, beginning in the 1980s, social movements once again appeared across Latin America, challenging dictatorial regimes in such countries as Chile, Brazil, Argentina, El Salvador, Nicaragua, and Venezuela. In 1994 came the Zapatista uprising against racism, poverty, and NAFTA.[22] In some cases, these movements included guerrillas or, at least, undergrounds. More often they took the form of mass explosions and strikes in the streets. In every case, they carried banners of Che. Seeking to understand this apparent resurrection of Che's spirit in new form, I visited Bolivia and Cuba on four occasions between 2000 and 2006.

What followed the death of Che in Bolivia was a long period of violent dictatorship, social movements only flickering at the margins. In the mid-1980s, Bolivia became a leading "success story"—a poster child, U.S. policymakers deemed it—of Western corporate globalization under the tutelage of financial institutions such as the World Bank and the International Monetary Fund and American economists such as Jeffrey Sachs. Then twenty-five years old, Sachs was something like a Che Guevara in reverse. "I did not know exactly where Bolivia was in Latin America," he wrote in his memoir, but it seemed an inviting place to carry out his goal of counterrevolutionary privatization in 1985.[23] "Bolivia gave me my first insights into the problems of economic development…. At the time, I thought that I knew just about everything that needed to be known about the subject."[24] Trying to match Germany's 1923 one-day killing of hyperinflation,[25] Sachs proposed a sharp spike in oil and gas prices, layoffs, and privatizations. *"Almost five-sixths of the tin workers eventually lost their jobs."*[26]

Over the next decade, as the price of basic necessities was driven up, people took to the streets in ever larger waves, led by the indigenous people who seemed "impenetrable as rocks" to Che. Some revolutionary nationalists were waging guerrilla attacks, but the vast majority of the indigenous were mobilized in direct street actions, road blockades, work stoppages, boycotts, even political parties. Their main leader was Evo Morales, an Aymaran Indian who headed the militant union of coca growers (known as the *cocoleros*). This was a many-sided social movement, not a *foco,* aimed at the seizure of power. How they surmounted and survived dictatorial repression was difficult to explain.

Perhaps the authorities felt constrained, at least slightly, by the globalization of human rights and media coverage. But at root the main factor appeared to be the indomitable will—a romantic phrase, but there is no other—of Bolivia's indigenous people, tin miners, *cocoleros*, women, and students who marched in the face of bullets, bayonets, and gas.

There was blood, inevitably, and during September and October 2003 the armed forces of President Gonzalo Sánchez de Lozada (known by all as "Goni," a Chicago-trained free-market champion) killed 65 people and wounded hundreds more, bringing the toll of dead protesters to 110, more than the number killed during the worst dictatorship of the seventies.[27] For Sachs, still in denial, Goni's flight was a sad event, considering "the notable achievements since 1985."[28] To my surprise, Goni's campaign consultants were not only American but also Democrats, none other than Bill Clinton's top operative, James Carville, and key pollster, Stanley Greenberg. They were active across Latin America for candidates espousing Clinton's neoliberal experiment in eliminating state barriers to private investment. Some of them would still be in Bolivia in 2008, trolling for presidential candidates.[29]

Bolivia's street protests drove Goni out of the country, resettling him in Miami. I was a fellow teaching at Harvard's Institute of Politics at the time and was shocked to learn that Goni was seeking a temporary appointment at the institute until the storms receded in Bolivia. Asked my opinion, I pointed out that it might be unseemly to appoint someone who had so recently killed so many of his countrymen. To its credit, Harvard saw the wisdom in declining the offer. It remained stuck in my mind, however, that this was the kind of leadership being sponsored by liberal Democrats forty years after the Bay of Pigs and Alliance for Progress. The learning curve seemed more like a treadmill.

I arrived in La Paz soon after and interviewed many of the survivors of the shootings in Villa Ingenio, the coldest and poorest neighborhood in El Alto, a vast ramshackle city of 1 million Aymara and Quechua people sitting one mile above the colonial city of La Paz. I toured the altiplano, met indigenous people in the remote heart of the Andes, and had many meetings with local economists, even a brief meeting with Morales, then the leader of the parliamentary opposition. It was the first time I ever experienced a prerevolutionary situation; Morales would be elected by 53 percent in 2005, the first indigenous leader to triumph since the conquest 513 years before.

By far the most interesting Bolivian intellectual I met was Alvaro García Linera, a white, native-born academic who had previously spent several years in a guerrilla *foco*—the Tupac Katari Guerrilla Army—and was captured, imprisoned, and tortured. One year after our meeting, to the surprise of many, he was elected vice president of Bolivia as Morales's running mate.

García Linera grew up in white neighborhoods oblivious to the existence of Bolivia's indigenous majority. His generation was the last to live through the last days of the Latin American dictatorships. As an adolescent, he was stunned to witness the Aymara carry out their first road blockade, which left La Paz isolated.

The struggles of Bolivia's miners were familiar to him, but as for the Aymara, "they were an actor I did not know, an actor that was very distant for me." As a growing intellectual, he suddenly realized that the "[indigenous] sector is not available in books." He would have to understand the indigenous reality by immersing himself, with the "intent to invent tools that were not in books but came out of these movements' own history."[30]

When I cautiously asked García Linera about Che's legacy, he was blunt, even irritated. Che's Bolivia campaign was a disaster, he said, because Che was as unconscious of the indigenous factor as García Linera had been in growing up. His description of Che as a misguided and elitist mestizo seemed subjective and harsh, but sent me scrambling back to Che's early *Motorcycle Diaries,* where the young Argentine exile, after completing a continental journey, gave a speech declaring that "the division of [Latin] America into unstable and illusory nations is completely fictional. *We constitute a single mestizo race,* which from Mexico to the Magellan Straits bears notable ethnographical similarities."[31]

There it was. The speech is the climactic moment of the 2004 film starring Gael García Bernal, whose executive producer, Robert Redford, was an adventurist hero of *Butch Cassidy and the Sundance Kid,* set in Bolivia. There was, I realized, a deep foundational ignorance of the indigenous reality of Bolivia. García Linera was right. Only now, decades later, he was building a dialogue between Marxism and what he called "indigenism." The Marxists of the sixties and seventies, the Cubans as well as the Bolivians, "saw the Indians as reactionaries because they wanted to talk about historical themes that weren't relevant to revolution, or they were petit bourgeois," primitive forces outside the apparatus of production. As a result, the Indian cultural revolutionaries of the period "rose up in a confrontation with Marxism," declaring they were "*ni Marx ni menos*" (neither Marx nor less). At the same time, Bolivian Marxism was losing ground as globalization imposed the closing of tin mines, and the indigenous were being courted and co-opted by nongovernmental organizations with promises of civil rights. The uprooted Aymara were becoming "urban Indians" in an informal family-based subsistence economy, whose needs could not be fully addressed by a traditional Indian nationalism or by an industrial trade union movement. Instead, they took the road of social movements and politically supported the tendency represented by Morales.

García Linera did not explain why the face of Che was omnipresent in these street movements or why, one year later, Morales would invoke Che's guerrilla campaign in his presidential acceptance speech. What was the cause? What was the effect? How had Che, the defeated martyr, become such a galvanizing symbol in the present? I was able to locate in La Paz Chanto Paredes, the surviving brother of two who had died in Che's campaign (Coco in 1966 and Inti, who was killed while trying to rebuild the core, in 1969).

The surviving Paredes, when I met him, was a senior member of parliament in the MAS (Movement toward Socialism) party, led by Morales. Paredes was living in a high-rise apartment complex in La Paz where I interviewed him, amid photos of his slain brothers and other memorabilia. As our conversation unfolded, the elderly Paredes took the view that the past could not be reversed, only built upon as prologue.[32] The death of Che, he recounted, was followed by an escalation of class wars, including the nationalization of Gulf Oil and the temporary government of Juan José Torres until 1971, when a military dictatorship took power. In the following decades, Che's name, image, and slogans accompanied every popular mobilization in Bolivia through the election of Morales.

What are we to make of this Che as icon, catalyst, precursor, martyr, hero of Hollywood films? Was he too idealistic, too radical, too adventurist? Or did he set a standard of commitment and open a pathway for later generations? If so, how?

Che is perhaps evidence of our hunger for iconic heroes. But he has become more than a best-selling t-shirt, more than a deity that millions worship. The story of his failures reminds us that he was human, flawed, mistaken, and perhaps more heroic as a result. He saw oppression, he saw suffering, and he fought with every fiber of his being. His sacrifice is impossible to forget or discount and drives some in later generations to stand where he fell. In his retrospective on Che, Debray, who became a French government official and writer, slips into the unfortunate metaphoric category of the Latino "blood group" to explain Che's passion, forgetting that the same stereotype has been imposed on the revolutionary French and Irish.[33] Debray adds that "it took me twenty years to break the taboo against admitting the paradox—corroborated by a mass of other indices—that Che Guevara went to Bolivia not to win, but to lose."[34]

This explanation is too facile. Che metamorphosed through elaborate facial surgery and disguises to enter Bolivia. He and Fidel painstakingly chose their initial cadre. Both held extensive meetings with Bolivian party leaders. These are not indicators of an intent to lose. Perhaps Che did know on the deepest level, in the words of Fidel, that "in order to die with dignity it is not necessary to be accompanied."[35] Certainly, he placed himself in the line of fire, but he had done so since the Cuban revolution. Clearly, he believed that wherever death might find him, others would pick up the banner and gun. The evidence suggests that the loss in Bolivia was based on too many false assumptions and concrete mistakes, perhaps including the sending of an identifiable Debray into the region.

What is clear, I think, is that Che arose as part of an entire generation of Latin American revolutionaries, not as an isolated Don Quixote. That generation of guerrillas failed to overthrow any governments after Cuba's in 1959 (except Nicaragua, briefly), and a time of American-backed death squads and dictatorships fell across the continent. Then at the very moment the cold war was ending and the United States was declaring itself a sole superpower, nation after nation in Latin America rejected the U.S. model and democratically elected a new generation of nationalists who, despite their various differences, paid homage to Che Guevara and their guerrilla predecessors. Starting with Venezuela, by 2008 the list included Brazil, Bolivia, Argentina, Uruguay, Chile, Ecuador, Guatemala, Nicaragua, El Salvador, Honduras, and Paraguay. Former guerrillas held presidential power in Nicaragua and Uruguay. The president of Chile was a woman whose father had been murdered and who herself had been tortured under the Augusto Pinochet dictatorship. The president of Brazil, and many of his colleagues, had been incarcerated and abused under martial law. A commandante of the Salvadoran revolutionary movement was director of intelligence for a reform government. This was Che's generation, now in power through peaceful transitions led by social movements carrying his banner.

There had been no continental revolution as Che once predicted. There were no new communist regimes. But the continent had moved to the Left, the center-Left perhaps, from the murderous Right. To the north, the United States still marshaled the largest military force on earth. Its drug war and counterterrorism campaign still dominated Colombia and the Mexican border and could spill over into Venezuela at any moment. But enormous events had happened. There no longer was a Soviet bogeyman to justify U.S. military interventions. Freer than ever to choose their own course, voters and political parties rejected corporate and financial trade agreements that favored the U.S. multinationals. They unanimously chose close diplomatic relations with Fidel's Cuba, leaving the United States isolated in the hemisphere.

The extreme visions of Marxism forged in the time of the guerrillas, too narrow now for electoral or civic society frameworks, were broadening into combinations of nationalism and economic democracy, perhaps a mosaic of social democracies. There were cries for participatory democracy from the streets of Caracas and for participatory constituent assemblies from people everywhere frustrated by the traditional mechanisms. The homeless and landless and children of the streets were marching with new demands for justice.

This was not exactly the Latin America of Che's and Fidel's utopian dreams, but neither was it the backyard of banana republics the North Americans preferred. It was something else, an outcome of their dream nonetheless.

Three decades after that late-night interview with Fidel, I visited Havana to make another assessment. My host and friend was Ricardo Alarcon, student leader at the University of Havana in the early sixties and a longtime Cuban diplomat and leader of the National Assembly. Alarcon's daughter, Maggie, was raised partly in New York City and is an excellent interpreter, one who will surely serve as a bridge between our two countries when the time comes.

To my surprise, Alarcon simply wanted to exchange thoughts about the decades we had passed through. It was just about "too old guys hanging out," Maggie joked. At the time Fidel was at the brink of his surgery, hospitalization, and resignation from office. Time was accomplishing what imperialism had not. Rather than living with nostalgia, however, Alarcon was actively discussing the possibilities of revolution in the new era. What, if anything, did socialism now mean? What was the post-Soviet era? What did globalization and immigration mean for progressives? He went on and on, talking aloud, over luncheons here and dinners there, for four days and nights. He even recorded an interview with me, for Cuba's historical archives, about everything I could recall about the events of the sixties.

Two comments by Alarcon remain fixed in my mind. First, under globalization, he said, the old distinctions between North and South, between the oppressor in "el norte" and the oppressed in Latin America, Africa, and Asia, were breaking down. Che's tricontinental formula, I interpreted him to mean, was no longer a single southern bloc, if it ever had been. Immigration was driving Central and Latin Americans into the United States by the tens of millions. America's working class was not benefiting from wars of occupation like Iraq. There were new possibilities for social change from *within* the United States. It was time for Latin America to stop viewing the land of the yanqui as a monolith.

Second, he disagreed with those elements of the Latin American Left who opposed elected leaders such as President Luiz Inácio Lula da Silva in Brazil for being too close to the United States and to international financial institutions such as the World Bank. Though Cuba was associated closely with more radical leaders like Hugo Chávez in Venezuela, the reelection of the more moderate Lula was the most important task of the Latin American Left, he said. There had to be Latin American unity against any new interventions by the United States.

What could not be denied, however, was that *extreme Latin American poverty and extreme resource pillaging continued in spite of the dramatic success of political democracy.* "At the beginning of the 21st century, wealth inequality was at an all-time high."[36] Perhaps Che was right after all in doubting any electoral salvation for the 40 percent of Latin America born in poverty. An expanded revolutionary guerrilla war seemed implausible. The "twenty-first-century socialist" governments of Venezuela and Bolivia were far from ending poverty and inequality. The threat of violent countermovements in those countries could not be dismissed, and U.S. special forces and drug warriors were active in Colombia and Mexico. The descendants of Che had come this far, and so far no further. Whatever its blueprint, the stage ahead would need to entail a far-reaching redistribution of power, resources, and wealth, something Washington—and, indeed, Latin America's own oligarchs—never before had agreed to. Indeed, many in the American establishment were moving in precisely the opposite direction, making Cuba, Venezuela, and Bolivia into an "emerging threat" linked to everything from cross-border gangs to Islamic fundamentalism. Their solution was deeper linkages with Latin America's military. Once again, the White House in the Bush years defined the enemy in Latin America as "leftists."[37]

Perhaps a key, according to Alarcon's thinking, was the rise of Latino/as within the United States alongside an anti-interventionist bloc of Americans fatigued by Iraq, amid an economic depression. Perhaps these forces might oppose the interventionist hand of neoimperialism and, with a realistic sense of interdependence, extend the hand once offered by Franklin Roosevelt's Good Neighbor policy of the 1930s.

FDR was a master Machiavellian. He came to understand the enormous costs of countless American military interventions in Central and Latin America. He realized that the revolutionary Mexican government could open commercial relations and sell oil to Japan, Germany, and America's European competitors. Facing an economic crisis of his own, FDR in 1936 declared a policy of military nonintervention and went forward to accept the nationalization of U.S. oil companies by Mexico. Social movements like the Anti-Imperialist League, featuring leaders such as Mark Twain, played an important role in turning public opinion away from proponents of an American invasion. Roosevelt's new U.S. trade policies benefited the American economy as well. Together the United States and Latin America's bloc achieved the important UN Universal Declaration of Human Rights and what FDR called an "economic bill of rights," including social security, health care, union rights, education, and equality for women. When Roosevelt died in 1946 and U.S. policy turned toward the cold war immediately thereafter, the promise of the Good Neighbor policy was finished.

The 1954 U.S. coup in Guatemala was "the first of its kind since the establishment of the Good Neighbor Policy," according to a State Department memo.[38] As it happened, Ernesto Guevara was a young doctor then serving in Guatemala who took refuge from the American bombs in the Argentine Embassy in Guatemala City. From there he won safe passage to Mexico, where, in time, he met Fidel Castro. How might history have been different, one must ask, if FDR's policies had been followed in Argentina, where a leftist politician, Jacobo Arbenz, was democratically elected on a pledge of land reform? It is possible that fifty years of misery, strife, bloodshed, and wasted resources could have been prevented.

In 2009, the Obama administration faced conditions not unlike those before Roosevelt in 1936. Whether the memory of Che Guevara is deeply understood may determine what path Barack Obama chooses in Latin America. Web sites on the American Right include Che's death scene altered to show a fascist officer tickling his chest as Che's toes twitter.[39] Boardwalks seemingly everywhere feature Che t-shirts on their racks. A bronze tower to Che has risen in Buenos Aires, the land of his birth. A British vodka company uses his image. A five-hour, two-part Steven Soderberg movie has been released, with Benicio del Toro as Che. Which Che memory will most interest President Obama? Will Obama's aides include anyone like the young Richard Goodwin, who brought back that coexistence offer to John Kennedy? Or will they be like the Green Berets Obama is sending into the jungles of Colombia?

An unfortunate gap in Obama's background concerns Latin America, where he has never traveled. As president, he will never be able to visit the region freely or engage in candid conversations with Latin Americans who see themselves on the path of Che today. His earliest formulations on Latin America included only a slight tweak of America's dead-end Cuba policy coupled with a robust pledge to continue the counterinsurgency in Colombia, pour millions in military resources into the drug wars on the Mexican border, and skirmish verbally with Venezuela's Hugo Chávez. His undersecretary of state for the hemisphere has spoken of "armoring NAFTA" instead of dismantling it. Obama may learn in time that "strategic" partnerships are defined by more than the possession of nuclear weapons and that the growing interdependence of Latin America and North America, with our Latino population becoming larger by the year, makes this relationship a strategic one as well.

I met Che's daughter, Aleida, by accident in 2005. We were crushed together in a throng of people listening to Hugo Chávez orate from a balcony at the World Social Forum in Brazil. I introduced myself, felt foolish, said nothing more. I knew she was living in Havana, a pediatrician; her brothers, Camilo and Ernesto, were lawyers there. I had read her writings, knew she was seven when her father died. Much as I wished to ask her a million questions, I wanted more to leave her alone, an anonymous person huddled there, listening to every word. I thought to myself how her dad would have loved the scene.

By now, as everyone knows, Che Guevara was a durable icon of the era, not one of the fallen forgotten. In a 1997 biography, *The Life and Death of Che Guevara*, Jorge Castañeda argues that the sixties failed as a revolutionary political project, but succeeded on a cultural level, with Che as the personification. What Che represented, and the sixties wrought everywhere, he writes, was, first, the existence of a sphere of moral and cultural power outside institutions and, second, the imperative to resist the authority of those institutions to the end. If the thrust of the sixties was defeated, "as Che was in the barren hills of Bolivia," its impact would be found, with Che, "in the niches reserved for cultural icons, for symbols of social uprisings that filter down deep into the soil of society, that sediment in its most intimate nooks and crannies."[40]

But have Che and the sixties he represents become commercialized and co-opted icons today? It is a hard question, if only because the 1960 photo of Che's face has become an international image subject to multiple commercial uses. Is this the trimph of consumer capitalism, the reexecution of Che?

There is another interpretation. Years ago I met and interviewed Alberto Korda, the Cuban photographer who had shot the famed photo of Che on March 5, 1960. The occasion was a mass funeral of eighty Cubans killed when a French cargo ship was sabotaged in Havana harbor. Che's gaze seems to be into the future. Korda has described the expression as *encabronadao y dolente*, "angry and sad." He labeled the photo "*guerrillero heróico*" (heroic fighter).[41] When we met in 1997, he told my son Troy that previously he had been a fashion photographer, but had been shocked and radicalized by photographing a little girl from a poor family playing with a stick of wood as if it were her doll. In the event, the Che photo hung on Korda's wall for one year, apparently until brought to Europe by Giangiacamo Feltrinelli, a left-wing Italian publisher. From there, it appeared in several European magazines until it caught the eye of Jim Fitzpatrick, a young Irish graphic artist.

It happened that as a young man tending bar in Ireland, Fitzpatrick had met Che while the Argentine was on a stopover from Moscow to Cuba. The teen-aged Fitzpatrick was struck by Che as "likeable and roguish, a descendant of Irish grandparents." Later, when Che was assassinated, Fitzpatrick was enraged. With the Che picture supplied by a Dutch provo, the Irishman went to work, sending countless reprints to activist groups across the world. "I deliberately designed it to breed like rabbits," he said later.

Fitzpatrick's motive was a rage against the oblivion intended for Che. "There was no memorial, no place of pilgrimage, nothing." Fitzpatrick was determined that Che would not be disappeared, but memorialized.[42]

He had no idea how universally the image would spread. By 2008, the art historian Trisha Ziff had collected hundreds of icons of Che into "Chevolution," an iconography of Che that opened in Barcelona in 2007 and arrived at Washington's Corcoran Gallery in January 2008. Ziff maintains that, even though Western commerce tries to separate the man from his message—Unilever distributed Che ice cream in Australia—the image of Che remains an *uncontrolled brand* of a kind of revolution, "and the brand's logo is the image, which represents change. It has become the icon of the outside thinker, at whatever level—whether it is anti-war, pro-green, or anti-globalization." The Che t-shirts worn across Latin America and among alienated young people around the world are more than commercial branding. They represent the open face of defiance staring into the future. Che has triumphed in memory. If he was not allowed to create his global revolution, according to Castañeda, "he was only destined, like so few others in his time, to die the death he wished, and live the life he dreamed."[43]

15

The Underground in America

The solidarity of the progressive world with the Vietnamese people has something of the bitter irony of the plebeians cheering on the gladiators at the Roman Circus. To wish the victim success is not enough; one must join him in his fate.

—Che Guevara[1]

How bright the future would be if two, three, many Vietnams flowered on the face of the globe.

—Che Guevara[2]

Wherever death may surprise us, let it be welcome if our battle cry has reached even one receptive ear, if another hand reaches out to take up our arms, and other men come forward to join in our funeral dirge with the rattling of machine guns and new cries of battle and victory.

—Che Guevara[3]

*A*s THE WESTERN DEMOCRACIES FAILED TO STOP the Vietnam War, and Che's calls for "two, three many Vietnams" grew more insistent, as the police repression of the Panthers grew bloodier, the once-peaceful New Left incubated small guerrilla networks "behind enemy lines." These were not the Latin Americans whose continent was sinking in poverty and repression. These were graduates of American universities who felt the pressure to do something more than voting, picketing, and knocking on doors. Children of privilege, it was privilege they wanted to destroy.

The most extreme of these was Germany's Red Army Faction (RAF), many of whose parents had been Nazis or "silent Germans" or who simply had failed to "do enough" against the evils of their time. The trigger was perhaps the June 1967 police shooting of Benno Ohnesorg, a German student protesting a visit by the shah of Iran.[4] By this time, German radicals were inspired by the American SDS slogan "from protest to resistance," which implied draft resistance specifically, but also something more radical against the state. A leading German journalist, Ulrike Meinhof, interpreted the slogan to mean, "Protest is when I say I don't like this. Resistance is when I put an end to what I don't like."[5] Characteristic of her generation, Meinhof expressed shame at being nothing more than a social critic. In a cynical essay called "Columnism," she wrote that being a columnist was serving as "a pressure relief valve." "Columnists are the blacks of the State Department, the women in the federal government, the fig leaves, the tokens, the alibis, the excuses."[6] She gave up on the democratic process. Speaking of women, she wrote, "They got the right to vote once no more social change could be wrought by the vote."[7]

In April 1968, radical youth burned down a department store in Frankfurt in order to "protest against the apathy of society in the face of the murders in Vietnam" and claimed that it was "better to set fire to a department store than run one."[8] In the same month, the charismatic leader of the German SDS, Rudi Dutschke—the equivalent of Berkeley's Mario Savio—was shot by an alleged lone assassin and suffered serious head injuries from which he died some fourteen years later. It was the month that Martin Luther King was murdered as well.

From these beginnings was born the Red Army Faction, also known as the Baader-Meinhof Gang, which carried out a guerrilla war until 1998, in which sixty people died directly, twenty-seven of them RAF members.[9] Meinhof died hanging in a prison cell on May 8, 1976, the anniversary of the end of World War II. Baader and two others died in their cells one year later, on October 17, 1977.

I knew none of these German revolutionaries, but I have interviewed and talked with many of their close contemporaries in the circles from which they came.[10] There were intellectual links between the German SDS and the American SDS.[11] A member of the German SDS, a visiting student named Michael Vester, drafted sections of the Port Huron Statement opposing the cold war. The slogan "from protest to resistance" was passed from the American SDS to the Germans. There was a common fascination, by the middle sixties, with the theories of Herbert

Marcuse. The Frankfurt School of German intellectual exiles had a profound influence on the New Left. The presence of massive American military bases on German soil made opposition to Vietnam and defense of GI war resisters major issues for the German students.

If we set aside the moral question of nonviolence, there was a certain logic, or pattern, to the violence that began in these advanced countries in the late sixties. First, there was the urgency of Vietnam's suffering and example, suggesting there was no time for gradualism. Second, there was deep disillusionment with the political default of Western democracies. Third, there was the growing belief that Machiavellian decisionmakers could understand nothing but Machiavellian logic, the logic of force. To "increase the costs" to the war-makers became a strategy among those disillusioned with public opinion and elections. All these views fit neatly with Che's call for tricontinental guerrilla war, which projected a role for white radicals "behind enemy lines." The Panthers held a related notion that "radicals in the Mother Country" could play an important role as allies behind the Panther vanguard. Marcuse's concept of a co-optive one-dimensional society made the very idea of reform suspect. By 1967, the Port Huron Statement itself was dismissed as "reformist," too. Even accepting gradualism as realistic was defined as accommodation to racism.

In the background of this hothouse of frustration, I believe, was the shadow of World War II and Nazism. It was no accident that Germany, Italy, and Japan, with their recent histories of fascism, became the centers of the greatest revolutionary violence in the West.[12] The younger generation carried the weight of the past most intimately. In America, the burden was slavery, lynching, and Jim Crow, no further in our past than the Ku Klux Klan networks awaiting us in the South. But our generation also was influenced by the images of gas chambers, concentration camps, weapons of mass destruction, and growing questions of how the Holocaust could have happened. Yes, the United States went to war. Yes, American troops helped liberate the camps. But it also was true that boatloads of Jewish refugees were turned away from American ports and the military response to evidence of the Holocaust was painfully slow. In my own story, the pastor of my Catholic suburban church was Father Charles Coughlin, an incendiary orator and anti-Semite. Down the road in Detroit was his close ally, Henry Ford, promoter of the American Nazi Party. When I first traveled south, the chairman of SNCC, Charles McDew, was a black Jew who continually asked, "If not now, when?" A large number of the early SDS and white SNCC activists were young Jews imbued with a passionate urgency never to repeat the moral crimes of indifference and apathy.[13]

The past was present. The trial of the organization man of the Nazi machine, Adolf Eichmann, opened in April 1961 and ended with his hanging on May 31, 1962. It was a morality play at the beginning of the sixties, raising questions that only the young can ask: *What were our parents thinking,* and *what would we have done?*

There is a *direct relationship between shame and violence,* according to Dr. James Gilligan, which may explain the eruption of armed actions by so many young people in the late sixties.[14] The shame of representing nothing of value, of living a meaningless life, can trigger the violent desire to lash out and leave a mark. This was the message of the Algerian psychiatrist Frantz Fanon, who left behind a series of stirring books after his early death in 1962, the most influential being *The Wretched of the Earth*.[15] Born in the French colony of Martinique, Fanon joined the Algerian revolution as a doctor treating what he called the "neuroses of colonialism." To shake off a feeling of death within life itself, he believed, required a violent act to make the self known. The birth of the new self sometimes required the death of the oppressor. Fanon, who did not live to evaluate the revolutions he helped foment, was an enormous influence on the sixties, especially on the Black Panthers and the Weather Underground. His concept of therapeutic violence was meant for people of color, but the condition of being *wretched* is one that fit the condition of young white people in the sixties as well. Not merely an economic or political status, to be wretched is an emotion connoting an internalized shame. Just as the colonized must rip out their feelings of inferiority, so must the colonizer deal with an internal shame when the original blessing of privilege is realized to be a curse. As it was for John Brown dealing with shame and guilt, so it would be for the Weather Underground.[16]

Those who became activists after the escalation in Vietnam and the black violence in northern ghettos were the second-generation SDS. They were not there for the birth of SDS or SNCC or for the period through Mississippi Summer. Shocked at first, perhaps, they swiftly absorbed the amoral and remorseless nature of the state. It was also a time of drugs (mainly pot) and sexual liberation, a greater flaunting of the authorities, a birthing of a youth culture at the margins.

There were stages when it might have been prevented, but the war kept escalating as domestic neglect worsened. There were thousands of draft resisters bound for Canada by underground paths. Then came the Catholic resistance. Then there were Panther fugitives. The model of SDS as a loose-knit, bottom-up participatory network did not match the perceived necessity of greater focus, commitment, sacrifice. The eclectic spirit of participatory democracy was replaced, to my surprise and helpless disappointment, by a dogmatic factionalism in the traditions of the Old Left from which the early SDS had broken. The youthfulness of the activists, combined with the higher stakes, seemed to require a less provisional, more doctrinaire explanation of all questions, a secular catechism. The intelligence services were certainly infiltrating their way into SDS circles as well, but I believe that we accomplished mostly on our own the chaos that the FBI and CIA only dreamed about.

The sense of becoming a vanguard was another cause of the crisis. The early SDS and SNCC believed they were vanguards mainly out of apathy and into activism. There was no such thing as a correct line. In fact, it was a joke. Differences were argued on the basis of evidence from the field, not formulations from the Red Book. Should nonviolent direct action continue to be the cutting edge? Was voter registration a more effective assault on southern segregation? Could there be interracial cooperation, a beloved community, and if so, how? Or was it better to organize along the lines of black power and form alliances from the basis of a greater equality? These were tough debates, and perhaps the participants erred at times. For example, the decision to ask whites to leave SNCC, made in the depression after Mississippi Summer, was by a one-vote margin, hardly a model of the early consensus mode. But at least the decision was made with the exhaustive input of those who took the risks and did the work.

What happened in the late sixties was more like a scene from a Fyodor Dostoyevsky novel, a white fever. At just the moment when the student movement was exploding on campuses like never before, the SDS leadership was attempting to extricate itself from its own class and racial status. One "line" instructed students to abandon their privileged lives by going to work in factories, in clandestine communist cells (following the Chinese line at the time). Another proposed occupations of university campuses in hopes of revolutionizing the institution on behalf of the Third World (the Cuban and Vietnamese tendency). Another favored dropping out to organize working-class youth. What all the emerging views shared were a significant shame over white, student, and bourgeois privilege and a desire to eradicate it.

I was facing trial in Chicago at the time and kept wondering when it had become a sound organizing principle to define being white, middle-class, or American as being the enemy. It seemed contradictory, even tending toward madness, though I indulged these very feelings myself at times. But the trial kept me anchored. As a defendant, it seemed plain to me that we had to win or neutralize the Chicago jury or, failing that, lay the foundation for winning an appeal, both objectives being dependent on winning over a large share of public opinion.

That was the point at which Billy Ayers; his future wife, Bernardine Dohrn; Terry Robbins; Mark Rudd; Teddy Gold, John Jacobs (J.J.); Jeff Jones; Cathy Wilkerson; Howie Machtinger; Diana Oughton; Kathy Boudin; Peter Clapp; and others of the second-generation SDS were pondering whether to form what became the Weather Underground. Most, if not all, of them were liberal or pacifist by background, all were gifted organizers, and they soon would leave SDS and the antiwar movement behind to relocate underground in America.

I first met my friend Billy Ayers—known by watchers of the 2008 presidential election as the bomber pal of Barack Obama—somewhere between the Vietnam escalation and the Chicago protests. The place was Ann Arbor, and I remember him sitting on the floor of a children's community school where he once had been the principal, with Diana Oughton, his partner just back from teaching in Guatemala. Bill was always smiling, and on this day his grin was especially wide and infectious. I could tell he delighted in raising a little schoolroom of nonconformists. Diana thought he was a Peter Pan.

The point of the meeting was to rally Bill and his friends to come to Chicago, prepared for the worst at the hands of the police. There was a danger that people would stay away because the authorities were denying permits and ordering up their body armor. I sensed that Billy and Diana would stand their ground against Chicago's finest. In his memoir, Bill recalls me as "our Captain Ahab" set to fight the great white whale.[17] I believed that street confrontations were inevitable and that surrounding the convention with throngs of protesters, like the Pentagon scene the year before, was desirable. He wrote that I "thought we might provoke the convention to implode," which was correct. There was a strategy of implosion in my mind. I believed that if the Chicago officials denied permits for sleeping in the parks and marching, there would be police occupying the streets in all directions, potentially disrupting the convention, which happened; that the federal troops called up from Fort Hood might mutiny, which they did; and that the disfranchised McCarthy-Kennedy-McGovern delegates might rebel inside the convention, or walk out, which they tried to do. I hoped that the convergence of all these imploding forces might make the Democrats change course on Vietnam, which did not happen, at least not in August 1968. Bill seemed interested in the fight, for which he had a growing aptitude. Bill had a joyous personality, a good brain, and, I have to say, a self-confidence that could spill over into cockiness. During the Chicago protests, I remember him sitting on a floor again, smiling again, this time with a gang of arrestees in a temporary holding area. He had been scrimmaging with his affinity group against the police, something that traced back, perhaps, to his experience of being a "scrappy" football guard. He carried a blackjack.

I had seen similar appetites in J.J. (John Jacobs) and Mark Rudd at Columbia that spring when it came to storming buildings. I joined their strike and chaired an occupied building myself. But they were miles ahead of me in practicing Georges Danton's slogan, adopted by Che, "audacity, audacity, and more audacity."[18]

As the Chicago trial began, SDS was disintegrating and brutally morphing into factions, one of which became Weathermen. We went on trial in late September, erasing any time for me to witness the ruins of the organization I had founded seven years before. The group that became Weathermen was busy over the summer organizing small, disciplined street-fighting collectives to prepare for something called the Days of Rage in Chicago that October. Days of Rage, Days of Resistance ... it all sounded like more of the same street skirmishes that had been breaking out since 1967. The Chicago conspiracy defendants were invited to speak at these Days of Rage, which were scheduled for a weeknight during the trial. I paid little attention to the date, October 11, the anniversary of Che's assassination just three years before.

By now I was becoming a bit nervous about this new SDS. Though I was five or six years older than the Weather generation, there was a huge generation gap, the same demarcation that divided the sixties as a decade. At Columbia, I noticed that these new SDSers exhibited a vanguard streak of brilliant militancy. They carried a defiant certitude that they could put the administrators "up against the wall, motherfuckers." In contrast, I was now the old guard, trying to keep up. The Columbia seizure of buildings had been carried out in spite of a recent campuswide student vote *against* the SDS demands. The new SDS belief was that social change would occur, not through plebiscites, but through students (the public, whomever) being *forced* to make choices they preferred to avoid. The tactics of direct action were said to create a mandate of their own, galvanizing much of the student body, faculty, and media into useful engagement. I shrugged off the tendency toward vanguardism; after all, I was in the vanguard.

Now, in October 1969, what began as an "action faction" at Columbia was turning into an improvised, and possibly deadly, manifestation of Che's *foco* theory. On October 5, the proto-Weathermen blew up a police monument in Chicago's Haymarket Square, a memorial to officers killed the century before in a controversial and ambiguous battle with local anarchists who subsequently were hanged.[19] Five nights later, on October 11, not fully realizing that something entirely new was about to happen, something I was not exactly briefed about, I decided to drive up to Lincoln Park for the rally billed as kicking off the Days of Rage. As I recall, Abbie Hoffman, John Froines, and Len Weinglass were with me.

I was not prepared for the scene when we arrived. A bonfire was already roaring. The numbers were quite small, perhaps one hundred or a few more, far less than the Weather forecast. They were painted up, dressed for combat, and probably on speed. I do not remember any placards with demands. As Abbie and John trickled away, someone handed me the bullhorn. Bill Ayers was standing there, hopping up and down, in a helmet and loose-fitting clothes. No one was paying any attention to the words. Bill says I was "caught up in the spirit of the moment and, shedding [my] careful demeanor from court, became the old inciter."[20]

That is not my recollection. I was experiencing a breakdown of reality in the presence of the unexpected and therefore felt there was nothing to say. I was familiar with young people fighting back after the police had assaulted and gassed them. But this was the reverse, a feverish preparation before an attack on the dark and shuttered neighborhood of the elite—and anyone in the way. I could not process this at all. I could understand civil disobedience with an objective, I could understand illegal activities conducted in secret, but I could not fathom why all these people were going to run amok straight into the guns and cameras. It was like a ritualistic initiation event.

Initiation into what? I truly did not know, but I still was not ready to break with the demonstrators—they were my younger sisters and brothers—even as it was evident that they were breaking from me. I said over the bullhorn that, contrary to reports, the Chicago conspiracy defendants had not denounced the Days of Rage, that we were not opposed to an escalation of militancy ... but I did not know what I was talking about. They were jumping up and down, pawing the earth, psyching themselves to charge whooping against the police protectors of the nearby boulevards of opulence. Then the crowd started running. I was left looking for the car I came in to take me back downtown. Feeling bypassed, either by history or insanity, I went back to my trial chore of preparing the cross-examination of witnesses.

Eight were shot and wounded by the cops that night, and at least 100 were arrested and brutally beaten. Over a four-day period, 287 were arrested, mainly for breaking some fourteen hundred windows of cars, stores, and homes.[21] The city's corporation counsel, Richard Elrod, broke his own neck trying to tackle a Weatherman. No one in the Weather crowd expressed any second thoughts about the small turnout or about the favorable public response to the police. Instead, there were dreams of Moncada, where Fidel had once led a handful into a suicide assault on an armory; of Fidel's and a dozen fighters in the Sierra Maestre; or of the Paris Commune, whose revolt, Bill later wrote, echoing Marx, "may have been futile, but to their eternal credit, they had stormed the heavens."[22]

Preparing for an underground life is not like going to trade school. Any army trains its young fighters by a process of breaking their individuality and remolding their loyalty and character. With an underground it is no different. The Weathermen believed they had to transform themselves utterly, smash their individualism, abandon all ties to others, overcome sexual possessiveness and monogamy, prepare for the likelihood of early death, master karate, harden themselves for the prospect of killing or wounding others, and study the use of weapons, the preparation of bombs and blasting caps, the obtaining of false IDs, the theft of cars and airline tickets, the location of safe houses, and, above all, the practice of discretion, evasion, and secrecy. It is an all-consuming way of life, detaching the individual from any on the outside. It is a commitment so total that it is imperative to feel that one has chosen rightly, which means that all others have chosen wrongly or are unenlightened.

I became a split personality during the trial. In my life thus far, I had been a decidedly public figure, a writer, a speaker, said to be an effective organizer. (As Judge Julius Hoffman would declare at my sentencing, "Fellows as smart as you could do awfully well under this system," adding, "I'm not trying to convert you, mind you.") Mine were not the habits of anonymity and selflessness necessary to nurture an underground lifestyle. So it seemed to me that I was not a candidate for such a life, although I often might now and again pass through the risky lines between the two worlds; one might study underground techniques, for example, in case they became necessary without necessarily embracing the strategy. In those years, I would learn how to use weapons and hide fugitives, while still spending most of my hours writing pamphlets and organizing projects such as a child care center staffed by men or collecting signatures for a referendum on community control of police in Berkeley (we lost, even in left-wing Berkeley).

It also troubled me that I might lack a necessary courage to face reality. Over and over it came down to that question—*What was reality in an unreal time?*—and here our differences were sharpest. I believed that the coming of a police state was an emerging *possibility* that could be prevented by political means, whereas the Weathermen believed it was the emerging *reality*. I believed we might win our court case; the Weathermen believed the courts were becoming more repressive by the day. I believed that property damage might embarrass the state, but that social change had to occur through organizing a mass movement, even if many of us were jailed.

Over dinner during the trial, Bernardine argued forcefully that the trial was a racist mockery, that the Nixon courts would reject our appeals, that we would serve our time in dangerous prisons. She thought we had no right to continue as white defendants alongside the chaining and gagging of Bobby Seale. The duty of the revolutionary was to smash the courtroom. Because the choices of liberal society were disappearing, she suggested, I should walk out of the trial and go underground.

I could not be certain that she was wrong. But I knew I could not join her. I would take my chances with the tools of persuasion, organizing, coalition-building, and the politics I had learned since 1960. I believed that we had a case to make and that Panther attorney Charles Garry, now recuperating from surgery in San Francisco, wanted Bobby's courtroom defiance to stand alone. I felt more useful aboveground than below. Perhaps I did leave the door open a crack in case Bernardine's worst prophecies became true. Unlike most of the organized Left, I believed that she, Bill, and the others were far from crazy or incomprehensible in their diagnosis. During those same weeks, the Chicago police, with the assistance of an informer, carried out the extrajudicial assassinations of Fred Hampton and Mark Clark. There were hunters out there with badges and guns, and we were all somewhere on their lists.

And so it was that the younger generation of SDS went underground, leaving the organizational wreckage behind. One of them said, "We offed the pig," meaning they had closed down the national office and thrown away the key. Their story has been recounted in many books and films, to which I can add little. J.J. and Terry Robbins, I think, pushed for the hardest line. As our trial was ending with hundreds of street protests around the country, they were forming a secret underground collective in New York, plotting to go beyond anything previously imagined. Some of them already had thrown a firebomb at the home of the judge in the Panther 21 trial, causing little damage and no casualties. It was the initiation of a "fifth column" strategy, modeled after the insurgent resistance behind enemy lines in the Spanish Civil War. The analogy was totally flawed, however, because the Spanish *brigadistas* were defending the *elected* Spanish Republic against a fascist military overthrow supported by Adolf Hitler.

Someone conceived the idea of attacking American military officers on American soil, in keeping with Che's dictum to haunt them in their sanctuaries. It was time, some in the New York underground collective believed, to cross the boundary from property destruction to deliberate killing.

This was in sharp contrast to movement sentiment at the time. The vast majority of activists were opposed to armed struggle, though they were not ready to turn anyone in to the police. The minority who were sympathetic drew the line at violence against property rather than persons. Later in 1970, for example, an underground unit bombed an army research center at the University of Wisconsin early in the morning, accidentally killing an innocent researcher, Robert Fassnacht. Shock, grief, and regret traumatized the Madison radical community at the time, and the event sent shock waves through the national antiwar movement.[23]

What was being planned in the New York townhouse was of a different moral character. This was meant to be war with collateral damage. The target would be a dance for military officers, their wives, and their girlfriends at nearby Fort Dix, over the river in New Jersey. Apparently, none of the handful of Weatherpeople who knew of the plan spoke out against it. According to one of Terry's closest friends at the time, Cathy Wilkerson, there was an atmosphere of "passivity" induced by the psychic "humiliations" Terry inflicted on others in the collective.[24] "When the proposal was floated about Fort Dix, no one argued against it, but the tension in the air seemed to crystallize into a fine mist," Wilkerson recalls.[25] Terry also was crossing an internal line, by which he accepted the inevitability of his own coming death. No longer a political organizer, he now was already a combatant in the war against the United States, somewhere between a young Che and Butch Cassidy. He was twenty-two years old.

Terry was a fanatic dreamer who believed that sheer will was more important than anything. He knew very little about dynamite, blasting caps, timers, and wiring, yet insisted he would take charge. It was decided to use nails in the pipe bombs, "with little discussion," although Wilkerson remembers Diana Oughton becoming "noticeably somber."[26] Bill Ayers's memoir imagines her "wobbling," murmuring, "I'm not sure," as Terry constructed the bombs.[27] If the purpose of the collective was the loss of individuality, it was accomplished. (I do not mean to demonize any of them here, because militaries and religions everywhere foster a similar group identity in place of critical thinking.)

Terry and Diana were in the basement when the wires crossed and blew them to bits of dust. Ted Gold was crushed at the front door. Wilkerson was upstairs, ironing. Boudin was showering. The two surviving women fled the house and staggered into the arms of a neighbor, Susan Wagner, a former wife of Henry Fonda. Another neighbor, Dustin Hoffman, stared in disbelief. Bill Ayers learned days later of Diana's death, the news delivered in an isolated phone booth on an empty road.

The remaining Weathermen, now deeply traumatized, escaped to a hidden whereabouts to consider what this all meant. A deepening divide among them became an uncrossible chasm. On one side, nearly alone, was J.J., who wanted to press on with escalating the military strategy. On the other was Bernardine, who, like Bill, was traumatized at the descent into insanity by close comrades and lovers.

J.J. was purged after a bitter argument. The remaining Weathermen, now hunted everywhere by the FBI, decided on a path that avoided all casualties. They chose to continue bombing selected physical targets—a violent guerrilla theater—while searching to understand how they could have detached themselves so badly from a blossoming mainstream activism. Their new actions were meant to be "immediately understood and timely, fire the imaginations of young people, inspire the movement, and make anyone of goodwill secretly smile—even if they denounce our tactics," Bernardine was to say.[28] In this way they could maintain their belief in an underground existence (as members of the FBI's ten most wanted list, they could not surface in any event). But they would focus on physical targets with propaganda value: Bombing a bathroom in the U.S. Capitol was in response to the 1971 invasion of Laos, for example; bombing the air force wing of the Pentagon in 1972 was a reaction to the mining of North Vietnam's harbors.

The problem was that the spectacle of the deed always overshadowed the political message. The deeds *were* the message, which was that there were underground bombers loose in America. The number of bombings and acts of arson in those years were vastly greater than anything the Weather Underground could have predicted. Even though the Weather actions were fewer than twenty-five, the overall estimates of arson, vandalism, and bombings in that period were in the thousands. There were 563 fraggings—throwing a fragmentation bomb into an officer's tent—by American troops in Vietnam in 1969–1970 and 363 courts-martial.[29] That level of violence by Americans against their authorities has been gutted from memory, especially the fraggings, which are mostly deleted from history or reduced to mindless anarchy. No doubt, therefore, a cost of sorts was inflicted on the reputation of the superpower. But the *method* of delivering the message trumped any attention to the issues. Thousands of people in the streets protesting the war were far more effective than damaging a Pentagon computer or a toilet in the House of Representatives. Army fraggings weakened the military's stability while bringing down repression on voiceless GIs. It was obvious that the primary way to convey a political message was through a political movement. In the case of returning Vietnam veterans, they could create the Vietnam Veterans Against the War, a political outlet for soldiers' rage. The Weathermen would have to fade away, like Japanese soldiers in caves after World War II, or find a method of return in the midst of a growing movement from the streets to the electoral arena.

As an intermediate step, perhaps, they produced communiqués, dispatches, pamphlets, even films with Haskell Wexler, Emile de Antonio, and Mary Lampson. In those years, I would see them occasionally by accident—once in a theater where Spike Lee's *Malcolm X* film was playing, another time munching on avocados in Death Valley. Our conversations were intense—they were movement family, after all, and carried a sorrow beyond words. It seemed that we would never reconnect again. By 1976 the sixties were ending; I was married to Jane Fonda, building organizations, running for political office; the Weather Underground was disintegrating "like a house of cards."[30] The future, I thought, would be an impossible challenge to memory, sorting facts from fantasies and secrets, maybe all of it simply sinking into oblivion like the story of other forgotten revolutionaries.

J.J., for whom the line between fanaticism and fury was never clear, felt betrayed when the collective expelled him after the townhouse explosion. He took himself to Vancouver in 1976, and in the same year he was diagnosed with a melanoma. In exile, he became Wayne Curry, agonized over what went wrong, trimmed trees, gardened, fathered two kids, contributed to a Buddhist retreat, and grappled with his relentless disease. After twenty years, he was found writhing in the throes of death in a Vancouver house. When a police officer touched his burning skin while trying to help him to his feet, J.J. launched a final punch in his war against the state. He died shortly afterward, and subsequently some of his ashes were spread beside Che's tomb, with the permission of the Cuban government.[31] I wonder what Che might have thought.

By the late seventies, most of the Weathermen had somehow navigated their return to civil society.[32] Two were even pardoned by President Bill Clinton. Bernardine was imprisoned for several months for refusing to name names before a grand jury. Then she was fined $1,500 and received probation for assault and battery in Chicago. Mark Rudd was fined $2,000 and placed on probation, too. Cathy Wilkerson pled guilty to possession of illegal explosives, served three years in prison, and became a mathematics teacher. The imprisoned Kathy Boudin succeeded in a twenty-year fight for clemency. The charges against Bill Ayers were dropped, reluctantly, according to prosecutors, for fear that the FBI's illegal undercover techniques might be compromised. It appeared that the very Watergate reforms that had seemed inconceivable when the Weathermen went underground were a major factor in the dropping of so many charges in 1973. *In fact, in 1978 federal prosecutors brought charges against the FBI for its Weathermen probes.*[33]

Bill and Bernardine, now a couple, birthed two children underground, surrendered to the FBI in 1980, adopted a child of two imprisoned Weather members in 1981 (Kathy Boudin and David Gilbert, still imprisoned for life), and forged careers again along the very paths they had been traveling just a decade before. She became a law professor at Northwestern, specializing in child and family law; he became a tenured professor at the University of Illinois, focusing on inner-city schools, juvenile halls, and teacher education. Both were respected not only as faculty members but also as players in Chicago's local political culture. Bill was an ally of Mayor Richard Daley, the son of the former mayor whose police Bill had fought in the streets in 1968. A key figure in school reform, Bill helped obtain a $60 million foundation grant for school reform projects in the inner city.

It seemed to be the American dream, and the Weather nightmare come true. Former revolutionaries forgiven by the state, living successful professional lives, raising their children, while torture from Chicago's jails to Guantánamo was still a norm for people of color.

Enter Barack Obama, and the world turned over again. For most of 2007–2008, the mainstream media pored over connections between Senator Obama and William Ayers. The core allegations, which were true, were that Obama had held a fundraiser at the Ayers-Dohrn home when he ran for state office in the nineties, that the two sat on a foundation board distributing Annenberg school funds, and that they occasionally socialized in the manner that most politicians do with their constituents. Obama read Bill's book on juvenile justice, as I did when I served in the state senate. Comparing perception to a camera lens, I am sure that Obama perceived Bill and Bernardine in their *foreground* lives, not the cloudy background.

After all, everyone around Hyde Park viewed them in terms of their present-day existence, and if they were allies of the mayor, distinguished professors, and good parents, what was the point of holding their pasts against them?

Then in 2001, the karma came with a vengeance. On September 10, Bill Ayers was being interviewed by the *New York Times* about his *Fugitive Days,* released that day. On September 11, terrorists attacked the United States, killing three thousand people. On the very same morning, the *Times* quoted Bill from the day before saying: "I don't regret setting bombs. I feel we didn't do enough."[34] Bill would try to retrieve and explain the quote in the subsequent days and years, but there it was.[35] It would become the foundation of a virulent attack in 2007 on Obama for ever having such a friend and on the radicals of the sixties as a whole.

As portrayed by the mass media and John McCain's campaign in 2008, William Ayers and his Weatherfriends were demons, potent hybrids of Eric Hoffer's true believers and the twenty-first century's terrorists. The key to this depiction of the Other is that they are the mutant offspring of evil, that their sudden appearance has no origin in American society or foreign policy. McCain could bomb North Vietnam twenty-four times, killing or wounding how many civilians no one knows, but that was authorized and legitimate violence, the following of legitimate orders. Barack Obama, however, was "palling with terrorists."

Establishing guilt by association was the tactic of the militant Machiavellians going back to the McCarthy period, even back to the Palmer raids of 1920. In the case of Ayers and Obama in 2008, the attacks failed in both the primaries and the general election. Why? Perhaps the Republicans were outspent. Perhaps other issues, such as a falling economy, trumped the old negative politics. Perhaps Obama's positive image was persuasive. I would like to believe that one factor was the gradual maturing of the American public away from the politics of demonization.

There is an enduring lesson here. It goes to the basic question of whether evil is simply the devil's seed, an inherent trait that must be eradicated, or whether evil has causes that must be addressed. Should Barack Obama, upon meeting Bill Ayers, have said words to the effect of "Get thee behind me, Satan!" or should he have accepted him as a reformed survivor of the madness of the sixties, with lessons to share, living in Obama's senate district?

Seen this way, the Weather Underground originated as one inevitable response to the Vietnam War by an alienated handful of the sixties generation. When the war was escalated to historic levels of violence against the Vietnamese, when Martin Luther King and Robert Kennedy were killed, when Democrats were issuing shoot-to-kill orders on American streets, some young people were driven mad by their comfortable privileges and struck back in a fury consistent with their shame. When the Vietnam War ended and Richard Nixon was forced out of power, the causes of their rage dried up and nearly all the Weather Underground floated back toward the paths they had been following only a few years before, now carrying unspeakable sorrows and unerasable stigmas. All over the world the pattern was the same, red armies and autonomous guerrilla *focos* rising in the extreme climate of the late sixties and falling as Vietnam murderous dictatorships, and the Nixon era faded out. The violence was sociological in origin, not the pathological result of permissive amorality.

Inflicting official violence and killing was not the way to teach the lesson to young people that violence and killing are wrong. Avoidance of Vietnam was the only way to avoid violence in the United States. It could be a useful lesson for the wars ahead.

❦ 16 ❦

The Old Revolutionaries of Vietnam

*D*URING CHRISTMAS 2007, I TRAVELED BACK IN TIME with my family, to Vietnam, for the first time in thirty-two years. I was feeling a deep need to see the place once more and a regret at having withdrawn from a country I had visited four times during the war. I wanted to understand the long-term lessons and, on a personal basis, track down the Vietnamese guides and translators, men and women, who had assumed an ideological faith in the American "people" they escorted through ruins inflicted by the American "enemy." They would become important diplomatic bridges between our two countries in the postwar period. Most were survivors of the French and American wars and would be in their eighties by now. Were they still alive? How had they suffered? After the exuberance at their victory and reunification after 1975, how had they adjusted to a Vietnam without war? Vietnam's consul in San Francisco, Chau Do, said many of these old revolutionaries were alive, excited by my return, and asking whom I wanted to see. I told him that my closest Vietnamese friend was a poet, musician, and translator, Do Xuan Oanh, who was perhaps forty in those days. "I can help you find him," Chau replied with a smile. "He's my dad." My eyes filled with tears. It would be quite a trip.

Before I would reunite with these old friends and contacts, however, I plunged into the shocking contrasts between past and present in Hanoi. Between Christmas 1965 and November 1972, when I made four unauthorized visits to Hanoi, the wartime city was unlit and ghostly. Most people had been evacuated to the countryside. Air raid sirens and public safety broadcasts were the only urban sounds. There was no economic development beyond the construction of pontoon bridges to replace those bombed by the Americans. The only motorized vehicles were military ones. Most residents rode bicycles or carried their meager wares on bamboo poles across their shoulders. Water buffalo pulled the heavier loads. To outward appearances, General Curtis LeMay's plan to bomb Vietnam back to the Stone Age was on track.

Finally came the Christmas bombing of Hanoi and Haiphong by 200 B-52s, from December 18 to December 28, 1972. After seven years and 120,000 B-52 bombing runs, the United States says that 15 of the giant Stratofortresses were shot down and 93 American airmen went missing in just eleven days (Hanoi says 34 B-52s and 81 fighter planes were put out of action).[1] Estimates of civilian deaths range from 1,600 to 2,368 in those eleven days, and Hanoi listed 5,480 buildings destroyed. In the American narrative, the Christmas bombing forced Hanoi to sign the Paris Peace Accords one month later. But under terms agreed to by the Nixon administration, North Vietnamese units remained positioned in the south, and in 1975 they stormed Saigon. What is beyond dispute is that crowded Hanoi neighborhoods and the Bach Mai Hospital were reduced to rubble during the Christmas B-52 raids. The last time I had seen Hanoi was in 1974, when Jane Fonda and I walked through the hospital debris and interviewed still-furious victims of the Christmas 1972 bombs.

Now, suddenly for me, it was Christmas 2007 and Vietnam was ablaze with festive holiday lights, from Hanoi to Ho Chi Minh City. Though billboards of Ho Chi Minh were pervasive, the most ubiquitous bearded one this Christmas season was Santa Claus, beckoning shoppers from department store doorways, seen incongruously riding a motorbike, waving to little children. Spectacular strings of red and green lights were draped over the streets and stores, blinking at thousands of Vietnamese rolling along on bicycles and motorbikes, parting smoothly like schools of fish around pedestrians crossing the street. Restaurant-goers applauded Christmas carols sung by young Vietnamese women strapped in Heineken Girls sashes. None of this was about Jesus—Christmas is not a tradition in this Buddhist and secular Marxist country—but all about corporate branding. The fancy Diamond department store next to Independence Palace was filled with shoppers, gawkers, and Santas wandering the aisles of Lego, Calvin Klein, Victoria's Secret, Nike, Converse, Estée Lauder, Ferragamo, and Bally. The nearby Saigon Center bore a billboard proclaiming, "More Shops, More Life."

Far be it from me to question the desire of Vietnamese to share our globalized consumer culture like everyone else or to reject their aspiration to be the next Asian Tiger or to freeze them in memory as icons of selfless revolutionaries. Gentrification and consumerism, after all, have damaged the character of my favorite American haunts, such as North Beach, Berkeley, Venice, and Aspen. It seems the way of the world. As I walked through the busy Christmas streets, however, I was gripped by the question of why the Vietnam War was necessary in the first place. Why kill, maim, and uproot millions of Vietnamese if the outcome was a consumer wonderland approved by the country's still-undefeated communist party? The whole wretched American rationale for the war, that Vietnam was a dangerous domino, a pawn in the cold war, seemed so painfully wrong. Was there any connection between destroying so much life and causing the Vietnamese to go Christmas shopping? Would the same outcome—a one-party socialist government leading a market economy—have occurred in any event, without the destruction? Now that U.S. naval ships were paying peaceful visits to Da Nang, this question nagged at me: Is it possible that Marxism and nationalism won the war, but capitalism and nationalism have won the peace?

Those who still believe Vietnam was a "necessary" war must take pleasure at seeing that country in the camp of corporate neoliberalism. A proud new member of the World Trade Organization (WTO), Vietnam was welcoming a $1 billion Intel project to Ho Chi Minh City when we visited and has accepted the wholesale privatization of telecommunications and other industries.

Some in Hanoi are dismayed by all this. An American expatriate, Gerry Herman, a former antiwar activist turned businessman and film distributor who has lived in Vietnam for fifteen years, told me the Vietnamese were so desperately eager to normalize relations with the United States that they accepted the most liberal market reforms of any developing country. Having some internal knowledge of the trade negotiations, he says bitterly that Vietnam was blackmailed by the U.S. negotiators. To gain export markets for their textiles, shoes, and seafood, the Vietnamese slashed subsidies and opened markets in banking, insurance, services, and advertising to private foreign investors. For Herman, the distressing prospect is that Vietnam may follow the failed model of the Philippines, not the more successful Asian Tigers whose development benefited from government subsidies.

China, Herman says, got a better deal than Vietnam, winning twenty years of protection for its telecommunications industry. "The American negotiators said to Vietnam that they were beaten by the Chinese on certain issues and would never do it again, and Vietnam could take the deal or leave it." The Americans, in deference to domestic political pressure, even demanded market access for Harley-Davidson, against the Vietnamese complaint that the larger, faster Harleys would worsen the high accident rates on their narrow, congested roads. "The Vietnamese negotiator broke down in tears," Herman said, over the Harley concession. I suddenly remembered the cynical 1960s strategy of Harvard's Samuel Huntington, that forced urbanization would transform the Vietnamese into a "Honda culture." It was coming true before my eyes, with the Honda Dream motorcycle and, sooner or later, the Harley. As a Vietnamese named Pham Thong Long blogged last July, "I have only one dream is buy one of brand new Harley-Davidson, now I waiting for Harley-Davidson deal to open in Saigon. I need a Fatboy."

It is difficult to discern the truth across these cultural divides. Scholars such as Gabriel Kolko have predicted the disintegration of the Vietnamese Communist Party for decades, but the political situation by most accounts is stable, even improved. Thao Griffiths, a thirty-year-old who directs the Hanoi office of Vietnam Veterans of America, reminded me of certain fundamentals on my first day adjusting to the new Hanoi. "Since thirty years ago when you were first here, we have motorbikes in addition to bicycles, cellphones more than land lines, an Internet, and most of our population like myself was born after the wars. It has been a time to catch up in peace." As for Hanoi's accepting the WTO, Thao said: "We knew the mechanism was not fair, but the strategic reason is that we had to get inside. We didn't really have 'normal' economic relations with the U.S. until 2006, for four decades. Even last year, Bush was saying America should have stayed the course in Vietnam." Thao herself reflected postwar Vietnam: Fluent in English and a former Fulbright scholar, she spent two years at the Vietnam veterans' office in Washington, DC, deeply involved in the normalization process. She has two children with her Australian husband, Patrick, a researcher for the United Nations. Her little boy, Liem, immediately befriended our seven-year-old, Liam, on sleepovers and trips to fabled Ha Long Bay.

Vietnam's annual economic growth of 7–8 percent in recent years has been remarkable, though it has come at the price of rising inequalities, a pattern in many other countries under neoliberalism. Per capita gross domestic product (GDP) rose from $200 in 1993 to $835 in 2008. That is still less than $2 per day for most Vietnamese, but it comes close to removing Vietnam from the World Bank's category of the poorest nations. The Vietnamese government estimated foreign direct investment at $13 billion in 2007, the highest investors being South Korea, the British Virgin Islands (a conduit for offshore Hong Kong money), and Singapore. Poverty has fallen from 58 percent to 20 percent, though the majority of ethnic minorities and rural Vietnamese still live in poverty, and growth has created catastrophic problems of infrastructure, traffic congestion, and pollution.

The party introduced its drastic *doi moi* market policies in 1986, a "renovation" plan that opened doors to private foreign investment and a Gorbachev-style internal perestroika. An exhaustive European study concluded in 2006 that a remarkable result of the *doi moi* reforms has been "the absence of organized social opposition among workers, peasants and youth. They are generally content with their growing economic opportunities."[2]

Of course, Vietnam is a one-party state that closely monitors the Internet and pockets of dissent among religious and ethnic groups. But the institutional controls have been steadily relaxed since the 1970s, with none of the uprisings that accompanied the fall of Soviet or Eastern European communism. Nor has there been a Tiananmen Square in Hanoi. "Democratic debate within the party and within the National Assembly, as well as personal freedoms, have made much progress since the war," observes John McAuliff, a reconstruction specialist who has made an estimated fifty trips to the country. "It's true that it wouldn't be wise to stand up on a soapbox and advocate the overthrow of the government," says Lady Borton, a longtime American expatriate and translator in Hanoi. "But there is widespread criticism of the party leaders on all levels in private and in the press," which she describes as "bulldogs." In an observation I shared, Borton described Vietnam as "a place of constant talk, all the time, and they talk freely." "Most Vietnamese simply felt that their lives were much better since the government … shed the heaviest baggage of Marxist-Leninism and abandoned central planning," wrote Robert Templer in his critical 1998 book, *Shadows and Wind*.[3]

A bizarre example of the evolving spirit of youth was provided in Templer's account of the first rock concert by a Western performer in Hanoi's special Giang

Vo exhibition center in the nineties. The singer, Patricia Kaas, was besieged by a throng of teenagers who pushed to the stage, ripped off their t-shirts, and chanted, "I want to fuck you."[4] The MTV virus thus creates an irrepressible youth culture from Brooklyn to Ho Chi Minh City, suggesting a withering away of the state that the Marxist dialectic never predicted.

Kent Wong, the director of UCLA's Labor Studies Center, discerns a positive spirit among Vietnam's working class based on his taking several union delegations to Vietnam. "I've seen poverty in many developing countries, and Vietnam is different. There are no shantytowns," Wong says. Vietnamese unions, Wong acknowledges, are not constituted as adversarial bargaining units, but the many members he has interviewed have high morale. "Four years ago when I was there, they had a plan to organize 1 million more workers in the public sector, and they actually met the goal," he says. Wide income disparities prevail in the private sector, but inequalities in the public sector are less pronounced. Wong, who wants to turn the AFL-CIO away from its lingering cold war (and CIA-financed) heritage of anticommunism toward Vietnam and China, is working to build direct worker-to-worker relationships to foster labor solidarity strategies in the age of globalization.

To make sense of the contradictions between Vietnam's grinding poverty and rising affluence, between defeating Americans in war and joining the WTO in peace, one must consider Vietnam's history. Perhaps no country in the modern world has suffered the sorrows of war more heavily and for a longer consecutive period than Vietnam. Even if we leave out the century of French colonialism, the Vietnamese survived, even prevailed, during the Japanese occupation in World War II, the nine-year war against French reconquest (365,000 battle deaths), the fifteen-year war with the Americans (2.1 million battle deaths), and the ten-year war with Pol Pot's Cambodia and China in the 1980s. Millions of Vietnamese died of famine as well or lived with hunger and deprivation as everyday experiences. After the American war, at least 38,000 more Vietnamese were killed by unexploded bombs and landmines, and countless numbers continue to live with the deformities resulting from 20 million gallons of dioxin-laced Agent Orange and other defoliants. Their sufferings are beyond Western imagination. All this sacrifice was accepted as either a duty in the war for independence or a reality to be accepted and survived. It was accompanied by the deep personalized pain of Vietnamese killing one another, not simply the French or American invaders. At least 185,000 Saigon soldiers died, for example, dishonored as the losing side.

Here, perhaps, is the explanation for Vietnam's two-decade quest to achieve something resembling a normal life, to avoid exclusion from the world community. This memory is why they believe normalization with the United States, accession to the WTO, and a (nonpermanent) seat on the UN Security Council are strategic "victories" on a long road to recovery. It is a matter of great pride that a Vietnamese Bronze Age drum is placed at the entrance to the UN Security Council today.

"No More War was the lesson after Vietnam for our people," says Bao Ninh, author of *The Sorrow of War*,[5] a 1993 antiwar novel that ranks in my mind with the classics of Erich Maria Remarque, Joseph Heller, Kurt Vonnegut, Norman Mailer, Tim O'Brien, and Philip Caputo, among war veterans. We visited Ninh one evening at his Hanoi residence, where he and his wife received us with tea, fruits, and cake. His first floor was a bright reception room with a couch, chairs, and, in one corner, a motorbike. Ninh's novel was banned at first for allegedly undermining the national consensus that the war had been patriotic, victorious, and glorious. But under *doi moi* the book gained a huge audience in Vietnamese and other languages, and soon it may be produced as a film.

When he was fifteen in Hanoi, Ninh saw his first American. It was John McCain, parachuting into Truc Bach Lake from his burning fighter-bomber after destroying a power plant. Ninh watched as McCain, drowning with two broken arms, was pulled from the lake by a local fisherman at a spot marked by a small monument today. Ninh later joined the army to fight in South Vietnam, was among the soldiers who liberated Saigon in 1975, and searched for the decomposing bodies of dead soldiers after the war. His book is more about man's inhumanity to man than a tale of triumphant revolution. I was stunned at the jacket's description of Ninh as 1 of 10 survivors of a youth brigade of 500. With a laugh, he surprised me by saying the numbers were made up by his publisher, Pantheon/Random House. "Not only governments but soldiers themselves make up war stories, too," he laughed again, not unlike sardonic American Vietnam veterans. "I like writing. I write about what I know. I wanted to tell a soldier's story, not a political or ideological one."

Ninh visited the United States in 1998 with other Vietnamese writers, gaining an impression of U.S. diversity, including surprise at how many Americans were "quite fat." That aside, even in conservative towns such as Missoula, Montana, he found Vietnam memorials and town officials who were veterans like himself. Ninh came away impressed that so many Americans still "remembered, discussed, and agonized over Vietnam," and he formed the opinion that this memory of Vietnam could be "a tower of strength from the past" on which to build better relations in the future.

Beneath his friendly bearing, Ninh carries the scars and guilt that only some war veterans are capable of expressing. The most painful, perhaps, is his "sorrow at having survived," the belief that the very best of his generation died for Vietnam's present peace: "Look carefully now at the peace we have, painful, bitter, and sad. And look who won the war. To win, martyrs had sacrificed their lives in order that others might survive. Not a new phenomenon, true. But for those still living to know that the kindest, most worthy people have all fallen away, or even been tortured, humiliated before being killed, or buried and wiped away by the machinery of war, then this beautiful landscape of calm and peace is an appalling paradox."[6]

Ninh was repelled by Vietnam's Marxist postwar policies. "In the war, I had lived like an animal. Now I couldn't stand this [the peace]. Some Americans may sympathize with communism, but I lived under it and couldn't stand it. Everybody was fed up with the hardship. That's what led to the *doi moi* in the '80s." One of

Bao Ninh's sons is making millions in the global high-tech industry and travels frequently to the United States. It is not the future he fought for at the same age, he says, but he is proud and happy for his son. "We Vietnamese are not like North Korea or China. If communism doesn't work, we move on. But North Korea, for example, has a very tough time because they keep going on with communism."

Not many Vietnamese today think of the war with America with Bao Ninh's profound cynicism, for that would mean questioning their country's very identity, much like questioning the Indian wars or the Revolution for Americans. Rather, the American war is perceived as a necessity forced on Vietnam by invading powers, as has happened for more than a thousand years, beginning with the Chinese. Vietnamese take pride in having defeated so many great powers and feel deeply about their losses. There is a suppressed anger that they were willing to join the search for American MIAs (missing in action) while the United States and Monsanto refused to take responsibility for Agent Orange.

The question is whether the future, aside from the obvious advantages of peace, will be worth the sacrifices of the past. Is the period of anticolonial revolution—which Vietnam symbolized and which so dominated our thinking in the 1960s and beyond—becoming an obsolete memory in the era of globalization? Has the promise of those inspiring revolutions faded with the decline of colonialism in its naked form and the emergence of so many corrupt authoritarianisms in the Third World? Or are the supposedly scientific models of history long embraced by the Left being replaced with a kind of chaos theory of unpredictability? Is this all that was ever possible? Perhaps this was why I had stayed away so long but had to return after so many decades. Much as I still opposed war and imperialism, from Vietnam to Iraq, I no longer expected joyous endings.

I wanted to see my oldest acquaintances in Vietnam for personal reasons but also as guides in sorting out these troubling questions. I will call these people, now in their eighties, Vietnam's old revolutionary generation. Their roots went back nearly a century, to young Ho Chi Minh's odyssey to the West—in particular, France and America—to study the spirit of republican revolutions for lessons he might bring home. Ho, then known as Nguyen Ai Quoc, presented a petition to the 1919 Versailles conference asking for Vietnam's inclusion in the call for self-determination. There he learned that Woodrow Wilson's Fourteen Points did not apply to the colonies. In the period of the Russian Revolution, Ho was waiting tables in Harlem and making diary notes on lynchings. He embraced Marxism-Leninism because of V. I. Lenin's opposition to colonialism. Twenty-five years later, Ho collaborated with American intelligence agents in resisting the Japanese occupation. Then he cited the U.S. Declaration of Independence in declaring Vietnam's freedom in 1945. From long tradition grew the practical, and even sentimental, belief that the "American people," in Walt Whitman's mythic invocation, could be appealed to against American imperialism.

Thus arose Viet-My (Vietnamese-American) solidarity committees and cultural exchanges from the very beginnings of the war with the United States, staffed by bright young Vietnamese who were asked to host American wartime visitors and in the process learned more about American culture and politics. Now long retired, many of these old revolutionaries went on after the war to become diplomats and ambassadors to European countries. These days in Hanoi many still arise at 5:30 for morning exercises at the Flying Dragon Club, an old building with a curved roof, and then, with bodies limber and spirits balanced, go out for tea and conversation.

In general, the old revolutionaries are busy, active in community affairs, proud, and nationalistic, and they shared with me the unanimous sense that Vietnam has become too materialistic and acquisitive. "The new generation lacks a balanced approach," said eighty-one-year-old Nguyen Ngoc Dung, who runs shelters for street children in Ho Chi Minh City. "The situation is out of balance," she added. "They are not looking—how do you say?—at the other side of the coin."

Dung is a former deputy to the most well-known of the old revolutionaries, eighty-one-year-old Nguyen Thi Binh, who presides over the Peace and Development Foundation in Hanoi. During the war, "Madame Binh," as she was known, was a striking global icon and nemesis denounced by Henry Kissinger in the Paris peace negotiations. When she welcomed me for tea, she seemed smaller than the woman I remembered, but her energy remained vibrant. The formality of the re-union was derailed by the arrival of the "two Liams," arm in arm. They sat on her grandmotherly lap while Binh held forth on the challenges of healing the damage of Agent Orange and developing Vietnam past the status of other poor countries. She showed a keen interest in sponsoring workshops with critics of globalization. Meanwhile, the two little Liams lobbied to be taken to the local Lego franchise.

On another morning, the sudden arrival of an older man in a blue windbreaker surprised me. He walked toward me peering carefully through wide spectacles. "Do you remember who I am?" he asked with an expectant look. Then he held before me a black-and-white photo of myself, ten pounds lighter and thirty-five years younger, staring at Vietnamese graves, notebook in hand. The man with glasses was Pham Khac Lam, an interpreter and photographer whom I last saw deep within a cave in rural North Vietnam in 1972.

Lam, now seventy-seven, was the top assistant to General Vo Nguyen Giap in preparing the battle plan for Dien Bien Phu in 1954. His father was a mandarin adviser to Emperor Bao Dai, the last Vietnamese king. Lam's father is said to have written Bao Dai's abdication speech in 1945. Lam, in other words, grew up in the absolute center of Vietnamese anticolonialism, joined the solidarity committees during the American war, and participated in the postwar process as director of the country's first television network. He was part of the Rose Garden ceremonies when Vietnam's leaders met Presidents Bill Clinton and George H. W. Bush. He takes modest credit for the idea of flying both Vietnamese and U.S. flags on the stretch limousine that carried Hanoi officials to the White House door. And he once told Civil War buff Ted Turner, who opened media relations between CNN and Hanoi, that "it was important to let the past be 'gone with the wind.'" Turner generously sold Lam the rights to broadcast CNN for a nickel.

Lam edits *Viet-My*, a glossy magazine that seems devoted to promotional reports on commercial and diplomatic ties with the United States, including critical commentary on issues such as Agent Orange. Occasionally Lam inserts a strategic analysis of the U.S. quandary in Iraq, buried amid advertisements beckoning tourists to such attractions as health clubs at the beach. How did he really feel, I wondered, about the world he had done so much to shape?

Lam seemed relaxed and diplomatic. His duties have included welcoming former Saigon dictator Nguyen Cao Ky, who has visited Hanoi frequently in recent years, against vociferous complaints from Vietnamese exiles in America. "Ky said that he always wanted to unify Vietnam, so I have to salute him," Lam said wryly. On the question of his country's deepening inequalities, however, Lam parted from the optimistic party line. "The government is trying to reduce poverty, but it's already a reality. The rich are getting richer because they have the means. And the poor don't. We are better off materially, but not mentally, ethically," he said, brushing his forehead.

The world had changed all around him, from the caves of resistance to welcomes in the Rose Garden, from Dien Bien Phu to the global media stage. The geopolitical balance was altered forever, with no more Soviet Union or "socialist camp" and with tensions simmering beneath the "fraternal relations" with China. "We and the Chinese used to call each other comrade; now it's mister," he reflected wryly. The most ironic piece of the puzzle before me was falling into place. Although it could not be said explicitly—and even though Vietnam inevitably would strive to maintain close relations with China, its giant northern neighbor—the United States could serve as a strategic balance in Asia for Hanoi, while Vietnam serves as a silent check on the expanding Chinese power Washington fears most. Ironically, this is the domino theory in reverse.

Finally, there was a visit to my oldest friend, Do Xuan Oanh, who first greeted me at Hanoi's airport on a December day forty-two years before. He went through a "bitter period" after retirement, someone told me, but he was feeling better, having recently translated into English an edition of Vietnamese women's poetry. He lived alone, his wife having died after many years of illness, his three sons all abroad. As I remembered him, Oanh loved America in unique ways. For example, after learning English from the BBC, he translated *Huckleberry Finn* into Vietnamese, a massive challenge. A musician, he could sing many American protest songs. A romantic, he wept easily and became close to many Americans.

Now, in a carload of old revolutionaries, I traveled along a narrow cement path past houses, until we came to the gate of Oanh's home of fifty years. He was standing in the door, a thin shadow of the Oanh I remembered. Taking my hand, he led me into a windowless room where a couch and piano were the most prominent fixtures. There were alcoves for painting and a kitchen. We sat and looked at each other. He held my hand on his knee, while the others sat in a quiet circle. It was more a last visit than a time to renew an old conversation.

"Do you want some booze?" Oanh asked with a low chuckle, pointing to a half-bottle of Jim Beam. I deferred, worried what might happen after a few drinks. My wife said Oanh seemed fit and energetic for an eighty-five-year-old. She asked if he would play the piano, and he performed an original piece in a classic European style. He gave me a copy of the song, signed to his "precious friend," and a small carving of a beautiful Vietnamese woman carrying a student briefcase, which he said reminded him of his wife "before the revolution." He repeated the phrase, then relaxed. Gradually, the others began to reminisce about the old days. I wondered if we would ever meet again. I remembered an e-mail from Oanh's son in San Francisco: "I believe God assigned my father and myself to serve the American people." His son would come for a visit in the summer, Oanh said.

We walked back along the dark path to the street filled with motorbikes and strolling couples out for a coffee. Oanh looked at me intently, pointing a finger for emphasis. "Nothing can be predicted" were his last words before we said good-bye.

17

Peace in Northern Ireland

*T*HE EVOLUTION OF NORTHERN IRELAND, from the 1968 revolt by a new generation of republican militants to the successful Good Friday Agreement of 1998, is a classic example of the movement model. However, it has received little attention on the traditional American Left or among national security thinkers. Left theorists, historians, and sociologists have tended to be either British-centric or suspicious of the anti-Semitic tendencies associated with traditional Catholic nationalism, sometimes justifiably so. The neutrality of the Irish state during World War II cemented this suspicion on the Left and Right.

But there is a long Irish revolutionary tradition that in the 1916 Easter Rising blended religion, nationalism, and socialism under the leadership of the trade unionist James Connolly. The roots of that tradition, known as republicanism, lay in the 1798 rebellion of the United Irishmen—Protestants, Catholics, and Dissenters—which was closely patterned after republican movements in America, France, the rest of Europe, and Latin America. Although succeeding in America and France, the Irish republican dream was deferred in the bloody defeat of 1798, where an estimated thirty thousand were killed by Crown forces and thousands were forced into exile to other lands, including America, where Thomas Jefferson welcomed the Irish refugees despite a ferocious Protestant-led backlash symbolized by the Alien and Sedition Acts.

One of those exiles was Thomas Emmet, who carried on the republican heritage in America after his brother's beheading by the British. I was named after this Thomas Emmet—Thomas Emmet Hayden IV—but in the amnesia caused by assimilation, my third-generation parents had no knowledge of Emmet to pass on to me. In Irish, the name Hayden derives from O hAodain, which roughly means "the person of the flame"; Garity (my mother's maiden name) came from Mag Oireachtaigh, or "the assembly man." I never knew a thing about this history of my own personal ghosts until the 1960s made me Irish. When I asked my mom why I was "the fourth" in my lineage, she only said it was because there were the first, second, and third.

On a cultural level, the 1960s constituted a process of reverse assimilation. People of color sought liberation from whiteness. Women liberated themselves from male cultural standards. Native people fought against reservation schools. Universities were forced to establish programs in black studies, Chicano studies, Asian studies, Native American studies, women's studies, even the formally designated queer studies. Just as Irish Americans celebrated assimilation with the 1960 election of John F. Kennedy, the fabric of identity was unraveling. As the 1968 Chicago confrontations subsided, I watched on television as marchers in Northern Ireland were beaten and hosed while singing, "We Shall Overcome." I discovered a heritage that, it turned out, was not so much lost as taken from me by a culture and school system that disparaged Irish culture as inferior to the white, Anglo-Saxon paradigm. The fully assimilated Irish Americans—the Catholic hierarchy, the Chicago police, legions of FBI agents, the conservative building trades—were on the other side of the blossoming culture wars.

The 1960s were sweeping across Britain's northern Irish colony as well. The Irish Republican Army (IRA) was a spent force, its last military campaign having stalled and stuttered through 1962. A climate of surface contentment prevailed, similar to the parallel assimilation of Irish Americans into suburban quietude. Beneath the surface was another matter. A new generation was awakening. A young Gerry Adams, then working in a Belfast pub, remembers being gripped by a "youthful, mistaken conviction that the revolution was happening all around us…. [There] was a feeling shared across countries, continents and religions."[1] Partly this sense came from the music, especially Bob Dylan's lyrics. But fundamentally, it was the global impact of the African American civil rights movement.

Adams was from a strong republican family, worked at a local pub, and involved himself in community organizing around housing discrimination. His hair was shaggy, his glasses large, his intelligence keen. Skeptics will claim that he already was a closeted revolutionary, ready to manipulate events to republican advantage. On the face of things, however, he was engaged in reformist activity to improve housing opportunity on the Falls Road. He was beaten up on one occasion for selling the republican newspaper. It would be more accurate to describe him as a new generational figure in an old tradition. As a youth, he became a natural leader in the nightly community meetings during the siege of Ballymurphy, a Catholic housing project in Belfast where in 1970, local people fought street battles against British troops firing CS gas and using armored cars mounted with barbed wire. He was among those interned—arrested and held without trial—aboard a British ship in Belfast harbor.

As for Martin McGuinness, he was a devout young Catholic who joined the IRA during the wave of street battles in Derry (which the British called Londonderry) in the late 1960s. When I first met him in the mid-1970s, he was twenty-eight years old, the same age I was during the Chicago street confrontations. McGuinness was not hidden in the shadows; he was a visible target of the British, openly taking part in community protests and, indeed, in the thick of spontaneous street fighting. Though traditionalist in certain ways, he shared a distinctive consciousness of the 1960s, complaining that the British were "trying to turn us all into golfers" in a consumer society. A third longtime friend, Danny Morrison, was waiting on tables and dreaming of classic literature when the 1960s struck his life. Another, Tom Hartley, was working in the Sinn Fein bookstore on the Falls Road, hawking leaflets and posters, and accumulating knowledge about the history of Belfast cemeteries. Like many others I met, they would survive to be leaders of their generation, supporting armed struggle, surviving terrible feuds with other factions, leading Sinn Fein toward a political strategy that abandoned violence, and arriving finally, after thirty years, in leadership positions in the communities to which they always belonged: Adams and McGuinness as the catalysts and negotiators of the peace process, Adams as president of Sinn Fein, McGuinness as minister of education and deputy first minister of the Northern Ireland Executive, Morrison as an accomplished author of many novels and essays, Hartley as the lord mayor of Belfast. Although considered "fenian bastards," criminals, incorrigible radicals, terrorists, and contaminated untouchables along the way, by any measure today they would have to be considered part of the "establishment," a term that surely makes them wince.

There already existed fertile nationalist ground in the Catholic ghettos, though fallowed with time. In his history of *The Troubles,* Tim Pat Coogan refers to *uisce fe talamh,* or "water under the ground," an Irish "consciousness of race and place, formed by history and circumstance, whereby one grows up knowing things without realizing where one learned them."[2] The infectious concept of a nonviolent struggle for civil rights was a new one. Previous generations of republicans had hewed to their physical force strategy on the grounds that the British colonial power was unreformable by peaceful means. To seek civil rights within the British empire was to abandon the long quest for national independence.

But now the images from the American civil rights movement drew a diverse array of factions and personalities into the Northern Irish Civil Rights Association (NICRA). Ending discrimination in employment and housing and sectarian gerrymandering were popular demands uniting Catholics of all class backgrounds while drawing fierce opposition from the Unionist state. Instead of rancorous debate, the unifying assumption was that the civil rights demand would test the limits of British rule. According to one historian: "The new strategy was inspired by the Black civil rights movement in the United States. The term 'civil rights' had not been used to define the aspirations of the minority community in Northern Ireland and it had never before adopted a strategy that was both militant and constitutional."[3] The sentiment was expressed bluntly in Roddy Doyle's 1988 *The Commitments*, in which Jimmy Rabbitte, the leader of a Dublin rock-and-roll band and devotee of James Brown, proclaims proudly that "the Irish are the niggers of Europe, lads."[4]

The civil rights demand allowed the movement, including radicals and republicans, to broaden its appeal to the Catholic mainstream, a significant number of Protestant liberals, the European Community, and Irish Catholics in the United States. Repeated attacks on peaceful civil rights marchers, including the moderate member of Parliament for Westminster Gerry Fitt on October 5, 1968, were transmitted globally by the media. Charismatic young leaders such as Bernadette Devlin were attracting the attention of journalists like Jimmy Breslin and stirring a global audience. "We Shall Overcome" was sung on the road to Derry.

There were two layers on the Machiavellian side. The first comprised the privileged Unionist community and the more extreme Loyalists, organized in agencies such as the Orange Order and leading a Protestant population then numbering more than 60 percent of Northern Ireland's 1.5 million people. The second was made up of the supporting organs of the British colonial state, which funded, gerrymandered, and provided one-sided security on all levels, organized through Westminster's Northern Ireland Office (known to republicans as the "securocrats"). The Unionists were threatened by a loss of privilege, the British by a loss of empire. The most well-known of the "no surrender" faction of unionism was the Armagh-born Reverend Ian Paisley, recipient of a divinity degree from the then-segregated Bob Jones University in South Carolina.[5] America's fundamentalist Right was a domestic ally of the Orangemen. In the background was the so-called special relationship between the United States and the United Kingdom, which treated Northern Ireland as the internal affair of the British, with the United States providing diplomatic and intelligence cover.

The Irish civil rights movement provoked an immediate and violent backlash from Orange mobs, including firebombings, shootings, beatings, even de facto pogroms. For a brief period, the dominant reaction in besieged Catholic neighborhoods was to call for intervention by British troops. Within a year, however, the British proved themselves to be so deeply tangled in the preservation of the Protestant status quo that they were regarded as an occupying army.

By 1969–1970, Catholic ghettos in Derry and Belfast had become communities of resistance, thus giving a new identity to everyday life. Barricades went up in Derry (home of McGuinness) and the Ballymurphy housing estate where Adams lived, and rioting occurred almost on a nightly basis. Along the Falls Road, colorful murals went up overnight. Community newspapers were invented underground. Black taxis replaced a burned-out bus system. Hundreds of community organizations were born. And in the face of the imminent threat of Loyalist attacks with British complicity, the self-defense networks gave birth to a new "provisional" Irish Republican Army.

The response of the British was the internment policy of 1971, in which hundreds of alleged IRA members were lifted from their homes to be imprisoned without charge on the prison ship *Maidstone* in Belfast harbor, in the newly created Long Kesh prison, and in jails in Crumlin Road and Armagh. The British introduced torture techniques that would remain in use during the Iraq war thirty-five years later, including hooding, high-pitched noise, sleep deprivation, standing spread-eagled against a wall, and simulations of being hurled out of a helicopter. In these harsh conditions, the militant republican identity was only solidified. According to young Gerry Adams's description of the change, "A *steely determination* entered many hearts, a feeling that if it was war they wanted, it was war they would get."[6]

A key transition occurred in Derry in 1969–1972, climaxing in the British Army killing of fourteen peaceful protesters on January 30, 1972, known as Bloody Sunday. Officially named Londonderry, but known to nationalists as Derry, the city's Bogside ghetto became a no-go, or liberated, zone proclaimed in huge murals as "Free Derry." The name was chosen because the young radicals had heard of "Free Berkeley," a romantic experiment in establishing an autonomous community in resistance to Ronald Reagan and the UC Regents at the time (I was involved then in one of the many Berkeley communes). Free Derry was more than a state of mind, however; the Bogside was the scene of perpetual confrontations with Loyalists, police, and British troops looking down on the ghetto from the ancient walls of the city. This was a genuine community of meaning that would be carried forward in the lives of thousands of its young rebels for three decades.

The killings on January 30, 1972, meant to suppress the rebellion and restore order, have been the subject of two lengthy inquiries, several films, numerous books and articles, John Lennon's "Sunday Bloody Sunday," and U2's 1984 song of the same name. The key facts are that the British forces shot and killed fourteen unarmed people and wounded thirteen more, falsely claimed that their troops were provoked by sniper fire, then engaged in a massive cover-up for decades. "*The state stood by its own,*" wrote a Derry radical of the time, Eamon McCann, referring to the fact that a lord chief justice had proclaimed that the killings were neither wrong nor illegal.

"Standing by its own" was a key Machiavellian maxim. As we shall see, the state interest changed in the course of the thirty-year war, but at the time the state "stood with its own," defending a "Protestant state for a Protestant people" and protecting the image and power of the United Kingdom. The apparent similarities between the American and Irish civil rights conflicts were becoming stark opposites. Within the segregated American South, blacks could appeal to the interest of the national state in ending unconstitutional practices in a section of the country; that is, civil rights meant equal rights as Americans. The Northern Ireland crisis was more like the eighteenth-century crisis between the American colonies and the British Crown; that is, the British would not accept a definition of civil rights that included the fundamental right to be Irish. Thus, "free Derry posed an unambiguous challenge to the authority of the state and the rule of law."[7]

According to internal documents, the British decided the following day, on January 31, to pursue a tribunal strategy that would "pile up the case against the deceased," even though there was no evidence that any of them had been armed.[8] After all, the Downing Street memo underscored, the state was "fighting not only a military war but a propaganda war."[9]

Bloody Sunday marked the shift from a civil rights movement to armed guerrilla warfare against British rule. In terms of our model, the militant social movement came to dominate, as did the militant countermovement against the moderate middle classes. In the three years previous to Bloody Sunday, 210 people were killed across Northern Ireland; nearly 500 died in the eleven months after Bloody Sunday; and more than 3,600 in the three decades to come, the rough equivalent of 600,000 Americans.[10]

The British never defeated the IRA or the larger force of Irish nationalism. Instead, their material costs and reputational power suffered as some seven hundred British soldiers were killed, along with larger numbers of Ulster regiments and Royal Ulster Constabulary (RUC) officers. Billions of pounds in property damage was inflicted, too. In April 1993, the IRA blew up London's financial district at an estimated loss of 800 million pounds.[11] Again, in 1996, when the peace talks were stagnating, the IRA blew up London's Canary Wharf and the center of Manchester.[12] Although open support for armed struggle was confined to a nationalist minority, the relevant fact is that a sufficient number of northern nationalists were anti-British enough to understand, tolerate, and give protection to the IRA's network of active-service units. In that sense, the organization was embedded within mainstream nationalist opinion in the north and, to an extent, in the legacy of the quieter southern state as well.

With the militant strategy prevailing, however, the option of a political strategy preferred by the Irish majority was postponed for years. Sinn Fein, the political party led by Adams and associated with the IRA, was limited to a dedicated hard-core constituency and was unable to make wider breakthroughs. Its moderate rival, the Social Democratic and Labor Party (SDLP), drew heavy support from the Irish establishment, including Irish American political leaders, but its nonviolent electoral strategy was no answer to the British occupation. According to the *New Statesman* in 1994, "British intelligence had played a vital role in the creation of the SDLP. Dusting off from the decolonization strategies of 1960s Africa, the objective was to create an acceptable, modern alternative to armed militant nationalism."[13] This sharp division between militants and moderates continued over the decades, ending sharply in the 1990s when Sinn Fein and the IRA captured the peace banner and thus middle-class Catholic support. This was unexpected news for the Machiavellians, one of whom said, "We were all taken by surprise by Hume-Adams." The *New Statesman* added that "the British government is surprised and somewhat alarmed by the progress that Sinn Fein and Gerry Adams have made in the key political constituencies of Dublin and Washington.... MI5 and the RUC Special Branch clearly have a major role to play in the continuing *political* struggle against the republican movement."[14]

A critical moment came with the 1981 republican hunger strikes, in which ten republican prisoners slowly and painfully died while demanding the restoration of their status as political prisoners. The British establishment, represented by Prime Minister Margaret Thatcher, held fast to a hard-line stand as Irish and world opinion turned against them. Irish people long divided over the IRA came together in urgent unity in support of the prisoners. It was not simply Thatcher's cruelty, but the sense of a purity of sacrifice among the strikers that deeply moved the population. The prisoners' leader, Bobby Sands, was a poet whose lines were smuggled to the outside world on toilet paper that had been passed to visitors. Sands condemned a world where journalists "wrote not a jot of beauty tortured sore," and he compared the prisoners to "flowers in the dark" or bluebells lifting their heads. With naked courage, eloquent writing, and an iconic face resembling that of Che Guevara or Jesus Christ, Sands touched the souls of many.

The political effect of the hunger strike was to make the unthinkable possible: Sands elected to the British Parliament while he lay dying. Two other strikers, Kieren Dougherty and Paddy Agnew, were elected to Leinster House, the seat of power in Dublin. For Sinn Fein, the explosion of public support was undeniable evidence that an electoral strategy of a new kind was possible, a combination of the ballot box and armalite (a gun), Danny Morrison said. Not only was there an unprecedented opening to the political mainstream, but also Sands and his comrades would endure in memory as global legends.[15]

There were many more dramas and deaths ahead, but the purpose here is to examine the process by which the actors were reconciled in an unusual peace agreement in 1998. Let me first describe the dynamics of the nationalist movement, then the Machiavellian response. The key notion is that the conflicting sides each came to the realization of a *stalemate,* that is, a strategic recognition that their maximum goals were becoming unreachable. On the nationalist side, Sinn Fein understood the impossibility of its aspiration of forcing the Unionist majority to either convert to Irish nationalism or be forced to emigrate from Ireland. The long war had been waged for two decades, and even though the IRA could not be defeated, a military victory also was out of the question. The reality of unionism would have to be accepted and therefore, some sort of connection with the UK. Reaching the holy grail of the republic would be delayed. President Bill Clinton cynically told Adams at the White House that a united Ireland would have to wait upon the Catholic birthrate, according to someone who was present.

For moderate nationalist leaders such as John Hume, it was equally clear that unity was needed with the republicans, despite principled differences over violence and revolution. The SDLP base, however opposed to violence, was strongly nationalist and shared much of Sinn Fein's agenda, including radical reform of the RUC. Just as Adams was limited by the IRA's military campaign, Hume was limited by having no leverage over the IRA. In January 1988, therefore, Adams and Hume sat down for secret open-ended discussions in search of a pan-nationalist strategy for power. The talks were strongly supported by an ally of Adams, Father Alec Reid, a priest at the Clonard monastery in West Belfast. The Adams-Hume approach at the time was deeply unpopular with large segments of their followings. For a social movement in particular to shift fundamental direction without convulsing into deadly factions is a testimony to the skills of Adams and the republican leadership, particularly their decision to continually convene lengthy, participatory, often confusing meetings of the membership at each decisive moment. There were defections, to be sure, but the memory of devastating splits in past republican campaigns might have influenced the character of internal debates during the peace process.[16]

On the British side, key strategists realized that the military war against the IRA could not be won. Two further developments permitted a modification of their worldview. First, the cold war came to an end, which meant that the IRA could never again be demonized as a communist threat, like Cuba, across the channel. Second, new pressure from an ad hoc network of Irish Americans had influenced the thinking and political calculus of Bill Clinton. Perhaps because he himself was a child of the sixties, perhaps because he had been impressed with Bernadette Devlin's speeches while he was a student at Oxford (in 1969, while Clinton was a graduate student, Devlin, then twenty-one, had been elected a rebel member of the House of Commons),[17] Clinton was persuaded to endorse an Irish peace process, appoint a peace envoy, and offer a visa to Gerry Adams. He did so against the strong opposition of his State Department, the CIA, and most of the Irish American establishment. It was even necessary for the White House to wrest control of Northern Ireland policy from the State Department. This decision meant rupturing a long-held "special relationship" with the British, under which Northern Ireland was considered an internal matter reserved to the United Kingdom. Why Clinton acted in this way may have been purely political, that is, his quest for white ethnic votes in the 1992 election. Or it might have been political payback for Prime Minister John Major's effort to help the Republican Party defeat Clinton with scurrilous attacks on his patriotism.

The split in the British-American axis was enormously helpful to Sinn Fein and Adams, creating a pronationalist U.S. counterweight to British colonial interests. Adams's visit to America in 1997 generated huge Irish American crowds and a media frenzy. Overnight a new Irish American movement became a factor in pressuring Clinton to move forward, which he did with the appointment of former senator George Mitchell as the envoy who eventually mediated the peace process.

There were many twists, turns, crises, and near-implosions and acts of unexpected leadership in the process that are well recounted in many books, but the point is that the outcome was a classic example of a new order being constructed through the Good Friday Agreement of 1998.[18]

For whatever mixture of reasons, in 1989 and 1990 the British secretary of state, Peter Brooke, gave two revelatory speeches on British strategy that broke "all the unwritten rules" of diplomacy.[19] In the first, Brooke acknowledged for the first time publicly that "it is difficult to envisage a military defeat [of the IRA]" and suggested that an "imaginative" alternative process would have to be "managed."[20] In the second, Brooke went further, declaring that "the British government has no selfish or strategic or economic interest in Northern Ireland ... [and] an Irish Republicanism seen to have finally renounced violence would be able, like other parties, to seek a role in the peaceful political life of the community."[21]

As the stalemate deepened, the British in June 1997 announced a new inquiry into Bloody Sunday, this time as a confidence-building measure in the peace process. The Dublin government released a damning assessment of Bloody Sunday for the first time on the same day. Tony Blair acknowledged the innocence of the fallen. It was a victorious moment for the victims' families, lonely researchers such as Don Mullen, and Irish nationalism, though twenty-five years in the making. Human rights issues had become central to the unfolding peace process. Two years later, in 1999, British documents released during the new inquiry revealed 1972 military proposals to "restore law and order" with "stronger military measures" that necessarily would include killing "innocent members of the crowd," the scenario that had played out in Derry that Sunday.[22] The countermovement had prevailed in 1972 over the handful of voices counseling gradual but fundamental reform of the British state.

There followed many unsuccessful efforts to undermine and split the republican movement, one British leader snidely proposing a "decontamination" period before Sinn Fein could be at the table. But the new nationalist alliance held firm, expanding to include the Dublin government and, to an extent, the Americans. The IRA declared a cease-fire, broke it in 1996 when talks were going nowhere, and reestablished it in 1997. The main Loyalist paramilitaries announced parallel cease-fires as well, signifying the indispensable support of the armed movements for the peace process. The apparently impossible contradictions were carefully managed through negotiations in which hundreds of British diplomats faced off against small groups of self-educated Sinn Fein cadres accountable to endless community feedback sessions. Politically, Clinton's 1996 reelection was followed by Tony Blair's Labor Party sweep in 1997, thus making "the Ulster unionists no longer a factor in the Westminster political equation."[23] What emerged was a brilliant example of conflict resolution that brought the cycle of killing to an end and opened a political path for nationalism to succeed.

On the Irish side, the rights of Irish nationality, culture, and language were guaranteed. The RUC was dissolved and replaced, in principle, by a police service committed to fundamental reform (as of 2009, the transfer of justice and policing powers to the Northern Executive was in the final stages of negotiation). The Irish tricolor could be flown everywhere. Border checkpoints were removed, and cross-border commissions were established between north and south. All political prisoners, Irish and Loyalist, were released to their communities. The IRA was committed to eventual decommissioning (putting out of use) of their weapons without any implication of surrender. Tribunals were established to seek the truth about Bloody Sunday and other cases. A system of power-sharing, based on proportional representation, allowed Sinn Fein representatives to essentially cochair the Stormont assembly and become mayors of numerous cities, including Belfast; Adams and others were elected members of the British Parliament, but still declined on principle to serve officially. Sinn Fein was free to organize in the south, where it soon achieved seats on municipal levels and the Dail (parliament), becoming Ireland's only islandwide nationalist party. The path was open to de facto reunification of Ireland as a whole, at least on a gradual step-by-step basis. It was less than a thirty-two-county Irish republic, but more like a transitional binational arrangement in which Irish nationalism was empowered for the first time in some eighty years.

On the other side, Blair could claim that the existence of Northern Ireland in the United Kingdom was preserved, though on an entirely new basis and only for the foreseeable future. It would no longer be a Protestant enclave, but the rights and property of the diminishing Unionist majority would be guaranteed. The British had found a formula for preserving both the appearance and reality of their core Machiavellian interest, their reputation as a credible guarantor, their writ of sovereignty intact, even if over a profoundly changed situation. There were moments when a mutiny of the British generals seemed possible, but it never transpired. Michael Oatley, a secret negotiator for the British MI6, wrote an unusual piece in the *Times* denouncing the conservative countermovement as the picador approach: "No doubt if sufficient barbs are thrust into its [the IRA's] flanks, the animal, with reluctance, will charge. The picadors then can claim the beast was always a ravening monster."[24]

The paradox is that a peaceful arrangement was achieved by the inclusion of the former "extremes" while the moderate parties gradually imploded. By 2007, the first minister of the north was Ian Paisley, and the second-in-charge was Martin McGuinness, whose concurrence was essential to the government doing business.

Sinn Fein has been little studied as a political party, but ten years after the Good Friday Agreement it has survived so far the fates usually predicted by political scientists. This may be because it remains more a movement than a party. It has been neither co-opted into loyalty to the British state nor sundered by significant factions. With leadership and some luck in timing, a pan-nationalist unity was cobbled together among Sinn Fein, the SDLP, the Dublin government, and Irish America, when divisions might easily have undermined the project. Sinn Fein has not come to power across the island, but neither is it a remnant of the past. It is the largest nationalist party in Ireland, holds scores of seats in the north and south, and has beaten back both the demonizers and the dividers. The key to its political rise was its leadership in the peace process. By one estimate, its vote rose from 78,000 in 1992 to 176,000 in 2001, and it doubled its elected northern councilors from 51 to 108.[25] It is true, as in the case of all social movements, that success in winning so much of its original agenda has led to some demobilization of its activist base and an uncertainty of purpose. With the borders open, the occupation ended, the detention camps emptied, Irish music and writing flourishing, the formal goal of a unified Irish state still seems years away. In the meantime, Sinn Fein must deliver on issues that originate beyond its scope in the globalized capitalist economy. When peace arrives, do revolutionary movements wither? When what was radical becomes mundane, what happens to the radicals?

But forty years after the British attempt to crush Sinn Fein's birth, a period of normalcy is to be expected and even deserved. Killings due to the Troubles have fallen nearly to zero, and Belfast is more peaceful than many big American cities. Sinn Fein remains a model of conflict resolution for revolutionary nationalist movements as well, having exceptionally close historic ties to the African National Congress and, more currently, direct engagement in roundtable dialogue among rival Sunni and Shia movements in Iraq.

I last saw Adams and McGuinness in August 2008, at the longtime Sinn Fein headquarters off the Falls Road. Outside is a wall-sized mural of Bobby Sands, smiling down, with the quotation, "Everyone has a part to play." McGuinness was essentially cochairing the executive with Peter Robinson, who had earlier vowed to "smash Sinn Fein" and donned a red beret to represent resistance to the Good Friday Agreement. I had just returned from City Hall, where Lord Mayor Tom Hartley presided over the official placement of the Irish Tricolor. The day before, I spoke to the Belfast Festival about the Good Friday Agreement as an example of compromise between Machiavellians and movements. When I commented on the unusual success of Sinn Fein in avoiding the splits that usually follow victories, Adams joked that it was not too late.

Inside the Sinn Fein building, I interviewed Martin McGuinness about his two recent trips to Baghdad, where he was trying to export the lessons of the Irish peace process. His traveling partners were a startling assortment: Jeffrey Donaldson, once a Unionist hard-liner and now part of Belfast's power-sharing arrangements; Cyril Ramaphosa, a former secretary-general of the African National Congress; and Roelf Meyer, once the key strategist in South Africa's white apartheid regime. The message was dramatic: If the bloodied foes in South Africa and Northern Ireland could achieve coexistence through power-sharing, so might the fractured factions of Iraq. The Iraqis were fascinated, McGuinness said, that archrivals such as Sinn Fein and the Democratic Unionist Party could sit at the same table. At the first Iraqi talks, competing factions would not talk to each other, he said, "but now they acknowledge each other, and it's interesting they showed up the second time." In their presentations to the roundtable gathering, the ANC leadership stressed that "the most important constituency to negotiate with is your own," he said. To all the words scribbled on the meeting's blackboard, McGuinness added only one: "leadership." The key to the Irish process, he believed, was the release of prisoners on both sides, whereas Iraq had evolved only from Saddam Hussein's dictatorship to a Shia gulag with thousands of Sunni prisoners. "It might all end in tears," he acknowledged. But several years into the Irish peace process, there were more British troops in the north than the United Kingdom deployed to Iraq, and yet an agreement had been reached. The Iraqis eventually would learn there was no alternative to dialogue and politics, and until then McGuinness would keep going back. Indeed, by the end of the Bush years, the Iraqis were negotiating a peace that would withdraw American troops and leave Iraq as a unitary state, a future that had seemed unlikely even one year before.

It seemed incredible to me that an IRA leader who had fought the British Army to a standstill would now be conducting foreign policy missions to Iraq, with the tacit acceptance of the British, and even George Bush. "The Brits and Americans wanted to help us, but I said no," McGuinness commented. "But every time I see Bush at the White House, he asks how it's going and he seems well-briefed." George Bush asking Martin McGuinness how to be helpful? Had Martin joined the Machiavellians, or had certain Machiavellians learned a better way than military occupation to cope with social movements? Gerry Adams was not sure, but he reckoned that Martin's mission might be useful in the long run, spreading Irish lessons to a world of stalemated ethnic wars. But there was more work to do in Ireland, he said. How can a social movement be kept alive when its leaders are in office? How can more elections in southern Ireland be won when peace was no longer the issue and the activist base was aging? At sixty years himself, Adams had been organizing on this road for forty-two years, and the work was by no means finished.

(No sooner had I finished these reflections than dissident republicans shot and killed two British soldiers and one policeman in Northern Ireland in a violent rebuke to Sinn Fein's politics, the peace process, and the continued partition of the island, where about four thousand British troops remained in barracks. Leaders across Northern Ireland, including McGuinness, were quick to unite against the violence, a remarkable display of nationalist-Loyalist unity. Although the renewed violence was dismissed as isolated, and the probabilities of going back to war extremely unlikely, the shooting was clear evidence that ancient hatreds were not erased by the compromise Good Friday Agreement. In addition to the three killings, there had been fifteen other attacks on troops or police in the previous seventeen months, and a 250-pound bomb had been defused outside a military barracks.)[26]

At least as serious, America's Wall Street meltdown late in 2008 led to a collapse of the "Celtic Tiger" experiment with neoliberal economics in the south of Ireland. Not only could Sinn Fein be strengthened as a force of peace, but also its supposedly obsolete rhetoric about the 1916 socialist republic, if translated into a progressive economic program, might gain the organization greater support across Ireland than ever before. And if the Machiavellians were interested only in ending the violence, their market-driven economic agenda would sow and reap a new discontent in the ghettos of Northern Ireland and beyond.

⌒ 18 ⌒

From the War on Poverty to the War on Crime

ROM 1960 THROUGH 1965, THE RACIAL ISSUE WAS FRAMED as one of civil rights, guaranteed by the Constitution, versus a backward system of segregation harbored in the Deep South. The 1963 agenda of "jobs and justice," the slogan of the March on Washington, was linking voting rights with economic opportunity as envisioned in the War on Poverty. But instead of pursuing this agenda, the cold war Democrats by 1965 were escalating the Vietnam War at the expense of addressing the domestic crisis. Antipoverty funding was slashed while large numbers of African American and Latino youth were drafted straight from urban poverty into jungle warfare.

Small-scale violence already had broken out in northern cities in 1964, but the volcano blew in Watts in August 1965, leaving forty-five people dead, more than one thousand injured, and $40 million in property damage.[1] The importance of Watts was reflected in the choice of John McCone, a former CIA director, to lead a blue-ribbon commission in its wake. The McCone panel emphasized immediate action to address underlying conditions that had set off the explosion, but little action occurred. The Los Angeles Police Department soon inaugurated its SWAT and CRASH units as a military model of ghetto control, armed with submachine guns, assault rifles with double banana-clips, semiautomatic shotguns, sniper rifles, and flash-bang devices.[2] The SWAT and CRASH models spread across the country as antipoverty budgets were reduced.

The next few years would bring race-based riots (or as some would say, police-based riots) in more than one hundred American cities, a greater wave of continual anger than had occurred during the previous riot peaks in 1919 and 1943. The Machiavellian response was two-pronged. On the one hand, SWAT teams spearheaded a campaign of suppression. On the other, moderates formed blue-ribbon commissions. The 1968 Kerner Commission, for example, concluded that most outbreaks had been triggered by an instance of police brutality against a backdrop of deeper economic disfranchisement. The commission's report made no reference to gangs or delinquency, but instead proposed immediate literacy programs and jobs for five hundred thousand hard-core unemployed people, including individuals with arrest records, followed by 2 million new jobs for the same population within three years.[3] The same authors advocated hiring young street leaders regardless of previous criminal records and stressed the need for "ghetto residents to participate in the formulation of public policy and the implementation of programs affecting them."[4] Instead, the subsequent war on crime, gangs, and drugs—including $100 million for counterintelligence operations—was launched in 1968 through the Crime Control and Safe Streets Act—and continued thereafter on a bipartisan basis.

From 1964 through 1968, I worked as a community organizer (preceding Barack Obama's Chicago phase by fifteen years) in Newark, New Jersey. By statistical measures, Newark was hell on earth.[5] When the ghetto erupted for five days and nights in July 1967, *Life* magazine called it "the predictable insurrection."[6] Twenty-four black people were gunned down by police and state troopers. One firefighter and one police officer were killed, possibly by friendly fire or unknown shooters. By the end of that year, whatever politics of hope I had maintained from the early sixties was soured. Nonviolence and community organizing had failed to correct the systemic abuses apparent in every northern city, and now the national Democrats were responsible. I believed that the wave of racial disruptions yet could "create possibilities of meaningful change" based on recommendations like those in the Kerner Report—though it would depend on whether stronger organizations arose out of the ashes.[7] "Violence can contribute to the shattering of the status quo," I wrote, "but only politics and organization can transform it."[8]

Without realizing it, I was anticipating the growth of organizations like the Black Panther Party, which first appeared in Lowndes County, Alabama, after the failure of the 1964 MFDP challenge but took root in Oakland, other northern ghettos, and prisons. If not for a militant political group like the Panthers, the vacuum would be filled by new street gangs.

Living in the late sixties near the Panthers' headquarters in Oakland, and especially through the experience of being on trial with Bobby Seale, I could tell that the organization had deep appeal among the young people, especially the dropouts, I had encountered for years in Newark. The Panthers also appealed to an older black middle class radicalized by the civil rights movement and to many in prison and the armed forces. They were more than a fringe, though less than the vanguard they aspired to be. Among whites, their appeal was deepest among campus radicals as well as artists, intellectuals, and writers. One had to admire their bravery in arming themselves for self-defense against police departments that for years had systematically intimidated the black community.

It was also true objectively that the Panthers lacked any capacity to withstand the force of the SWAT teams, prosecutors, FBI counterintelligence, mainstream political structures, and sensationalist media aligned against them. This was painfully true in the many instances of black prison rebellions inspired, if not organized, by the Panthers, from San Quentin to Attica.[9] One could admire and support these prison revolutionaries, which I did, while agonizing over the isolation that made them doomed martyrs. The Panthers' efforts at alliances with Hollywood celebrities or white radicals fell far short of the backing they needed, and their admirable social programs, free breakfasts for children, were too little to offset their controversial military posture and arsenals. In retrospect, however, even a *nonviolent* Black Panther Party or prisoners' movement would have been opposed as threats to the distribution of wealth and power, just as Dr. King's 1966 Chicago civil rights crusade went nowhere and the long history of reform efforts has shown.

With militant organizations battered by the police and counterintelligence programs, and community antipoverty programs underfunded and hampered politically, the void would increasingly be filled by street gangs and a vast underclass of young people who became fodder for the criminal justice system. As longtime gang researcher Louis Yablonsky wrote: "[There was] a hiatus in gangs, gang violence and warfare during the late 1960s through the early 1980s, partly as a consequence of various quasi-political groups like the Black Panthers and the Brown Berets. These groups and others channeled many black and Chicano youths who might have participated in gangbanging violence into relatively positive efforts for social change through political activities."[10] Another respected researcher, James Diego Vigil, concluded that "the abrupt destruction of the Panthers and the cutbacks in War on Poverty programs probably contributed to the acceleration of street gangs in the early 1970s."[11] Poet and former gangbanger Luis Rodriguez wrote from his own life experience that "in the 1960s a lull in gang activity coincided with the apogee of the civil rights struggles and the advent of groups like the Black Panthers, the Brown Berets, and the Young Lords."[12]

A new sort of organization—*the modern street gang*—filled the inner-city vacuum as Vietnam escalated, inner-city development declined, and political opportunity structures shriveled. In Watts, where young men previously formed car clubs and skirmished over access to parks and swimming pools, suddenly the Crips and Bloods were exploding everywhere.

The reasons for gang formation were well-known to sociologists and community advocates. Typically, they were young men, school dropouts, lacking economic skills, caught in a revolving system of criminal justice, abused by police and jailers, who joined gangs for street money, protection, and identity in the absence of other socializing structures. Earlier in the century, the white ethnic gangs—Jews, Irish, and Italians in particular—were defined as ruthless incorrigibles by law enforcement and the property-owning classes. But as Prohibition ended and the New Deal promoted jobs and unions for the white immigrant underclass, the issue of gang violence diminished sharply. Professional mobsters continued to operate, but their mass base was absorbed in the skilled trades and other jobs that could raise their hopes for a middle-class future for their children. The end of Prohibition eliminated the need for violence to settle jurisdictional disputes.

After the sixties, the same stereotypes were imposed on a new generation of street gangs—"superpredators" and "urban terrorists" being the most potent labels—and a new conservative politics overwhelmed the old liberalism. Instead of improvement in schools, drug treatment programs, job training, and economic opportunities, the favored "solutions" became SWAT teams and prison expansion.

The power structures feared any evolution of the street gangs into the political arena, although this was precisely the path taken by the white ethnics, including Chicago's mayor Richard J. Daley, who as a teenager had been active in the Hamburg gang in Canaryville.[13] "It was the political threat posed by black gangs in the 1960s that led Daley to declare war on them in 1969," according to Chicago historian John Hagedorn.[14] That year, the Panthers' Fred Hampton was holding talks with the Blackstone Rangers about merging with the Panthers; by year's end, Hampton was killed by the Chicago police.

Law enforcement remained suspicious even when street gang members tried to quell their own suicidal violence through cease-fires and truces. The most famous of these was the truce between Crips and Bloods in 1992, the same year that another insurrection swept Los Angeles, taking the lives of forty-five people, destroying seven hundred local businesses, and leaving $1 billion in property damage.[15] Immediately afterward, a formal effort to "Rebuild LA" was launched with the goal of $6 billion in largely private investments to create approximately seventy-four thousand new jobs in five years.[16] The unique feature of the plan was its reliance on the *privatization of inner-city development*, an approach already known as neoliberalism in its application to Latin America. The effort failed completely, folding up in two years with little civic acknowledgment. Instead of receiving thousands of new jobs, the South Central area actually lost a net fifty thousand jobs in the 1992–1999 period.[17]

Nevertheless the Crips-Bloods truce carried on for several years before wilting from internal tensions and external neglect. Under the headline "Ex-gang Members Work to Bring Peace to the Streets," the *Los Angeles Times* reported that killings in South Los Angeles declined from 466 in 1992 to 223 by 1998, while gang-related homicides dropped by 36.7 percent citywide and drive-by shootings by 27 percent.[18]

Gang homicides are not included in the national mortality data published in *Vital Statistics of the United States* or in the *Uniform Crime Reports* collected by the FBI, as if gang body counts do not count. Using law enforcement data, however, I was able to calculate that at least *eleven thousand gang members died in Los Angeles County alone in the two decades, 1980–2000.*[19] This war at home went unnoticed, although a 1995 study for the *Journal of the American Medical Association* profiled the pattern for a single year in LA:

- The median age of those killed was twenty-one (in 1995).
- One-third of those killed were not affiliated with violent gangs.
- The motivation in 62 percent of the cases was "rivalry"; only 5 percent were drug related.

- Of an amazing total of 807 killings, 390 were Latino on Latino, 170 were black on black, fewer than 50 were either black on Latino or Latino on black, and only 35 were white victims of largely nonwhite assailants.[20]

This was not a crime wave, but an unchecked intratribal war, the sort of divide-and-conquer death spree promoted by the British empire in Africa or the United States on its western frontier.

By 2000, while gang-related violence was declining from its peak in 1992, police budgets and incarceration rates were rising across the country. In the city of Los Angeles, the police obtained 30 percent of the city's budget funds. Across California, the numbers in state prison rose from twenty-eight thousand in 1983, the year I joined the legislature, to one hundred fifty thousand when I retired in 2000, three-quarters of them identified as gang members.[21]

Soon America was leading the world in building prisons and locking people up, reaching a total of *25 percent of all inmates globally.* In 2008, the United States held 2.3 million people behind bars, whereas China had 1.6 million. From imprisoning approximately 100 persons per 100,000 in the late sixties, the United States had 690 per 100,000 people in jail by 1998 and 751 in 2008—compared to rates of only 125 and 45, respectively, in England and Japan.[22] These prisoners, nearly all of them young people, were not simply "doing their time"; they were, instead, subjected routinely to forms of punishment including isolation, lockdowns, numbing medications, inmate-on-inmate violence, sexual abuse, and sadistic guards. In California, guards were forcing young inmates to stage "Friday night fights" against each other; between 1989 and 1999 alone, California prison guards shot and killed thirty-six inmates and wounded more than two hundred.[23]

The reason for the persistent issues of gangs and unemployment could be found in the new pattern of globalization, accepted ideologically as the post–New Deal viewpoint of both parties. "Deindustrialization," "privatization," and "deregulation" became policy buzzwords; the Reagan decade resulted in cuts in the social safety net; and Bill Clinton followed by declaring that "the era of big government is over." The New York City region lost five hundred thousand manufacturing jobs and slashed social services; Atlanta became the crime capital of the South.[24] Besides locking in unemployment and a low-wage service economy, the loss of manufacturing jobs eliminated the traditional opportunity for former gang members to "mature out" of the street life into jobs in local industry.

The globalization of street gangs also began to metastasize as doctrines of neoliberalism took hold in Latin America, South Africa, and other countries where safety nets were slashed and protectionist strategies were replaced by the "free"-trade protocols of the General Agreement on Tariffs and Trade; its successor the WTO; NAFTA; and the global apparatus of what George Bush called "the new international order." If that drove the gangs into the bottom rungs of the drug economy, the solution was simply to expand the global War on Drugs, which militarized the addiction crisis while doing little to dent the flow to American and European consumers.

Politics lay behind all this, peaking in the 1988 Republican campaign charging presidential candidate Michael Dukakis with being soft on crime for furloughing Willie Horton (a release program that Bush had once supported himself). Behind the politics, however, was an ideology that sought to blame the gang crisis on the sixties.

The master work on official gang data for the period 1970–1998 was by Walter Miller, under the auspices of the Office of Juvenile Justice and Delinquency Prevention.[25] In explaining the presence of seven hundred fifty thousand gang members in America, Miller never mentioned economic or political disfranchisement. Instead, he listed drugs, broken homes, immigration, and, especially, the culture of the sixties, which fostered tolerance of "many of the *customary practices* of the inner cities."[26] This was code for "language patterns" (slang, hip-hop lyrics), "family arrangements" (fatherless homes), and the growth of street gangs that were "recognized as legitimate community groups,"[27] apparently by the earliest War on Poverty programs.

The neoconservatives were more explicit than Miller in identifying the sixties as the cause. A godfather of the neoconservatives, James Q. Wilson, claimed that there were no "root causes" of gang violence.[28] He wrote that the "moral relativism" of the sixties supplied gangbangers with a theory of social causation for crime.[29] He also fostered a theory of inevitable superpredators by predicting that the nineties would produce thirty thousand more "young muggers, killers and thieves than we now have." What was his policy advice? "*Get ready.*"

In *Body Count* (1996), Ronald Reagan's drug and education czar, William Bennett, antidrug warrior John P. Walters, and a research protégé of Wilson's, John Dilulio, elaborated the preposterous notion that "a new generation of street criminals is upon us—*the youngest, biggest and baddest generation any society has ever known.*"[30] Dilulio wrote an article entitled "The Coming of the Super-Predators" in the *Weekly Standard,* the house organ of the neoconservatives, projecting that there would be a spike of an additional two hundred seventy thousand "junior super-predators" raised in "practically perfect criminogenic environments" who would "terrorize our nation" by 2010.[31] To make matters worse, President Clinton adopted the neoconservatives' analysis, warning that "we have about six years to get ahead of this juvenile crime and drug problem that will be almost unbearable, unmanageable, and painful."[32]

Although the superpredator prediction was politically successful, the problem was that it was pure propaganda lacking any serious evidence. It was the demographic equivalent of the neoconservative claims about Saddam Hussein's weapons of mass destruction. There was no there there. The doctrine was based on the false premise that a mere demographic increase would result in a parallel crime increase, the equivalent of saying children in certain zip codes were born as criminals. An obvious alternative model might include childhood interventions such as better

Table 18.1

Year	Total	Latino	African American
1990	251	100	107
1991	220	146	70
1992	208	151	47
1993	164	91	68
1994	114	56	51
1995	148	88	42
1996	90	53	27
1997	75	46	17[1]

[1]Criminal Justice Statistics Center, California Department of Justice, 1998; from Michael Males, *Framing Youth*, Common Courage, 1999, p. 98.

schools, books, and teachers, along with jobs and greater family incomes. The superpredator thesis fit nicely with bell-curve arguments of the era, implying an actual genetic predisposition to crime.

During the period in question, in fact, there was a decline in teenage homicides in LA County (see Table 18.1). Dilulio himself later admitted regret at having published the faulty superpredator thesis, but it was too late.[33] Bennett et al. had achieved two purposes: first, to discredit the idea of rehabilitation, which they said "emasculated" the prison system; and second, to demolish any notions that poverty causes crime or that the United States was imprisoning a disproportionate number of its citizens.[34] Their loudest political champion became New York mayor Rudy Giuliani, who flatly declared that "there has never been a proven connection between the state of the economy and crime, and there is absolutely no correlation between unemployment and crime."[35]

How did this happen? Essentially, the conservative countermovement discredited the War on Poverty at birth, replacing it with wars against crime, gangs, drugs, and shadowy foreign enemies similar in character to domestic gangs. A leading neoconservative hawk, Robert Kaplan, warned of "armies of murderous teenagers ... angered by the income disparities that accompany globalization."[36] In his Darwinian view, "It means economic survival of the fittest—those groups and individuals that are disciplined, dynamic and ingenious will float to the top, while *cultures that do not compete well technologically will produce an inordinate number of warriors [driven by] the thrill of violence.*"[37] Neither Kaplan nor the neoconservatives had any nonmilitary suggestions for government intervention to head off this coming anarchy, because they ideologically discounted government as a positive force and believed the fault to lie in the "moral poverty" of the poor.

The Bush administration, dominated by Karl Rove, opportunistically seized on the gangs/crime issue for political reasons. Rove chose the theme "that we faced this generation of juvenile criminals" to elect Bush governor of Texas even though most crime rates had fallen in Texas and the incumbent governor, Ann Richards, had mounted a historic prison-building program.[38] Bush also became a devotee of Marvin Olansky, a Marxist from the sixties who became a born-again Christian in the seventies and who counseled that religious orphanages and charities should replace jobs and antipoverty programs.[39]

By 2008, a small faction of neoconservatives had succeeded not only in fabricating the grounds for a stalemated war in Iraq, despite a military budget greater than the next dozen countries combined, but also in exaggerating the crisis of drugs and gangs to fill the largest prison system in the world, with American incarceration rates five to ten times greater than those of any other advanced country.[40] Police policies of door-to-door sweeps, preventive incarceration, and mass detention began to characterize domestic and foreign policy alike, leading neoconservative ideologue Paul Wolfowitz to comment that "I think it'd be interesting if we could find some real experts on attacking gangs and send them to Iraq to work on this operation."[41]

By these measures, the sixties generation had failed shamefully. If the Kennedy brothers and Dr. Martin Luther King had lived, this ever-escalating war on youth would not have happened. But the decline of the civil rights movement, undergirded by Clinton's acquiescence in privatizing the New Deal functions of government and creating the WTO and NAFTA, combined with understandable Democratic defensiveness on the politics of crime, made the outcome inevitable.

The sixties contributed to the 2008 consensus that Americans were ready for a black president, marking a major victory over racism, but at the same time leaving behind an enormous crisis of the underclass in ghettos, barrios, juvenile halls, and prisons. The crisis of the underclass was addressed as one of crime and pathology, not of the failed legacy of the civil rights endeavors and antipoverty programs.

Enter Barack Obama. As a community organizer and Illinois state senator, he displayed a sharp understanding of racial profiling and mass incarceration. His expedient support of more police on the streets at least was accompanied by calls for police and prison reform. A remarkable fact about his presidential campaign was that the Republicans were unable to attack Obama for being "soft" on crime and gangs. The potential attacks were prepared by the same forces who had effectively questioned John Kerry's military credentials in 2004. But either because Obama adroitly finessed the issues or, more likely, because the American public's priorities had shifted away from mass incarceration and toward economic and foreign policy issues, the question of the wars on gangs and drugs was never debated between Obama and John McCain.

Obama's attorney general, Eric Holder, has confided to visitors that he and the president intend to reverse previous policies toward juvenile justice and incarceration at some point in the years ahead.[42] There is no doubt that Obama demands a stronger emphasis on treatment rather than more military escalation of the drug wars. Congress has shown signs of interest as well, particularly in the proposed youth "promise act" of Representative Bobby Scott, a Democrat from Virginia, the first legislation in a generation to fund prevention and gang intervention programs without adding more resources to prosecutors.

But Obama now faces the entrenched interests of police, prosecutors, and prison authorities, whose public support is as significant as Pentagon support for foreign policy. Some of Obama's own policy proposals, moreover, show a penchant for continuing the war against gangs and drugs, as evidenced in the highly militarized Plan Colombia and its offshoot, Plan Mérida, at the Mexican border. For example, in a Miami speech in November 2008, he pledged to continue the counterinsurgency in Colombia and added that "we'll crack down on the demand for drugs in our own communities.... We must win the fights on our own streets if we're going to secure the region."

This analysis is upside down. The much-feared Latino street gangs, Mara Salvatrucha in particular, were born and bred in the United States among Salvadoran refugees from Reagan-sponsored civil wars in Central America. Deporting tens of thousands of gang members back to Central America is extremely destabilizing for the region, setting off a permanent cycle of violence. Integrating U.S. drug warriors with the Mexican military does nothing to block the flow of economic refugees from Mexico, the flow of guns purchased in the United States for Mexican cartels, or the apparently insatiable demand of American consumers for marijuana grown south of the border.

An alternative path—legalization of marijuana, regulating, taxing, and recycling revenues obtained from a medical approach to the drugs crisis—lacks majority support, partly because so few political leaders will advocate it. An alternative policy on gangs is blocked for the same reason. Obama may understand that the present policies perpetuate a cycle of madness but believes he lacks sufficient public and institutional support for serious change. If so, a renewed social movement taking on these issues is a precondition to meaningful presidential or congressional action. Winning the fight for civil rights was a huge achievement; reversing economic deindustrialization, drug, and incarceration policies may be even more difficult.

To his credit, Obama repeatedly criticizes the failed model of market fundamentalism and promises the revival of a stronger role for government. The Wall Street meltdown of 2007–2009 might alter policy priorities, given the unsustainable budget burdens of the gang and drug wars, mass incarceration, deportations, and rising expenditures for counterinsurgency in Colombia and Mexico. Such budgetary issues already have forced reconsideration of New York's harsh Rockefeller-era drug sentencing laws.

The wars on gangs and drugs will be ended not by backdoor means, but by different socioeconomic policies with popular support. Instead of scapegoating gangs, it is better to recall the diagnosis of Jacob Riis, the chronicler of New York's slums in the late nineteenth century: "The gang is a distemper of the slums, a friend come to tell us something is amiss in our social life."[43]

Frederick Thrasher's 1927 classic on the gangs of Chicago charted an alternative approach that arose from the settlement houses and continued through the era of community organizations and antipoverty programs in the sixties. Suppression and intimidation were scorned. Government measures to support rehabilitation, training, and jobs were strongly endorsed. Central to this philosophy was the notion that young people could change for the better through their own efforts. Demography was not destiny. Adolescent lives were malleable, not fixed. Thrasher believed that "the problem of redirecting the gang turns out to be giving life meaning for the boy."[44] He added that former gang members could be role models and part of the solution: "I would spend a large part of the money expended on institutions in hiring 'Boy Men' to cover the city and spend their entire time with gangs."[45]

This is not meant to glorify inner-city dropouts or to argue that police should not arrest them when they commit serious crimes. They are traumatized children raised in war zones, needing respect, dignity, role models, rehabilitation, education, and training. When they are arrested, they should be respected, not treated as subhumans, which only keeps alight the slow-burning fuse of their rage. They have stories to tell that the public needs to hear. They can be role models, as members of the Alcoholics Anonymous community are to each other. The case for former gang members as intervention workers rests on the assumption that those who initiated the madness can contribute to ending it. But they have been defined as untouchables for thirty years, economically redundant, politically scapegoated. Their numbers represent the sixties' greatest failure and may be Obama's greatest challenge.

19

Liberation Theology

Have I, then, escaped from the opportunism of a decadent church to end up in the Machiavellianism of a political sect?

—Ignazio Silone[1]

THE SOCIAL MOVEMENTS OF THE SIXTIES were tied together by the threads of a new spirituality. Arising at the margins, the new sentiment gained considerable popular force, challenged and altered the mainstream religious institutions, and created a lasting spirituality outside the traditional religious molds.

The institutional religious hierarchy is itself Machiavellian and, at its worst, fully integrated into the larger Machiavellian order. The essential story of Christianity reveals the pattern. Jesus, his friends, and his followers represented a dissenting social movement on the edge of the Roman Empire. They were ridiculed, demonized, persecuted, and crucified alongside thieves. Like Che Guevara, Jesus became immortalized, his core teachings disseminated, his network transformed into a new church. (In this inexact analogy, think of Fidel as Peter and Cuba as the rock of Che.) After four centuries, the Roman state accepted as its new state religion the movement it had once persecuted as an illegal cult. From the catacombs, Christianity ascended the throne. The cross of the crucifixion became the cross of the Crusaders, the witch-burnings, the colonialists, and the slave trade.

But radical, dissenting Christianity intermingled with native traditions to become a syncretic platform for lasting social movements against the empire. The slaves, the abolitionists, the suffragists, and numerous other movements of the oppressed embraced the Jesus of the social movement. Progressive currents carrying on the Jesus movement—the Social Gospel tradition, black churches from Atlanta to Soweto, the Catholic workers' movements, for example—took hold as powerful, though minority, traditions within the institutional religious world. The Jewish tradition supplied countless prophets, organizers, and advocates for social justice. Buddhism and Asian spiritualities grew within the American counterculture from the time of Henry David Thoreau and the Transcendentalists to the ashrams of the sixties. The counterculture was fertile ground for spiritualities associated with an age of Aquarius, the New Age, or simply "the religion of no religion" as embraced at retreat settings such as the Esalen Institute in Big Sur.

The most powerful of these currents in the sixties were the movements associated with Latin American liberation theology, on the one hand, and the rise of Zen Buddhism in America, on the other. Their sharp differences can be traced to class differences that affected the sixties as a whole: Liberation theology asserted a "preferential option for the poor," whereas Zen tended to flower in the middle-class counterculture. Occasionally, their agendas overlapped. In the end, both followed the pattern of all social movements from the margins through the mainstream, to triumphal experiences but also co-optation into the Machiavellian realm of the "powers and principalities."

As the sixties dawned in America, Protestant Christianity was the de facto state religion, under pressure at the top from Catholics such as presidential candidate John F. Kennedy and at the bottom from the radical Christianity of prophetic ministers such as Martin Luther King. At the highest levels, however, from Billy Graham's evangelizing to Cardinal Francis Spellman's anticommunist crusades, American seemed to be a stable, conservative, often right-wing, Christian country on nearly every level. But as the atheist Karl Marx once wrote, "All that is solid melts in the air."[2]

The searchers of the sixties who became community organizers, like myself, were enthralled by Ignazio Silone's short novel, *Bread and Wine*. Written in 1936, the time of Italian fascism, the main character is Pietro Spina, a political revolutionary who wants to mobilize the rural peasantry. To do so under the repression, he must adopt another identity, that of a Catholic priest, Paolo Spada. This former student leader comes to believe that the peasantry will never be moved by political speeches, but perhaps only by human deeds. He wants to be a kind of saint, but without the ceremonial trappings and belief in a distant god; he wants to live the simple life of simple deeds as Jesus did. Only such an example might awaken others from their lethargy, he says. *Bread and wine* are not only the body and blood of the crucified Jesus, but also the substances that sustain the life of the poor.

Albert Camus, another icon of our generation, had asked a similar question: whether it is "possible to become a saint without believing in God." In *The Plague*, the character Tarrou sums up the challenge of dealing with a systemic plague (which for us was racism or nuclear war): It was to organize sanitation teams without regard for expediency or reputation. "All I maintain is that on this earth there are pestilences and there are victims, and it's up to us, so far as possible, not to join forces with the pestilences."[3]

These were seeds of the liberation theology movement, which swept through the church in Latin America and echoed across the civil rights, farmworkers', and other social movements during the sixties. In his excellent sociological text on liberation theology, Christian Smith writes that liberation theology originated within the theological schools of the mainstream church, a top-down transformation of doctrine. Trained young theologians brought the nascent doctrine with them to Latin America, where the Second Vatican Council had opened the doors to reformers; Protestant missionaries, too, were working on a theology of revolution.[4] In Latin America, the precursors included Brazilian bishops such as Dom Helder Camera as early as the fifties and the consciousness-raising pedagogy (*conscientization*) of Paulo Freire's literacy training movement.

"The story of liberation theology," as theologian Harvey Cox observes, "is about how in less than twenty years a quiet conversation among a few out-of-the-way Latin Americans became a worldwide theological movement."[5] Those conversations took place against a backdrop of grassroots continental and global social movements that were sparked without anyone's prediction.

It is notable that the organizers of this movement were community organizers by commitment. Peru's Gustavo Gutiérrez, whose theology was central to the movement, worked as an organizer in a Lima slum.[6] Brazil's Clodovis Boff spent six months each year in the Amazon jungle.[7] Liberation theology priests and nuns were central to the revolutionary process in El Salvador and Nicaragua. Bishop Samuel Ruiz was transformed by his contact with Mayan people in the mountains of Chiapas. These religious men and women risked their lives (one thousand would be variously excommunicated, silenced, kidnapped, arrested, tortured, and killed during three decades).[8]

The organizing approach of liberation theology was different from the vanguard approach common to both religious and political proselytizers, where the gospel or party line is transmitted to the masses from an ideological center, whether Rome or Moscow. The priests instead formed "base communities" (base ecclesiastical communities, or BECs) among the poor, where the Bible was translated, often for the first time, from Latin into Spanish or indigenous languages, allowing people to read the Jesus story for themselves, not hear it told through an intermediary from a pulpit.

The biblical stories of the poor, of exploitive tax collectors and usurers, of Roman soldiers, of crucifixion and martyrs, of the struggle with Satan, could be easily applied to their lives. A people's church arose in tension with the church of privilege.

No one knows the true number of these grassroots communities, but the estimate was one hundred fifty to two hundred thousand by the seventies.[9] In Chiapas alone, a Congress of the Indigenous in 1974 was organized in four Mayan languages. In translation, the indigenous told Ruiz and his colleagues they wanted the world turned upside down. The new "old testament" would have to include the old stories, symbols, and rites of the indigenous. The clergy would have to include the indigenous, too. From these roots grew a vast movement that would be the springboard for the Zapatistas two decades later, when Ruiz became the chosen mediator between the state and the rebels of Chiapas.

The sixties experience, from debates over the Alliance for Progress, to the Cuban revolution, to innumerable student, labor, and guerrilla risings, had turned most of the continent on a progressive, even radical, quest. By 1968, liberation theology and practice were becoming accepted at the highest levels of a Latin American church that previously had anchored the status quo. From August 24 to September 6, 1968 (the same time period as the Chicago antiwar demonstrations), 130 Latin American bishops formally endorsed liberation theology at their meeting in Medellín, Colombia. Their Medellín statement began with a denunciation of the poverty and "inhuman wretchedness" afflicting Latin America and declared that "a deafening cry pours from the throats of millions of men, asking their pastors for a liberation that reaches them from nowhere else."[10]

The bishops' analysis was a radical one. They denounced the structures of power as sinful and declared the need for "a global organization, where all of the peoples, but more especially the lower classes, have, by means of territorial and functional structures, an active and receptive, creative and decisive participation in the construction of a new society."[11]

The Latin American church, once integral to the Machiavellian order, was being transformed. Its legitimizing power, its resources, and its structures were extended to preaching and programs giving "preference to the poorest and most needy sectors." This remained official policy for another decade, through the bishops' 1979 gathering in Puebla, Mexico. During that time, revolutionary priests played key roles in the 1979 overthrow of the old regime in Nicaragua and the 1970s insurgency in El Salvador. Both revolutions had occurred soon after the Puebla conference; in both situations the revolutionary movements were strongest in the base communities.[12] The movement spread into North America, Europe, Africa, and Asia.

The countermovement was swift, brutal, and global. Military coups swept through Chile, Brazil, Bolivia, Uruguay, Peru, Ecuador, and Argentina, all backed by the United States and conservative church elements. The liberation theology movement was demonized as procommunist, even though its spirituality set it apart from its Marxist rival. It threatened the landowners, the privileged, the military, and elements of the middle class in country after country. It threatened the Vatican, with its intricate web of political and financial arrangements with the powerful. It threatened the Reagan administration so greatly that the White House allied itself with the Vatican in an effort to shut down the movement in the eighties. Pope John Paul II expressed outrage that priests were participating in the Sandinista movement. At the same time, a State Department task force issued the "Santa Fe Declaration" defining liberation theology as a threat to American interests.[13]

These combined efforts to stall liberation theology were successful; under John Paul II the conservative hierarchy prevailed. Conspiratorial right-wing groups such as Opus Dei rose to power within the church. Radical reformers were silenced (Leonardo Boff in Brazil), killed (Archbishop Oscar Romero, priests, and nuns in San Salvador), or replaced (Bishop Ruiz in Chiapas). Church resources were withdrawn from insurgent movements, and solidarity programs were dismantled. Jesus the agitator was forgotten, even denied. The pope in 1979 criticized those who would "depict Jesus as a political activist, as a fighter against Roman domination and the authorities, and even as someone involved in class struggle. This conception of Jesus as a political figure, a revolutionary, as the subversive from Nazareth, does not tally with the Church's catechesis."[14]

A central figure in this countermovement was Joseph Ratzinger, now Pope Benedict XIV. When the student movement swept through Germany in 1969, Ratzinger was teaching theology at the university at Tubingen. He was shocked and offended at the defiant politics and manners of the students, twenty-five of whom took over the faculty lounge and interrupted classes by shouting slogans. Most important, according to one student leader looking back, was the conflict over Ratzinger shutting down abortion counseling centers operated by Catholic women on campus.[15] Ratzinger rapidly rose as a doctrinal enforcer against the winds of the sixties threatening the church. The former Holy Office of the Inquisition was renamed the Congregation for the Doctrine of the Faith, with Ratzinger named its prefect in 1979. "With the doctrine of liberation theology," he declared in 1984, "we are clearly facing a fundamental danger for the faith of our church." His was the voice of a militant countermovement whose powers ranged from silencing theologians to promoting Opus Dei members to key posts at pinnacles of power. As recently as 1994, Ratzinger authored an edict that American Catholic voters were guilty of "formal cooperation in evil" if they voted for presidential candidate John Kerry, a Catholic whose views on abortion were liberal. The increased Catholic vote in Ohio, Iowa, and New Mexico was decisive in Kerry's defeat.[16]

But in spite of the doctrinal suppression and purges, liberation theology had become deeply rooted in the popular base of the church. Weakened, deprived of resources and blessings from the pulpit, the movement continued to spread. Theologians and grassroots Catholic communities were vital in the rise of the Workers Party in Brazil and similar networks across the continent. In a milder form, liberation theology can be said to be "in power" in many countries today. In 2008, the voters of Paraguay, after sixty years of one-party military rule, elected as their president a sandal-wearing former priest and bishop, Fernando Lugo, who had immersed in liberation theology in the seventies and had worked for years on land reform in rural areas.[17] In 2009, where liberation theology and its martyrs had left a lasting legacy, the voters chose as president the candidate of the Farabundo Martí National Liberation Front, Mauricio Funes, who immediately pledged to carry out "preferential actions" for the poor, the exact language of the original liberation theology movement, and visited the gravesite of Archbishop Romero on the morning of his inauguration, June 1, 2009.

⁓ 20 ⁓

Reverend Jeremiah Wright and Black Liberation Theology

FOR CENTURIES BEFORE LIBERATION THEOLOGY, of course, the African American community had birthed a spirituality of its own, blending African tradition with the Exodus story and the Old Testament prophets to form a religious community of succor, service, and resistance. Martin Luther King was the most important of a new generation of ministers who challenged the racism and conformity of mainstream churches in the early sixties, drawing on Mahatma Gandhi's *satyagraha* (truth power) philosophy for his civil disobedience campaigns as well.

But the general rise of liberation theology stirred a new doctrine, *black liberation theology*, that would reverberate unexpectedly in the Obama presidential campaign, centering on the preaching of Barack Obama's pastor of twenty years, Reverend Jeremiah Wright. Black theologian James Cone "informed and inspired Wright,"[1] who passed through the sixties first in the Marines, then "dabbling with liquor, Islam, and black nationalism," in the account of Barack Obama.[2] Wright became minister at Trinity United Church of Christ in 1972, when its Chicago congregation numbered fewer than one hundred. Nearly forty years later, Wright still cited James Cone's influence in an interview with PBS's Bill Moyers.[3] Cone was the seminal theorist, writer, and advocate in a movement that began publicly when fifty-one black pastors signed a full-page ad in the July 31, 1966, *New York Times*.[4] Primarily inspired by the black power movement, the theologians inserted themselves in a sharp dialogue with those from Latin America, who were mainly white and of European heritage. In conferences and correspondence, Cone argued forcefully that liberation theology must rest on *race*, not simply on *class*, in contrast to the Latin American view that the oppressor was imperialism.[5] Cone and others argued that Christianity was not Christianity unless it identified with the struggle and religious tradition of black people. Concretely, he wrote, "the violence in the cities, which appears to contradict Christian love, is nothing but the black man's attempt to say Yes to his being defined by God in a world that would make his being into nonbeing."[6]

Relying on a historical analysis of the Bible, which identified the enslaved as Hebrews, black liberation theology insisted that black people had become the new slaves who would be saved from the fiery furnace, the lion's den, and Egyptian bondage: "Didn't my lord deliver Daniel, deliver Daniel, deliver Daniel, didn't my lord deliver Daniel, and why not every man."[7]

Liberation theology emphasized a spiritual, or nonmaterial, dimension to the theory of social movements. In explaining the sudden, unexpected, and unpredicted origin of a social movement, liberation theology relied on the instrument of the spirit, or grace, as agency:

> Amazing grace! How sweet the sound …
> 'Tis grace hath brought me safe thus far
> And grace will lead me home.

> The Spirit of the Lord is upon me,
> Because he has anointed me to preach good news to the poor.[8]

> The wind blows where it wills and you hear the sound of
> it, but you do not know whence it comes nor whither it
> goes; so it is with everyone who is born of the Spirit.[9]

From this viewpoint, social movements cannot be launched by material or organizational forces alone; they arise from feelings inherent in being a child of God, or creation. The Machiavellian enemy, or Antichrist, is embedded in "the powers and principalities" in a struggle that is transcendent, not simply limited in time. The movement arises at the extreme margins:

> He was despised and rejected by men;
> A man of sorrows and acquainted with grief;
> And one from whom men hid their faces
> He was despised, and we esteemed him not.[10]

In liberation theology, the social movement is sustained on its journey by a community of meaning expressed in the spirituals and the blues culture (Cone writes, "I am the blues and my life is a spiritual; without them, I cannot be"[11]) as well as symbolic stories, especially the struggle against the Pharaoh, the vision of the promised land, along with the inevitability of divisions, temptations, and corruptions along the way. Victories are won on the battlefields of the world, but never permanently. The struggles begin again and again, in memory and life thereafter. In the time of James Cone, and his follower Jeremiah Wright, there was a swelling desire to wrest and reclaim Jesus from a Christendom that was racially segregated and stratified—as it continued to be even through 2008, when certain fiery snippets of Reverend Wright's sermons were edited and released and sounded like Old Testament ravings against the soothing decade of Ronald Reagan.

"I think it was Hannity and Holmes, I think they searched it out, I'd be interested to know," James Cone told me when I interviewed him in early 2009. Jeremiah Wright, he said, was from the second generation of black liberation theology. "He read my stuff as most of them did and was influenced by it." Cone was struggling as a theologian to "bring together Martin and Malcolm," the struggle of black people at the heart of the Christian faith along with a cultural acceptance of the African heritage. From the theology came a practice, typified by Jeremiah Wright's creation of Trinity Church as a way to embrace the central themes, cultural and political, of black liberation theology. "He's a good man," Cone said of Wright, "but like all of us there are negative sides. I think he got caught up in the media, and now they have no more use for him."

Barack Obama, according to Cone, "represents a new group," seeking an identity in the churches created from black liberation theology. Searching for himself, Obama "discovered that Trinity was the place that best expressed his cultural and political vision." As a theologian, Cone does not think that Obama is particularly familiar with liberation theology, because "you don't get it in a university." Cone does not know Obama, but adds that "he seems to be connected with a spiritual force that makes him calm and conveys that he's the person for this moment."

As Obama tells the story, he first visited Wright's church as a community organizer in search of church endorsements for his project. At Trinity, the young religious skeptic, who was "having too many quarrels with God to accept a salvation too easily won," gradually found an essential spirit force that went beyond faith in either his isolated self or the methods of community organizing. The heart attack of Mayor Harold Washington, whose historic campaign heavily influenced Obama's decision to move to Chicago, now left Obama feeling vulnerable in a universe of chance. He saw the local Machiavellians making their plans for restoration in the wake of Washington's death: "But power was patient and knew what it wanted; power could outwait slogans and prayers and candlelight vigils.... [Power] was large, fleshy men in double-breasted suits with the same look of hunger in their eyes—men who knew the score."[12]

Obama, turning thirty, was facing deep personal questions about whether leaving Chicago for law school was a form of escapism that simply repeated his own thwarted father's return to Kenya some twenty-eight years before. Was it true that "power was unyielding and principles unstable"? Was a black man's life about escape, "emotional if not physical, away from ourselves, away from what we knew, flight into the outer reaches of the white man's empire—or closer to its bosom"?

It was the theory and practice of black liberation theology at Reverend Wright's church that solidified young Obama's identity and fortified his position in the

African American community. Without Trinity, it was impossible for him to become "black enough." Two messages by Reverend Wright had a profound effect. One was a Trinity policy of "Disavowal of the Pursuit of Middleclassness," sounding very typical of the sixties spirit. The other, "The Audacity of Hope," was the sermon that Obama credits with his moment of conversion. The minister summoned up an image from a painting of a woman sitting on a mountain with a harp. At closer look, the harp has only one string and the woman looks down upon a valley of famine, deprivation, and war. The woman, Wright preached, has the audacity to make music on the one string she has left. In this transformative moment, writes Obama, the stories of David and Goliath, Moses and Pharaoh, the Christians in the lion's den, Ezekiel's field of dry bones, "became our story, *my* story.... This black church on this bright day, seemed once more a vessel carrying the story of a people into future generations and into a larger world. Our trials and triumphs became at once unique and universal, black and more than black."[13]

I describe this transformation in detail not only because the author is now our president only twenty years later, but also because it illustrates a vital dimension of social movements: the conversion experience the organizer often passes through. Barack Obama in this story channels the spirit of Silone's character, who evolves from a radical skeptic into a priest who finds himself becoming an exemplary kind of saint, one with a quality that liberation theology defines as a "charism," or gift, not a personal achievement. Every great social movement, while rising from the bottom up, is also known for its charism, in exceptionally creative leaders who seem to appear, like the movement itself, out of nowhere. Silenced theologian Leonardo Boff, writing at approximately the time of Obama's conversion, said that "power can be a *charism* as long as it serves everyone and is an instrument for building justice in the community."[14]

In his 2008 speech on race, Obama made an important distinction between the sixties and the present in attempting to explain his relationship with Reverend Wright. On the one hand, Obama's distancing himself from his reverend was a classic Machiavellian tactic, doing what he considered necessary to win the presidency. His preacher made exactly the same point when asked by Bill Moyers about Obama's speech: "I don't talk to him about politics.... He's a politician, I'm a pastor. He says what he has to say as a politician. I say what I have to say as a pastor."[15]

On the other hand, Obama offered a deeper analysis, of the *sixties as a context* producing a completely different state of mind between the two generations. He spoke of "the reality in which Reverend Wright and other African-Americans of his generation grew up" as shaping their radical, revolutionary, or at least incendiary views.[16] The extremisms of the sixties generation, the future president and self-described child of the sixties was saying, were caused by the extreme context faced by black Americans and others. When people feel they are chronically marginalized, when no one is listening, the rage and "irrationality" of their rhetoric inevitably rise in compensation, taking the militant form of social movements.

"The profound mistake of Reverend Wright's sermons," Obama went on, "is not that he spoke about racism in our society. It's that he spoke as if our society was static, as if no progress has been made, as if this society is still irrevocably bound to a tragic past."[17] In the proper context of the long sixties, Barack Obama represented an evolving new consensus, which could include and transcend Reverend Wright at the same time.

Enough Americans had evolved through the long sixties to make Obama's story seem credible, in accord with their own understanding of the generation gaps during and after the sixties. Something profound was taking place as the countermovement to demonize the reverend—and with him the entire sixties once again—unraveled and sputtered to failure.

How far was Obama willing to go in distancing himself from Reverend Wright? Was he, as president, going to abandon the minister who was so influential in his life? Was that a metaphor for abandoning the sixties? Obama drew considerable outrage by asking the conservative Reverend Rick Warren, an opponent of gay marriage, to offer the inaugural invocation. Reverend Warren appeared to be the pastoral and polar opposite of Reverend Wright. But Obama performed a balancing act that might characterize his presidency, choosing Reverend Joseph Lowery to offer the benediction. Lowery, an original associate of Martin Luther King, a leader of the Southern Christian Leadership Conference, a supporter of gay marriage, offered more than balance. He tipped the scales, calling on the Lord: "Deliver us from the exploitation of the poor and least of these, and from favoritism to the rich, the elite of these," and "We ask you to help us work for that day when black will not be asked to get in back, when brown can stick around, when yellow will be mellow, when the red man can get ahead, man, and when white will embrace what is right."

Reverend Jeremiah Wright was not at the inauguration. But black liberation theology was there at the benediction, the last Word.

21

The Spirituality of the Counterculture

THAT THE 1960S MARKED A LONG CULTURAL REVOLUTION is suggested by the flowering of literature and music that still resonate. At the heart of this new culture was a spirituality, a "religion of no religion," an explosion of alternative spiritualities.[1] Liberation theology took perhaps the most institutional form. Others rose more or less autonomously. Black liberation theology, according to James Cone, appeared before the works of Latin American theology were translated into English. Women's spirituality, ecospirituality, and the revival of Eastern mysticisms rapidly followed. In the face of homophobia, gay, lesbian, and transgender people fought for their spiritual identity. Spanning all these separate outbreaks was a resurgence of the Old Religion, diffusing all of creation with magic and holiness, even if often described and disparaged as paganism. There was a profound misunderstanding among critics about the pronouncement "God is dead." The 1960s were an era in rebellion against the top-down authority of institutional religion, but they were not an atheistic decade. Instead, the old gods came alive.

The spiritual revolts were about restoring an excluded Other, or the subaltern, to proper recognition, in ways parallel to the political revolts of the time. Black theology, women's theology, and ecotheology were incorporated into schools of theology. But at the deepest level, they were not simply seeking chairs in the divinity schools, but a new sense of the sacred, in the oneness of humankind with the earth and universe and with a humbling mystery felt to be flowing through all things, a mystery made more mysterious, not less, by the endless discoveries of science. The photos of Earth from the moon were a dazzling revelation of discoveries that seemed beyond the limited imaginations of artists. Like all of the sixties, this spirituality was a quest.

If one looks back fifty years, the story of the counterculture follows one of two narrative lines. The historic one charts a path from the bohemians through the beats to the drug culture, rock-and-roll, the musicians, crash pads and communes, trips, crack-ups, and co-optations. That story, included in earlier chapters and the Timeline in the last part of this book, is presented as a tale of excess and privilege, a frenzy that gave rise to a right-wing countermovement, leaving little but debris, regret, and musical nostalgia.

Overlooked in this narrative is the substantial degree to which the counterculture successfully became the culture itself. The 1960s counterculture largely won the so-called culture wars of the past two decades. Sixties music and artists still retain a dominant influence. The general public is supportive of the decriminalization of marijuana and a treatment-centered approach to drugs. Things organic, food and medicines, hold vast sway. Above all, environmental programs such as renewable energy and conservation derive from approaches that were considered part of the extreme fringe thirty years ago.[2] California governor Jerry Brown, for example, in the seventies overcame a "Governor Moonbeam" image, identified with Zen Buddhism, and appointed Gary Snyder, Peter Coyote, and Jane Fonda to the California Arts Council. The deepening American embrace of diversity was a precondition for the 2008 election of an African American president who had sampled pot and cocaine in his youth and had been raised by a white countercultural mother. Among many symbols of the Barack Obama triumph was the appearance at his inauguration of ninety-three-year-old Pete Seeger, accompanied by Bruce Springsteen, singing, "This Land Is Your Land," complete with the once-censored lyrics dismissing private property.[3]

As happens, of course, the rough and radical edges of the counterculture were left behind in its absorption into the mainstream, raising fair questions about the triumph of co-optation and commercial values. Green politics still remains white politics. Disturbing questions still linger, cloud, and shadow counterculture history as well, especially the role of the CIA in drug development and experimentation. It was clearly in the interest of the intelligence agencies to push sixties radicalism in the direction of an alienated nonpolitical fringe (and to redefine the crisis as drug related rather than political). But the counterculture played its own role in that demise, many assuming that it was enough to change their heads instead, that the revolution was exclusively internal. As Tim Leary once said: "The cause of social conflict is usually neurological. The cure is biochemical."[4]

I never ingested acid myself. There was a time when I could not make this statement without, on the one hand, disbelief from conservatives and, on the other hand, scorn from Yippies. But I have to say, in retrospect, that it was difficult to work on a daily basis with people who were tripping at all hours, whether in courtrooms or in the streets. Marijuana was another matter, although I came to believe that it made no sense to be stoned when under police surveillance. Long after the sixties, I experienced ayahuasca in the Amazon jungle, which reinforced an existing bond with nature and with my son. But I never joined the underground ayahuasca cult in Los Angeles, believing it was too escapist. At the same time, I have experienced numerous moments of unexpected vision—natural highs—in everyday life or while in dramatic natural vistas like the Sierras. Therefore, I may underestimate the lasting importance of the drug experience per se in opening the doors of perception of which Aldous Huxley wrote. And I understand what he described as a "principal appetite of the soul," the need to transcend the limited boundaries of the self.[5] And I will never forget listening to him, spellbound, as he spoke to a packed audience in Ann Arbor in the late 1950s. So the legacy of the counterculture is surely a mixed one, in which self-centered, self-destructive, and largely white fantasies need to be weighed against the profound changes in cultural norms that nevertheless occurred. In keeping with the model, we can say that there was cultural *reform*, if not revolution.

There is still another narrative of the counterculture, a metanarrative perhaps, that requires a deeper look at *the underlying spiritual and moral quest* of the era. In original, uncontaminated, remarkable form, I believe, it is all there in Jack Kerouac's *The Dharma Bums* (1958).[6] Kerouac's more well-known classic, *On the Road* (1957), was published the year I graduated from a middle-American high school, and it inspired me to write short stories and to go hitchhiking north, south, east, and west. Kerouac was a deeply spiritual, highly disciplined writer who lived at the invisible margins for almost a decade before being discovered and canonized by the mainstream media. His audacity was a challenge. Kerouac literally invented a new form of writing free of the restraints of punctuation, and he insanely produced the manuscript of *On the Road* on a single massive scroll of paper that he unfurled on his publisher's floor! That he could succeed at all sent a wake-up call to thousands of young high school and college idealists like myself who were ready to settle for less in life, since less was all we knew. Kerouac's *The Dharma Bums* contained the audacity—what respectable writer, after all, would invent a title and self-description like "dharma bum" in 1958?—while also dreaming the essential story of the counterculture before it had unfolded. The book was novel and prophecy.

Kerouac endows his real-life characters with pseudonyms to tell what seems to be a true story. Kerouac is the narrator, Ray Smith, a self-taught Buddhist seeker who visits the West Coast beat scene as a visitor from the East Coast. The main character is Japhy Ryder, Gary Snyder, then a Berkeley graduate student, a mountaineer from the American Northwest, an inheritor of Wobbly, miner, and native traditions, preparing for rigorous Zen training in Japan (which lasted for most of a decade). Allen Ginsberg is present as Alvah Goldbook, joining Ray (Kerouac) and Japhy (Snyder) on a long march up the Matterhorn, the central event of the book.

Kerouac's Ray tells the story of a real event far more important than the Port Huron convention in jarring the sixties generation out of apathy. He follows a "gang of howling poets" down to San Francisco's Six Gallery for what becomes "the night of the birth of the San Francisco Poetry Renaissance,"[7] or what has been called "the spiritual underground of Cold War America."[8] Kerouac whips the crowd into a shouting frenzy by passing out glasses of red wine and shouting, "Go, go, go," while Ginsberg reads *Howl* for the first time, as "scores of people stood around in the darkened gallery straining to hear every word of the amazing poetry reading."

Ginsberg's epic is both personal and political, spiritual and howling against the military-industrial complex. The "Moloch" repeatedly denounced in "Howl" is the Machiavellian spirit, symbolized by the glowing eyes (windows) of the Francis Drake Hotel that Ginsberg, on peyote, once beheld while in San Francisco.

I talked with Gary Snyder, now age seventy-nine, in Oakland on March 3, 2009, about looking back on that night in San Francisco. "It was hard for Allen, Jack, Philip Whalen, and myself and others to get our poetry published, so we said, 'Why not just hold a poetry reading?' So Allen and I rented the Six Gallery and sent out postcards to our lists. To our surprise, an amazing number of people showed up. The wonderful thing was the feeling in the room when Ginsberg read 'Howl.' I realized this was a new game. The power of poetry reading is that it brings people together in a new way. So all of a sudden people started having poetry readings all over." Snyder compares the fifties experience to modern poetry slam contests, which he has been asked to judge. ("Those kids are really good.")

Ginsberg was a remarkably complicated person who played an influential role all through the sixties and beyond, until his death of heart failure in 1997. More than any other witness at the Chicago trial, he drove the prosecutors wild, leading U.S. Attorney Tom Foran to rant that "we are losing our children to the freaking fag revolution." (When I called Ginsberg to invite him to a reunion at the 1996

Chicago Democratic National Convention in Chicago, he declined, simply sharing his preoccupation with a failing heart.) Somewhat ironic given his Buddhist values, he was a systematic promoter and archivist of himself, his friends, and an endless Rolodex range of contacts among the high and mighty. What he promoted, however, was as radical and threatening as any message of the sixties. One outraged critic of *Howl* was Norman Podhoretz, who hurled himself into a fifty-year culture war against the counterculture while mentoring the next generation of neoconservatives. Ginsberg was radically antiestablishment in his orientation to issues, but more deeply, he was psychologically and spiritually at odds with the mores of civilization at the time. He spent eight months in a New York psychiatric institute. He was a gay man when that orientation was criminalized and taboo. He and I disagreed on certain matters, my bent being far more political and confrontational and having little use for zazen as a strategy against authority. But I was awed by the Buddhist bonzes who immolated themselves in Vietnam, and I respected the knowing depths of Ginsberg's spiritual explorations and his role in conveying Buddhist sensibility to a considerable audience. This orientation of detachment from desire was something he struggled with, leading away from involvement in trying to reform the system he despised and instead toward what he called "the secret, or hermetic tradition of art 'justifying' or 'making up for' defeat in worldly life."[9] It was a fatalism that resonated with my Catholic experience. In *The Dharma Bums,* however, the Ginsberg character becomes decidedly secondary to Snyder and Kerouac, an intellectual follower, not yet awakened to the Buddhism of the High Sierras, to which Snyder attempts to introduce Kerouac.

Shortly after the famous San Francisco poetry reading, Ray (Kerouac) makes his way to Japhy's (Snyder's) little rented house in Berkeley, then shared with Ginsberg. After many nights of talking Buddhism, drinking, and openly sharing sex with a girlfriend of Snyder's, they agree on a trek to the summit of the Matterhorn, high in the Sierras, around whose peak much of the novel unfolds. Snyder is Kerouac's hero, though their temperaments are significantly different. Kerouac is from the eastern cities, Snyder from the great Northwest mining country, where the dharma is revealed in the clouds and high reaches. Kerouac is Buddhist in a more general sense, whereas Snyder is a disciplined, already studious follower of Zen. In addition, Snyder wants to be "enlightened by actions," not just "words, words, words."[10]

Kerouac records the prophetic vision of Japhy (Snyder) as a great "rucksack revolution":

> The whole thing is a world full of rucksack wanderers, Dharma Bums refusing to subscribe to the general demand that they consume production and therefore have to work for the privilege of consuming all that crap they didn't really want anyway such as refrigerators, TV sets, cars, at least new fancy cars, certain hair oils and deodorants and general junk you finally always see a week later in the garbage anyway, all of them imprisoned in a system of work, produce, consume, work, produce, consume, I see a vision of *a great rucksack revolution* of thousands or even millions of young Americans

wandering around with rucksacks, going up to mountains to pray, making children laugh and old men glad, making young girls happy and old girls happier, all of 'em Zen Lunatics who go about writing poems that happen to appear in their heads for no reason and also by being kind and also by strange unexpected acts keep giving visions of eternal freedom to everybody and all living creatures.[11]

Here is truly an exception to the general rule that the sixties movements were unpredictable. Here was Snyder, in his early twenties, predicting exactly what would happen in a few short years, the "rucksack revolution" of back-to-the-land environmentalists who sensed a Buddha nature in the wild and who sought to dissolve the artificial boundaries between self and nature. In 2009, Snyder recalled his story somewhat more fully, believing that his environmentalism was rooted in a combination of Northwest influences, from Wobbly grandfather to mountaineering to growing up near Japanese American farmers' children who were interned and never seen again.

In any generation, he believes, a group of young people feels alienated, looks around, and wonders if they want to be part of society. They "realize they are in a different story, that the mainstream story is not their story." From there they hear about alternatives. "Everyone who gets into alternative politics or culture has a story, like for example an orthodox Jew hearing a story from a Marxist uncle, until they become little islands of sensibility who find each other."

Snyder loved City Lights Bookstore the moment he wandered in. "I found a really great collection of fugitive small poetry publications. Across the alley was a place for beer, and Miss Smith's tea house, which was a hard-core lesbian bar where you could be subject to glaring looks." He attached himself to poet Kenneth Rexroth, a mountaineer and anarchist, who he thought wrote about Pacific Coast landscapes as Robinson Jeffers did. Snyder differed from his beat friends like Ginsberg by his continuing attachments to the mountains and clouds, where he felt the Zen experience to be most palpable.

"I could see how much freedom a backpack gave you from the presumptions of what you have to be in America. And I learned to hitchhike. I could see a backpack revolution in our future. Then I got into the rucksack, which came from World War II European soldiers. We were all buying surplus rucksacks for a dollar-fifty at the army surplus. All-white Tenth Mountain Infantry tents. Then we would camp in the middle of the winter."

But Kerouac faltered. The drinking described as a personal fault in *The Dharma Bums* became a fatal alcoholism by 1969. He could not cope with the fame bestowed on him or the invitations to become a "spokesman for a generation." (Similar pressures would affect personalities as diverse as Mario Savio and Bob Dylan.) The term "beat," which he had invented as early as 1948, now became the brand for his generation.[12] In the beginning, the term meant to him "to be in a state of beatitude, like St. Francis, trying to love all life ... [despite] our mad modern world of multiplicities and millions."[13] But later Kerouac wrote, "What horror I felt … to suddenly see 'Beat' being taken up by everybody, press and TV and Hollywood Borscht circuit … and so now they have beatnik routines on TV, starting with satires about girls in black and fellows in jeans with snap-knives and sweatshirts and swastikas tattooed under their armpits."[14]

The early Kerouac wrote of "characters of a special spirituality," subterranean heroes "who'd finally turned from the 'freedom' of the West and [were] taking drugs, digging bop, having flashes of insight, 'the derangement of the senses,' talking strange, being poor and glad, prophesying a new style for American culture," [and] "talking madly about that holy new feeling out there in the streets."[15] But when the sixties hit full force, he already was turning forty and turning off. Perhaps it was the onslaught of interviewers or his Buddhist detachment, but he did not like what "the road" had become, a boulevard of wild and colorful protests. He still disliked the hypocrisy at the upper echelons of America, but he also rejected the Yippies and the antiwar movement. He revered the freedom of the road under capitalism, doubting that he would enjoy the same right "to hitchhike half-broke through 47 states of this union and see the scene with my own eyes, unmolested."[16] In one of his later writings, he said, "You can't fight city hall, it keeps changing its name."[17] He died, consumed by fame and "alcohol-related hemorrhaging" just as the Chicago conspiracy trial was under way in October 1969.

Snyder, although as remote as Kerouac in his own way, lived much of the sixties in Japan and, on return, found himself at the Gathering of the Tribes in Golden Gate Park, where he blew a conch to open the event. He remembers it as being "slightly decadent, instead of the cutting edge of something beginning, more like approaching an ending." He thought the combination of drugs, materialism, and individualism deeply problematic: "My experience with psychedelics was with peyote, mushrooms, hashish, and with LSD only slowly and occasionally. I found it a very deep and demanding study, an education in the content of the mind, the unpredictable unconscious, not so much a way to really dissolve the self. Leary, I thought, was overenthusiastic."

Snyder never lost his disciplined individualism, unusual for the counterculture. Over the years he continued to deepen his spirituality; built a home, a zendo, and a community on San Juan Ridge in the Sierra foothills; won a Pulitzer Prize for poetry; and served effectively on Jerry Brown's iconoclastic arts council handing out millions of dollars in grants. In 1969, he had identified the sixties revolt as part of "the Great Subculture," tribal in nature, going back to the Paleolithic, spanning peasant revolts, witchcraft, the illuminati, the Gnostics and alchemists, all the way to Golden Gate Park.[18] At the time, I wished he had identified more with the antiwar movement and his populist working-class roots instead of defining the counterculture in such an esoteric mode. He says he "took on the thankless task of trying to talk to politically Left people about the importance of nature. One of Marxism's primary errors was the labor theory of value. *Nature creates value.* The other error was thinking you could deal with people as underprivileged classes, not as minorities, because to the Marxists everyone was eventually part of a single class." As for radical political commitment, "I wasn't making predictions; I was doing Crazy Horse—we can't beat the white man, but by God we are going to fight him!" He had learned from the Bhagavad Gita the answer to expediency: "Act without thought for the fruits [outcomes] of your actions. Gandhi got that from the Gita, and I had come to it as a basic spiritual teaching."

I saw Snyder a decade ago at his place called Kitkitdizze, a native term for the groundcover bush everywhere in that part of the Sierras. It was snowing heavily. Gary and his wife, Carole Koda (who died in 2006), were living their nature philosophy to the greatest extent possible. Deer wandered the open space surrounding their home, a reminder of the Buddha's original deer park. Photovoltaic energy and candles supplied the power and light. Ponderosa pine looked down upon fruit trees. With one of his sons, Gary was mapping the ridge to fully understand its place in the Sierra ecosystem. He was pioneering the concept of the *bioregion*, an effort to conform the political maps to the truer contours of watersheds, wetlands, old-growth forests, deserts, and other natural habitat. The ridge where Gary lived was a link in a larger ecosystem of the Sierras, not just a physical dot on a county map. A community, or "node in the net," had formed around the ridge, composed of people trying to reinhabit nature and restore themselves in the same process.

The reason for my visit (accompanied by my wife, Barbara, and three dogs) was to walk the nearby Yuba River watershed, where developers were seeking to dam a wild stretch of the river. With Senator Byron Sher, I was trying to block their scheme. As it happened, the battle was won, but it was only one of many against the machinery of dams, deforestation, and development. Gary had a longer view, summarized years later, that the counterculture "can be said to have triggered deeper changes," like the gradual support his neighboring environmentalists were winning. "They are no longer trashed by the right wing. They are stakeholders, respected by the media, and their ideas are taken into account. They have some clout," he reckoned.

Later in the year we hiked the Yuba Gary joined Mike Davis and me at readings to support the restoration of the cemented and disparaged "river" running through Los Angeles. Millions of dollars for restoration were obtained from voter-approved bonds, and public sentiment runs strongly in favor of a renewed river, but the battle is far from over. LA has cemented some fifty miles of flowing river into a flood control channel that protects property and pollutes Santa Monica Bay, and the developers and the Army Corps of Engineers want to keep it that way.

I was going deeper where Gary had led the way, holding hearings and drafting legislation requiring that an *inherent value* of ancient forests, watersheds, and other habitats be incorporated in California law, a step toward extending spiritual regard to the natural world. Previous California law defined redwood forests and naturally flowing water for their *utilitarian* value, as if nature was only an external storehouse, in the backyard of civilization, containing raw materials for development and use. Our fish and game code, for example, was based on the utilitarian declaration that "fish and wildlife are the *property* of the people and provide a major contribution of the *economy* of the state" (emphasis added). State timber policy declared "maximum sustained production of high quality timber products" the main priority. And so on. The model was based on a bipartisan consensus on growth, with liberals and conservatives disagreeing only over the distribution of "resources" obtained from exploiting the environment. Even the self-described "stewards" of the environment, latecomers by millions of years in evolution, felt a strange entitlement to manage nature's fate as if they were overseers. I was indebted to Gary Snyder, the Zen Lunatics, the longhair dropouts, and shamans like the Dalai Lama, Thich Nhat Hanh, and Joan Halifax for having achieved a change of perception and practice.

Once I crawled over the impossible roads, little changed in thirty years, it was clear that Gary was a sociable hermit, but still something of a Zen Lunatic. He had not retreated from the world so much as reimagined it. The barriers used by the mind to separate the self from nature and the universe had dissolved long ago, as they had for millions of people since the sixties. Everything from his carpentry to his poetry was elegant, sparse, harmonious with the ridge.

The New Left had carried out Dr. King's 1963 message that all God's children are sacred. But our human community could not hew to an exclusive claim to special status, dependent as we are on air, water, soil, and the natural web that sustains us. The counterculture at its best had extended Dr. King's credo to assert that a sacred value is intrinsic in God's creation, too, one beyond the rules of humans. Nature thus has rights. Just as the state was being changed by social movements into a respecter of greater social diversity, the counterculture was dissolving artificial barriers to biological diversity and the unity of all being. Starting with the sensibility of the counterculture, the maturing work of the environmentalists was yielding fruit in the work of those such as Al Gore and, in 2009, even President Obama, who spoke fluently and persuasively to a global majority of things renewable and sustainable. These were the outgrowths of the counterculture transformed into a new political consciousness, not exactly that of the dharma bums, but reflecting an understanding that the nature of the state must be based on respect for the state of nature, not the other way around.

PART IV

The Sixties in the Obama Era

Obama
Robert Cohen, November 4, 2008

A thin man comes along
Out of nowhere
A black man comes along
Out of everywhere
Against all odds
Comes along
Materialized young and whole
Out of our very selves.

He is saying what's on the tip of our tied tongues
Finishing our tortured sentences
With possibilities
Of hope in a hopeless time.

This one
Understands
What we want
Some of what we want
Enough of a fraction of what we want
And need
To send us
Singing joyous alive tonight
Dancing in the streets with history
Embracing neighbors and strangers
All round the wounded world.

Impossible man
Made of dignity and calm.

Put your incredulous trust in him
Against your better reason
Extract it like a diamond from the dark column
Of your spine
Awed at yourself
You're *doing* this
Polish and deposit it
Thankful
In the hands of this man.

Fiercely protect and challenge him.

Give him pieces of yourself
Friends
All of us common from Africa
Give him your gold-flecked little strengths
Give him air from your deep chest
Your stubborn beating heart
Turn your fists into working hands now.

❧ 22 ❧

A Call to Progressives for Obama
with Barbara Ehrenreich and Bill Fletcher Jr.
(March 10, 2008)

ALL AMERICAN PROGRESSIVES SHOULD UNITE for Barack Obama. We descend from the proud tradition of independent social movements that have made America a more just and democratic country. We believe that the movement today supporting Barack Obama continues this great tradition of grassroots participation drawing millions of people out of apathy and into participation in the decisions that affect all our lives. We believe that Barack Obama's very biography reflects the positive potential of the globalization process that also contains such grave threats to our democracy when shaped only by the narrow interests of private corporations in an unregulated global marketplace. We should instead be globalizing the values of equality, a living wage, and environmental sustainability in the new world order, not hoping our deepest concerns will be protected by trickle-down economics or charitable billionaires. By its very existence, the Obama campaign will stimulate a vision of globalization from below.

As progressives we believe this sudden and unexpected new movement is just what America needs. The future has arrived. The alternative would mean a return to the dismal status quo party politics that have failed so far to deliver peace, health care, full employment, and effective answers to crises like global warming.

During past progressive peaks in our political history—the late thirties, the early sixties—social movements have provided the relentless pressure and innovative ideas that allowed centrist leaders to embrace visionary solutions. We find ourselves in just such a situation today.

That Barack Obama openly defines himself as a centrist invites the formation of this progressive force within his coalition. Anything less could allow his eventual drift toward the Right as the general election approaches. It was the industrial strikes and radical organizers in the 1930s who pushed Franklin Roosevelt to support the New Deal. It was the civil rights and student movements that brought about voting rights legislation under Lyndon Johnson and propelled Eugene McCarthy's and Bobby Kennedy's antiwar campaigns. It was the original Earth Day that led Richard Nixon to sign environmental laws. And it will be the Obama movement that makes it necessary and possible to end the war in Iraq, renew our economy with a populist emphasis, and confront the challenge of global warming.

☙ 23 ❧

Dreaming Obama in North Carolina: A Story of Race and Inheritance

*D*R. JOHN HOPE FRANKLIN WAS NINETY-FOUR YEARS OLD and still a formidable progressive historian, having lived through two world wars, five decades of segregation, the sixties civil rights movement, and Barack Obama's presidential campaign when I sought to see him during the North Carolina presidential primary. (He passed away on March 26, 2009.) Because there was no comparable or greater authority alive, I was eager to ask him to evaluate this long history. I ventured to North Carolina for meetings and dinner with Dr. Franklin in Raleigh-Durham, where he kept office hours at Duke's John Hope Franklin Center. It was April 16, and Barack Obama was rolling through North Carolina that week, the state where the student sit-in movement had begun three years before Obama's birth. I was especially wondering where Dr. Franklin placed Obama in African American history.

Dr. Franklin was dark-skinned, tall, and angular, with the strong handshake of a man deeply grounded. He was very present, but his presence also invoked the presence of an ancestor, the kind Barack Obama searches for in *Dreams from My Father* (1995). Dr. Franklin was living history himself as well as the author of such classics as *From Slavery to Freedom: The History of African Americans.* This was a man who had volunteered to fight in World War II but was rejected for military service on grounds of race, a man who became a Ph.D. while having to personally integrate segregated libraries, a defender of W. E. B. Du Bois and Junius Scales during McCarthyism, a key social researcher behind *Brown v. Board of Education,* the first black chairman of a major history department (Brooklyn College, 1956), a man who lived the bitter decades even before the Reverend Jeremiah Wright came along.

His wife, Aurelia, died in 1999 after fifty-nine years of marriage. Dr. Franklin was walking with a cane when we met, but he was extremely alert, curious, and possessed of a mirthful smile. During our dinner, admirers kept approaching our table to wish him well, introduce their families, and share stories.

Dr. Franklin had received a call from Barack Obama the day before, he said, but the two had not connected yet. "The person who took the call in my office is a Hillary supporter," he softly chuckled.

The Clintons showered many honors on Dr. Franklin, including a Presidential Medal of Freedom in 1995, the year that young Barack Obama published his *Dreams.* Dr. Franklin spent many hours in the White House during the Clinton years and still in 2008 remained a ranking academic charged with molding the history presented in the new African Art Smithsonian Museum on the Mall. Dr. Franklin told me he would announce his support of Barack Obama despite several personal entreaties from both Clintons to at least remain neutral.

"Don't know Obama, never met him," he said. What was it about Obama that drew Dr. Franklin away from the Clintons? I asked. "I thought he was exceptionally bright and qualified, with more potential for growth in office" than what he had seen the Clintons achieve in the years he had watched them.

Then, after starring at the table intently, Dr. Franklin said that Obama's recent speech on racism was "the Sermon on the Mount, the Declaration of Independence, and the Emancipation Proclamation, all combined into one."[1] Sensing that this was quite a pronouncement, he then bit off a small portion of meat, saying that he was on a low-salt diet these days. It was as if his evaluation of Obama's historic place were an everyday statement of fact. We went on to discuss the size of black bass in North Carolina creeks.

I missed a front-row opportunity to see Obama's Raleigh rally that week, though I arrived in time to listen from the parking lot. I was late because I was exploring another chapter of the pre-Obama era. Back in 1961, I had been in North Carolina at a gathering of early SDS and SNCC activists discussing a strategy of realigning the Democratic Party through direct action and voter registration. The catalyst for that brainstorming was the 1960 Greensboro, North Carolina, sit-in, which spread the wildfire of nonviolent direct action across the South. Here I was in 2008 missing Obama in the present because I was visiting the Greensboro lunch counter site where the activism of my generation had first begun.

Flashbacks briefly affected me as I arrived in Greensboro with two friends from Duke, both graduate students and community organizers. Greensboro is an old textile and insurance town with a couple of historically black colleges, Bennett and North Carolina A&T, where the four original sit-in leaders had been enrolled. A railroad track bisects the town of two hundred fifty thousand, which is just under 30 percent black. The look of many buildings and streets has changed little. When we briefly became lost, an old caution about whom to ask for directions came over me. When I glimpsed white pedestrians walking along the street where the sit-ins had occurred, a former sense of high alert briefly returned, too. I felt something like a ghost.

The old Woolworth's was still there, on the corner of a street now renamed February 1st, its shell being reconstructed, slowly, as an international civil rights museum. The lunch counter, swivel chairs, and serving area have not changed since 1960. I sat down where David Richmond, Ezell Blair (now Jibreel Khazan), Franklin McCain, and Joseph McNeil—and others—had been arrested for politely asking for cups of coffee so long ago; then I shared coffee and conversation with local people trying to complete the work of memory. They called themselves the Beloved Community Center of Greensboro (www.belovedcommunitycenter.org).

One of them, Louis Brandon, had been a participant in those first sit-ins while a junior studying biology at A&T. Reverend Nelson Johnson and Joyce Johnson directed the development efforts. Henry Fry, a Greensboro native first elected to the state legislature in 1968, later the state's appointed chief justice, and now back teaching at A&T, seemed to be a living example of progress. But all said their struggle had been a hard one. Fifteen years ago, the Woolworth property was slated to become a parking garage. Two black leaders were able to purchase the structure. Then a 1999 $3 million bond referendum to fund restoration failed by a close margin along racial lines (85 percent of the town's blacks voted yes, while 75 percent of the white majority were opposed). Another referendum was attempted and failed again. Someone placed a headless skunk on the entrance.

The prospects improved, starting in 2001. The story of 1960 began to incorporate a handful of white students who joined the sit-in from a private women's college, Bennett. (Two of them, exchange students from Mt. Holyoke, were among those arrested.) The state legislature, now reflecting African American constituencies, eventually provided $2.5 million, with downtown developers and large corporations such as tobacco firms pledging several million more.

As a 2004 *New York Times* story on such civil rights museums noted, "The lure of tourism money has helped overcome the shame." The tourism potential of such sites "has shown that *the history of the 50s and 60s is a valuable commodity.*"[2] Meanwhile, project costs had risen from an initial $7 million to $18 million, largely due to renovation of the 1929 building.

With the history of civil rights being commodified, had things really changed as much as Barack Obama was suggesting? Surely there had been deep shifts since the time of John Hope Franklin. How did they feel about the Woolworth's lunch counter being both legacy and tourism magnet?

The responses were ambiguous. Memories remain bitter over Klan and Nazi killings of five activists during a textile workers' march in 1979.[3] Louis Brandon quickly asserted that "the town has not changed, and if you want any change, you have to protest." Fry, the former legislator and judge, had learned over time that "there's more than one way to skin a cat; you need the radicals, some conservatives, and people in the middle to get it done," though he agreed that "everything here is a struggle" because "the people making laws are careful to give so many advantages to the people at the top."

The power of the textile and insurance interests remains "tenacious," said Reverend Johnson, who had been a principal organizer of the 1979 march. But, he noted, "what is changing is the community encroachment on power." For a time in the seventies, he said, Greensboro became "the center of the southern black power movement," with a thriving culture of radicals, nationalists, black Marxists, and publications such as the *African World* (what I describe as the militant wing of the social movement). Gradually, he said, community empowerment had grown through turbulent strikes by cafeteria workers, renters, and textile workers. In the absence of a strong labor movement, he noted, the community itself was the union, linked by meetings at the church every Monday (two of the original four sit-in students were "anchored," he thought, by attending the same church). Now "pieces of all these movements are on a cusp of change."

The debate about what memory should be preserved was at times heated. "The power dynamic is unchanged, but the disguise constantly changes in order to prevent change. This gets told," the reverend said, pointing to the Woolworth's site where we sat, "so that the rest of the history of strike and struggle doesn't get told." History, he said, ought to be "a servant, an agent, of transformation," not a servant of the tourism industry. "That's exactly what Dr. King would not want." Indeed, the common image of North Carolina as a liberal southern state masked a long nightmare of racist and antilabor violence. Greensboro itself was the home of Junius Scales, an antiracist, prolabor activist who had joined and later left the Communist Party in the thirties and forties. In 1954, Scales was tried in Greensboro for simply belonging to the party. He was found guilty and, when the Supreme Court reversed his conviction, was tried and convicted again in 1958. Scales, a World War II veteran, went to prison in 1961, abandoned by his former party comrades. John F. Kennedy commuted Scales's sentence in 1962, though not pardoning him, in response to a petition from liberal leaders, including John Hope Franklin.

Did Obama represent the "cusp of change" for these deeply rooted and savvy community leaders in Greensboro? During his presidential campaign, Obama had not visited the Woolworth's site when I was there, as he did the historic Selma, Alabama, bridge. But the senator held a town meeting at the Greensboro coliseum in March 2008, filling twenty-one hundred seats and spilling outdoors. "The more he talked," said Fry, grinning, "the better I felt. It was like Shirley Chisholm running for president back in those days; she lifted my spirits. And when I got elected to office in 1968, there was a radical black running for governor who lost, but he got a lot of new voters out. *Everything builds on everything else.*"

That notion of history, of everything building on everything else, echoed the personal testimony of another little-remembered North Carolina civil rights heroine, Pauli Murray, who organized a comprehensive sit-in strategy in the 1940s and later forced the desegregation of the university at Chapel Hill. Looking back on her life from the late 1970s, Murray recalled that "in not a single one of these little campaigns was I victorious. In each case, I personally failed, but I have lived to see the thesis upon which I was operating vindicated. *I've lived to see my lost causes found.*"[4]

A postscript, November 2008: On the Friday before Obama's election, I called Jessica Levy on her cell in Brunswick County, North Carolina. I had been in e-mail contact with her partner, Jason, a few days earlier, who had encouraged the call. Jessica was working full-time in the reddest zones of North Carolina, and all plans were on hold. Jessica had dropped out of her Ph.D. program at Chapel Hill to join the Obama training program and become a full-time organizer working 9 a.m. to midnight in towns where the Klan is still a live presence. I was very moved by this echo of history going back to 1960, when young, white, often Jewish students dropped out of universities to knock on doors in the back country, beginning the slow process of change that ultimately enabled Barack Obama's candidacy. "So you chose Brunswick County to get a feel for what it was like back in the day, did you?" I asked her. Jessica laughed, then replied, "Oh God, without your generation, I wouldn't be here right now."

Jessica volunteered for Brunswick County, was told she had to raise her own money, and promptly did so, $3,000 for a campaign office and supplies. Local people, on both sides, were shocked that the Obama campaign even showed up in such a right-wing stronghold. The very existence of Obama posters was a disruption of the traditional status quo in Brunswick. But in less than two months, Jessica employed her community organizing training to build a network of hundreds of active volunteers, who then reached out to thousands of voters. She refused to talk to any reporters, concentrating on the ground war like no one had seen in the county before.

She invited me down for the last week, gaily saying, "I'll put you on doors!" Jason would be consumed with legal voter protection teams to prevent last-minute intimidation. We would have a great time, and I could see and record history being made all over again. I said no, with regret, sadly thinking of myself as a burden on the energy of the young. But I called.

As the election approached, voter registration had reached all-time highs, and now Jessica was focused on the early vote. "We're trying to run up the Obama numbers as far as we can, whether or not we can win here." Thousands of volunteers were making the same effort in red states, pushing Obama toward a national voter majority. On that Friday, Jessica already had exceeded the expectations of the Obama campaign, getting more than 30 percent of the new Obama voters to cast their ballots before Tuesday. "We're trying for over 50 percent by Monday," she said, with proud excitement in her voice.

On election day, Obama won North Carolina by a 0.4 percent fraction, 49.9 to 49.5 percent. An invisible tide, from Jessica and Jason in their twenties to John Hope Franklin in his nineties, had made a difference. Virginia and Florida went for Obama, too, and not simply due to northern migrants. The Old Confederacy, the very heart of the American countermovement, was straining under the pressures of a unified black community and a new generation of young voters and organizers. Forty years late, a realignment was perhaps under way.

24

Bobby and Barack

*A*S SOMEONE WHO HAS EXPERIENCED BOTH ERAS, I think the current movement for Barack Obama has achieved a living remembrance of Bobby Kennedy's campaign in this week when RFK's murder is painfully remembered. On June 4, 1968, I watched from a New York townhouse the second murder of a Kennedy in five years. Martin Luther King already was gone. Vietnam and our cities were burning. I was in the midst of chaotic planning for antiwar demonstrations at the Democratic National Convention coming up in August.

I drifted off with friends to St. Patrick's Cathedral, where Kennedy staffers let us through the doors late at night. After sitting a while in silence, I found myself a member of a makeshift honor guard standing next to his simple coffin. I was wearing a green Cuban hat and weeping. The last political hope of the sixties vision—a movement-driven progressive government—was finished, whether by chance or by plot, I would never know. The violence I had resisted under white racism in the South was seeping across the nation and into my veins. Like many who took their rage even further, I was hardening, and I never dared again to recover the idealism of my youth.

"Dad, don't you recognize anything of yourself in this movement?" asked an angry e-mail from my son Troy, nearly forty years later. He was working 24/7 with his (now) wife, Simone, for Barack Obama, spreading the boundless energy of the young and an artist's flair for silkscreens. "How could I share your giddy utopianism," I wanted to respond, "after the murders of the sixties icons—John Kennedy, Robert Kennedy, Martin Luther King, Malcolm X, Medgar Evers—all of whom I had known as a young man?" As if those killings were not enough, we suffered the Nixon and Reagan eras of counterrevolution aimed at everything our generation had achieved. Then came the war and sanctions and war again for control of the Persian Gulf. During the coming decades, I was limited every day by the sordid realities, as well as the occasional modest achievements, of electoral politics.

I did not see Obama coming. When I heard of the young Illinois state senator with a background in community organizing who wanted to be president, I was interested. When I read *Dreams from My Father*, I was taken aback by its depth. This young man apparently gave his first public speech, against South African apartheid, at an Occidental College rally organized by Students for Economic Democracy, the student branch of the Campaign for Economic Democracy, which I chaired in 1979–1982. The buds of my curiosity quickened. Soon I was receiving e-mails from David Peck, an organizer of the Occidental rally, who now was coordinating "Americans in Spain for Barack Obama."

One of Bobby Kennedy's qualities, or perhaps it was a quality of the times, was an easy and growing familiarity with the New Left. He evolved between 1961 and 1963 from viewing the freedom riders as a dangerous nuisance to seeing them as a prophetic minority. By 1967, he even wanted to copy SDS community organizing projects—a forerunner of Barack Obama's path—as a template for a national war on poverty.

He had a talent for engaging outsiders while trying to remain presidential. When Staughton Lynd and I met with him in late 1967, we sparred with RFK over his still-forming position on the madness of Vietnam. He mocked the

Vietnamese communist position on free elections, for example, but realized there was no answer to the evidence that Ho Chi Minh would have won 80 percent of the national vote in 1956—in elections that France and the United States had prevented. He wanted to be the antiwar candidate, but hoped for peace through negotiations, not a unilateral withdrawal. Yet his thoughts seemed free-floating, driven by curiosity.

I sensed there was no fixed version of Robert Kennedy. He was evolving, improvising, feeling his way, from former counsel to Senator Joseph McCarthy, to his brother's attorney general, to a dissenter from the Democratic establishment.... It was unclear where he was headed, perhaps even to himself, but it was my sense that he was on some deep level, astonishingly, ultimately, on our side.

For this intuition I was sharply criticized from all directions. FBI memos suggested that I was a Kennedy "agent" in the movement, though our positions were quite different. Many in the revolutionized (and fragmenting) SDS held the same suspicions. The Yippies considered calling off the Chicago protests for fear that Bobby Kennedy would co-opt them with his lengthening hair. The McCarthy volunteers were livid that he was stealing their dream.

But he was the only one who could bridge the chasm between the traditional Democrats and the disaffected young, the striking farmworkers, the rebellious blacks, even the utterly disfranchised Native Americans. I learned from that experience that, like it or not, a charismatic and willing candidate, not just a linear program, is needed to mold a diverse majority.

So it was with great interest that I attended a Robert Kennedy human rights event in Washington in 2007, featuring Barack Obama as the honored speaker. I sat in a small audience that included Senator Ted Kennedy; Bobby's widow, Ethel; and several of her grown sons and daughters. Obama's written remarks were heartfelt, thoughtful, read through rather quickly. What struck me was how enthralled the Kennedys were, especially Ethel. He definitely seemed to be the one they had been waiting for.[1]

There are vast differences between Bobby Kennedy and Barack Obama, owing to circumstance, though both have followed hero's journeys of the classic sort. Kennedy was shaped by his brother's murder and the climate of his times, which drove all but the most robotic toward alienation from their government. Barack is a product of globalization, immigration, even slavery, but nonetheless a privileged inheritor of the movements for which Bobby Kennedy stood. Both have believed, with Camus, that greatness lies in touching and uniting both ends of the arc of experience. Both were cautious in formulating policy positions that seemed to placate everyone while leaving little solid ground revealing their specific beliefs. It was hard to believe at times that this was their way, not just calculated opportunism.

My hopes for Robert Kennedy might have been dashed by his subsequent policies if he had lived to be president, but I do not think so. The best evidence is the progressive course consistently pursued by those closest to him, Ethel and Ted Kennedy, and his children, to this day. It is hard to imagine him abandoning all those poor people, fervent antiwar activists, and early environmentalists who swarmed his rallies—and who, like the farmworkers, carried him to victory on the ground in California.

The most impressive parallel between Bobby and Barack is the reappearance of a unified African American community along with an inspired new generation of activists and voters. Win or lose, the Obama movement will shape progressive politics, and our racial climate, for a generation to come.

Those who denounce Obama—and the possibilities of all electoral politics—should ponder the effectiveness of sitting judgmentally on the sidelines while an Unexpected Future arrives through the sheer will of a new generation. They should consider whether politics and history can be reduced to a fixed determinism that is endlessly repeated, as if there were no surprises. We can have our differences with Obama's specific policies, as I certainly do, but those should be measured against the prospect that a movement might transform him even as his very rise continues to transform the rest of us.

25

Barack Obama between Movements and Machiavellians

I WAS STARTLED UPON READING THE FOLLOWING from Barack Obama in the *New York Times* in late 2007: "The Democrats have been stuck in the arguments of Vietnam, which means that either you're a Scoop Jackson Democrat or *you're a Tom Hayden Democrat and you're suspicious of any military action*. And that's just not my framework."[1] On first reading, this made no sense. Senator Henry "Scoop" Jackson, known as "the Senator from Boeing," favored spending on vast military budgets and the Vietnam War itself and had fostered the original clique of neoconservatives. Jackson had institutional power in his grasp. Against this power, why would it be extreme to be "suspicious of any military action," as I was, along with tens of millions of other Americans? Should not Barack Obama, as commander in chief, harbor "a suspicion of any military action," given the history of false promises and failures from Vietnam to Iraq? Or was this a shorthand political formula to distance Obama from the radical connotations of the sixties and define him instead as a committed centrist? Assuming this is the case, we have a key to understanding the Obama presidency.

Something like a math principle, Obama's center is a midpoint between two poles, as measured by polling data and contending political forces. Therefore, progressives will have to become a force that pulls the center toward the Left so that President Obama will follow. The parallels are familiar, from the radical labor movement pressuring FDR in the 1930s to the civil rights movement pressuring Lyndon Johnson in the 1960s. Social movements, and the force of public opinion, become critical in this equation.

But unfortunately, polling numbers are not enough to ensure results. If, for example, elected officials simply followed public opinion surveys, America would have a universal health care system modeled after Social Security. The force of private lobbies can trump, contain, or at least delay the force of public opinion for decades. Machiavellians will settle for delaying the inevitable. Poor FDR, for example, thought it would be only a few short years before national health insurance was added to Social Security; instead thirty years passed before Medicare came into existence. Now Obama, who in the past has favored a Canadian-style single-payer system, is settling for what he thinks is achievable, an expansion of health care to children and a $650 billion down payment on an expanded system that includes a "public option" as well as private plans (the insurance companies are fiercely attacking the "public option" on the ironic grounds that it will be cheaper and therefore more popular). Pushing the single-payer option, according to this formula, will help make the "public option" more centrist.

Or consider the wars in Iraq, Afghanistan, and Pakistan. Candidate Obama defined his distinctive difference with Hillary Clinton and John McCain around ending the Iraq war. Public antiwar sentiment surged between 2006 and early 2008, directly affecting congressional elections and the presidential primaries. Obama adjusted accordingly, used Clinton's 2002 vote to authorize the Iraq war against her, then took up the centrist proposals of the Baker-Hamilton Study Group in 2007, and finally embraced the notion of a withdrawal deadline in 2008, as the primaries were becoming intensely competitive. But his 2008 proposal included a gaping hole for keeping fifty thousand "residual" trainers, advisers, and counterterrorism personnel in Iraq indefinitely. Then, just before Obama was inaugurated, the outgoing Bush administration finalized a curious pact with the Iraqi government that pledged a staged withdrawal of all American troops and bases by the end of 2011 (the Iraqis called this "the withdrawal agreement"; the Bush administration labeled it a "status-of-forces agreement"). From the Machiavellian view, this pact would allow Obama to assert that he was only carrying out a withdrawal agreed to by the Bush administration and Baghdad. Surprisingly, that is what he did in March 2009 in a speech at Camp Lejeune.

This was a major victory for the peace movement, though most activists were understandably unimpressed and doubtful. But the peace movement, broadly defined, was a key constituency making Obama's close primary and general election victories possible. It was the local Chicago peace coalition that gave Obama the platform for his October 2002 speech. There were hundreds of thousands of peace activists who demonstrated, kept vigil, knocked on doors, campaigned, and voted for him. At the same time, Obama's actions were an illustration of the centrist formula in motion: Obama continually positioned himself between the peace advocates chanting, "Out now," and McCain, who never recovered from the comment that he might keep the United States in Iraq for one hundred years.

As for Afghanistan and Pakistan, Obama chose an opposite tack. Early in the primaries, he locked himself into the position that he would escalate in Afghanistan and attack militants in Pakistan if given "actionable intelligence." Few noticed that this was a violation of the sovereignty of two countries, a secretive and preemptive war. The president presumably believed that as commander in chief he was obligated to maintain an offensive against al Qaeda as long as there were plots afoot to attack America or Europe. As Daniel Ellsberg argues in his brilliant *Secrets,* the main reason for past escalations was "not to lose."[2]

President Obama surely knows the dangers of a quagmire in Afghanistan, in Pakistan, and, perhaps once again, in Iraq. He has issued an official new policy based on the secretive deliberations of a group of advisers known as the Committee of Principals. Once again, he will position himself between the antiwar base of his own Democratic Party and the Republican Party and the generals and the neoconservatives at the American Enterprise Institute. He is escalating in Afghanistan by at least twenty-one thousand additional American troops, slightly fewer than his commanders and the neocons propose, a deployment unlikely to have much impact on a battlefield much larger than Iraq. He will fund and train a huge expansion of the Afghan armed forces and police, a process the Pentagon says will take up to ten years. Military expenditures will continue to outpace any funds for development. Obama, however, is sensible enough to insist on an exit strategy, though undefined, a position that by itself draws fire from the neocons demanding a military "victory." In 2009, he lobbied against even that modest rhetoric when it was proposed by Congressman Jim McGovern of Massachusetts, because an initiative coming from Congress might make the new executive seem "weak."

The American war in Afghanistan has driven al Qaeda into Pakistan, where American policy since 2001 has involved spending $11 billion on a military dictatorship (Pervez Musharraf's), and Obama plans to invest $1.5 billion for the next five years. Obama is killing hundreds of civilians with airpower, including Predator strikes in Pakistan's tribal areas, where $450 million is budgeted to raise a tribal "freedom force" to battle the Taliban and al Qaeda. If Obama somehow manages to capture or kill Osama bin Laden or Mullah Omar, he will enjoy a significant surge in popularity, though the dynamics that produce anti-Western terrorism may not diminish. If, as is more likely, the attacks on Pakistan continue inconclusively, the insurgents will take their fight deeper into Pakistan's populated centers and Pakistani opinion will grow even more anti-American.

In Iran, Obama's prudent proposals for diplomacy may create constructive openings, but sooner or later he is likely to be coping with Israeli pressures for a strike against Tehran's nuclear facilities, with unpredictable volatility in the region as the consequence. Meanwhile, Iran's geopolitical influence has risen because of the American interventions, and Obama will have to depend on Iran to help stabilize both Iraq and Afghanistan before the crises are over. Contrary to thinking of Iran as a power to topple with military force, in 2009 a powerful social movement arose in Iran that might reform the mullah-based regime in time to come—but not under Western direction. As Juan Cole, an analyst at the University of Michigan, predicted to me in 2008, "Bush and the Republicans are leaving more than one poison pill behind for Obama."

At the root of Obama's inheritance is a new model of the "global war on terror," described at the Pentagon as "the long war," replacing the cold war as the framework of American strategic thinking. In his 2007 comment, Obama declared that the former arguments of the sixties—between "Scoop" Jackson the hawk and Tom Hayden with his "suspicion of any military action"—were not his framework. But to fearlessly unleash Predators and drones on tribal areas is no "framework" at all. Neither is inflicting war or occupation on two of the world's poorest countries. A younger Obama would not have approved.

Though downplaying the terminology, Obama is sliding into the antiterrorist framework in the absence of any other. This framework commits American forces to a "long war," in the words of General John Abizaid, along the vast "arc of crisis" that defines the Muslim world and oil resources. Like the cold war, there is no consensus on American goals beyond military containment and access to oil. Like the cold war, the North Atlantic Treaty Organization will expand to south Asia and the Russian borders. Like the cold war, alliances with friendly police states are guaranteed. Like the cold war, the United States will establish permanent military bases near oil reserves and any countries such as China considered "potential competitors." Like the cold war, military expenditures will continue to undermine the capacity for domestic social change. Like the cold war, an atmosphere of paranoia and fear will seep into the public climate. Like the cold war, the threat of terrorism and brinksmanship will increase.

There happens to be an alternative, beginning with Obama's welcome willingness to begin talks and open relations with perceived rivals. More important would be a genuinely crash program in energy conservation and renewable sources of energy, which Obama says he is poised to undertake. Whereas the Bush-Cheney years were only a scramble in support of Big Oil's agenda, Obama promises a parallel energy track, including everything from green jobs to renewed global treaty negotiations. His environmental appointments are among his best, reflecting the deep influence of Al Gore and a generation of global warming activists. Their efforts might energize the environmental constituency for several years, but an ultimate impasse will grow as the oil industry fights off the challenge of alternative energy as a competitor. Already, Exxon-Mobil and other energy corporations are dismissing the urgency of investments in solar, wind, or renewables, and Congress can be expected to renew its political support for coal, perhaps even nuclear power.

Obama's problem is his desire to equally pursue the wars on terror (and drug wars in Colombia and Mexico) and the war for energy independence, but this is no more possible than Lyndon Johnson's vain pursuit of guns and butter during Vietnam. If Obama de-escalates the use of military force while radically escalating an energy alternative, however, he will be improvising a crucial new paradigm that breaks with the lingering ones of the cold war and the war on terror. He will be opening space for a new "good neighbor policy" toward Latin America, for example, a continent that cannot fit or be reduced to either of the current paradigm choices. Unfortunately, a lack of previous experience with Central and Latin America leaves Obama dependent on failed paradigms—the war in Colombia, the embargo against Cuba, the war of words against Venezuela, the insistence on privatization strategies—at a time when Latin American democracies are blooming and nearly half of the U.S. population soon will be, in the phrase of Juan Gonzales, "the fruit of empire." The new unity of Latin American opinion, coupled with the legacy of solidarity movements from the Reagan era, may enable him to make better choices.

None of these concerns carries the threatening weight of the American economic crisis, however, a direct result of market philosophies indifferent to the growing scale of inequality (the greatest of any advanced country) and worshipful of the deregulated private financial and corporate sectors. Ironically, it was public outrage at Wall Street, beginning in August 2008, that created the final momentum for Obama's victory over McCain. Having relied primarily on organized labor, environmentalists, and peace and civil rights champions for his close electoral margin, Obama then stunned many of his partisans by appointing as economic advisers many of those responsible for the Wall Street calamity, a close-knit group of Ivy Leaguers resembling the ill-fated "best and brightest" team that had led the United States into the Vietnam quagmire. (The comparison is not a rhetorical one. In fact, Edward Liddy, the stumbling CEO of the American Insurance Group, has said that he will not be able to *retain the best and brightest* without massive bonuses for those in his financial products division.[3])

Obama's top economic adviser, Larry Summers, a former treasury secretary and Harvard president, was responsible for legislation in the Clinton era ensuring that the gigantic derivatives market remained beyond government regulation.[4] Summers himself has been part of an exclusive hedge fund, D. E. Shaw. Given such a circle of advisers, it is no accident that Obama's fiscal solutions lean heavily on profitable rewards for the Wall Street elite while taxpayers fund the most massive subsidies in financial history. He needs populism to make his program possible, but turns to anyone but populist advisers when governing.

Fortunately, Obama is following a Keynesian spending path on the federal budget, with nearly $1 trillion to increase jobs and purchasing power and innovative initiatives toward a green economy and expanded health care and greater federal investments in education. In comparison to the banking bailouts and foreign wars, which are projected to reach several trillion dollars in cost, his domestic budget priorities are the best since Roosevelt or Johnson, even if they are produced more by necessity than by choice. But they are not feasible given the budgets for the "long war" and might produce an effective countermovement based on right-wing economic populism.

It is dangerous to make predictions at such an early date, especially when one hopes Obama will succeed, but there is one conclusion that seems certain to loom over the future: Obama's priorities are unsustainable and unprovable. Pentagon planners are projecting ten years or longer for the fighting in Afghanistan/Pakistan, while hedging on withdrawals from Iraq. Administration officials are moving more slowly on global warming than their Kyoto counterparts want them to. Wall Street is complaining about new regulations and restrictions on executive pay. No one expects the deep recession to end soon. *Obama is caught between the movements that helped him come to power and the Machiavellian elites that all presidents need to placate.*

Once I asked President Jimmy Carter if he felt that the unelected multinational corporations had more power than the elected president of our country. His reply was clear, swift, and chilling: "I learned that my first year in office." If Barack Obama did not already know this, he is learning it now.

The decline of populism began long before Obama's presidency. I remember sitting through Senate hearings in the 1990s that bailed out conservative Orange County in a derivatives scandal. I remember the California legislature being misled into utility deregulation. My oddest memory is receiving a phone call from Michael Milkin when I was trying in the 1990s to legislate modest controls over junk bonds. I had never met Milkin, but he complained loudly that I was going conservative. Junk bonds, derivatives, the deregulation of financial markets, he said, were a revolutionary completion of the original project of Students for a Democratic Society! I am sure he was sincere in his raving. But citing the Port Huron Statement to justify the overthrow of regulations meant the Sixties were being used against the Sixties.

Obama is trying to navigate between the Machiavellians he has either inherited or appointed—the generals, military contractors, national security elites, Wall Street bankers, and hedge fund speculators—and a public opinion of high hopes and growing anger, which has not yet been channeled into powerful social movements. As the Wall Street crisis deepened, I wrote in *The Nation* that "rage is good," a turn on Gordon Gekko's declaration in the nineties movie *Wall Street* that "greed is good." Aroused and conscious public opinion is the primary force that Obama and Congress need if there is any chance to reregulate Wall Street and override the plutocrats and generals who seem to regard democratic elections as an interference in their game plans for the world.

To permanently shift the American balance of power in a progressive direction, the Obama administration needs to encourage both structural shifts and cultural ones, not policy changes alone:

- First, reforms that will create a more progressive balance of forces in the marketplace and political system, such as a growing labor movement as a counterweight to corporate power in the marketplace through passage of some form of the Employees Free Choice Act and political reforms that expand the electorate among Democratic-leaning and independent voters, such as automatic registration and weekend voting.

- Second, relentless pressure against the right wing by necessary blame-placing initiatives, such as public investigations of the Bush administration policies that promoted torture of detainees, resulted in fabricated claims of "weapons of mass destruction," and invaded constitutional rights through domestic spying on social movements; and public investigations into the roots of the Wall Street scandal modeled after the hearings following the Crash of '29 led by Senate investigator Ferdinand Pecora.
- Third, the reregulation of Wall Street and of corporate America, including global policies that currently foster sweatshops and offshore banking havens. Unlike previous regulatory mechanisms that were expert-dominated and bureaucratic, these should be more populist, including citizen participation in policymaking and oversight.
- Fourth, tacit support for Al Gore's insistence that a massive social movement, including civil disobedience in the Martin Luther King tradition, will be needed to address the global warming and environmental crisis.
- Fifth, he needs to recognize and legitimize the peace movement that helped elect him president, not depend on the new "best and brightest" while marginalizing millions of progressive activists.
- Sixth, a conscious rejuvenation of the community organizing culture of the early sixties that was taken up by Barack Obama and his generation, ensuring that the Obama generation will be the cradle of social activism for the next two decades.

Throughout my fifty years of activism, both inside and outside the system, one hard lesson has become clear to me from experience: *Domestic progress has been continually derailed by dubious wars.* When civil rights activists fought for voting rights in Mississippi, often alone, the government dispatched five hundred thousand troops in the name of "freedom" to Vietnam. When Jimmy Carter tried to focus on energy conservation, the United States wound up in Central America and Iran. When I entered state and local politics, the United States was still intervening in Central American wars; when I joined the state senate, we sent hundreds of thousands of troops to protect Kuwait. Unlike any other country in the world, we always seem called to a new manifest destiny of saving civilization from the latest rogue threats. Our prosperity depends on it, it usually is added. Is this true? Certainly, there are plenty of monsters to slay abroad, as John Quincy Adams eloquently noted, but there also are times to set our house in order. Empire and democracy are increasingly irreconcilable. Now it is becoming clear as well that Marxism was wrong, that empire and prosperity are at odds. So, too, empire is toxic for the natural environment. And yet some expect the white man's burden to be carried by our first African American president.

What he needs, then, and what we need, is a New Left.

PART V

A Sixties Timeline

The 1960s

1960

January 16, 1960: One thousand students occupy Tokyo airport to protest Prime Minister Nobusuke Kishi's trip to sign a security treaty with the United States.

January 19, 1960: Forty students are arrested in New Delhi at Lucknow University while protesting the closure of the university, which was handed over to the state police.

January 24, 1960: A state of siege is declared after insurrection against French rule breaks out in Algeria.

February 1, 1960: North Carolina A&T students Ezell Blair Jr., Joseph McNeil, David Richmond, and Franklin McCain stage a sit-in at a whites-only lunch counter at Woolworth's in Greensboro, North Carolina; a series of sit-ins ensues over the next two months, spreading to fifty-four cities in nine states.

February 15–21, 1960: Aviator Jerrie M. Cobb is the first woman to qualify to become an astronaut. Twelve other women later pass the test and together with Jerrie Cobb become known as the "Mercury 13."

February 27, 1960: Seventy-seven black and five white protesters are arrested for disorderly conduct for demonstrating against segregated stores in Nashville, Tennessee.

March 9, 1960: Students of the Atlanta University Center, made up of Atlanta University, Clark College, Morehouse College, Morris Brown College, Spelman College, and the Interdenominational Theological Center, draft "An Appeal for Human Rights," which is published in the Atlanta *Constitution* and other national newspapers.

March 15, 1960: Three hundred fifty African Americans are arrested for participating in sit-ins in Orangeburg, South Carolina.

March 15, 1960: Julian Bond and more than 200 Atlanta University Center students of the Committee on Appeal for Human Rights hold their first sit-in in Atlanta. Sit-ins also begin in Corpus Christi, Texas; St. Augustine, Florida; and Statesville, North Carolina.

March 16, 1960: San Antonio, Texas, becomes the first major southern city to integrate its lunch counters.

March 17, 1960: President Dwight Eisenhower approves a secret CIA plan titled "A Program of Covert Action against the Castro Regime," which will train Cuban exiles to invade Cuba and overthrow the Fidel Castro government.

March 21, 1960: Black South Africans demonstrating in Sharpeville (near Johannesburg) against mandatory passes clash with police, who employ armored cars and automatic weapons; 69 demonstrators are killed, including 8 women and 10 children, and 180 are injured.

March 29, 1960: Blacks in Capetown and Vereeniging, South Africa, initiate a general strike.

March 30, 1960: A state of emergency is declared in 122 magisterial districts in South Africa, which will not be lifted for another five months.

March 31, 1960: Sit-ins begin in Birmingham, Alabama.

April 1960: Ernesto "Che" Guevara publishes *Guerrilla Warfare*, his handbook on guerrilla strategy and tactics.

April 13, 1960: Eighteen distinguished nationalists in South Vietnam petition President Ngo Dinh Diem to reform his repressive, nepotistic, and Catholic-controlled regime. Diem instead closes several opposition newspapers and arrests journalists and intellectuals.

April 15, 1960: The Student Non-Violent Coordinating Committee is formed by black students on the campus of Shaw University in Raleigh, North Carolina, as a means of coordinating sit-ins, freedom rides, marches, and voter registration.

April 17, 1960: Sit-ins begin in Biloxi, Mississippi.

April 19, 1960: Massive riots occur in Seoul, South Korea. One hundred twenty-seven people are reported killed, and more than 1,000 are wounded as the police fire into the crowd of protesters, who are protesting the election policies of the Syngman Rhee administration.

April 19, 1960: The home of black Nashville lawyer Z. Alexander Looby is destroyed with dynamite. Twenty-five hundred people march silently to City Hall, where student leader Diane Nash confronts Nashville's mayor, Ben West, and asks if he believes segregation is wrong. West answers yes. Shortly after, six lunch counters are desegregated downtown.

April 23, 1960: Sit-ins continue to proliferate, now in Starkville, Mississippi.

April 24, 1960: Sit-ins begin in Charleston, South Carolina.

April 24, 1960: Rioting erupts after a group of African Americans move onto a beach in Biloxi, Mississippi, reserved for whites only. Armed whites gather and shots are fired, causing the injuries of eight blacks and two whites. City leaders blame the NAACP for inciting the violence.

April 26, 1960: Syngman Rhee resigns as president of South Korea, following the protests of April 19.

April 27, 1960: Togo gains its independence from France.

April 28, 1960: Sit-ins begin in Dallas, Texas.

April 28–May 1, 1960: The newly formed Students for a Democratic Society holds its Act Now Conference on Human Rights in the North, in Ann Arbor.

May 1, 1960: A CIA operative flying an American U-2 spy plane over Soviet airspace is shot down and captured. Eisenhower denies any knowledge of aerial reconnaissance. The Paris summit between Nikita Khrushchev and Eisenhower breaks down.

May 2, 1960: "Red-Light Bandit" Caryl Chessman is executed at San Quentin Prison, California. His coming execution had ignited debate over capital punishment, with pleas on his behalf from notables such as Eleanor Roosevelt and Ray Bradbury.

May 6, 1960: President Eisenhower signs the Civil Rights Act of 1960, which includes token steps allowing individual African Americans to appeal a "pattern and practice" resulting in denial of their voting.

May 11, 1960: The Food and Drug Administration (FDA) approves the first contraceptive pill, Enovid, created by G. D. Searle & Co., after years of lobbying of the FDA by Margaret Sanger and Katherine McCormick.

May 13, 1960: Berkeley students, organized by the student political party SLATE, protest the closed hearings of the House Un-American Activities Committee (HUAC) in San Francisco. They sing, "We Shall Not Be Moved" before being attacked by police with fire hoses and clubs on the marble stairs of San Francisco City Hall.

May 14, 1960: Fidel Castro attends the opening session of the United Nations, staying in Harlem at the Hotel Theresa, where he meets with Malcolm X. Eighteen are arrested after several hundred supporters and opponents of Castro clash in front of the Cuban consulate.

May 27, 1960: Young military generals take control of the government in Turkey in a coup. The premier ousted in the coup is Adnan Menderes, who has become increasingly unpopular for censoring journalists and the media and violating the constitution.

June 15, 1960: In a massive Tokyo demonstration against the U.S.-Japan security treaty, 270 students and 600 police are injured; 1 female student is killed.

June 20, 1960: Mali and Senegal gain independence from France.

June 26, 1960: Madagascar gains independence from France.

June 30, 1960: The Congo wins independence after being a Belgian colony since 1908 and is renamed the Democratic Republic of the Congo under Prime Minister Patrice Lumumba and President Joseph Kasavubu.

July 1, 1960: Somalia gains independence from Italy and Britain.

July 6, 1960: Esther Peterson of the AFL-CIO heads an alliance to prevent the Democratic convention from endorsing the Equal Rights Amendment in its 1960 platform.

July 14, 1960: Jane Goodall, at twenty-six, becomes the first person to study chimpanzees in their natural habitat, in Tanzania.

July 20, 1960: Demonstrations, riots, and arrests occur in British-controlled Southern and Northern Rhodesia.

July 24, 1960: Police shoot and kill eleven nationalist protesters in Bulawayo, Southern Rhodesia.

July 29, 1960: The Democratic Party, the foe of Syngman Rhee, wins in the South Korean election.

July 31, 1960: Elijah Muhammad, leader of the Nation of Islam, calls for the creation of a separate all-black state.

August 1, 1960: Benin gains independence from France.

August 3, 1960: Niger gains independence from France.

August 4, 1960: The FBI's counterintelligence program, COINTELPRO, issues a directive to disrupt Puerto Rican independence groups.

August 5, 1960: Burkina Faso gains independence from France.

August 7, 1960: Côte d'Ivoire gains independence from France.

August 9, 1960: Timothy Leary takes psilocybin mushrooms for the first time.

August 11, 1960: Chad gains independence from France.

August 13, 1960: The Central African Republic gains independence from France.

August 15, 1960: The Republic of the Congo attains independence from France.

August 17, 1960: Gabon gains independence from France.

September 1960: At the Olympic Games in Rome, African American runner Wilma Rudolph of Clarksville, Tennessee, wins three gold medals. Cassius Clay of Louisville, Kentucky, wins the light-heavyweight gold medal in boxing.

September 1960: Young Americans for Freedom is founded at the Connecticut estate of William F. Buckley Jr. in an effort to challenge SNCC, SDS, and campus radicalism and to provide a conservative voice on university campuses.

October 1, 1960: Nigeria gains independence from Britain.

October 14, 1960: John Kennedy announces his proposal of the Peace Corps on the steps of the Student Union at the University of Michigan in Ann Arbor.

October 17, 1960: Four national chain stores—Woolworth's, Kress, W. T. Grant, and McCroy-McLellan—desegregate lunch counters in about 150 stores in 112 cities in North Carolina, Virginia, West Virginia, Kentucky, Texas, Tennessee, Missouri, Maryland, Florida, and Oklahoma.

October 19, 1960: Martin Luther King Jr. is arrested during protests in Atlanta. King is held due to a previous traffic violation and sentenced to four months in a Georgia prison.

October 27, 1960: King is released after efforts by John F. Kennedy and Robert F. Kennedy. JFK calls Coretta Scott King after she reaches out to him.

October 31, 1960: Cuban foreign minister Raúl Roa, at the UN General Assembly, exposes the CIA recruitment and training of Cuban exiles, whom he refers to as "mercenaries and counterrevolutionaries."

November 8, 1960: Kennedy wins the presidential election by 0.2 percent, or 118,574 votes, becoming the first Irish Catholic president.

November 14, 1960: Four black girls attend class at two white schools in New Orleans, the first black children to attend as a result of court-ordered desegregation.

November 16, 1960: Two thousand whites demonstrate against school desegregation at New Orleans City Hall; protests are broken up with fire hoses.

Late 1960: "Operation Abolition," an antiprotester film by HUAC on the HUAC hearings in San Francisco, May 12–14, 1960, is released.

November 25, 1960: CBS broadcasts *Harvest of Shame,* a Thanksgiving news special by journalist Edward R. Murrow exposing the exploitation of millions of migrant farmworkers.

November 28, 1960: Mauritania gains independence from France.

December 5, 1960: The U.S. Supreme Court, in *Boynton v. Virginia,* rules that segregation in interstate bus terminals is unconstitutional.

December 30, 1960: North Vietnamese troops invade Laos to provide themselves with territory and a supply route in the war against South Vietnam.

1961

January 1961: President Kennedy appoints Esther Peterson head of the Women's Bureau in the Department of Labor. Women hold only 2.4 percent of all executive positions in the Kennedy administration.

January 1961: Robert Zimmerman, known later as Bob Dylan, hitchhikes to New York from Hibbing, Minnesota, to meet his idol, Woody Guthrie, then hospitalized with Huntington's disease.

January 9, 1961: Charlayne Hunter-Gault and Hamilton E. Holmes enter the University of Georgia under a barrage of jeers, rocks, and burning effigies. Hunter-Gault becomes the first black staffer at the *New Yorker* magazine and later a national correspondent for the *MacNeil/Lehrer Newshour* on the Public Broadcasting Service.

January 17, 1961: Eisenhower's Farewell Address warns of a "military-industrial complex" that is "new in the American experience."

January 17, 1961: Patrice Lumumba is assassinated by agents of Belgium with U.S. complicity.

February 6, 1961: SNCC sends Charles Sherrod, J. Charles Jones, Diane Nash, and Ruby Doris Smith to implement a "jail, no bail" strategy in Rock Hill, South Carolina, to flood the jail system, joining nine other students who were arrested on February 1, 1961.

February 15, 1961: African Americans disrupt the UN Security Council chamber in response to the coup and assassination of Lumumba in the Congo.

February 23, 1961: The National Council of Churches endorses birth control, access to abortion, and homosexuality.

March 1, 1961: President Kennedy signs Executive Order 10924 establishing the Peace Corps.

March 7, 1961: The city of Atlanta agrees to integrate lunch counters, ending a boycott.

March 8, 1961: Kennedy creates the President's Committee on Equal Employment Opportunity under Executive Order 10925.

March 23, 1961: Kennedy changes U.S. policy from military intervention to neutrality in Laos.

April 15–19, 1961: Kennedy launches a CIA-led invasion of Cuba by exiles, but refuses a recommendation to send U.S. combat troops. The covert Bay of Pigs operation, with U.S. bombing, CIA operatives, and Cuban exiles, ends in complete defeat. Of the approximately 1,400 anti-Cuban forces, 118 are killed and 1,189 are captured. Of the 15,000 Cubans fighting, 176 members of the regular army are killed and between 4,000 and 5,000 militia are killed or missing.

April 25, 1961: Sierra Leone gains independence from Britain.

May 4, 1961: The freedom rides begin, led by Nashville students and by SNCC and CORE volunteers. By the end of the summer, 1,000 freedom riders participate.

May 14, 1961: White racists force one of the freedom ride buses off the road near Anniston, Alabama, and firebomb it. Ku Klux Klan (KKK) members meet another bus in Birmingham and beat the freedom riders with pipes and clubs.

May 16, 1961: A military coup led by Major General Park Chung-hee ends the Second Republic of South Korea.

May 20, 1961: Nashville freedom riders arrive in Montgomery, Alabama, along with the U.S. Justice Department's John Seigenthaler, assistant to Attorney General Robert Kennedy. The freedom riders and Seigenthaler are attacked by a white mob.

May 20, 1961: Martin Luther King Jr. speaks at the First Baptist Church in Montgomery, Alabama, while thousands of white racists surround the church, smashing its windows. Attorney General Robert Kennedy sends in federal marshals, who disperse the crowd with tear gas.

May 24, 1961: Twenty-seven freedom riders leave Montgomery for Jackson, Mississippi. Two days later, they are arrested and sentenced to sixty days in the state penitentiary at Parchman. Among them is Stokely Carmichael.

May 30, 1961: Dominican Republic dictator Rafael Trujillo is assassinated. It is revealed in 1973 that the CIA had involvement in the killing.

July 1961: Robert Moses becomes SNCC field secretary in Mississippi and establishes the first SNCC voter registration outpost in McComb, Mississippi.

July 1961: The Frente Sandinista de Liberación Nacional (FSLN) is founded by Nicaraguan teacher Carlos Fonseca along with Tomas Borge. Inspired by the Cuban revolution, the FSLN's goal is to overthrow the dictatorship of Anastasio Somoza through armed struggle.

September 12, 1961: Philosopher Bertrand Russell is arrested and sentenced to seven days in prison for inciting civil disobedience at a nuclear-disarmament demonstration in London.

September 22, 1961: The Interstate Commerce Commission (ICC) bans segregation at interstate travel facilities, a policy that will become effective November 1, 1961.

November 1, 1961: Bella Abzug and Dagmar Wilson found Women Strike for Peace. Thousands of women march in Washington, DC, and other cities in the United States.

November 1, 1961: Openly gay drag performer Jose Sarria runs for San Francisco City supervisor on a platform opposing police raids on gay bars. He does not win, but he gets close to 7,000 votes.

November 22, 1961: Kennedy orders U.S. advisers to South Vietnam but rejects recommendations to send combat troops.

December 9, 1961: Tanzania gains independence from Britain.

December 10, 1961: Freedom riders from Atlanta are arrested while testing the ICC order at the Albany, Georgia, railroad station. The Albany civil rights movement is launched.

December 11, 1961: The U.S. Supreme Court unanimously reverses the conviction of sixteen African American demonstrators arrested at a lunch counter sit-in in Baton Rouge.

December 12, 1961: Police arrest 267 civil rights activists in Albany, Georgia.

December 14, 1961: President Kennedy establishes the President's Commission on the Status of Women under Executive Order 10980.

December 17, 1961: Martin Luther King Jr. and Reverend Ralph Abernathy are arrested in Albany, Georgia, for obstructing the sidewalk and parading without a permit.

1962

January 1, 1962: The repeal of sodomy laws in Illinois goes into effect. It is the first state to overturn them.

February 16, 1962: The Committee for a Sane Nuclear Policy of Boston and SDS organize the first antinuclear march in Washington, DC; thousands participate.

March 1962: Uprisings spring up in Guatemala. Military dictator Miguel Ydigoras Fuentes unleashes the country's U.S.-trained military and welcomes a U.S. base on his nation's soil.

March 2, 1962: The Burmese Army, led by General Ne Win, overthrows the sitting government in a bloodless coup.

April 3, 1962: The U.S. Department of Defense, under Deputy Secretary of Defense Roswell Gilpatric, orders complete racial integration of all military reserves except the National Guard.

April 11, 1962: The health risks of thalidomide are exposed. Thousands of women protest and seek abortions in Europe.

April 25, 1962: The United States resumes atmospheric nuclear testing for the first time in three years at Christmas Island in the Indian Ocean.

May 5, 1962: Tupamaro guerrillas, formed and led by Marxist lawyer and activist Raul Sendic, attack and burn the Union Confederation Building in Montevideo, Uruguay.

May 9, 1962: Venezuelan president Romulo Betancourt engages in repression against the Communist Party and suspends civil liberties. The Fuerzas Armadas de Liberación Nacional is formed as a Marxist guerrilla force in response.

June 1962: U.S. Fish and Wildlife biologist Rachel Carson publishes warnings about DDT and other pesticides in the *New Yorker*.

June 11–15, 1962: SDS holds its founding convention in Port Huron, Michigan. Tom Hayden drafts the Port Huron Statement, a manifesto adopted by SDS calling for greater participatory democracy, an end of racism, and a reversal of the cold war.

June 25, 1962: In *Engel v. Vitale*, the Supreme Court votes 6–1 that daily prayer in New York public schools is unconstitutional.

July 1, 1962: Rwanda and Burundi gain independence from Belgium.

July 3, 1962: Algiers gains independence from France.

July 7, 1962: Fifteen students are killed and 27 are wounded in a protest at Rangoon University in Burma against "oppressive" new dormitory regulations.

July 23, 1962: Jackie Robinson becomes the first African American inducted into the Baseball Hall of Fame.

July 23, 1962: The United States and thirteen other nations at Geneva approve negotiations for a neutral Laos.

September 25, 1962: Mississippi troopers prevent twenty-nine-year-old African American James Meredith, accompanied by Justice Department representatives, from registering at the University of Mississippi.

September 27, 1962: Rachel Carson publishes *Silent Spring*. The book becomes a best seller. Critics and the chemical industry attack the book as a "hysterical" outburst.

September 30, 1962: César Chávez creates the National Farm Workers Association in Fresno, California.

September 30, 1962: James Meredith, backed by 500 federal troops, is admitted to the University of Mississippi after a court ruling and an executive ruling from President Kennedy.

October 1, 1962: Twenty-three thousand federal troops end rioting in protest of James Meredith's admission to the University of Mississippi. One hundred sixty marshals are wounded, and two other persons, including French journalist Paul Guihard, are killed in the process.

October 9, 1962: Uganda gains independence from Britain.

October 22, 1962: Kennedy reveals Soviet missile sites in Cuba and imposes a quarantine on any military equipment headed for the island.

October 27, 1962: A U-2 reconnaissance plane is shot down over Cuba by Soviet missiles. Kennedy rejects a retaliatory invasion and accepts a proposal by the Soviets to withdraw their missiles in exchange for a noninvasion pledge.

November 20, 1962: Kennedy signs Executive Order 11063, banning discrimination in government-sponsored housing.

1963

1963: Mayor Robert Wagner of New York City and his administration begin a crackdown on gay people to make them "invisible" by the time of the 1964–1965 World's Fair to be held in New York City.

February 1963: Betty Friedan's *The Feminine Mystique* is published. Her book helps launch the second wave of the feminist movement and becomes a national best seller.

February 24, 1963: A. Philip Randolph announces that the Negro American Labor Council will plan a mass "pilgrimage" to DC in August to dramatize the African American employment crisis.

February 25, 1963: The U.S. Supreme Court reverses the convictions of 187 African Americans arrested in March 1961 in Columbia, South Carolina.

February 27, 1963: Madalyn Murray, an atheist, sues to ban the Lord's Prayer and Bible reading in Baltimore's public schools, bringing the case *Murray v. Curlett* to the U.S. Supreme Court.

April 3, 1963: Martin Luther King Jr. and the Southern Christian Leadership Conference (SCLC) begin their Birmingham, Alabama, campaign. King releases the "Birmingham Manifesto."

April 11, 1963: The Vatican releases Pope John XXIII's "Pacem in Terris" encyclical, opposing the nuclear arms race and liberalizing church doctrines, laying a foundation for diplomacy between adversaries and Kennedy's later American University address.

April 12, 1963: Martin Luther King Jr., Ralph Abernathy, and Fred Shuttlesworth lead marchers to the Birmingham City Hall and are arrested. King is placed in solitary confinement.

April 15, 1963: Seventy thousand march in London's Hyde Park to ban the bomb.

April 16, 1963: King writes a "Letter from Birmingham Jail," in which he explains why the movement cannot wait any longer and calls on the church to "meet the challenge of this decisive hour."

April 23, 1963: William Moore, a white postal worker and CORE member, is shot and killed during a solitary freedom walk from Alabama to Mississippi. He staged several lone marches to state capitols and delivered antiracism letters to white governors. Phil Ochs celebrated Moore on his album, *A Toast to Those Who Are Gone.*

May 2, 1963: James Bevel leads a Birmingham march of children between the ages of thirteen and eighteen. More than 900 are arrested.

May 3, 1963: Birmingham police chief Eugene "Bull" Connor orders police and firefighters to attack student protesters with fire hoses, billy clubs, and police dogs. The events are televised.

May 6, 1963: Kennedy issues National Security Memorandum 239, which orders a nuclear test ban treaty as a step toward disarmament.

May 8, 1963: Buddhists in South Vietnam riot when denied the right to display flags during the Buddha's birthday celebrations.

May 10, 1963: Birmingham city officials agree to desegregate downtown stores and release all prisoners if the SCLC ends all boycotts and demonstrations.

May 10, 1963: KKK members in Birmingham riot against the settlement. They firebomb the Gaston Motel, where most of the demonstrators, including King, are staying, as well as the home of A. D. King, Martin's brother.

May 15, 1963: Hundreds of demonstrators are arrested in Greensboro, North Carolina.

May 18, 1963: President Kennedy condemns the violence in Birmingham and sends federal troops to Alabama.

May 28, 1963: After twenty years, the Equal Pay Act is passed by Congress, amending the Fair Labor Standards Act to provide equal pay for equal work without discrimination on the basis of sex. Bills to achieve this goal were first introduced in Congress in 1943.

June 10, 1963: Kennedy signs the Equal Pay Act, making it law.

June 10, 1963: Kennedy delivers the commencement address at American University in which he calls for the end of the cold war and announces a unilateral suspension of atmospheric nuclear tests.

June 11, 1963: Vivian Malone and James Hood become the first African Americans to enroll at the University of Alabama in Tuscaloosa. Governor George Wallace stands in the university door in defiance.

June 11, 1963: Kennedy announces that he will push Congress to enact strong civil rights legislation.

June 11, 1963: Seventy-three-year-old Buddhist monk Thich Quang Duc immolates himself in Saigon to protest against President Ngo Dinh Diem and his brother, Nhu.

June 12, 1963: NAACP field secretary Medgar Evers is shot and killed in his front yard in Jackson, Mississippi, by Byron de la Beckwith.

June 16, 1963: Soviet Valentina Tereshkova becomes the first woman in space.

June 17, 1963: In *Murray v. Curlett,* the U.S. Supreme Court rules 8–1 that no state or locality can require prayer in public schools.

June 19, 1963: Kennedy submits a civil rights bill to Congress.

June 22, 1963: Kennedy reverses his earlier opposition and agrees to support the proposed August March on Washington and meet with civil rights leaders.

July 1, 1963: The United Brotherhood of Carpenters, the largest trade union in the United States, orders its locals to end racial discrimination.

July 15–25, 1963: The United States and the USSR negotiate the Treaty Banning Nuclear Weapons Tests in the Atmosphere, in Outer Space, and Under Water.

July 24, 1963: The Clean Air Act allocates $95 million for research and cleanup efforts.

July 30, 1963: Sixty thousand Buddhist activists in South Vietnam demonstrate against the Diem government.

August 18, 1963: James Meredith graduates from the University of Mississippi.

August 28, 1963: Two hundred fifty thousand people join the March on Washington for Jobs and Freedom. At the Lincoln Memorial, Martin Luther King Jr. gives his "I Have a Dream" speech.

September 1, 1963: One hundred thousand Japanese demonstrate in Yokosuka against the proposed visit of U.S. nuclear-powered submarines.

September 9, 1963: Federal district court judges prohibit Alabama governor George Wallace from blocking school integration in Tuskegee, Birmingham, and Mobile. Concurrently, President Kennedy federalizes the Alabama National Guard, preventing Governor Wallace from using the troops to block desegregation.

September 15, 1963: Klan member Robert Chamblis bombs the Sixteenth Street Baptist Church in Birmingham, Alabama, killing four girls—Denise McNair (eleven), Addie Mae Collins (fourteen), Carole Robertson (fourteen), and Cynthia Wesley (fourteen)—and injuring twenty-three others. Governor George Wallace told the *New York Times* one week before that Alabama needed a "few first-class funerals" to stop integration.

October 11, 1963: Kennedy endorses "American Women: The Report of the President's Commission on the Status of Women," which documents widespread sex discrimination. Edited by Margaret Mead and Frances Bagley Kaplan and published in 1965, 64,000 copies of the report are sold in less than a year.

October 11, 1963: Kennedy issues National Security Memorandum 263 withdrawing 1,000 military personnel from South Vietnam in 1963 and "the bulk" of U.S. personnel by the end of 1965.

October 22, 1963: To protest de facto school segregation, 225,000 public school students in Chicago stay home.

November 1–2, 1963: With U.S. foreknowledge, Saigon generals overthrow and kill South Vietnamese president Ngo Dinh Diem and his brother, Ngo Dinh Nhu.

November 10, 1963: Malcolm X delivers his speech "Message to the Grassroots" in Detroit.

November 22, 1963: President Kennedy is assassinated in Dallas, Texas, while in a motorcade with his wife, Jackie; Texas governor John Connally; and Texas First Lady Nellie Connally. Governor Connally is seriously wounded. Lee Harvey Oswald, the assumed killer, is soon arrested on circumstantial evidence after fatally shooting a Dallas police officer.

November 24, 1963: Suspected Kennedy assassin Lee Harvey Oswald is killed by nightclub owner Jack Ruby after declaring to reporters that he was "just a patsy!"

November 26, 1963: The new president, Lyndon Johnson, approves a national security memorandum green-lighting secret operations against North Vietnam.

December 1963: The Tupamaro guerrillas begin a campaign of stealing goods, money, and food from the rich and giving all of it to the poor. A food truck is stolen, and turkey and wine are handed out to the poor in Montevideo, Uruguay.

December 12, 1963: Kenya gains independence from Britain.

1964

1964: Native American activists stage "fish-ins" to preserve off-reservation fishing rights and are later active in helping the occupiers on Alcatraz. Fishing and land rights protests continue throughout the 1960s and early 1970s.

January 9, 1964: Students in Panama try to hoist their national flag over the Canal Zone, resulting in violent clashes with U.S. troops. Twenty-one Panamanian students are shot and killed in the clash, and at least three American soldiers are killed as well. Accounts of the day are still under dispute.

January 13, 1964: The U.S. Supreme Court rules that a Louisiana statute requiring the race of political candidates to be listed on electoral ballots is unconstitutional.

January 26, 1964: May Craig, a lifelong feminist member of the White House press corps, asks Representative Howard W. Smith of Virginia if he would put equal rights for women in Title VII of the Civil Rights Act. On February 8, Representative Smith proposes to add "sex" to the list of prohibited discriminations in a "southern strategy" to defeat the Civil Rights Act.

January 27, 1964: Senator Margaret Chase Smith from Maine becomes the first woman to seek the nomination of a major political party, announcing her candidacy for the 1964 GOP presidential nomination.

February 1964: The Bracero program, which utilized Mexican labor in the agricultural sector of the United States, is ended.

February 25, 1964: After winning the heavyweight championship, Cassius Clay declares his devotion to the Nation of Islam and renames himself Muhammad Ali.

March 1964: The Movimiento de la Izquierda Revolucionaria (Revolutionary Left Movement) of Peru begins a guerrilla campaign inspired by the Cuban revolution.

March 2, 1964: The National Indian Youth Council holds a fish-in on the Puyallup River in Washington to protest interference in native treaty rights. Actor Marlon Brando is arrested.

March 8, 1964: Malcolm X leaves the Nation of Islam.

March 9, 1964: Five Sioux Indians claim Alcatraz Island under the 1868 Fort Laramie Sioux Treaty enabling Indians to take possession of surplus federal land.

They occupy Alcatraz for four hours, calling for the island's transformation into a cultural center and an Indian university.

March 12, 1964: Fifteen thousand white parents march from the Brooklyn Bridge to Manhattan in protest of a plan to bus New York City students to achieve racial balance.

March 16, 1964: President Johnson proposes a $1 billion "War on Poverty," including maximum feasible participation of the poor.

March 23–24, 1964: An African American woman, Johnnie Mae Chappell, is killed and one white reporter is severely beaten during a police assault on a civil rights demonstration in Jacksonville, Florida.

March 26, 1964: Martin Luther King Jr. and Malcolm X hold a cordial meeting in Washington DC.

March 31, 1964: The elected Brazilian government of João Goulart is overthrown by a U.S.-backed military coup. Books are burned, political parties are banned, and students are arrested and harassed en masse.

April 3, 1964: Malcolm X delivers his speech "The Ballot or the Bullet" in Cleveland.

April 13–May 21, 1964: Malcolm X tours Africa and the Middle East.

April 26, 1964: The Mississippi Freedom Democratic Party is formed by SNCC members as an alternative political party in Mississippi.

May 25, 1964: The U.S. Supreme Court rules unanimously in *Griffin v. County School Board* that Prince Edward County, Virginia, must reopen those public schools that have been closed since 1959 in resistance to racial integration.

May 28, 1964: The Palestinian Liberation Organization (PLO) issues its founding charter. A parliament in exile soon follows.

June 1964: Malcolm X, after leaving the Nation of Islam in March, founds the Organization of Afro-American Unity.

June 1964: The California State Department of Education releases a report, "The Negro in American History Textbooks," that finds that the history of African Americans is often distorted in textbooks to appease southern school districts.

June 11, 1964: Police in St. Augustine, Florida, arrest civil rights demonstrators, including Martin Luther King Jr.

June 12, 1964: South African antiapartheid activist Nelson Mandela is sentenced to life imprisonment for sabotage.

June 19, 1964: The civil rights bill is passed by a U.S. Senate vote of 73–27.

June 21, 1964: The first 200 recruits of the Freedom Summer Project led by SNCC's Bob Moses leave from Ohio for Mississippi. Thousands of people, including many white college students, participate. The campaign is made up of a coalition of CORE, NAACP, and SNCC members, collectively called the Mississippi Council on Federated Organizations. Moses says the goals of Freedom Summer are to expand black voter registration in the state, to organize a legally constituted "freedom democratic party" to challenge the Mississippi Democratic Party, to establish "freedom schools" to teach black children, and to open community centers where blacks can obtain legal and medical assistance.

June 21, 1964: Activists Andrew Goodman, Michael Schwerner, and James Chaney are beaten, tortured, shot, and thrown in a swamp near Philadelphia, Mississippi.

July 1964: SDS sends more than 100 activists to become community organizers in nine northern cities.

July 1964: An armed black self-defense group, made up mostly of veterans, is formed in Jonesboro, Louisiana, and is soon called the Deacons of Defense and Justice.

July 2, 1964: President Johnson signs the Civil Rights Act of 1964. The act includes a ban on employment discrimination based on sex.

July 6, 1964: Malawi gains independence from Britain.

July 18–21, 1964: Race riots erupt in Harlem and Brooklyn after a white police officer kills a black teenager.

August 2–4, 1964: Race riots break out in black and Puerto Rican neighborhoods in Jersey City, New Jersey.

August 4, 1964: The bodies of Goodman, Schwerner, and Chaney are found in an earthen dam on a farm near Philadelphia, Mississippi.

August 4, 1964: The U.S. destroyer *Maddox* in the Gulf of Tonkin claims attacks by North Vietnamese torpedo boats during secret U.S. covert operations in the Gulf (Op Plan 34-A and Operation DeSoto). The United States announces attacks on North Vietnam later that day.

August 7, 1964: The Gulf of Tonkin Resolution authorizing the Vietnam War passes the U.S. Senate 88–2 (Senators Wayne Morse of Oregon and Ernest Gruening of Alaska voting no) and the House 416–0.

August 11, 1964: Race riots erupt in Elizabeth and Paterson, New Jersey.

August 22–27, 1964: The MFDP arrives in Atlantic City, New Jersey, seeking to be seated at the Democratic National Convention. The party rules that only two of the sixty-eight MFDP delegates will be seated and only as nonvoting, at-large members. The MFDP refuses the offer.

August 29, 1964: Philadelphia mayor James Tate quarantines 125 city blocks in response to race riots.

September 1964: Berkeley president Clark Kerr bans all political advocacy at tables on Sproul Plaza, igniting the Free Speech Movement.

September 3, 1964: President Johnson signs the Wilderness Act, creating the National Wilderness Preservation System of more than 9 million acres of national forests.

September 19, 1964: The first gay rights demonstration is held by the New York League for Sexual Freedom and the Homosexual League of New York at the Whitehall Army Induction Center in Manhattan.

September 29, 1964: UC Berkeley students set up tables on campus and refuse to leave. University officials order five protesters to disciplinary hearings on September 30. Instead, five hundred, led by Mario Savio, march to the administration building demanding that they be punished, too.

October 1, 1964: UC Berkeley graduate student Jack Weinberg is arrested for setting up a CORE information table on campus. Berkeley students surround a police car, holding Weinberg and police officers for thirty-two hours.

October 14, 1964: Martin Luther King Jr. receives the Nobel Peace Prize. At age thirty-five, he is the youngest ever to receive the award.

October 24, 1964: Zambia gains independence from Britain.

November 10, 1964: Five thousand students participate in a day of protest at UC Berkeley, held to coincide with the monthly meeting of the Regents.

November 15, 1964: Governor Luis Muñoz Marín pardons Puerto Rican rebel leader Pedro Albizu Campos. The nationalist leader and his band of rebels were notorious for shooting up the U.S. House of Representatives and plotting to assassinate President Harry S Truman.

December 2, 1964: UC Berkeley students sit in on campus to protest the suspension of the FSM activists. More than 1,000 people fill administrative building Sproul Hall, including folk artist Joan Baez, who sings, "We Shall Overcome." Governor Pat Brown calls in 600 police officers, who arrest 773 demonstrators, the largest peacetime arrest in the United States to that point in time.

December 4, 1964: Fifteen thousand people rally at UC Berkeley's Sproul Hall.

December 4, 1964: Twenty-one white men are arrested by the FBI for suspected involvement in the murder of Freedom Summer activists Andrew Goodman, Michael Schwerner, and James Chaney.

December 4, 1964: President Johnson issues an executive order banning discrimination in federal aid programs.

December 7, 1964: The U.S. Supreme Court rules in *McLaughlin v. Florida* that Florida's laws prohibiting the cohabitation of interracial couples are unconstitutional.

December 7, 1964: UC Berkeley president Clark Kerr convenes an outdoor meeting for all students, faculty, and staff, held in the campus Greek Theater. Twenty thousand people are in attendance, and FSM leader Mario Savio is apprehended by police before he can speak at the podium. Savio is released after the crowd demands that he speak. A rally of 20,000 then occurs at Sproul Hall Plaza.

December 8, 1964: The UC Berkeley Academic Senate affirms the goals of the Free Speech Movement in a vote of 824 to 115.

December 11, 1964: Che Guevara addresses the UN General Assembly.

December 12, 1964: Buddhist leaders begin a hunger strike to protest the Saigon government.

December 14, 1964: The U.S. Supreme Court upholds the power of Congress to prohibit discrimination in privately owned motels in *Atlanta Motel v. United States*.

December 14, 1964: The UC Regents affirm that university rules must be consistent with U.S. Supreme Court decisions on free speech.

1965

January 1965: The Colombian rebel group Ejército de Liberación Nacional makes its presence known by taking over the town of Simacota. One member of the group is priest Camilo Torres Restrepo, later to be killed. He then becomes an early martyr of liberation theology.

January 11, 1965: African American football players arriving in New Orleans for the American Football League All-Star Game are denied access to social clubs, some at gunpoint, and subsequently threaten to boycott the game. The game is moved to another city.

January 15, 1965: Senator George McGovern of South Dakota opposes the escalating Vietnam War.

January 27, 1965: Congress passes the Water Quality Act, establishing the government's first clear environmental quality standards for water.

February 1–2, 1965: More than 700 protesters, including Martin Luther King and many children, are arrested in Selma, Alabama.

February 14, 1965: In the early morning hours, the Queens home of Malcolm X is firebombed. He is able to escape safely with his wife and four children; however, his home is seriously damaged. That night in Detroit, he delivers his speech "After the Bombing" at the Ford Auditorium, urging unity within the African diaspora movement.

February 18, 1965: Gambia gains independence from Britain.

February 21, 1965: Malcolm X is assassinated by a faction of the Nation of Islam before an audience at the Audubon Ballroom in New York City.

February 26, 1965: Twenty-six-year-old Jimmy Lee Jackson, of Marion, Alabama, is shot and killed by an Alabama state trooper while trying to protect his mother and grandfather from police attack during a civil rights demonstration. The killing was the primary catalyst for the first Selma to Montgomery march, culminating on March 7.

February 26, 1965: Trans World Airlines union members strike for higher wages and shorter hours. They also demand a change in the airline's policy of requiring stewardesses to retire at age thirty-five.

March 7, 1965: Six hundred protesters, led by SNCC chairman John Lewis and SCLC organizer Hosea Williams, begin a fifty-four-mile march from Selma to Montgomery, Alabama. While crossing the Edmund Pettus Bridge out of Selma, they are attacked with tear gas, chains, clubs, and electric cattle prods by state paratroopers and local police in an event known as Bloody Sunday.

March 8, 1965: U.S. Marines arriving in South Vietnam mark the first combat troops of the war.

March 9, 1965: King leads a symbolic march of ministers and other supporters to Selma's Edmund Pettus Bridge. The marchers do not attempt to cross police lines, but rather say a prayer and return.

March 9, 1965: James Reeb, a white Unitarian Universalist minister from Boston, is beaten after the Selma march, dying two days later.

March 15, 1965: President Johnson requests a comprehensive voting rights bill in a speech delivered to a joint session of Congress.

March 16, 1965: Alice Herz, an eighty-two-year-old Quaker, immolates herself in Detroit in protest of the Vietnam War. "I wanted to burn myself like the monks in Vietnam did." She dies ten days later.

March 21–March 25, 1965: A third attempt to march from Selma to Montgomery is launched, beginning with 3,200 marchers on March 21, walking nineteen miles per day, and ending with a force of 25,000.

March 24, 1965: SDS and university faculty organize the first "teach-in," at the University of Michigan, where students and teachers hold an all-night discussion of the Vietnam War. More than 3,000 show up.

March 25, 1965: Civil rights activist Viola Liuzzo, a white woman from Detroit who participated in the March to Montgomery, is murdered by KKK members while she is driving across Alabama.

Spring 1965: Eighty-five farmworkers on a McFarland rose farm in California strike for higher wages with the help of César Chávez's National Farm Workers of America. They win the wage hike but are prohibited from unionizing.

Spring 1965: The Agricultural Workers Organizing Committee leads a walkout of hundreds of Filipino and Mexican grape pickers in Coachella Valley. After ten days, the workers are given a $1.25-an-hour raise, but no union contract.

April 1, 1965: Che Guevara leaves secretly on an expedition to the Congo. He gives Fidel Castro his farewell letter.

April 17, 1965: Twenty-five thousand people participate in an anti–Vietnam War demonstration in Washington, DC, organized by SDS, the largest antiwar protest in memory.

April 17, 1965: The Mattachine Society demands equal rights for gays in a protest outside the White House. The society's grievances include the less-than-honorable discharges given to gays in the armed forces and the government's refusal to hire homosexuals.

April 21, 1965: Puerto Rican nationalist leader Pedro Albizu Campos dies after claiming that radiation testing was inflicted on him in prison. The testing on prisoners occurred from the 1950s to the 1970s.

April 28, 1965–September 22, 1966: The United States invades the Dominican Republic under the guise of rescuing American citizens in the midst of a potential leftist takeover of the government. The final U.S. troops leave in late September 1966 after a former Trujillo puppet president, Joaquín Balaguer, is elected over the Left-leaning Juan Bosch.

May 15, 1965: A national Vietnam teach-in is held in Washington, DC, broadcast to 122 college campuses.

June 7, 1965: On the basis of the right to privacy, the U.S. Supreme Court in *Griswold v. Connecticut* invalidates an 1879 Connecticut law prohibiting birth control. The right to privacy becomes the basis for the Court's striking down abortion laws in *Roe v. Wade* in 1973.

June 8, 1965: Seventeen thousand protest at an antiwar rally at Madison Square Garden in New York City.

Summer 1965: Project Head Start, under the U.S. Office of Economic Opportunity, runs for eight weeks, providing education and nutritional opportunities for low-income preschool-age children.

July–August 1965: Antiwar student demonstrators in Berkeley's Vietnam Day Committee hang on to troop trains and lie on railroad tracks in an attempt to stop the trains from leaving the Bay Area.

July 30, 1965: Johnson signs legislation establishing Medicare, a social insurance program that provides the elderly with comprehensive health care coverage at an affordable cost.

August 5, 1965: CBS reporter Morley Safer reports on GIs burning Vietnamese villages with Zippo lighters.

August 6, 1965: Johnson signs the Voting Rights Act of 1965, containing enforcement provisions targeting areas of the country with the greatest potential for discrimination. He declares, "We shall overcome," at the signing ceremony.

August 11–16, 1965: Thirty-four people are killed and 4,000 are injured in week-long riots in the Watts ghetto of Los Angeles.

August 20, 1965: Episcopal divinity student Jonathan Daniels is shot and killed by an Alabama deputy in Fort Deposit. Daniels was trying to protect seventeen-year-old Ruby Sales, the target of the assailant. In the same incident, Father Richard Morrisroe is shot and wounded. Daniels had come for the Selma march several months earlier, and chose to remain in the movement. As a result of the killing, SNCC and local activists adopt an explicit policy of armed self-defense, a tactic that previously was in informal use in rural areas.

August 29, 1965: The Spanish poet José María Valverde resigns from the University of Barcelona in protest over the dismissal of several professors accused by the Franco government of taking part in antigovernment political activities.

August 30, 1965: Johnson signs legislation prohibiting the destruction or mutilation of a draft card.

September 16, 1965: The NFWA (what later becomes the United Farm Workers) votes to join the Agricultural Workers Organizing Committee strike against California grape growers.

September 28, 1965: Executive Order 11246 requires federal agencies and contractors to overcome employment discrimination through affirmative action.

September 30, 1965: Indonesian generals install a military dictatorship and unleash a massacre of 500,000 people. The U.S. Embassy in Jakarta provides many of the names and locations of communist and dissident leaders to the military and is given nightly information about the names of those killed. An official human rights inquiry is not launched until 2008.

October 12, 1965: Student organizations converge to form the Movimiento de Izquierda Revolucionaria (MIR) in Chile. One of the early leaders is Andrés Pascal Allende, nephew of future Marxist president Salvador Allende. MIR's purpose is to promote leftist, revolutionary change in Chilean politics.

October 15, 1965: During International Days of Protest against the war in New York City, twenty-two-year-old David Miller is the first to publicly burn his draft card.

October 16, 1965: More than 100,000 demonstrate against the war in Vietnam during the International Days of Protest.

November 2, 1965: Quaker Norman Morrison immolates himself in front of Robert McNamara's Pentagon office in protest of the Vietnam War. Morrison has brought his one-year-old daughter, Emily, with him, who remains safe from the blaze.

November 9, 1965: Roger Allen LaPorte, twenty-two and an active member of the Catholic Worker Movement, immolates himself in front of the UN building in New York.

November 18, 1965: "Sex and Caste: A Kind of Memo" is written by Casey Hayden and Mary King, raising the first questions about sexism within the civil rights movement.

December 1965: The grape boycott begins in Delano, California, targeting the Schenley Industries and DiGiorgio Corporations.

December 1965: The U.S. Selective Service inducts 40,200 men for military service (up from the 5,400 inducted in January). Troop levels reach 184,300 in Vietnam.

December 1965: Antiwar activists Tom Hayden, Herbert Aptheker, and Staughton Lynd meet with North Vietnamese officials in Hanoi.

Winter 1965–1966: With a Black Panther as its symbol, the Lowndes County Freedom Organization becomes a third party at a convention of 900 people. The idea followed rejection of the Mississippi Freedom Democratic Party at the 1964 Democratic Convention. The Black Panther Party is formed in Oakland as a direct result. SNCC leader Stokely Carmichael is the catalyst for the Lowndes County Freedom Organization.

1966

1966: The first gay community center is opened in San Francisco by the Society for Individual Rights.

1966: Between 400 and 1,000 Americans migrate to Canada to refuse the draft.

1966: The first Mexican American history class is taught in Los Angeles by Rodolfo Acuña, at California State University at Northridge.

Early 1966: The Pentagon estimates that the war in Vietnam is costing the United States $1 billion a day.

January 3, 1966: SNCC worker and Vietnam veteran Sammy Younge is murdered by a white gas station attendant for trying to use the restroom. Three days later, SNCC issues its first statement of opposition to Vietnam War.

January 30, 1966: Senator J. William Fulbright's televised Senate Foreign Relations Committee hearings question the legality of U.S. involvement in Vietnam.

January 31, 1966: Senator Robert Kennedy criticizes Johnson's decision to resume bombing in Vietnam after a thirty-seven-day moratorium.

March 10–11, 1966: Student protests erupt in Spain following the Ministry of Education closure of the University of Barcelona after students start a sit-in. One thousand students shout slogans and throw stones at police. Riot police arrest several students.

March 17–April 11, 1966: The National Farm Workers Association marches from Delano to Sacramento, calling for better wages and working conditions.

March 25–27, 1966: Antiwar protests are held in eight U.S. cities and seven foreign capitals. In New York, 25,000 participate, including veterans who burn or destroy their discharge papers.

March 28, 1966: There are school walkouts in East Los Angeles in protest against cuts in educational aid.

April 12, 1966: Activists flood the New York Stock Exchange with antiwar leaflets.

April 23, 1966: Heavyweight boxing champion Muhammad Ali refuses draft induction and applies for conscientious objector status as a Muslim, saying "I ain't got no quarrel with those Vietcong. Ain't no Vietcong ever called me a nigger." Ali is convicted of draft evasion, stripped of his heavyweight title, and banned from American boxing. The draft decisions are overturned by the U.S. Supreme Court eight to zero in 1971.

May 12–13, 1966: Students at the City College of New York and the University of Chicago attempt to seize the colleges' administration buildings.

May 13, 1966: Twelve school districts in Louisiana, Mississippi, and Alabama in violation of school desegregation guidelines are denied federal funding.

May 15, 1966: Fifteen thousand antiwar protesters gather in Washington, DC; 8,000 circle the White House.

May 26, 1966: Buddhist students burn the U.S. Cultural Center and library in Hue, South Vietnam.

May 30–31, 1966: Students in Yokusuka, Japan, demonstrate against the visit of a U.S. nuclear submarine. In Tokyo, members of the Japanese Diet march in protest as well.

June 1966: Selective Service chief Lewis Hershey testifies that he prefers drafting high school dropouts and underprivileged youth to give them "educational, physical, and moral training."

June 5, 1966: The *New York Times* prints a three-page ad signed by 6,400 academics calling for an end to the war.

June 5–6, 1966: James Meredith begins a "march against fear" from Memphis, Tennessee, to Jackson, Mississippi. On his second day, he is shot and wounded.

June 7–26, 1966: Led by Martin Luther King, Stokely Carmichael, and Floyd McKissick of CORE, thousands complete the James Meredith march. They are clubbed and tear-gased in Canton. Carmichael voices a demand for "black power."

June 16, 1966: Stokely Carmichael calls for "black power" during Meredith march. Carmichael later said he "he had no idea … Black Power was going to take off the way it did."

June 29, 1966: The National Organization for Women is founded in Washington, DC, by twenty-eight women, including Betty Friedan, who each contribute $5 to its formation. NOW is created in response to the failure of EEOC enforcement of Title VII of the Civil Rights Act.

July 4, 1966: President Johnson signs the Freedom of Information Act into law.

July 18–23, 1966: The National Guard is called to the Hough ghetto of Cleveland after racial violence occurs.

Late July–August 1966: Puerto Ricans battle police in Perth Amboy, New Jersey, after the passage of an antiloitering law.

August 5, 1966: The *New York Times* publishes portions of the SNCC "black power" manifesto.

August 13, 1966: The Cultural Revolution in China is announced to the world.

August 22, 1966: The National Farm Workers Association merges with the Agricultural Workers Organizing Committee to become the United Farm Workers. The AFL-CIO executive council admits the UFW.

September 2, 1966: Alabama governor George Wallace signs a bill declaring that the U.S. Office of Education guidelines for school desegregation are "null and void" in his state.

September 18, 1966: Secretary General of the United Nations U Thant criticizes U.S. policy in Vietnam in a report to the UN General Assembly.

September 28–October 1, 1966: A San Francisco police officer shoots and kills a black youth who ran from a stolen vehicle. Riots erupt, the National Guard is called, and 359 people are arrested and 51 injured.

September 30, 1966: Botswana gains independence from Britain.

October 1966: Bobby Seale and Huey Newton announce the creation of the Black Panther Party in Oakland, California.

October 1, 1966: Secretary of Defense Robert McNamara launches "Project 100,000" to lower the mental and physical requirements of draftees in order to increase manpower in the war.

October 4, 1966: Lesotho gains independence from Britain.

October 6, 1966: LSD is banned.

October 22, 1966: For the second weekend in a row, members of the New Mexico Alianza, led by Reies Tijerina, take over part of the Kit Carson National Forest. They claim the land from a Spanish treaty. One hundred fifty cars and vans enter the park, refusing to pay fees. Two park rangers are "arrested" by the group, put on trial, and charged with trespassing and being a public nuisance. The rangers are then released. The event ends in Tijerina's arrest, along with that of his brother and three other members of the group.

October 29, 1966: Pope Paul VI refuses to change the Vatican's position on birth control.

October 29–30, 1966: The founding conference of NOW is held in Washington, DC, by its 300 members. Betty Friedan is elected president. NOW pushes for aggressive enforcement by the EEOC.

November 8, 1966: Attorney General of Massachusetts Edward Brooke, a Republican, is elected to the U.S. Senate, the first African American senator since Reconstruction.

December 1966: SDS decides to embrace draft resistance on campuses.

December 22, 1966: The Tupamaros are forced to go underground after a deadly shootout with Uruguayan police that claims the life of Carlos Flores, twenty-three.

1967

1967: The National Mobilization to End the War in Vietnam, also known as the MOBE, is founded.

1967: By the end of the year, 952 men are convicted of draft violations.

January 5, 1967: The U.S. Department of Defense announces that 5,047 U.S. soldiers died in Vietnam during 1966.

January 14, 1967: A human be-in involving tens of thousands of young people is held in Golden Gate Park, a public birthing of the counterculture. The be-in attempts to unite Bay Area radicals with the new generation of "hippies" flooding Haight-Ashbury. Present are the Grateful Dead, Timothy Leary, Gary Snyder, Allen Ginsberg, Jerry Rubin, and Richard Alpert (later Ram Dass).

January 16, 1967: Lucius D. Amerson becomes the first black sheriff in the South since Reconstruction, winning an election against a white male incumbent in Macon County, Alabama.

February 1967: The March issue of *Ramparts* magazine reveals how the CIA subsidizes the National Student Association.

March 4, 1967: The Selective Service recommends that graduate student deferments to the draft be ended and that a lottery system be created in which nineteen-year-olds will be selected first for military service.

March 13, 1967: United Mexican American Students is formed at a gathering of approximately 250 students from seven colleges and universities in Los Angeles.

April 1, 1967: Secretary General U Thant urges the United States to declare a unilateral truce in Vietnam.

April 4, 1967: At Riverside Church in New York City, Martin Luther King speaks out publicly against the war in Vietnam for the first time. He calls for a boycott of the war, citing the disproportionate burden placed on blacks and the poor during wartime.

April 14, 1967: Former vice president Richard Nixon declares after visiting Saigon that U.S. antiwar protests are "prolonging the war."

April 15, 1967: The Spring Mobilization sponsors antiwar marches. In San Francisco, 50,000 attend. In New York, more than 100,000 participate. Martin Luther King is among the speakers.

April 19, 1967: Katherine Switzer and Roberta Gibb are the first women to run in the all-male Boston Marathon. Officials try to forcibly remove Switzer, and she is unable to finish. Gibb makes it to a foot away from the finish line but is removed.

April 21, 1967: U.S.-backed Greek generals stage a military coup against the "threat" of communists being included in a reform government coming to power through elections and establishing Greece as nonaligned in the cold war.

April 24, 1967: General William Westmoreland says that antiwar demonstrators give the North Vietnamese the hope "that [they] can win politically that which [they] cannot accomplish militarily."

April 25, 1967: Colorado becomes the first state to liberalize abortion laws, legalizing abortion if pregnancy occurs during rape, incest, or other specific conditions.

April 28, 1967: Muhammad Ali reports for induction in Houston, claiming an exemption as an Islamic minister. He tells the press, "I ain't got nothing against them Vietcong," and "the real enemy of my people is right here." The World Boxing Association strips Ali of his heavyweight title for being "a very poor example" for the world's youth.

May 2, 1967: Bobby Seale and Huey Newton lead thirty armed Black Panthers into the California state capitol claiming the right of self-defense against police brutality.

May 2–10, 1967: Bertrand Russell organizes an unofficial "International Tribunal on War Crimes" in Stockholm, Sweden. The trial criticizes the U.S. bombing of civilians in North Vietnam in particular.

May 5, 1967: Abortion laws in North Carolina are liberalized.

May 12, 1967: H. Rap Brown succeeds Stokely Carmichael as the SNCC chairman. He becomes famous for the statement that "violence is as American as apple pie."

May 27, 1967: In Australia, a referendum granting indigenous rights and citizenship is carried, thereby stripping the state's power over issues involving Aborigines.

June 2, 1967: During demonstrations against the shah of Iran, organized by German SDS, the police shoot and kill twenty-year-old Benno Ohnesorg, taking part in his first demonstration. The event has a radicalizing effect on the German student movement.

June 5, 1967: Twenty armed members of the Alianza in New Mexico attempt to detain District Attorney Alfonso Sanchez in a citizens' arrest. The attempt takes place at the Tierra Amarilla Courthouse and is in response to Sanchez's illegal blocking of a planned Alianza meeting. Two officers are injured, and the group flees to the nearby mountains with two hostages—Associated Press journalist Larry Calloway and Deputy Sheriff Pete Jaramillo. Calloway escapes, and Jaramillo is soon released unharmed. Those involved turn themselves in after a manhunt, which includes 2,000 National Guard troops. Tijerina is later acquitted of fifty-four charges stemming from the incident.

June 5–10, 1967: The Six-Day War results in Israeli occupation of east Jerusalem, the West Bank, the Gaza Strip, the Sinai Peninsula, and the Golan Heights. The result is a spreading Palestinian militancy across the region. In the United States and the West, divisions begin within the New Left and Jewish communities over recognizing the Palestinian right to self-determination and condemning the U.S.-funded Israeli occupation.

June 12, 1967: Antimiscegenation laws prohibiting interracial marriage are repealed in sixteen states by the U.S. Supreme Court in *Loving v. Virginia.*

June 15, 1967: California liberalizes abortion laws.

June 16–18, 1967: The Monterey Pop Festival is held at the Monterey County Fairgrounds, considered to be the first great rock music festival.

June 20, 1967: Muhammad Ali is found guilty of draft evasion by an all-white jury and is sentenced to five years' imprisonment and a $10,000 fine.

June 20, 1967: *One Hundred Years of Solitude,* by Gabriel García Márquez, is published in Argentina. An early work of magical realism, the book is based on the 1928 massacre of Colombian workers striking against the United Fruit Company. In the end, the event is "exiled from the memory of men" by a whirlwind set in motion by the company's representative.

July 1967: The first conference of the Organization of Latin American Solidarity is held in Havana, Cuba. Representatives from 27 countries attend and announce their solidarity and support for national liberation struggles in the continent against U.S. imperialism.

July 2, 1967: Congress ends deferments for graduate students.

July 12–17, 1967: Newark erupts in five days of rioting against police abuse and ghetto conditions. There are 26 deaths, 1,200 injuries, and 1,400 detentions.

July 18, 1967: The House of Representatives passes the "Rap Brown" amendment, making it a federal offense to cross state lines to incite violence. The amendment, attached to a fair housing bill, becomes the basis of the Chicago conspiracy trial in 1969–1970.

July 19, 1967: Race rioting occurs in Minneapolis.

July 20, 1967: The first National Black Power Conference is held in Newark.

July 23–28, 1967: Riots break out in Detroit for five days in response to a police raid on an after-hours club. Forty-three are killed, 1,000 injured, 4,000 arrested. U.S. Vietnam combat troops are used in crowd suppression.

July 24, 1967: In Cambridge, Maryland, H. Rap Brown says that "if America don't come around, we're going to burn America down." Chaos erupts later. Brown is arrested the following day by the FBI and charged with flight to escape prosecution for inciting arson.

July 27, 1967: Johnson appoints the National Advisory Committee on Civil Disorders, headed by Illinois governor Otto Kerner, to investigate causes and remedies for racial violence.

August 1, 1967: FBI director J. Edgar Hoover tells Johnson that "outside agitators" played key roles in the race riots of the summer.

August 1, 1967: Riots erupt in Washington, DC.

August 14, 1967: H. Rap Brown is indicted by a grand jury in Maryland for inciting a riot in Cambridge on July 24, 1967.

August 15, 1967: Martin Luther King calls for a massive nonviolent poor people's campaign to climax in 1968.

August 17, 1967: Stokely Carmichael, broadcasting from Havana, Cuba, tells African Americans to arm for "total revolution."

August 19–23, 1967: A riot happens in New Haven, Connecticut.

August 25, 1967: Counterculture radicals Abbie Hoffman and Jerry Rubin shower the New York Stock Exchange trade floor with 300 $1 bills, disrupting business as usual as traders scramble for the bills.

August 25, 1967: Hoover signs authorization for COINTELPRO against black nationalist groups. Hoover also directs counterintelligence to "expose, disrupt, misdirect, [and] discredit" the Black Panthers.

August 30, 1967: The New York chapter of NOW pickets the *New York Times* for its sex-segregated job listings.

August 31–September 4, 1967: Three thousand progressive delegates hold a national convention for new politics in Chicago, but fail to agree on a presidential strategy or a candidate for 1968. Also, a strong women's rights plank is rejected by the conference.

September 1967: The first national gay and lesbian newsmagazine, the *Los Angeles Advocate,* is published.

Fall 1967: New York Radical Women is formed. The group is credited with introducing "consciousness-raising" techniques and the phrase "The personal is political."

October 1, 1967: The Environmental Defense Fund is founded.

October 2, 1967: Thurgood Marshall becomes the first African American Supreme Court justice.

October 8, 1967: Two thousand students in Tokyo protest to prevent Prime Minister Eisaku Sato from visiting South Vietnam. One student is killed in the melee.

October 8, 1967: Che Guevara is captured and executed by Bolivian soldiers, with CIA advisers present.

October 16, 1967: "Stop the Draft" begins in Oakland and cities nationwide, representing a change "from protest to resistance." Downtown Oakland is paralyzed for two days.

October 17, 1967: Father Philip Berrigan, Tom Lewis, David Eberhardt, and James Mengel enter the Baltimore Customs House and pour blood over draft records. They become known as the "Baltimore Four."

October 18, 1967: Students at the University of Wisconsin–Madison force job recruiters from Dow Chemical, a manufacturer of napalm, to leave campus.

October 20, 1967: Michael Ferber, Dr. Benjamin Spock, Reverend William Sloane Coffin Jr., Mitch Goodman, Robert Lowell, Dwight MacDonald, and Marcus Raskin return hundreds of draft cards to the U.S. Justice Department. Spock, Coffin, and Raskin are indicted by Attorney General Ramsey Clark.

October 21, 1967: One hundred thousand march on the Pentagon, a template for the proposed Chicago protests the following year. Speakers include Jerry Rubin, David Dellinger, Rennie Davis, and Norman Mailer. Four hundred are arrested. Worldwide, protests occur in every Western European capital city, in Japan, and in Australia.

October 26, 1967: The government eliminates draft deferments for those who violate draft laws or interfere with recruitment.

October 28, 1967: Black Panther founder Huey Newton is accused of murdering Oakland police officer John Frey. Newton, wounded in the shootout, is hospitalized and imprisoned.

November 7, 1967: African Americans Carl Stokes and Richard Hatcher are elected mayors of Cleveland, Ohio, and Gary, Indiana, respectively.

November 11, 1967: Twenty-five student leftist protesters in Japan attempt to block Prime Minister Eisaku Sato from departing on a trip to the United States. One hundred thirty-two are injured and 330 are arrested.

November 16, 1967: The Senate Foreign Relations Committee approves a resolution that would restrict U.S. involvement in Vietnam and send the conflict to the UN Security Council for resolution.

November 18–19, 1967: NOW adopts a platform supporting the Equal Rights Amendment, the creation of publicly funded child care, and the repeal of all abortion laws, becoming the first national organization to endorse legal abortion. The UAW withdraws its support of NOW over the issue of the ERA.

November 23, 1967: A black youth conference endorses the boycotting of the upcoming 1968 Olympics. Among them is UCLA basketball player Lew Alcindor (later Kareem Abdul-Jabbar).

November 27, 1967: The first gay bookstore in the United States, the Oscar Wilde Memorial Bookshop, is opened in Manhattan.

November 30, 1967: Southern Yemen, a British colony, becomes the People's Republic of South Yemen after an armed struggle.

December 1967: The Brown Berets are founded in Los Angeles.

December 4, 1967: Martin Luther King announces the organization of the national Poor People's Campaign.

December 12, 1967: NOW holds simultaneous demonstrations at EEOC field offices across the country.

December 31, 1967: Abbie Hoffman, Jerry Rubin, Paul Krassner, Dick Gregory, and others declare the formation of the "Yippies" and announce plans for a "festival of life" at the 1968 Democratic National Convention in Chicago.

1968

January 15, 1968: The Jeanette Rankin Brigade (named after the first U.S. congresswoman, Jeanette Rankin) holds an antiwar demonstration in Washington, DC. New York Radical Women stage a "burial of traditional womanhood" action in which the phrase "Sisterhood is powerful" is first used.

January 19–21, 1968: Japanese students battle riot police after storming the U.S. naval base at Cape Iorizaki to protest the visit of the nuclear-powered aircraft carrier USS *Enterprise*.

January 23, 1968: Filipino protesters burn an effigy of President Johnson in front of the Congress building in Manila, protesting the presence of Philippine troops in Vietnam.

January 26, 1968: MOBE meets in New York to discuss demonstrating at the Democratic National Convention in Chicago. David Dellinger, Rennie Davis, and Tom Hayden are the key organizers.

January 30, 1968: Thousands march in protest against the Warsaw regime's ban of a famous nationalist play entitled *Forefather's Eve* (*Dziady*).

January 30–31, 1968: The Tet Offensive is launched in South Vietnam. North Vietnamese troops and National Liberation Front guerrillas attack thirty-nine of forty-four provincial capitals, as well as the American Embassy, Tan San Nhut airbase, the presidential palace, and Hue's Imperial Citadel. General William Westmoreland, commander of 500,000 troops, says, "The extent of this offensive was not known to the U.S.... The timing was not known.... I did not anticipate that they would strike in the cities."

February 8, 1968: One hundred black students protest against a segregated bowling alley in Orangeburg, South Carolina. State troopers fire into the crowd, killing South Carolina State University students Henry Smith, nineteen, and Samuel Hammond Jr., eighteen, along with DeLano Middleton, a seventeen-year-old high school student. Twenty-seven others are wounded.

February 10, 1968: The official "Report for Action: An Investigation into the Causes and Events of the 1967 Newark Race Riots" finds that the National Guard and state and local police used excessive and unjustified force against black citizens.

February 14, 1968: A student in Santo Domingo, Dominican Republic, is shot and killed by police following a sit-in demonstration to increase monthly subsidies paid to the National University. The police occupy the campus for a week following the incident.

February 15, 1968: César Chávez begins his first fast.

February 16, 1968: The U.S. government abolishes occupational and graduate student draft deferments.

February 17, 1968: A Vietnam congress sponsored by West German students attracts 5,000 from across Europe.

February 17, 1968: Five guerrilla fighters (three Cubans, two Bolivians), the last survivors of Che's failed Bolivian expedition, cross the border into Chile seeking asylum. They are given shelter and medical care with the help of Salvador Allende, then president of the Senate.

February 25, 1968: Pete Seeger performs his Vietnam War parody song "Waist Deep in the Big Muddy" on *The Smothers Brothers Comedy Hour,* a song CBS refused to allow Seeger to perform in September 1967.

February 27, 1968: After visiting Vietnam in the wake of Tet, CBS News anchor Walter Cronkite announces that the war is a "stalemate," the first such acknowledgment by a major public figure.

February 29, 1968: The National Advisory Committee on Civil Disorders (the Kerner Commission) issues its report, blaming the race riots of the summer of 1967 on poverty, discrimination, unequal enforcement of the law, substandard education, and inferior housing and public services. The report comes to the conclusion that "our nation is moving toward two societies, one black, one white—separate and unequal."

March 1, 1968: Thousands of Italian students on strike since February blockade universities and fight police in the streets for several weeks. They oppose the Vietnam War and demand radical university reforms.

March 3, 1968: Tens of thousands of Chicano youth walk out of Eastside Los Angeles schools, demanding student power and a reversal of educational inequalities.

March 4, 1968: Student leaders Adam Michnik and Henryk Szlajfer are expelled from the University of Warsaw. On March 28, students issue their Declaration of the Student Movement, demanding an end of censorship, self-government for workers, and an independent judiciary.

March 10–11, 1968: César Chávez breaks his fast, with Robert Kennedy at his side.

March 12, 1968: Mauritius gains independence from Britain.

March 16, 1968: Though not revealed to the American public until 1969, American troops slaughter 300 civilians in the hamlet of My Lai in South Vietnam. The story is broken by Seymour Hersch of Pacific News Service on November 12, 1969.

March 19–23, 1968: Students at Howard University occupy the school's administration building to demand more African American studies courses and programs.

March 22, 1968: French students at the University of Nanterre strike to demand a "critical university" and a dropping of disciplinary charges against eight students. The French May '68 has begun.

March 26, 1968: The Yippies submit an application to the Chicago Parks Department to allow them to sleep in Lincoln Park during the Democratic National Convention. As with all permit applications, it is denied.

March 26, 1968: The "wise men"—a formal advisory body of cold war diplomats, generals, bankers, and businessmen, including Dean Acheson, Averell Harriman, George Kennan, John McCloy Jr., Charles Bohlen, and Robert Lovett—meet with President Johnson and recommend U.S. withdrawal from Vietnam.

March 28, 1968: Martin Luther King marches with striking sanitation workers in Memphis, Tennessee. A sixteen-year-old boy is killed and 280 people are arrested in the violence that follows.

March 31, 1968: Johnson announces that he will not run for reelection. In the same statement, he halts the bombing of North Vietnam above the twentieth parallel, rejects the Pentagon request for 200,000 more troops, prioritizes the training of Saigon troops, and proposes immediate peace talks.

April 3, 1968: The United States and North Vietnam agree to open direct contact between diplomatic representatives.

April 3, 1968: Martin Luther King Jr. gives his final speech, "I've Been to the Mountaintop," in Memphis.

April 4, 1968: Martin Luther King Jr. is assassinated by a sniper while on a motel balcony in Memphis, Tennessee. His alleged assassin, James Earl Ray, leaves the United States through Canada for Europe.

April 4–mid-April 1968: Rebellions erupt in more than 130 U.S. communities in response to Martin Luther King's death. More than 700 fires burn in Washington, DC, alone. In Chicago, Mayor Richard Daley issues directives to "shoot to kill" arsonists and "shoot to maim" looters. Nationally, 46 people are killed (41 of whom are black), more than 7,000 are injured, and more than 20,000 are arrested.

April 6, 1968: Two days after King's murder, the Oakland police kill seventeen-year-old Black Panther "Little Bobby" Hutton and wound Black Panthers Eldridge Cleaver and Warren Wells. Hutton and Cleaver are shot while surrendering. Cleaver, then a parolee, returns to prison, and eight other Panthers are arrested.

April 11, 1968: Johnson signs legislation giving civil rights workers federal protection, and Title 8 of the bill, the Fair Housing Act, prohibits discrimination in the sale, rental, and financing of dwellings based on race, color, religion, sex, or national origin. Title 18 of the Act, the "Anti-Riot Act," makes it a felony to "travel in interstate commerce ... with the intent to incite, promote, encourage, participate in and carry on a riot." Title 18, the "Rap Brown law," is used to prosecute the Chicago Eight.

April 11, 1968: German student leader Rudi Dutschke is shot by a young German house painter, Joseph Bachmann; Dutschke suffers brain damage but lives until 1979. After the assassination attempt, German students blaming Axel Springer's press for negative publicity of their protests unleash thousands of demonstrators in twenty cities trying to block Springer office entrances; two more die in these events.

April 16, 1968: Chicanos boycott the Coors brewery in Denver for discriminatory hiring practices.

April 23–24, 1968: SDS and the Black Student Union lead a strike at Columbia University after King's murder. Students protest the building of a Columbia gymnasium on land in Harlem, the university's contract with a military corporation, and the university's disciplinary action against SDS leaders. The campus is closed as students occupy five buildings. Student strikes protesting the war break out at hundreds of college and university campuses.

April 26, 1968: The Department of Defense creates a riot-control center at the Pentagon.

April 27, 1968: During protests in Tokyo against the U.S. occupation of Okinawa and other Ryukyu islands since the end of World War II, 214 protesters are arrested.

April 30, 1968: More than 1,000 New York police arrest hundreds of Columbia students and restore administrative control of the campus.

May 1968: At Brussels University, students occupy buildings for fifty days, demanding participation in university decisionmaking.

May 2, 1968: The Mexican American Legal Defense and Education Fund is founded in San Antonio, Texas, with Ford Foundation funding.

May 3–10, 1968: French students rebel at police occupation of an inner courtyard of the Sorbonne. They occupy campus buildings, battle police in the Latin Quarter, and erect barricades on May 10–11. These actions lead to a spontaneous strike by 7–9 million workers, paralyzing French institutions.

May 9, 1968: FBI director J. Edgar Hoover instructs COINTELPRO to disrupt New Left activities throughout the United States.

May 10, 1968: Vietnam peace talks commence in Paris. Delegates include W. Averell Harriman of the United States, Le Duc Tho of North Vietnam, and Xuan Thuy of the National Liberation Front.

May 13, 1968: The general strike continues in France, consisting of hundreds of thousands of university students and French workers. President Charles de Gaulle retreats to an air force base and calls for new elections.

May 16, 1968: Student protests erupt in Corrientes, Argentina, over school privatization measures. A student, Juan José Cabral, is shot down by the police. The university is shut down.

May 17, 1968: Catholic priests Daniel and Philip Berrigan, along with seven others, invade the Selective Service office in Catonsville, Maryland. They steal 600 draft files and burn them outside using homemade napalm before being arrested. In the process, they discover files revealing the FBI's COINTEL program. The group becomes known as the Catonsville Nine, and they are tried and convicted in federal court in October.

May 18, 1968: Thousands of Spanish students protest dictatorship, holding unauthorized assemblies, "boycotting exams, proclaiming communes, paying homage to Che Guevara, occupying the dean's office, and smashing Franco's portraits on university premises."

May 20, 1968: France is crippled as 10 million workers, two-thirds of the French workforce, strike, taking control of factories, mines, and offices.

May 30, 1968: In Japan, 4,500 students protest in ten cities against the war in Vietnam and the U.S. control of the Ryukyu Islands; 46 are arrested.

June 1968: José Sánchez, a nineteen-year-old native of East Los Angeles, is the first Chicano to openly resist the military draft.

June 1968: In Czechoslovakia, communist reformers and independent intellectuals and artists circulate "2,000 Words," a manifesto calling for moral courage and grassroots resistance. Students adopting Western lifestyle symbols march demanding, "We want light!"

June 1968: Uruguayan president Jorge Pacheco declares a state of emergency. Political movements are repressed, and dissidents are tortured. The Tupamaros begin to conduct political kidnappings.

June 6, 1968: Robert Kennedy is assassinated in Los Angeles moments after declaring victory in the California primary. He is forty-two. The killer is identified as Sirhan Sirhan, a Palestinian angry at Kennedy's support for Israel. Doubts are raised about the lone assassination theory due to multiple gunshot wounds and bullet casings found at the site.

June 7, 1968: The Basque separatist group Euskadi Ta Askatasuna (ETA) carries out its first assassination when ETA guerrillas shoot down Guardia Civil member José Padines Arcay.

June 10, 1968: Dr. Benjamin Spock, on trial for conspiracy to aid draft resistance, testifies: "We have been destroying a country which never intended the U.S. any harm. We have been killing hundreds of thousands of men, women and children. My own belief is that this was a totally outrageous and abominable thing that the United States has been carrying on."

June 14, 1968: Dr. Benjamin Spock, Reverend William Sloane Coffin Jr., Mitchell Goodman, and Michael Ferber are convicted in a Boston federal district court of federal conspiracy to aid draft deserters. Marcus Raskin is acquitted. Although Attorney General Ramsey Clark urges suspended sentences, the four are sentenced to two years in prison and fined $5,000, with Ferber being fined $1,000. One year later, an appeals court overturns the convictions.

June 15, 1968: Twenty-five thousand Japanese university students demonstrate against U.S. involvement in Vietnam and the U.S.-Japan alliance. As riot police in Osaka attempt to turn back demonstrators, 141 police and 70 students are injured.

June 17, 1968: Japanese police are called in to remove protesting medical students at Tokyo University. A strike lasts for months.

June 19, 1968: The Poor People's Campaign holds a solidarity day march of 50,000 in DC.

June 24, 1968: Police tear-gas and shut down Resurrection City, DC, the primary encampment for the Poor People's Campaign.

June 26, 1968: Thousands of students, priests, nuns, teachers, writers, and workers march in Rio de Janeiro to protest police brutality and other antidemocratic practices.

July 1968: The American Indian Movement is founded in Minneapolis by 200 Native Americans led by Dennis Banks and Clyde Bellecourt, among others. Its purpose is to protect the city's American Indian community from police abuse and to create job training, housing, and education programs.

July 1, 1968: The United States, Great Britain, and the Soviet Union sign the Treaty on the Non-Proliferation of Nuclear Weapons.

July 22–26, 1968: Members of NOW picket the *New York Times* for sex-segregated job listing, chanting, "The *New York Times* is a sex offender!"

July 23, 1968: A shootout occurs between African Americans and police in Cleveland. Seven African Americans and three police are killed. The National Guard occupies the city.

July 29, 1968: In Pope Paul VI's encyclical "Humanae Vitae," the Vatican bans the use of artificial methods of birth control and voluntary sterilization.

July 30, 1968: Students from the National University of Mexico and the National Polytechnic Institute engage in antigovernment demonstrations in Mexico City. Federal troops and police battle the students.

August 5, 1968: Chicago deputy mayor David Stahl refuses to grant a permit to the Yippies allowing them to sleep in the park (for the Democratic National Convention).

August 7, 1968: Tupamaro guerrillas kidnap Ulises Pereira Reverbel, an ally of President Jorge Pacheco and considered the "most hated man in Uruguay."

August 13, 1968: One hundred fifty thousand protesters, mainly students, march to the Zócalo in Mexico City, demanding the release of political prisoners.

August 21, 1968: Soviet tanks and heavy armor invade Czechoslovakia amid massive peaceful resistance. The Soviet goal is to crush independence and reform within the USSR's cold war bloc, opposing the Prague Spring democratic reforms advocated by Czech party leader Alexander Dubček on behalf of a new social movement.

August 22, 1968: A seventeen-year-old Native American, Jerome Johnson, is shot and killed by Chicago police in Lincoln Park as hundreds of young people arrive for the week of protest. Police say the young man threatened them with a knife. There is no independent investigation.

August 26, 1968: The Democratic National Convention opens in Chicago. Eugene McCarthy delegates and peace activists propose a Vietnam peace plank in the platform. According to a Gallup Poll, 53 percent of Americans think the war is a mistake, double the percentage of two years before. About 3,000 demonstrators gathered in Lincoln Park after the 11 p.m. curfew are attacked by police with clubs and tear gas.

August 27, 1968: Demonstrators in Chicago hold an indoor "Unbirthday Party" for President Johnson in an attempt to discourage him from attending the convention. Phil Ochs sings, "I Ain't a Marchin' Anymore." Allen Ginsberg, William Burroughs, Terry Southern, and Dick Gregory speak, in addition to MOBE and Yippie representatives. Earlier Bobby Seale gives a brief militant speech in Lincoln Park, before a peaceful crowd, for which he is later indicted. That night in Lincoln Park a march led by ministers carrying a wooden cross is met by heavy tear gas attacks. After the Vietnam peace plank is voted down, many Democratic delegates join the street protest.

August 28, 1968: On the day of Hubert Humphrey's nomination, ten thousand rally at the Grant Park bandshell at noon. After a protester lowers the American flag to half-mast, a wave of police attack the crowd with batons and tear gas. One protest column is blocked from marching peacefully to the park across from the hotels. Others form small groups seeking to evade arrest and return to the Hilton by way of Michigan Avenue. As dusk descends, they are blocked and beaten by police while chanting, "The whole world is watching."

September 6, 1968: Swaziland gains independence from Britain.

September 7, 1968: The National Organization for Women (NOW) and other women's organizations demonstrate against the Atlantic City Miss America beauty contest. They throw bras, high heels, and girdles into a "freedom trash can." Despite common myths, no bras were burned that day.

September 8, 1968: Black Panther Huey Newton is found guilty of voluntary manslaughter of Oakland police officer John Frey and is sentenced to two to fifteen years in prison.

September 9, 1968: Arthur Ashe becomes the first African American tennis player to win the U.S. Open.

September 18, 1968: Army troops invade University City in Mexico City after students propose a negotiated solution to a standoff with the government.

September 24, 1968: Mexican students strike against police at the National Autonomous University of Mexico. In response to police repression, the chancellor resigns. Demonstrators plan a global message during the coming Olympic Games.

September 25, 1968: In Lima, Peru, police dispel protesters with tear gas and water cannons.

October 2, 1968: Hundreds of students are killed and "disappeared" by police at the Plaza de las Tres Culturas in Mexico City, ten days before the opening of the Olympics. The event dominates Mexican politics, culture, and memory for thirty years. Some of the surviving student radicals later organize the Zapatista network in Chiapas in the nineties.

October 12, 1968: Equatorial Guinea gains independence from Spain.

October 14, 1968: Dissenting soldiers at the Presidio Stockade in San Francisco sing antiwar songs as they are read the army's Mutiny Act. Similar acts of GI defiance take place at Fort Jackson, South Carolina, and at Fort Ord, California.

October 16, 1968: American sprinters Tommie Smith and John Carlos, after winning gold and bronze medals, give the black power salute from the Olympic podium. They are suspended from the U.S. team and banned from the Olympic Village.

October 21, 1968: Nixon leads Humphrey in the Gallup Poll, 44–31.

October 21, 1968: In Japan, 800,000 demonstrate in cities against the war in Vietnam and U.S. relations with Japan.

October 27, 1968: Fifty thousand demonstrators assemble in London to protest the war in Vietnam.

October 31, 1968: Johnson announces a bombing halt over North Vietnam and pledges peace talks. Through intermediaries, Nixon convinces the Saigon government to delay entering peace talks so as not to help Humphrey's campaign.

November 1, 1968: Nixon's lead is cut to 40–37 in Gallup and Harris surveys.

November 1, 1968: The United States announces it will intensify its bombing effort along the Ho Chi Minh Trail in Laos.

November 4, 1968: A progressive Latino activist named Rosalio Muñoz is elected UCLA student body president on an antifraternity platform.

November 5, 1968: Richard Nixon is elected president by a 0.7 percent margin. According to Theodore White, if the prospect of peace had become clearer in the last three days of the election of 1968, "Hubert Humphrey probably would have won the election."

November 5, 1968: NOW member Shirley Chisholm from New York becomes the first black woman elected to the House of Representatives. After the 1968 elections, ten women are serving in the House and one in the Senate.

November 6, 1968: The Third World Liberation Front (a coalition of African American, Latino, and Asian American groups) begins a student strike at San Francisco State University that lasts 134 days and results in America's first College of Ethnic Studies. Danny Glover is a leader of the campus Black Student Union.

November 7, 1968: Students trigger an uprising of several million for five months against Pakistan's Ayub dictatorship. They brandish spoons against leaders thought to be sucking up to Washington. At least 210 protesters are killed between November and March 1969.

December 1, 1968: The National Commission on the Causes and Prevention of Violence (the Walker Report) concludes that a "police riot" occurred in Chicago at the Democratic National Convention.

December 18, 1968: To protest U.S. restrictions on the free movement of Native Americans between the United States and Canada, Mohawk Indians form a blockade at the Cornwall International Bridge. Many demonstrators are arrested. The Canadian government dismisses charges.

December 18–19, 1968: Five thousand students and union laborers in Japan protest the visit of a U.S. nuclear-powered submarine at Sasebo harbor outside of Tokyo.

December 24, 1968: The photograph "Earthrise" is taken from the Apollo 8 spacecraft while orbiting the moon.

1969

January 7, 1969: California governor Ronald Reagan asks the state legislature to "drive criminal anarchists and latter-day Fascists off the [state college and university] campuses."

January 16, 1969: Student leader Jan Palach burns himself to death in Prague in protest of Soviet occupation; a huge funeral takes place on January 25.

January 17, 1969: Members of the United Slaves (US) shoot and kill Black Panthers Alprentice "Bunchy" Carter and Jon Huggins at UCLA's Campbell Hall. The conflict began in a dispute over leadership of UCLA's new black studies program. Evidence indicates the Panther–United Slaves conflict was partly triggered by the FBI's COINTELPRO program. An FBI report states the bureau's hope for "a 'U.S.' and BPP vendetta."

January 29, 1969: Union Oil Company spills 200,000 gallons of crude oil into the Santa Barbara Channel. Oil spreads into an 800-square-mile slick, covering thirty-five miles of coastline. The massive protest that follows is seen as the birth of an activist environmental movement against offshore drilling. The protest organization is named Get Oil Out.

February 9, 1969: NOW takes action at "men-only" restaurants, bars, and other public spaces (such as the Oak Room in New York City, Stouffers Grill in Pittsburgh, and the Polo Lounge in LA) during its "Public Accommodations Week."

February 14–16, 1969: The National Association for the Repeal of Abortion Laws is established at the First National Conference on Abortion Laws, which is held in Chicago.

February 16, 1969: An anti-U.S. protest by leftists in Istanbul turns violent during clashes with police and nationalist conservative counterprotesters. Twenty thousand are involved in the melee, and 2 people are killed.

February 27, 1969: Police at the University of California, Berkeley, charge student picket lines and arrest and club two Chicano student leaders, Manuel Delgado and Ysidro Macias.

March 9, 1969: One hundred families of the unemployed in Chile seize some private, unenclosed, and unused land located near Puerto Montt. The Ministry of the Interior sends 200 troops to dislodge settlers and set fire to their huts and belongings.

March 20, 1969: The "Chicago Eight"—Rennie Davis, David Dellinger, John Froines, Tom Hayden, Abbie Hoffman, Jerry Rubin, Lee Weiner, and Bobby Seale—are indicted by the Justice Department for crossing state lines with the intent of starting a riot at the Democratic National Convention.

March 22, 1969: Antiwar activists break into Dow Chemical's DC offices, splashing blood and destroying files in protest of Dow's manufacture of the war weapon napalm.

March 30, 1969: Detroit police engage in a shootout with the black separatist group the Republic of New Afrika. One police officer is killed.

April 1969: The Movimiento Estudiantil Chicano de Aztlan is formed by Chicano students seeking curriculum reform and educational opportunities.

April 2, 1969: The Panther Twenty-one are arrested and indicted in New York on charges of planning to bomb various department stores around the city. One of the Panthers arrested is Afeni Shakur, mother of Tupac Shakur. On May 13, 1971, they are acquitted.

April 9, 1969: SDS seizes the main administration building at Harvard University, protesting Vietnam and the campus Reserve Officers' Training Corps (ROTC) program. Four hundred police end the occupation the following day.

April 19, 1969: Eighty African American students, some of them bearing arms, occupy the administration building of Cornell University in Ithaca, New York. They protest against a burning cross left on the doorstep of a black sorority, demand greater security, and call for the creation of a black studies program.

April 22, 1969: Harvard faculty vote to create a black studies program and allow students a role in its faculty selection.

April 22, 1969: Blacks and Puerto Ricans occupy campus buildings at the City College of New York, demanding greater minority enrollment. The college is forced to close temporarily.

April 28, 1969: Students in Japan march in Tokyo against seventeen years of U.S. occupation of Okinawa; 800 people are arrested.

May 4, 1969: Former SNCC leader James Forman interrupts Sunday services at Riverside Church in New York City to present a "black manifesto" demanding reparations for slavery.

May 5, 1969: The Harvard ROTC building is damaged by fire, ruled an arson.

May 15, 1969: Berkeley police and the highway patrol invade People's Park in Berkeley, an organic garden and gathering place established one month earlier on vacant university land. A crowd of 6,000 students moves toward the park after a campus rally. Alameda County sheriff's deputies use lethal 00 buckshot, blinding bystander Alan Blanchard and killing James Rector. One hundred twenty-eight people are injured, and more than 1,000 are arrested. Governor Reagan declares a state of emergency. Thirty thousand march one week later.

May 20, 1969: Black Panther Alex Rackley is murdered outside of New Haven by fellow Panther member Warren Kimbro on suspicion of being an informant. On May 22, eight Black Panthers—Warren Kimbro, Ericka Huggins, Frances Carter, Rose Smith, George Edwards, Margaret Hudgins, Maude Francis, and Jeannie Wilson—are arrested in connection with the murder.

May 21, 1969: Antiwar activists throw paint on draft files and destroy equipment in Selective Service offices in Silver Spring, Maryland.

May 22, 1969: Canadian prime minister Pierre Elliott Trudeau says Canada will welcome U.S. military deserters on the same grounds as it admits other immigrants.

May 25, 1969: Antiwar activists burn draft board files on Chicago's South Side.

June 8, 1969: President Nixon announces the first troop withdrawals of the war, stating that 25,000 troops will be sent home by the end of August.

June 8, 1969: Two-thirds of Brown University's graduating class ceremony, wearing black robes and white armbands, turn their backs on Secretary of State Henry Kissinger.

June 18, 1969: SDS fragments into three factions at its Chicago convention: the Worker Student Alliance (dominated by the Progressive Labor Party), the Revolutionary Youth Movement, and the Weathermen. The Weathermen statement, based on Bob Dylan's "Subterranean Homesick Blues," calls for revolutionary action against racism, imperialism, and white skin privilege. The document, which is followed by a bombing campaign against military and corporate targets, is authored by John Jacobs, Jeff Jones, Mark Rudd, Karen Ashley, Bernardine Dohrn, Bill Ayers, Jim Mellen, Terry Robbins, Gerry Long, and Howie Machtinger.

June 22, 1969: Cleveland's Cuyahoga River, laden with heavy chemicals, catches fire.

June 28, 1969: Gay activists riot for several nights against police raids and abuse at the Stonewall Inn, a community bar in Greenwich Village. "Stonewall" becomes known as the opening shot of the gay liberation movement. On July 24, in the wake of the riots, the Gay Liberation Front is formed in New York City, announcing, "Homosexuals Are Coming Together at Last."

July–October 1969: In France, Gauche Prolétarienne forms an armed wing, which carries out eighty-two direct actions, such as detentions of politicians, between July and October.

July 1969: The National Coalition of American Nuns is founded to support civil rights and antiwar movements and to pressure for women's equality within the Catholic church.

July 4, 1969: Violent antiwar protests occur in five Australian cities outside of U.S. consulates. More than 100 are arrested.

July 20, 1969: Apollo 11 lands on the moon. Neil Armstrong, followed by Buzz Aldrin, walks on the moon as Michael Collins orbits in the command module. Photos of Earth from the moon instantly create a new global environmental consciousness.

July 27, 1969: A small group of radicals, led by Sam Melville, later to be killed during the Attica prison uprisings, bomb Grace Pier in Manhattan, owned by United Fruit Company. This is the first in a series of bombings that take place in Manhattan into November. In late August, the group bombs the Marine Midland Building. In September, it bombs a federal office building. In October, the Whitehall Army Induction Center is bombed. On November 11, these radicals bomb the Chase Manhattan headquarters, the General Motors building, and the Standard Oil offices in the RCA building. On November 12, the group carries out the last bombing, at the New York City Criminal Courts Building, where the Panther Twenty-one trial is being held. Melville and an FBI informant named George Demerle are arrested while attempting to plant dynamite at an armory. Jane Alpert and Dave Hughey, who assist in the bombings, are also arrested at the apartment the group operated out of. Charges against Demerle are quickly dropped, and Melville is found guilty and sentenced to Attica prison.

July 31, 1969: Chicago police raid the Panthers office, destroying medical supplies and food, and setting fires. Panther Pete Hayman is arrested and charged with attempted murder and is severely beaten.

August 2, 1969: Civil rights marchers in Northern Ireland, based partly on America's civil rights model, are attacked by Protestant paramilitaries, police, and British forces.

August 8, 1969: Nixon's Executive Order 11478 mandates affirmative action programs in federal employment.

August 12, 1969: Battles continue between young Irish republicans and Crown forces in Derry, Northern Ireland.

August 15–18, 1969: The Woodstock music festival draws a rain-drenched 400,000 people at a 600-acre farm near Woodstock, New York. The event becomes a turning point in the arrival of the counterculture.

August 19, 1969: Bobby Seale is apprehended by the FBI in Berkeley in connection with the Alex Rackley murder in New Haven.

September 3, 1969: North Vietnamese leader Ho Chi Minh dies in Hanoi at seventy-nine.

September 5, 1969: Army lieutenant William Calley is accused of killing 109 Vietnamese civilians in the My Lai massacre, March 19, 1968. In 1971, he is convicted of twenty-two murders and sentenced to life in prison. Nixon reduces Calley's life sentence to three years.

September 16, 1969: Former UCLA student body president Rosalio Muñoz refuses the draft publicly and accuses the United States of genocide against the Mexican American people.

September 19, 1969: UCLA fires philosophy professor Angela Davis for her social activism, including her involvement with the Black Panthers and her membership in the Communist Party.

September 24, 1969: The Chicago Eight go on trial in Chicago for plotting to incite a riot at the 1968 Democratic National Convention.

October 1, 1969: Daniel Ellsberg, a military analyst and former U.S. Marine Corps officer, walks out of the Rand Corporation office in Santa Monica, California, with a briefcase full of documents that become known as the Pentagon Papers. They are part of a top secret study on American conduct in the Vietnam War. The underground movement of Ellsberg and the papers before their release is coordinated by an antiwar network including Howard Zinn.

October 6, 1969: The Weathermen blow up a police statue in Chicago's Haymarket Square, "the only such monument erected to the constabulary in the entire nation," commemorating deadly battles among police, anarchists, and labor radicals the century before.

October 8, 1969: The Weathermen carry out their "Days of Rage" in Chicago, storming commercial and residential streets on the affluent Gold Coast, south of Lincoln Park. Six Weathermen are shot and wounded, 28 policemen are injured, and 68 people are arrested. Two days later, they battle police again, with 36 policemen and 123 Weathermen hurt. Chicago Corporation counsel Richard Elrod is paralyzed from smashing into a wall while tackling a demonstrator.

October 15, 1969: More than 1 million Americans join the moratorium against the war, including huge demonstrations in Washington, DC, and the Bay Area. With the Democrats out of power and Nixon continuing the war, the scale of the grassroots movement expands vastly.

October 21, 1969: Students in Japan observe International War Day, protesting the Vietnam War. Violent protests spring up in almost 100 cities across Japan. Fourteen hundred people are arrested.

October 29, 1969: The U.S. Supreme Court unanimously rules that thirty Mississippi school districts must immediately integrate.

October 29–November 3, 1969: Bobby Seale insists on a constitutional right to represent himself because his attorney, Charles Garry, is absent in a Bay Area hospital. Denied the right, Seale insists on preserving his protest on the record whenever his name is entered in testimony. Finally, Judge Julius Hoffman orders Seale handcuffed to a chair and gagged. After a two-day confrontation, the judge severs Seale from the case for contempt and resumes the trial. The case now becomes known as the trial of the Chicago Seven.

October 31, 1969: An antiwar group known as the Beaver Fifty-five claims credit for the shredding of records in forty-four Selective Service offices in Indianapolis.

November 3, 1969: Nixon announces his "Vietnamization" plan, which, on a secret timetable, calls for U.S. combat troops to become advisers to South Vietnamese troops while increasing U.S. air bombardment. Lower American casualties, the administration believes, will undercut antiwar sentiment at home.

November 5, 1969: Bobby Seale, after being chained and gagged for seeking to represent himself, is severed from the Chicago Eight defendants. The court declares a mistrial, and Seale receives a four-year sentence for contempt of court. The image of a defiant black defendant in chains is flashed around the world. Eventually Seale is cleared of all charges.

November 7, 1969: Antiwar demonstrators disrupt Dow Chemical offices in DC and erase magnetic tape holding biological and chemical research at Dow's data center in Midland, Michigan.

November 7, 1969: Antiwar activists break into six Selective Service offices in Boston, splashing ink and chemicals.

November 9, 1969: Mohawk Indian Richard Oakes leads seventy-five Native Americans on a second attempt to occupy Alcatraz Island, reclaiming the abandoned prison facility in the name of "Indians of All Tribes."

November 13, 1969: Fifty thousand demonstrate at the White House, reading the names of Americans killed in Vietnam.

November 15, 1969: The largest antiwar demonstration in U.S. history takes place when 250,000 people march down DC's Pennsylvania Avenue and sing for peace at the Washington Monument. An additional 200,000 assemble in San Francisco's Golden Gate Park.

November 15, 1969: The Chinese government complains of unrest and the spread of anarchism in Tibet.

November 18, 1969: Rosalio Muñoz, a former student body president at UCLA, again refuses to be drafted at an induction center in downtown Los Angeles.

November 20, 1969–June 11, 1971: Seventy-nine Native Americans of the ad hoc group Indians of All Tribes, mostly college students, take over Alcatraz Island in the San Francisco Bay to bring attention to issues of discrimination and treaty disputes. They occupy Alcatraz for nineteen months.

November 20, 1969: The Nixon administration orders a stoppage to the use of DDT in residential areas.

November 26, 1969: Nixon signs a bill to establish a draft lottery.

November 29, 1969: Panther members Frances Carter, Ericka Huggins, Rose Smith, and Margaret Hudgins, along with Panther George Edwards, are denied bail in connection with the murder of Alex Rackley. All later receive acquittals or the dropping of charges.

December 1969: Jane, an underground service for women to obtain safe and affordable abortions, opens in Chicago.

December 1, 1969: The first draft lottery since World War II is conducted by the Selective Service.

December 4, 1969: Fred Hampton, twenty-one, founder of the Chicago Black Panthers, is riddled with forty-four bullets, and Peoria leader Mark Clark, twenty-two, is also killed in an early-morning Chicago police raid. Both Panthers are asleep at the time. An informant provided the police with a floor plan of the apartment. Later evidence points to an extrajudicial assassination.

December 8, 1969: The FBI attempts a similar ambush in Los Angeles, apparently targeting Elmer "Geronimo" Pratt of the Black Panthers. The initial police gunfire aims at Pratt's bed, while he is sleeping on the floor. Six Panthers are wounded and thirteen are arrested.

December 12, 1969: The U.S. Justice Department says that it will investigate the killings of Black Panthers Fred Hampton and Mark Clark by Chicago police.

December 15, 1969: "A Matter of Simple Justice," a report by President Nixon's Task Force on Women's Rights and Responsibilities, is transmitted to Nixon but not released publicly until April 1970. It becomes the basis of the Women's Equality Act of 1971.

December 31, 1969: The U.S. death toll in Vietnam reaches 40,024.

The 1970s

1970

January 1, 1970: Former civil rights activist and Newark community organizer Carl Wittman drafts and publishes "A Gay Manifesto," which becomes a defining document of the gay liberation movement.

January 13, 1970: Guards at Soledad state prison shoot and kill three black inmates and wound a white inmate in the maximum security yard. After a hearing in which black inmates are not permitted to testify, the shootings are ruled justifiable homicide. Thirty minutes later, a white guard, John Mills, dies after being thrown from a third-floor tier.

January 20, 1970: Timothy Leary is sentenced to ten years in prison on marijuana charges.

February 14, 1970: Three Soledad inmates—George Jackson, Fleeta Drumgo, and John Cluchette—are indicted for first-degree murder of prison guard John Mills. They become known as the Soledad Three.

February 20, 1970: A jury finds five of the Chicago Seven defendants not guilty of conspiracy but guilty of incitement and two defendants, John Froines and Lee Weiner, not guilty of any charges. The verdicts and contempt citations are later addressed by the Seventh Circuit Federal Court of Appeals. Street demonstrations and battles break out across the country in response to the verdicts; in Isla Vista, a California Bank of America branch is burned to the ground.

February 25, 1970: San Quentin inmate Fred Billingslea is tear-gased in his cell, beaten, and dies. Inmates petition for a hearing.

February 28, 1970: The U.S. Seventh Circuit Court of Appeals overturns Judge Hoffman's denial of bail; the Chicago Seven are freed on appeal.

March 2–4, 1970: Students at the University of Illinois at Champaign protest on-campus recruitment by General Electric, General Motors, Dow Chemical, Lockheed, U.S. Steel, and Standard Oil. The National Guard is called in.

March 6, 1970: Three Weathermen—Terry Robbins, Diana Oughton, and Ted Gold—die in a New York townhouse explosion from nail bombs being prepared for possible use at a New Jersey military base. Two survivors, Cathy Boudin and Kathy Wilkerson, escape the blast.

April 22, 1970: Twenty million Americans join celebrations and rallies for the first Earth Day. Nixon prepares a major environmental legislative package.

April 23, 1970: Yale president Kingman Brewster says he is "appalled and ashamed that things should have come to pass that I am skeptical of the ability of Black revolutionaries to achieve a fair trial anywhere in the United States." Brewster is commenting on the New Haven murder trial of Bobby Seale and seven Panthers accused in the death of Alex Rackley on May 20, 1969. Brewster is also speaking in anticipation of a huge May 1 "Free Bobby" rally led in part by the Chicago Seven.

April 28, 1970: Vice President Spiro Agnew calls for Kingman Brewster's resignation.

April 30, 1970: U.S. troops invade Cambodia with American airpower and advisers alongside South Vietnamese ground troops. The operation stalls and becomes the focus of an international outcry.

May 1–3, 1970: A nationwide student strike is called in response to the Cambodian invasion. Hundreds of campuses shut down for the semester. Fifteen thousand rally at the New Haven Green, expanding their protest of the Panther trial to Nixon's invasion of Cambodia.

May 4, 1970: On the fourth day of anti-Nixon, anti–Cambodia invasion protests, the occupying Ohio National Guard shoots four Kent State University students and wounds nine others. The victims are shot in the back or from a significant distance. The four killed are Allison Krause, Jeffrey Miller, Sandra Scheuer, and William Schroader. Those wounded are Alan Canfora, John Cleary, Thomas Grace, Dean Kahler (paralyzed), Joseph Lewis, Douglas MacKenzie, James Russell, Robert Stamps, and Douglas Wrentmore. Crosby, Stills, Nash, and Young compose "Ohio" in response. Nixon and law enforcement authorities blame a sniper, an allegation known to be false.

May 6, 1970: The escalation of the war into Cambodia and the shooting at Kent State stir protests across the world. Students demonstrate in Montreal, Calcutta, Caracas, Canberra, and Auckland. From Vatican City, the pope denounces the escalation of the war.

May 8, 1970: In Australia, the first moratorium against the Vietnam War is held; 120,000 Australians participate across the nation.

May 10, 1970: The National Guard Association in Washington, DC, is bombed by the Weathermen as a response to the recent killings at Kent State. In June, they set off a bomb at the New York Police Department headquarters. In late July, the Weathermen bomb the U.S. Army post at the Presidio in San Francisco to commemorate the eleventh anniversary of the Cuban revolution. In October, they bomb the Marin County Courthouse in response to the murders of Jonathan Jackson, William Christmas, and James McClain. That same month, a traffic court in Queens is damaged by a Weather bomb set off in response to prison riots at the adjacent Queens Branch House of Detention. Days later, an all-women faction of the Weathermen bomb the Harvard Center for International Affairs in response to the arrest of Angela Davis.

May 14, 1970: Phillip Lafayette Gibbs, a twenty-one-year-old Jackson State University student, and James Earl Green, a seventeen-year-old high school student, are killed by Mississippi police and troopers. About 100 students protesting the killings at Kent State were inflamed by a false rumor that civil rights leader Charles Evers and his wife had been killed. In addition to two deaths, twelve other Jackson State students are hit by gunfire: Fonzie Coleman, Redd Wilson, Leroy Kenter, Vernon Weakley, Gloria Mayhorn, Patricia Ann Sandrers, Willie

Woodard, Andrea Reese, Stella Spinks, Climmie Johnson, Tuwaine Davis, and Lonzie Thompson. More than 460 police rounds strike the building, including every window facing the street on every floor.

May 15, 1970: Tom Charles Huston, a young right-wing activist on the White House staff, recommends stepped-up illegal counterintelligence operations against antiwar activists and radicals "who pose a major threat to internal security." Huston believes that FBI programs under Hoover are inadequate and proposes circumventing them. "The campus is the battleground of the revolutionary protest movement," he writes. The plan advocates burglary, electronic surveillance, and even opening of the mail of individuals determined to be domestic radicals by the administration.

July 1, 1970: The most liberal abortion laws to date go into effect in the state of New York. The law provides a referral system for women seeking abortions and lowers the cost of services. Women without insurance are provided free services.

July 14, 1970: H. R. Haldeman, on behalf of Nixon, approves Huston's recommendations. Seeking to avoid conflict with Hoover, "[Nixon] would prefer that the thing simply be put into motion on the basis of this approval."

August 7, 1970: Several of the inmate petitioners in the Billingslea case are in a Marin County courtroom where one of them, James McClain, is on trial for assaulting a San Quentin guard shortly after Billingslea's death. Two others, Ruchell Magee and William Christmas, are present as witnesses.

August 7, 1970: Seventeen-year-old Jonathan Jackson enters the Marin courtroom and attempts to free the three men, "and all political prisoners," by force. He takes five hostages, including Judge Harold Haley and three women jurors, and leaves the courthouse in a van. Guards open fire at the van, killing Jackson, McClain, and Christmas. The judge is killed as well. Ruchell Magee is wounded. Jonathan Jackson is the younger brother of twenty-eight-year-old Soledad prisoner George Jackson, serving a term of one year to life—his criminal record consists of driving without a license as a juvenile, theft of a motorbike, and accessory in a $70 armed robbery. Because he is serving a potential life sentence, he will receive a mandatory death penalty if convicted in the murder of a Soledad guard on January 13. George Jackson is now a Panther field marshal and the leader of a widespread insurgent prisoner movement. Guns carried by Jonathan Jackson are registered to Angela Davis.

August 14, 1970: A warrant is issued for Angela Davis, charging her with kidnapping and murder. Angela Davis disappears. FBI and police raids occur in several black communities.

August 24, 1970: Sterling Hall at the University of Wisconsin at Madison is bombed by four radical students, in the 3:00 a.m. hour. One physics researcher, Robert Fassnact, is killed in the blast, and four others are injured. Brothers Dwight and Karl Armstrong and David Fine, three of the four bombers, serve time in prison and are later paroled. The fourth bombing suspect, Leo Burt, is never found.

August 29, 1970: *Los Angeles Times* reporter Ruben Salazar is killed by a tear gas canister fired by a Los Angeles sheriff's deputy into the Silver Dollar Café during a Chicano Moratorium march of 30,000 in East Los Angeles. Two others are killed—Gustav Montag and Lynn Ward—and hundreds are arrested in a tear gas barrage. The coroner's jury rules there is no cause for action against the deputy who shot Salazar, a well-known critic of the police and authorities.

September 1970: The trial of the Panther Twenty-one begins in New York.

September 4, 1970: Senator Salvador Allende is elected president of Chile, the first socialist democratically chosen in Latin America.

September 13, 1970: Timothy Leary escapes from the California Men's Colony West in San Luis Obispo. His escape is aided by the Weathermen, who are funded by the Brotherhood of Eternal Love, a network of acid dealers in Southern California.

September 18, 1970: The second moratorium against the Vietnam War is held in Australia, with 120,000 participating; 300 are arrested.

October 1970: George Jackson's book of prison writings, *Soledad Brother,* becomes a best seller.

October 13, 1970: Angela Davis is arrested by FBI agents at a Holiday Inn near Times Square.

October 20, 1970: Timothy Leary is granted asylum in Algeria with his wife, Rosemary. Leary is harbored initially by the Black Panthers and Eldridge Cleaver, who is also in exile in Algeria.

October 22, 1970: Chilean Army officers with CIA support shoot and kill General Rene Schneider, commander of the Chilean Army and a defender of constitutional process.

October 24, 1970: Chile's parliament confirms Allende as president, 153–35.

November 4, 1970: Nixon orders a coup against Allende. The CIA director quotes President Nixon saying, "Make the economy scream." The CIA plans to foster "a coup climate by propaganda, disinformation, and terrorist activities."

1971

March 1, 1971: In response to the recent invasion of Laos, the Weather Underground bombs the U.S. Capitol Building in Washington, DC, damaging a bathroom, a congressional barbershop, and tables in a dining room. In August, Weather bombs the Office of California Prisons in Sacramento and the Department of

Corrections in San Francisco. The bombings are in response to the murder of George Jackson. In September, the Weather Underground bombs the New York Department of Corrections building in Albany in response to murders at Attica state prison. In October, the government-funded Center for International Studies at MIT is bombed by Weather.

May 1–3, 1971: May Day antiwar demonstrations in Washington, organized primarily by Rennie Davis, utilize mobile tactics on a mass basis, spreading nonviolent direct action by small groups. Seven thousand are arrested and held in preventive detention in Robert F. Kennedy Stadium.

May 13, 1971: The Panther Twenty-one trial ends in jury acquittals on all charges.

May 24, 1971: Jurors in the case against Ericka Huggins and Bobby Seale declare a mistrial in the murder case of Alex Rackley.

May 25, 1971: New Haven judge Harold Mulvey drops the charges against Ericka Huggins and Bobby Seale, citing massive publicity as the reason he cannot retry them.

June 13, 1971: The *New York Times* begins publishing the Pentagon Papers, a classified multivolume history of the Vietnam War that vindicates the critics' case.

Mid-June 1971: In response to the Pentagon Papers, Nixon creates the White House "plumbers' unit" tasked with plugging all national security leaks, wiretapping suspected leaders, neutralizing Ellsberg, and breaking into his psychiatric files in Beverly Hills. Nixon aide Charles Colson says, "We might be able to put this bastard into a helluva situation and discredit the new left." The unit hires G. Gordon Liddy, a former FBI agent, and E. Howard Hunt, a former CIA agent. Both are later involved in the Watergate break-in at the offices of the Democratic National Committee in 1972.

June 28, 1971: Daniel Ellsberg turns himself in for illegally possessing secret documents. Before he surrenders, he announces that he has given the Pentagon study to the press.

June 30, 1971: The right of anyone eighteen years old to vote in federal elections is approved by Congress and ratified by the states as the Twenty-sixth Amendment. The proposal, introduced in every congressional session since World War II, had never previously passed either house of Congress.

July 28, 1971: E. Howard Hunt, a key figure in both the Bay of Pigs and the Watergate break-in, sends a memo to presidential counselor Charles Colson on the subject of "Neutralization of Ellsberg," recommending the theft of psychiatrist's files, among other actions.

August 16, 1971: A memo from presidential adviser John Dean to H. R. Haldeman and John Ehrlichman, "Dealing with Our Political Enemies," says, "Stated a bit more bluntly—how can we use the available federal machinery to screw our political enemies." The list includes names of peace activists, civil rights leaders, George McGovern staff, labor leaders, elected officials, celebrities, and business-men against the war.

August 21, 1971: George Jackson, leaving a meeting with his lawyer at San Quen-tin, is involved in a contested confrontation with guards, who claim he is armed and attempting to escape. Three guards and two inmates are killed. Sprinting across the yard, Jackson is shot twice in the leg, then in the back while crawling on all fours. Guards claim he is hiding a gun under an Afro wig. His lawyer, Steve Bingham, charged with passing the gun, fears assassination and goes underground for fourteen years.

August 22, 1971: Hundreds of inmates in Attica state prison in upstate New York engage in a silent fast to protest the killing of George Jackson in San Quentin. In July, the Attica inmates issued a manifesto against prison conditions modeled after one written in Folsom prison. It said in part, "The program which we are submitted to under the façade of rehabilitation, is relative to the ancient stupidity of pouring water on a drowning man, inasmuch as we are treated for our hostilities by our program administrators with their hostility as medication." The manifesto called for peaceful change and received no response.

September 9, 1971: Twelve hundred inmates take over Attica prison, holding hostage thirty-eight guards and personnel. The incident is spontaneous, triggered by an incident in the yard the day before. The inmates choose a negotiating com-mittee to promote their July demands.

September 12, 1971: A committee of observers, including Clarence Jones, the publisher of the *Amsterdam News*; political leaders Arthur Eve and Herman Ba-dillo; journalist Tom Wicker; and attorney William Kunstler predict an Attica "massacre" if Governor Nelson Rockefeller fails to commence talks.

September 13, 1971: Seventeen hundred New York troops, police, and prison guards attack the Attica strikers at dawn. Forty-three people, including 34 inmates, are killed, and 200 are wounded. Sixty-two inmates are ultimately indicted on 1,289 counts; one state trooper is indicted for reckless endangerment. Among the dead is Sam Melville.

October 1, 1971: The late George Jackson is indicted for murder in the confronta-tion in which he died. First-degree murder indictments are issued for six survivors of August 21, 1971: Hugo Pinell, John Spain, Luis Talamantez, David Johnson, Willie Tate, and Fleeta Drumgo. They become the San Quentin Six.

1972

January 27, 1972: Operation GEMSTONE, G. Gordon Liddy's $1 million proposal for taking out the political Left and other opposition, includes mugging and kidnapping antiwar leaders, breaking in and surveilling Democratic targets, and using prostitutes at the Democratic National Convention. The plan is rejected by Attorney General John Mitchell. Liddy continues as general counsel of the Committee to Re-elect the President. Nixon insists that parts of Gemstone be implemented.

February 18, 1972: The California Supreme Court abolishes the death penalty. The decision has an immediate impact on Angela Davis, who has been denied bail because she is charged with capital offenses. If the death penalty is stricken, the rationale for bail is erased. She receives bail on February 23.

February 21–28, 1972: President Nixon visits China, signaling the normalization of relations with a communist nation.

February 28, 1972: The Angela Davis trial begins in Northern California. Charges against her are conspiracy, kidnapping, and murder. Two hundred defense committees form across the U.S., 67 more in countries around the world.

March 22, 1972: The Equal Rights Amendment is approved by Congress after passing in the Senate. It is then sent to the states for ratification, where it falls one state short of two-thirds after a seven-year deadline.

March 27, 1972: The two surviving Soledad defendants, John Cluchette and Fleeta Drumgo, are found not guilty on murder charges. They return to prison to continue serving indeterminate sentences. Cluchette is later released on May 23, 1972; Drumgo, on August 25, 1976.

May 3, 1972: Ellsberg transfers hundreds of classified pages of the Pentagon Papers to Representative Ronald Dellums's aide, Mike Duberstein, to place in the *Congressional Record* for May 10 and 11.

May 19, 1972: The Weathermen bomb the Pentagon in response to increased air attacks in Vietnam.

May 28, 1972: James McCord and a team of Cuban exiles loyal to E. Howard Hunt break into Democratic National Headquarters in the Watergate building, place electronic bugging devices in phones, and steal documents from files.

June 4, 1972: Angela Davis is found not guilty on all three charges of conspiracy, kidnapping, and murder.

June 17, 1972: The Liddy team carries out a second Watergate break-in. A security guard discovers a taped door and calls the police, who arrest five burglars. Four Nixon officials plead guilty eventually to cover-up, destruction, and secretion of documents; obstruction of official investigations; subornation of perjury; and offers of money and executive clemency to secure silence.

July 1972: The first issue of *Ms.* magazine is released.

November 7, 1972: President Nixon defeats opponent George McGovern in a landslide reelection victory.

1973

January 22, 1973: The Supreme Court rules in *Roe v. Wade* that access to abortion in the first three months of pregnancy is a constitutional right for women.

January 27, 1973: The Paris Peace Accords are signed, guaranteeing the presence of North Vietnamese troops in South Vietnam, talks with the Provisional Revolutionary Government, and the release of all U.S. POWs.

January 28, 1973: The espionage trial of Daniel Ellsberg and Anthony Russo begins.

February 27–May 8, 1973: Members of AIM occupy the hamlet of Wounded Knee and are surrounded by tribal police, state troopers, FBI agents, and undercover U.S. Army commanders. The siege lasts for seventy-one days. Two of the occupiers, Frank Clearwater and Lawrence Lamont, are fatally shot by federal agents on April 17 and April 27, respectively.

March 29, 1973: The last U.S. combat troops leave Vietnam.

April 3, 1973: A jury votes 11–1 to acquit Ruchell Magee of his murder charge, finds him not guilty of aggravated kidnapping, and votes in favor of a lesser charge of simple kidnapping. Nevertheless, he is retried for aggravated kidnapping. In 1974, he pleads guilty, then states that he was coerced. Finally, in August 1974 he pleads guilty to the kidnapping charge and is sentenced to life imprisonment. In 1976, the trial of the San Quentin Six—the longest at that point in California history—ends with not guilty (on forty-six counts) for Luis Talamantez, Fleeta Drumgo, and Willie Tate; a single count of simple assault for David Johnson; felony assault for Hugo Pinnell; and first-degree murder for John Spain. Spain is later released in the mid-1980s, and Pinnell remains in prison along with Magee.

April 27, 1973: Pentagon Papers trial judge William Byrne releases an April 15 disclosure that G. Gordon Liddy and E. Howard Hunt burglarized the offices of Ellsberg's psychiatrist on September 3, 1971.

May 10, 1973: The House votes for the first time to cut off all funding for U.S. combat, including bombing. Nixon promises to veto and then agrees to compromise, which permits bombing to continue until August 15. An effort to cripple the measure dies on a 204–204 tie vote in the House after heavy activist lobbying.

May 11, 1973: All charges against Ellsberg and Russo are dismissed by Judge William Byrne after the government claims to have lost evidence of wiretapping against Ellsberg.

May 17, 1973: The Senate Watergate committee opens televised hearings into the Watergate break-in.

May 18, 1973: The Weather Underground bombs the 103rd Police Precinct in Queens, damaging three police cruisers. The bombing is in response to the murder of a black ten-year-old, Clifford Glover, by a white police officer. A nearby off-duty Transit Authority patrolman is slightly injured by the blast. In late September 1973, Weather bombs the Latin American section of the International Telephone and Telegraph Corporation in New York, in response to the U.S.-backed coup against Allende in Chile.

August 15, 1973: The congressional deadline is reached for ending any further direct or indirect funding of U.S. combat forces in South Vietnam.

September 11, 1973: With U.S. support, General Augusto Pinochet launches air and ground operations against Chile's presidential palace, overthrowing Allende's government and leaving Allende dead in the process. Within days, the Pinochet dictatorship rounds up, tortures, and executes at least 4,000 targeted Chileans, largely leaders and activists in social movements.

October 2, 1973: Senators Ted Kennedy, Tom Harken, and others launch hearings into the U.S. role in the Chilean coup. In 1975 and 1976, Congress establishes human rights as a legal criterion in U.S. foreign policy and bans military assistance, credits, and cash sales of weapons to Chile. The administration ignores the new laws.

October 17, 1973: The Arab oil-producing nations in the Organization of Petroleum-Exporting Countries announce that they will embargo oil from nations allied with Israel, impacting the United States, Western Europe, and Japan.

November 17, 1973: The Greek military, using tanks, crushes 5,000 protesters occupying Athens Polytechnic University, killing 24 civilians. "The memorialization of the Polytechnic was the major legitimizing incident of the democratization process in Greece." Shortly after, a new guerrilla group is formed, named "November 17" after the date of the 1973 military repression. It continues until 2004, killing approximately the same number as died at the hands of the military in November 1973.

1974

March 6, 1974: The Department of Health, Education, and Welfare office in San Francisco is bombed by the Weathermen in response to the forced sterilization of poor women and cuts in welfare funding. In June, they bomb the Gulf Oil building in Pittsburgh in response to the company's involvement in the Portuguese colonial war in Angola.

March 18, 1974: The oil embargo against the United States is lifted, ending the five-month oil crisis. Syria and Libya do not agree to end the embargo.

July 27–30, 1974: The House Judiciary Committee votes for three impeachment counts after nine months of investigation, charging Nixon with obstruction of justice, abuse of authority while in office, and impeding impeachment proceedings by defying eight subpoenas for recorded White House conversations and other evidence.

August 9, 1974: President Nixon resigns, and Gerald Ford takes office.

December 6–11, 1974: Tens of thousands mourn U Thant; Burmese students take his coffin and bury it at the former Rangoon University Student Union, which was previously destroyed by Ne Win. Students and monks guard the makeshift burial site until Burmese troops are sent in to recover the body. Nine are killed in protests following the removal of Thant's body.

1975

January 28, 1975: The Weather Underground bombs the State Department building in DC in response to an increase in aid to South Vietnam. No one is injured.

Spring 1975: A right-wing covert assassination network, Operation Condor, is formed in Latin America under Chilean leadership. The intelligence services of Argentina, Brazil, Bolivia, Chile, Paraguay, and Uruguay take part. They carry out killings, abductions, disappearances, and torture across the Southern Cone of Latin America.

May 1, 1975: The Vietnam War ends with the complete collapse of the Saigon regime.

May 11, 1975: Charges against Daniel Ellsberg and Anthony Russo are dismissed by Federal Judge Matthew Byrne in Los Angeles. The dismissal is based on new evidence of a secret White House "plumbers" unit, wiretapping, break-ins at Ellsberg's psychiatrist's office, and files improperly removed upon presidential orders. On the same day, it is announced that Attorney General John Mitchell has been indicted, to be followed by H. E. Haldeman, John Erlichman, Charles Colson, and others. The U.S. Senate Watergate hearings begin one week later.

June 26, 1975: Shooting between AIM members and FBI agents on the Pine Ridge, South Dakota, reservation leaves three dead—AIM member Joseph Stuntz and FBI Agents Ron Williams and Jack Coler. AIM leader Leonard Peltier is convicted of the murders of the FBI agents and is sentenced to two consecutive life terms.

1976

September 21, 1976: Right-wing Cuban exiles, acting for Pinochet, kill Chilean diplomat Orlando Letelier and his twenty-six-year-old American aide, Ronni Moffitt, with a car bomb in Washington, DC. Moffitt's husband, Michael, survives the explosion. CIA director George Bush falsely blames the killings on a Chilean leftist faction. Letelier was foreign defense minister under Allende and the leader of a global human rights lobby against Pinochet.

December 1976: The remaining members of the Weather Underground disband. In total, they conducted approximately twenty bombings of various corporate and military sites.

Research on this Timeline was done by Emily Louise Walker.

Additional assistance was given by Alci Rengifo and Rachel DiFranco.

For a comprehensive timeline on European movements in the 1960s, visit http://www.1968ineurope.sneakpeek.de/index.php/chronologies.

❧ Notes ❧

NOTES TO INTRODUCTION

1. Kristin Ross, *May '68 and Its Afterlives* (Chicago: University of Chicago Press, 2002), 1.

2. Jay Stevens, *Storming Heaven* (New York: Grove Press, 1998), xix, cited in Carol Brightman, *Sweet Chaos: The Grateful Dead's American Adventure* (New York: Simon and Schuster, 1999), 24–25.

3. *SF Chronicle,* June 9, 2002.

4. Barack Obama, *The Audacity of Hope* (New York: Crown, 2006), 29.

5. Bill Clinton, *My Life* (New York: Knopf, 2004).

6. The phrase may have risen in collective conversation among scholars looking back. One source might have been the late Arthur Marwick, who employed the phrase to refer to 1958–1974 in his book *The Sixties* (New York: Oxford University Press, 1998). There is no book titled "The Long Sixties." Mark Hamilton Lytle's *America's Uncivil Wars: From Elvis to the Fall of Richard Nixon* (New York: Oxford University Press, 2006) covers the extended time period. The phrase appears as the subtitle in Mim Scala's *Diary of a Teddy Boy*: *A Memoir of the Long Sixties* (Dublin: Lilliput Press, 2001), and also as the title of a proposed curriculum on gay/lesbian/transgender studies by Ian Lekus, in Organization of American Historians' *Magazine of History* 20, no. 2 (March 2006): 32–38.

7. The top counterinsurgency adviser to Gen. David Petraeus, Lt. Col. David Kilcullen, advocated a "global Phoenix program" in the *Small Wars and Insurgencies Journal* (September–November 2004). Congressional hearings in 1971 established that the Phoenix program, created by the CIA, resulted in the killing of 20,587 Vietcong suspects in two years, with truncheon and electric shock treatments widely used. Kilcullen wrote in 2004 that Phoenix was "unfairly maligned" and "highly effective."

8. Obama, *The Audacity of Hope,* 36.

9. Obama told the *New York Times Magazine* on November 4, 2007, that "the Democrats have been stuck in the arguments of Vietnam, which means that either you're a Scoop Jackson Democrat or you're a Tom Hayden Democrat and you're suspicious of any military action. And that's just not my framework."

10. *NY Times,* May 15, 2009.

11. Certainly other periods from the American Revolution through the New Deal were equally or more critical in American history, but these earlier times were focused on one grand issue, such as independence or abolition, whereas the sixties were multi-issue and thoroughly global.

12. Although named for the fifteenth-century court adviser Niccolò Machiavelli, they have arisen in monarchies, dictatorships, and democracies, though in differing forms. The Machiavellians are broader than a ruling class. They are not simply the owners of major wealth or the heads of large institutions. The Machiavellians are the strata of power-wielders among the elites that C. Wright Mills described in *The Power Elite* (New York: Oxford University Press, 1956). Typically, they move easily within the overlapping circles of the political, economic, military, media, entertainment, and university elites.

13. Harvey Mansfield, "Introduction," in Niccolò Machiavelli, *The Prince* (Chicago: University of Chicago Press, 1998), vii.

14. Machiavelli, *The Prince,* 71; emphasis added.

15. Ibid., 70.

16. Mansfield, "Introduction," x, xiv.

17. Assistant Secretary of Defense John McNaughton, memo to Robert McNamara, in *The Pentagon Papers* (1967). McNaughton's other reasons included 20 percent to keep South Vietnam from Chinese control and 10 percent "to permit the people of SVN to enjoy a better, freer way of life."

18. Marxists speak of "contradictions within the ruling class" with reference to clashing material interests at the highest levels, an important concept. The economic differences between Northern industry and Southern agriculture over free versus slave labor in the nineteenth century was only one such example. The sharpest differences are often over the policy interests of the state and nation. Although the Kennedy-Hoover conflicts were personal, they were also over differing views of the nature of the Soviet threat and the importance of civil rights to the country's global image. The Kennedys and Hoover managed to agree over illegally wiretapping Dr. Martin Luther King while still plotting to remove each other from power.

19. John Lewis Gaddis, *The Cold War: A New History* (New York: Penguin, 2005), 165; emphasis added.

20. Ibid., 162.

21. Ibid., 163. See National Security Council memo, "National Security Council Directive on Office of Special Projects," June 18, 1948, in *FRUS: 1945–1950: Emergence of the Intelligence Establishment* (Washington, DC: GPO, 1996), 714, cited in ibid.

22. Gaddis, *The Cold War,* 163.

23. The Chicago conspiracy trial, for example, is remembered as a continual stream of chaos in the courtroom. In fact, the hundreds of contempt citations were imposed in a few short days over the course of a five-month trial. The federal appeals court, reviewing the record, found both the judge and prosecutors guilty of misconduct. A later federal trial on the contempt citations resulted in virtually all of them being erased. Bobby Seale, who was chained and gagged in the most confrontational moment of the trial, was severed from the case, never tried again, and acquitted of conspiracy to murder charges in New Haven for which he had been held in custody for three years.

24. "Restless Youth," September 4, 1968, was presented by CIA director Richard Helms to the president and his adviser Walt Rostow, who had requested the report. Helms noted the "peculiar sensitivity" of a report that violated a law prohibiting the agency from domestic spying. Rather than refuse the assignment, however, Helms urged Johnson to authorize the FBI, the domestic spy agency, to utilize "more advanced techniques" to surveil the New Left. See CIA, "Restless Youth," no. 0613/68, September 1968, sanitized version in files of Walt Rostow, Box #13, Lyndon B. Johnson Library and Museum, Austin, Texas.

25. Jacques Derrida, quoted in Kirby Dick and Amy Ziering Kofman, *Derrida: Screenplay and Essays on the Film* (New York: Routledge, 2005), 62. Derrida, an eminent French philosopher, took the side of the students during May 1968 in Paris.

26. Marcuse, who was my friend and political supporter, had a more complex view than that conveyed in the image of a one-dimensional society. He appealed to those who felt that permissiveness itself was a mode of social control, that all protest movements had been contained, and that such soft power was the mode of social control. That was a prevailing perception in the fifties and midsixties, but it simply could not predict the eruption of social movements on a global scale. Marcuse meant to analyze both the forces of containment and the forces that might "break this containment and explode the society," but he became known for the former. See Herbert Marcuse, *One-Dimensional Man* (Boston: Beacon Press, 1991), xxxii, xxxiii.

27. September 14, 2008, interview.

28. A discussion of Bloody Sunday in terms of complexity theory occurs in Tom Herron and John Lynch, *After Bloody Sunday: Representation, Ethics, Justice* (Cork, Ireland: Cork University Press, 2007), 21–22.

29. Freud, in *Civilization and Its Discontents,* discussed this oceanic feeling as a "bond with the universe" that had to be broken so that the ego/self could begin to subject nature to its will. See Sigmund Freud, *Future of an Illusion* (New York: Norton, 1989), 16; and Sigmund Freud, *Civilization and Its Discontents* (New York: Norton, 1961), 2: 15, 16, 27.

30. Walter Isaacson and Evan Thomas, *The Wise Men* (New York: Simon and Schuster, 1986), 736–737; emphasis added.

31. Richard Flacks, *Making History: The American Left and the American Mind* (New York: Columbia University Press, 1988), 244.

32. Ibid., 246.

33. Jacques Gilard, *Veinte y cuarenta años de algo peor que la soledad* (1988), quoted in Forrest Hylton, *Evil Hour in Colombia* (London: Verso Books, 2006), 1.

34. This view is shared both by the conservative Michael Lind and the progressive *Nation* writer Jonathan Schell in his *The Unconquerable World* (New York: Metropolitan Books, 2003), 95. Schell's analysis seems tilted by his thesis that nonviolence, not revolutionary warfare, is the more powerful force. It may be true that the Tet Offensive did not unfold as planned and that the Vietnamese suffered grievous losses. But it does not follow that an armed offensive dealt only psychological and political blows against the United States and its client regime. It could be as easily argued that the U.S. Vietnam policy, like the Iraq war policy, was designed primarily to impact the American people politically with false promises, official lies, and manipulated body counts.

35. On Korean War history and domestic politics, see David Halberstam, *The Coldest Winter* (New York: Hyperion, 2007); on "the informer as patriot," see Victor Navasky, *Naming Names* (New York: Viking, 1980).

36. On the notion that there are layers of creation myths, from the cosmic to the community level,

I am most indebted to theologian Thomas Berry, *The Dream of the Earth* (San Francisco: Sierra Club Books, 1988), xi. He argues that human beings need a viable creation myth to understand the meaning of their role in the universe; "the deepest crises experienced by any society are those moments of change when the story becomes inadequate for meeting the survival needs of the present situation." The same can be said of national creation myths.

37. See, among many others, Howard Zinn, *A People's History of the United States* (New York: HarperCollins, 1983); James Loewen, *Lies My Teacher Told Me* (New York: Touchstone, 1995); David Stannard, *American Holocaust: The Conquest of the New World* (Oxford: Oxford University Press, 1993).

38. Zinn, *A People's History*, 509.

39. *NY Times*, September 22, 2008

40. Tom Brokaw, *Boom! Voices of the Sixties: Personal Reflections on the '60s and Today* (New York: Random House, 2007).

41. John M. Broder, "Shushing the Baby Boomers," *NY Times*, January 21, 2007.

42. Zinn, *A People's History*, 558–560.

43. Christopher Hitchens, *NY Times Book Review*, December 19, 2004.

44. *NY Times Book Review*, March 27, 2005, in a review of Richard Bradley's *Harvard Rules*.

45. Nina Easton, *Gang of Five: Leaders at the Center of the Conservative Crusade* (New York: Simon and Schuster, 2000), 25–27.

46. Lt. Col. John Nagl, an Iraq battlefield veteran and coauthor of the army's counterinsurgency manual, believes that Vietnam could have been won and that 9/11 proves that "*instability anywhere can be a real threat to the American people here at home.*" Cited in Andrew Bacevich, "The Petraeus Doctrine," *The Atlantic* (October 2008).

NOTES TO CHAPTER ONE

1. Eric Hobsbawm, *Revolutionaries* (New York: New Press, 2001 [1973]), 106.

2. Larry Cable, "Reinventing the Round Wheel: Insurgency, Counterinsurgency, and Peacekeeping Post Cold War," *Small Wars and Insurgencies Journal* (Fall 1993): 230–231.

3. Blair later became Jibreel Khazan.

4. Charles Payne, *I've Got the Light of Freedom: The Organizing Tradition and the Mississippi Freedom Struggle* (Berkeley and Los Angeles: University of California Press, 1995), presents the case for local organizers and movements as the unseen motors of change.

5. Jacquelyn Dowd Hall cited in the excellent work by Glenda Elizabeth Gilmore, *Defying Dixie: The Radical Roots of Civil Rights, 1919–1950* (New York: Norton, 2008), 2.

6. *Hernandez* was a step away from the official U.S. government classification of Latinos as "white persons of Spanish surname" in the 1960 census. *Hernandez* required evidence that persons of Mexican descent constituted a separate class in each given case. Frustrated with the previous generation's failure to win equal treatment by defining themselves as racially "white," the sixties Chicano movement would demand justice as a race distinct from whites and African Americans.

7. Decades later, David Freund, in *Colored Property* (Chicago: University of Chicago Press, 2007), 243–246, documented how business leaders boasted of Royal Oak, my hometown, being "virtually all white," in part due to restrictive zoning. In 1956, when I was a high school junior, a black woman in Royal Oak Township was beaten by masked men in her home and threatened with death. Homeowner associations were mobilized to prevent the sale of homes to blacks or the building of rental housing.

8. Taylor Branch, *Parting the Waters* (New York: Simon and Schuster, 1988), 272; emphasis in original.

9. Ibid., 273.

10. Charles Cobb, *On the Road to Freedom* (Chapel Hill, NC: Algonquin Paperbacks, 2008), 96, is a must-read as a "guided tour of the civil rights trail."

11. Ibid., 142.

12. Branch, *Parting the Waters*, 303. See also Ahmed Kathrada, *Memoirs* (Cape Town, South Africa: Zebra Press, 2004).

13. The United Nations declared 1960 the "Year of Africa," when sixteen independent new African states were admitted, up from four just seven years before.

14. After Lumumba's assassination, black protesters appeared at the UN Security Council chamber chanting Lumumba's name and engaging in a shoving match with guards. Arrested that day were LeRoi Jones and Calvin Hicks. The media were told, for perhaps the first time, that "Negroes" would call themselves "Afro-Americans" from that point on. James Baldwin was emerging as a black prophet

of "the fire next time," reaching mainstream audiences through the *New Yorker* and the *New York Times*. Maya Angelou and Abbey Lincoln, among others, began a dialogue with a young minister named Malcolm X, who until then had avoided voicing support for demonstrations in keeping with Nation of Islam policy. See Peniel Joseph, *Waiting til the Midnight Hour: A Narrative History of Black Power in America* (New York: Owl, 2006), 41–43.

15. Eugene Schwarz, ed., *American Students Organize: Founding the National Student Association after World War II* (New York: Praeger, 2006), 565–566. Praeger received CIA funding during the cold war. For a biography of Allard Lowenstein, see Richard Cummings, *The Pied Piper: Allard Lowenstein and the Liberal Dream* (New York: Grove Press, 1985). Cummings speculates that the CIA arranged a draft deferment for Lowenstein in the early fifties, although he later served in the armed forces. Cummings also builds a case that Lowenstein's many associations with CIA personnel and fronts constitute evidence of secret ties. For more on Lowenstein, see David Harris, *Dreams Die Hard: Three Men's Journey through the Sixties* (San Francisco: Mercury House, 1982). Harris carefully describes the complex web of Lowenstein's ties with CIA-connected individuals and front groups, but draws no definitive conclusion, perhaps because Lowenstein was too individualistic to fit the mode of anyone's agent.

16. Howard Phillips remained a key activist in the Far Right, in the Republican Party, and in the Reagan administration, at one point charged with dismantling antipoverty programs. Tom Huston was the adviser to Richard Nixon who drafted the plan, named after himself, for the mass detention of alleged radicals in time of emergency. See Rick Perlstein, *Nixonland* (New York: Simon and Schuster, 2008).

NOTES TO CHAPTER TWO

1. Albert Camus, *The Rebel* (New York: Vintage, 1956), 15.
2. Henry David Thoreau, *On Civil Disobedience* (New York: Dover, 1993), 9. Thoreau added, in words that would be paraphrased by Mario Savio, that "a minority is powerless while it conforms to the majority; it is not even a minority then; but it is irresistible when it clogs by its whole weight."
3. Tom Hayden, *The Port Huron Statement* (New York: Thunder's Mouth Press, 2005), 45–46.
4. Some of those young liberals remained active for fifty years, including Marcus Raskin and Arthur Waskow, who founded the Institute for Policy Studies.
5. Michael Harrington, *The Other America* (New York: Scribner, 1962); John Kenneth Galbraith, *The Affluent Society* (New York: Houghton Mifflin, 1958).

NOTES TO CHAPTER THREE

1. The funding was to be channeled through the Voter Education Project based in Atlanta. Kennedy officials were "important people in the complex arrangements," demanding "strict secrecy" about the plans. Taylor Branch, *Parting the Waters* (New York: Simon and Schuster, 1988), 515.
2. Ibid., 476.
3. For JFK's comments on "radicals" and "sons of bitches," see Zachary Karabell and Jonathan Rosenberg, *Kennedy, Johnson, and the Quest for Justice: The Civil Rights Tapes* (New York: Norton, 2003), 172.
4. Scott Stossel, *Sarge: The Life and Times of Sargent Shriver* (Washington, DC: Smithsonian Institution Press, 2004), 476.
5. Richard Parker, *John Kenneth Galbraith: His Life, His Politics, His Economics* (New York: Farrar, Straus and Giroux, 2005), 404.
6. The telegram asked, in question 5, "What is your position on the proposals, mentioned by two congressmen, for a national youth corps serving in constructive peacetime activity abroad in place of military service?" It was signed, in order, by Thomas Hayden, editor, *Michigan Daily*; John Veenstra; David Macleod; Reverend J. Edgar Edwards; and Harold Duerkson, program director, University of Michigan Office of Religious Affairs.

NOTES TO CHAPTER FOUR

1. For credible evidence that RFK established a secret team to investigate his brother's murder and planned to reopen the investigation if he was elected president in 1968, see David Talbot, *Brothers: The Hidden History of the Kennedy Years* (New York: Simon and Schuster, 2007).
2. A huge subculture of conspiracy explorers, including Mark Lane and Staughton Lynd, grew through the late sixties, much like the later culture of questioning around the events of September 11, 2001.

NOTES TO CHAPTER FIVE

1. The congress was a coalition of Mississippi civil rights groups.

2. An exhaustive study of Freedom Summer, based on interviews with the volunteers, was published by Doug McAdam, *Freedom Summer* (New York: Oxford University Press, 1988).

3. There are numerous accounts of Freedom Summer, including the murders of the civil rights workers. See Taylor Branch, *Pillar of Fire: America in the King Years, 1963-65* (New York: Simon and Schuster, 1999); McAdam, *Freedom Summer*; Charles Payne, *I've Got the Light of Freedom* (Berkeley and Los Angeles: University of California Press, 1996).

4. Michael Beschloss, *Taking Charge: The Johnson White House Tapes, 1963–64* (New York: Simon and Schuster, 1997), 439.

5. The Popular Front was a major influence on the New Deal, for example, and Franklin Roosevelt even campaigned in 1936 against left-wing writer Upton Sinclair, who had won the Democratic primary for governor that year.

6. John Dittmer, *Local People* (Champaign: University of Illinois Press, 1994), is an authoritative history of the MFDP in Mississippi.

7. Ibid., 273.

8. Kay Mills, *This Little Light of Mine: The Life of Fannie Lou Hamer* (Lexington: University Press of Kentucky, 2007), 5.

9. Beschloss, *Taking Charge,* 511, Sunday, August 9.

10. Ibid., 498, Monday, August 3.

11. Ibid., August 4.

12. Ibid., 517.

13. Ibid., 516.

14. Reuther had come out of radical social movements in the 1930s to be the leading labor liberal of his time. He and the UAW donated their facility in Port Huron to SDS for its founding convention. One of SDS's founders was Sharon Jeffrey, whose mother, Mildred, was UAW vice president.

15. Dittmer, *Local People,* 293, cites the 1976 Senate Church Committee hearings, book II, final report, 117.

16. William Julius Wilson, *The Declining Significance of Race* (Chicago: University of Chicago Press, 1978). I agree with Payne, *I've Got the Light of Freedom,* who questions Wilson on this point.

NOTES TO CHAPTER SIX

1. Tom Hayden, *The Port Huron Statement* (New York: Thunder's Mouth Press, 2005), 57.

2. For example, in Ann Arbor the rules included what to wear to dinner, curfew times in dorms, the number of feet (three) that had to be on the floor when two people were engaged in open coupling hours. In 1961, we at *The Daily* exposed a dean of women who spied on white coeds seen having coffee with blacks, informed their parents, and in several cases caused their removal from the university. Our exposé led to her resignation. In 1962, curfews were abolished for senior women, and for juniors in 1965. By January 1968, the University of Michigan Regents voted to eliminate all curfews for women in residence halls and liberalized visitation hours. My former colleague on student government, John Feldkamp, opined that "personally, I can't imagine that any mature woman could have intercourse in a dormitory." The regimented system of house mothers soon collapsed. See James Tobin, "The Day *in Loco Parentis* Died," *Michigan Today* (November 2007).

3. Minutes of a meeting between Kerr and the UC legal counsel on November 10, 1964, in which Kerr argued "that we have a responsibility to put people on notice on what becomes subsequently unlawful ... for example[, the notes go on, the] Palace hotel incident." The counsel, Thomas Cunningham, rebuked the president, saying it was "prior restraint to threaten action to be taken at a subsequent time which at the time of its inception was lawful." These and other valuable notes, documents, and interviews are from Robert Cohen, *Freedom's Orator: Mario Savio and the Radical Legacy of the Sixties* (forthcoming).

4. PHS, 60.

5. Bettina Aptheker, *Intimate Politics* (Emeryville, CA: Seal Press, 2006), 153.

6. Clark Kerr, *The Uses of the University* (Cambridge, MA: Harvard University Press, 1966), 86–91.

7. Kerr wrote that research was "so absorbing that faculty efforts can no longer be concentrated on undergraduate instruction as they once were." Ibid., 65.

8. John Dittmer, *Local People* (Champaign: University of Illinois Press, 1994).

9. Mervin Field Poll, cited in Cohen, *Freedom's Orator.* See also Seymour Martin Lipset and Sheldon Wolin, *The Berkeley Student Revolt* (New York: Anchor Doubleday, 1965), 199.

10. Aptheker, *Intimate Politics*, 125.

11. *SF Examiner*, December 4, 1964.

12. The faculty committee was chaired by law professor Ira Michael Heyman, who later became a Berkeley chancellor. Cohen, *Freedom's Orator*, 244.

13. *SF Chronicle*, June 9, 2002, F1.

14. Ibid.

15. Ibid., F3.

16. Ibid.; emphasis added.

17. Cohen, *Freedom's Orator*, 228.

18. Ibid., 232.

19. Ibid., December 6, 1996.

NOTES TO CHAPTER SEVEN

1. See Martin Lee and Bruce Shlain, *Acid Dreams: The Complete Social History of LSD: The CIA, the Sixties, and Beyond* (New York: Grove Press, 1993), 146. The authors describe LSD hitting the streets of Haight-Ashbury on a mass scale in February 1965. They also cite the levels of consumption in 1965 (196). Robert Stone's elegant memoir, *Prime Green* (New York: Ecco Press, 2007), discusses LSD research at the CIA-funded Stanford Research Institute as well.

2. CIA, "Situation Information Report," July 30, 1970, obtained by Carol Brightman in a Freedom of Information Act request years later. See also Carol Brightman, *Sweet Chaos: The Grateful Dead's American Adventure* (New York: Simon and Schuster, 1999), 262, a classic about the Grateful Dead.

3. In modern times, for example, Israel chose to support the growth of Hamas and Islamic student movements in the West Bank so as to undermine the secular nationalism of the Palestine Liberation Organization. In addition, Israel helped the Muslim Brotherhood overall. See Robert Dreyfuss, *Devil's Game: How the U.S. Helped Unleash Fundamentalist Islam* (New York: Metropolitan Books, 2005). There is no doubt that the CIA launched MK-ULTRA, a drug-based mind-control program during the cold war. The program included the use of acid and schemed to dose "socialist or left-leaning politicians in foreign countries so that they would babble incoherently and discredit themselves in public." Lee and Shlain, *Acid Dreams*, 27, 35.

4. Kevin Phillips, *The Emerging Republican Majority* (New York: Arlington House, 1969). This work was first drafted as a memo, "Middle America and the Emerging Republican Majority."

5. Kesey's notion was to "systematically [set] up sudden, unexpected, and downright edgy situations to see what would happen," according to the supportive Charles Perry, *The Haight-Ashbury* (New York: Wenner Books, 2005), 13. The premise was that the "straight" world could not be reached by politics or reason and so had to be rattled and shocked. The corollary was that it did not matter much if straights were "turned off," because they were hopeless anyway.

6. Blurb by Norman Mailer on Jean Stein with George Plimpton, *Edie: American Girl* (New York: Grove Press, 1982). Stein herself continues to be quite principled and progressive and believes the Edie Sedgwick story to be one of the American gone decadent.

7. Interview with Gary Snyder, Berkeley, March 3, 2009.

8. Peter Coyote, *Sleeping Where I Fall* (Berkeley, CA: Counterpoint, 1998), 124.

9. See Mark Hamilton Lytle, *America's Uncivil Wars: The Sixties Era from Elvis to the Fall of Richard Nixon* (New York: Oxford University Press, 2006).

10. John Bryan, *Whatever Happened to Timothy Leary? An Unauthorized History* (Renaissance Press, 1989), 282–284. The Leary speech was in Berkeley on January 11, 1977. He died May 31, 1996, shortly after Kesey told him, "The sixties ain't over til the Fat Lady gets high." Robert Greenfield, *Timothy Leary: A Biography* (New York: Harcourt, 2006), 595.

11. Betty Friedan, *The Feminine Mystique* (New York: Norton, 2001), 20.

12. See Casey Hayden and Mary King, "Sex and Caste: A Kind of Memo," November 18, 1965, in *Liberation* (April 1966).

13. Mark Hamilton Lytle, *America's Uncivil Wars: The Sixties Era from Elvis to the Fall of Richard Nixon* (New York: Oxford University Press, 2006), 287.

14. See Susan Hartmann, *From Margin to Mainstream: American Women and Politics since 1960* (Philadelphia: Temple University Press, 1989).

15. Howard Zinn, *A People's History of the United States* (New York: HarperCollins, 1983), 509.

16. Lytle, *America's Uncivil Wars*, 281.

17. The proposed ERA simply stated that "equality of rights under the law shall not be denied or abridged by the United States or by any State on account of sex."

18. Lytle, *America's Uncivil Wars,* 287. See also Ruth Rosen, *The World Split Open* (New York: Penguin, 2000).

19. See Estelle Friedman, *No Turning Back* (New York: Ballantine Books, 2002), 10.

20. Susan Ferris and Ricardo Sandoval, *The Fight in the Fields* (New York: Harcourt, 1997), 43.

21. The histories include ibid.; Peter Matthiessen, *Sal Si Puede (Escape If You Can): Cesar Chavez and the New American Revolution* (New York: Random House, 1972); and Jacques Levy et al., *Cesar Chavez: Autobiography of La Causa* (New York: Norton, 1975).

22. Marshall Ganz, "The Power of Story in Social Movements," draft copy, Kennedy School of Government, August 2001.

23. Interview with UFW member Jessica Govea, in Arturo Rosales, *Chicano! The History of the Mexican American Civil Rights Movement* (Houston: Arte Público Press, 1997), 142.

24. Ibid., 147.

25. They were not wrong or unpopular. The 1848 treaty, which cut a border through ancient Mexico, guaranteed Mexicans the right to their property, language, and cultural institutions. Over time, however, the federal courts delegated the interpretation of the treaty to the states, the equivalent of the federal government delegating race and reconstruction issues to the Confederate states.

26. The *Los Angeles Times* declared the birth of brown power; see Carlos Muñoz, *Youth, Identity, Power* (London: Verso Books, 1989), 64.

27. Rosales, *Chicano!* 201–203. Salazar, a critic of the Los Angeles police, was shot and killed by a tear gas canister while he was inside the Silver Dollar Café.

28. FBI memo, June 14, 1969.

29. FBI memo, July 27, 1973.

30. Rosales, *Chicano!* 206, citing Edward Escobar, "The Dialectics of Repression: The Los Angeles Police Department and the Chicano Movement, 1968–1971," *Journal of American History* 79 (March 1993): 1505.

31. As a 1981 motion picture, the *Zoot Suit* character was played by Edward James Olmos.

32. As many as 12,000 died in London in 1952, BBC, December 5, 2002. Eighty died in New York City from an inversion in the summer of 1966; Kirkpatrick Sale, *The Green Revolution* (New York: Hill and Wang, 1993), p. 18.

33. Ibid., p. 15.

34. Paul Erlich, Random House, 1968.

35. Lytle, p. 327.

36. Robert Gottlieb, *Forcing the Spring: The Transformation of the American Environmental Movement* (Washington, DC: Island, 2005), p. 145. According to the author, the media reported 1,000 urban communes in New York City alone.

37. Ibid.

38. Industry trade journal quoted in ibid., p. 154.

39. Perlstein, p. 461.

40. Gottlieb, *Forcing the Spring,* p. 183.

41. Roderick Nash, American Environmentalism, p. 257.

42. Ibid., p. 227.

NOTES TO CHAPTER EIGHT

1. According to the Pentagon Papers study, in September 1964 there was "an administration consensus that military pressures against the North would be required at some proximate future date for a variety of reasons ... [and] it is interesting to note that ... one of the preconditions to such strikes had been generally acknowledged as a unity of domestic public opinion in support of such Presidentially authorized action. During the November debates, this is no longer an important factor. Indeed, it is openly conceded that such action is likely to evoke opposition in both domestic and international public opinion. Another interesting aspect of this policy debate was that the question of Constitutional authority for open acts of war against a sovereign nation was never seriously raised." On November 3, Lyndon Johnson was reelected; on the same day the president's interagency task force on Vietnam, headed by Walt Rostow, began drafting policy options that would escalate the war, Senator Gravel, ed., *The Pentagon Papers: The Defense Department History of United States Decision-Making on Vietnam* (Boston: Beacon Press, 1971), 111: 13, 113, 116. See also Daniel Ellsberg, *Secrets: A Memoir of Vietnam and the Pentagon Papers* (New York: Viking, 2002).

2. Senator John Stennis of Mississippi, for example, was chairman of the Senate Armed Services Committee.

3. On JFK's plans for Vietnam, see Richard Parker, *John Kenneth Galbraith: His Life, His Economics, His Politics* (New York: Farrar, Straus and Giroux, 2005), 405; and James K. Galbraith, "Exit Strategy: In 1963, JFK Ordered a Complete Withdrawal from Vietnam," *Boston Review* (October–November 2003). On October 4, 1963, a memo from General Maxwell Taylor declared that "all planning will be directed toward preparing RVN [Republic of Vietnam] forces with the withdrawal of all US special assistance units and personnel by the end of calendar year 1965." In a conversation with Daniel Ellsberg, Robert Kennedy said his brother "was absolutely determined not to send ground troops.... We would have fuzzed it up. We would have gotten a government that asked us out or that would have negotiated with the other side. We would have handled it like Laos." Ellsberg, *Secrets*, 195. Robert McNamara confirmed Kennedy's plan for withdrawal by 1965 in a speech at the LBJ Library, May 1, 1995.

4. Ellsberg, *Secrets*, 50–51.

5. In John Lewis Gaddis, *The Cold War: A New History* (New York: Penguin, 2005), 257; also December 7, 1964, LBJ memo in *FRUS: 1964–1968*, I, document 440.

6. Peter Dale Scott, "The Kennedy Assassination and the Vietnam War," in *The Pentagon Papers*, vol. 5, *Critical Essays*; also in Peter Dale Scott et al., *The Assassinations, Dallas, and Beyond* (New York: Vintage, 1976), 407.

7. McNamara notes from June 2, 1964, Honolulu conference, in Ellsberg, *Secrets*, 63.

8. Ellsberg, *Secrets*, 195.

9. John Carter Vincent, director of Far Eastern Affairs, in memo to Dean Acheson, December 23, 1946, cited in Ellsberg, *Secrets*, 252.

10. William Polk, *Violent Politics* (New York: HarperCollins, 2007). Polk was a member of the State Department Policy Planning Council in 1961. Polk's analysis is that Franklin Roosevelt, before his death, opposed the restoration of French power in Vietnam because "the people of Indo-China are entitled to something better than that" (164). After Roosevelt's death and the heating up of the cold war, Polk says, the United States decided to reject Ho Chi Minh's diplomatic feelers and instead finance most of the French military effort at reconquest through 1954 (167). According to the Pentagon Papers secret history, "US insistence on Ho's being a doctrinaire communist may have been a self-fulfilling prophecy.... The US offered Ho only limited options" (166).

11. Pentagon Papers, in *NY Times*, June 15, 1971.

12. *The Pentagon Papers*, 3: 559.

13. Virginia Carmichael, *Framing History: The Rosenberg Story and the Cold War* (Minneapolis: University of Minnesota Press, 1993), 3; emphasis added.

14. Mark Hamilton Lytle, *Uncivil Wars: The Sixties Era from Elvis to the Fall of Richard Nixon* (New York: Oxford University Press, 2006), 250.

15. Polk, *Violent Politics*, 169.

16. State Department, "Youth and Revolt—Depth and Diversity," November 8, 1967, LBJ Library, University of Texas, RG 59, IAYC records, IATC meeting, Box 1.g.

17. Rick Perlstein, *Nixonland* (New York: Scribner, 2008).

18. In October 1967, I returned from Cambodia with three American prisoners of war (POWs) released by the National Liberation Front (the Vietcong). One of them, Sgt. James Jackson, told me of massive Vietcong and North Vietnamese force preparations in the Mekong Delta where he was held by the guerrillas. Back in Washington, he personally told White House officials that a vast army was moving down the Ho Chi Minh Trail into the south.

19. Tim Wiener, *Legacy of Ashes* (New York: Doubleday, 2007), 285.

NOTES TO CHAPTER NINE

1. Tom Hayden, *Reunion: A Memoir* (New York: Random House, 1988); Jerry Avorn et al., *Up against the Ivy Wall* (New York: Atheneum, 1968); Michael Klare et al., *Who Rules Columbia?* (self-published, June 1968); James Simon Kunen, *The Strawberry Statement* (New York: Wiley Blackwell, 1995); Kirkpatrick Sale, *SDS* (New York: Random House, 1973); and Mark Rudd, *Underground* (New York: William Morrow, 2009).

2. For example, the students exposed the university's ties to the Institute for Defense Analysis, which worked on nuclear weapons and did research on jungle defoliants such as Agent Orange. University defense and foreign policy contracts were nearly one-half the university's overall budget.

3. Rudd, *Underground*, 60.

4. These grievances/demands were as follows: Stop construction of a Columbia gym in Harlem, cut ties to the Institute for Defense Analysis, permit indoor demonstrations, drop criminal charges over

protests at the gym site, rescind academic probation for six students arrested over the institute, and grant amnesty as part of resolving the campuswide strike.

5. Thirteen police were injured, one with a permanent spinal injury, and several hundred students were hurt, eighty-seven of them treated at St. Luke's Hospital adjacent to the campus.

6. See Mitchell Jose Yangson, "The Philippine American Collegiate Endeavor and the San Francisco State College Strike," http://userwww.sfsu.edu/-runamuck/PACEPAPER.htm.

7. William Orrick, "Shut It Down! A College in Crisis," staff report on the SF State strike to the National Commission on the Causes and Prevention of Violence, June 1969, 78.

8. Across the Bay, another TWLF strike was erupting in Berkeley. (Students in Berkeley had initiated a course known as Social Analysis 139x, with Eldridge Cleaver as a lecturer; when Cleaver went into exile, I became his replacement.)

9. Orrick, "Shut It Down!"

10. Ibid., 27.

11. Ibid., 29.

12. Ibid., 29.

13. Ibid., 29–30.

14. Ibid., 120.

15. Ibid., 33.

16. Ibid., 43.

17. Ibid., 45.

18. Yangson, "The Philippine American Collegiate Endeavor," 18.

19. Orrick, "Shut It Down!" 56.

20. Ibid.

21. Rick Perlstein, *Nixonland* (New York: Scribner, 2008), 383.

22. Ibid., 358.

23. Orrick, "Shut It Down!" 59. According to the study team: "It soon became apparent that public relations was a strong suit for the new president.... He appeared to seize upon every opportunity to obtain news coverage and to give broad expression to his point of view on the campus disturbances" (58).

24. Ibid., 52.

NOTES TO CHAPTER TEN

1. Memo from J. Edgar Hoover, "Counter-Intelligence Program, Internal Security, Disruption of the New Left," May 14, 1968, May 17, 1968; emphasis added. I obtained the Hoover memos cited in these pages under a 1976 Freedom of Information Act suit.

2. Hoover memo, March 4, 1968.

3. Hoover memo, October 23, 1968.

4. *Time,* October 18, 1968. Wallace, according to *Time,* was supported by 38 percent of all southerners in mid-October, which meant a larger number of whites.

5. Ibid.

6. On October 21, the Gallup Poll showed Nixon leading by 44 percent to 36. Later that week, Hanoi agreed to talks if the U.S. bombing stopped. On October 31, LBJ announced the halt, and the talks were ready to begin. On November 2, Nixon's lead was shaved to 42–40. According to Theodore White, *The Making of the President* (New York: Scribner, 1978), "had peace become quite clear, in the last three days of the election of 1968, Hubert Humphrey probably would have won the election."

7. Rick Perlstein, *Nixonland* (New York: Scribner, 2008), 545.

8. Ibid., 526. Perlstein's account has him drunk, but Rosen has him overheard describing student radicals as "stupid bastards." According to Rosen's version, Mitchell's words were "Listen, there is no such thing as the New Left. This country is going so far right you are not even going to recognize it." James Rosen, *The Strong Man: John Mitchell and the Secrets of Watergate* (New York: Doubleday, 2008), 104. Rosen is a Washington correspondent for Fox News.

NOTES TO CHAPTER ELEVEN

1. James Rosen, *The Strong Man* (New York: Doubleday 2008), 98. Rosen's biography of Attorney General John Mitchell, which attempts to shift blame for Watergate to John Dean, is based on numerous White House memos released for the first time.

2. Charles A. Thomas, "Blood of Isaac" (e-book), Charles A. Thomas Papers, Kent State May 4 Collection, http://speccoll.library.kent.edu/4May70/IsaacThree.htm.

3. James Moore and Wayne Slater, *Bush's Brain: How Karl Rove Made George W. Bush President* (Hoboken, NJ: Wiley, 2003), 124. Rove's entry-level job consisted of stealing a Chicago Democratic candidate's stationery and inviting one thousand people to a fake party with beer and girls in a local slum. Rick Perlstein, *Nixonland* (New York: Scribner, 2008), 630. Tom Charles Huston, a veteran of the early sixties Young Americans for Freedom organization, prepared an administration plan for opening mail, tapping phones without warrants, breaking into homes, infiltrating student movements, and so on. Nixon was not aloof from these plans; once, he told his staff to "find out who controls [the demonstrators, and] get our guys to rough them up at demonstrations" (519).

4. Philip Caputo, *13 Seconds: A Look Back at the Kent State Shootings* (New York: Penguin, 2005), 98.

5. *NY Times,* May 10, 1970.

6. Ronald Reagan speech to Council of California Growers, April 7, 1970; emphasis added.

7. *NY Times,* May 2, 1970.

8. Helen Thomas, in e-book by Charles Thomas, chap. 3, "Lost Crusades," Charles A. Thomas Papers, Kent State May 4 Collection.

9. Richard Nixon, address to the nation, April 30, 1970, public papers of the president of the United States, Richard Nixon, 1970 National Archives, Washington, DC, 405–409; emphasis added.

10. H. R. Haldeman notebooks, Charles A. Thomas Papers, Kent State May 4 Collection.

11. Haldeman notebooks, "O805 K&Z," ibid. "K&Z" refers to Henry Kissinger and Ron Ziegler, who met with the president that morning.

12. Caputo, *13 Seconds,* 22; emphasis added.

13. Thomas, "Lost Crusades."

14. *NY Times,* May 2, 2007. The tape, originally kept by the Justice Department, was retrieved from materials donated to the Yale archives by a lawyer who had defended the shooting victims. The order may have come from General Robert Canterbury of the Ohio National Guard, who first ordered the students to disperse, then directed the troops to advance with M-1 rifles locked and loaded, according to the *Times* account. Thirty minutes before the killings, Canterbury told a Kent professor that "these students are going to have to find out what law and order is all about." Peter Davies, in Scott Bills, *Kent State/May 4: Echoes through a Decade* (Kent, OH: Kent State University Press, 1988), 153.

15. Caputo, *13 Seconds,* 71.

16. Ibid., 177. The full name of the Scranton Commission was the President's Commission on Campus Unrest to the American People, 1970.

17. FBI report, sixth increment released, vol. 3, 746, Charles A. Thomas Papers, Kent State May 4 Collection.

18. Bills, *Kent State,* 152.

19. Bork's grand jury resulted in indictments of eight National Guardsmen. But they were acquitted by the judge in 1974 when the federal prosecutor admitted a lack of ballistics evidence and other deficiencies in the case. By acquitting the guardsmen instead of dismissing the charges, the judge effectively prevented the case from ever being brought again. See Davies essay in ibid., 157–158.

20. Caputo, *13 Seconds,* 111.

21. James Michener, *Kent State* (New York: Fawcett Press, 1971).

22. Ibid., 56.

23. On Mitchell, see Rosen, *The Strong Man,* 105. On Viorst, see James Rosen, *Fire in the Streets: America in the 1960s* (New York: Simon and Schuster, 1979), 543.

24. For Orangeburg, see Charles Cobb, *On the Road to Freedom: A Guided Tour of the Civil Rights Trail* (Chapel Hill, NC: Algonquin, 2008), 143–150. For Jackson State, see "Jackson Police Fire on Students," *NY Times,* May 15, 1970, 1.

25. Caputo, *13 Seconds,* 179.

26. Ibid., 181.

27. Ibid., 190.

28. Ibid., 183; emphasis added.

NOTES TO CHAPTER TWELVE

1. *Senate Watergate Report* (New York: Carroll and Graf, 1974), exhibit 35, 720.

2. Ibid., 198.

3. Rick Perlstein, *Nixonland* (New York: Scribner, 2008), 583.

4. Ibid., 583.

5. According to Liddy's autobiography, the plan was to emulate the Texas Rangers by identifying the leaders, kidnapping and drugging them, and holding them in Mexico until the convention was over. G. Gordon Liddy, *Will: The Autobiography of G. Gordon Liddy* (New York: Macmillan, 1996), 197.

6. *Senate Watergate Report*, 88.

7. The 1973 Paris Peace Accords accepted the presence of North Vietnamese combat troops inside South Vietnam, a major American concession two decades after the Geneva conference. This acceptance of reality sheds light on Kissinger's earlier reference to a "decent interval" in his secret talks with Chinese leaders, which meant an opportunity to declare "peace with honor" and withdraw American troops before allowing South Vietnam to collapse. Kissinger's 1971 official briefing book stated to the Chinese that "we want a decent interval. You have our assurance. [Marginal notation in Kissinger's hand.] If the Vietnamese people themselves decide to change the present government, we shall accept it. But we will not make that decision for them." Kissinger then informed Nixon that "we've got to find some formula that holds the thing together a year or two, after which—after a year, Mr. President, Vietnam will be a backwater. If we settle it, say, this October, by January '74, no one will give a damn." "Memorandum of Conversation with Zhou Enlai, June 20, 1972," National Security Archive, George Washington University, 27–37. Kissinger's conversation with Nixon was recorded on White House tapes. *Asia Times Online*, November 23, 2006.

8. Indochina Peace Campaign, "Watergate and the War," 1973.

9. Gerald Nicosia, *Home to War: History of the Vietnam Veterans Movement* (New York: Carroll and Graf, 2004), 106. See also Robert Lifton's classic *Home from the War: Learning from Vietnam Veterans* (New York: Simon and Schuster, 1973).

10. A banner reading "Vietnam Veterans against the War" first appeared in a 1967 New York peace march *before* an influential GI organization of the same name, VVAW, appeared. VVAW's presence was felt at major Washington demonstrations in 1971, in petitions from thousands of naval officers, in rebellions on military bases worldwide, in GI coffee shops near bases, in hundreds of underground GI-oriented newspapers, and even in a giant peace symbol carved in the Mekong Delta. Overall disruption in the armed forces included two hundred thousand draft refusals, ninety-three thousand army desertions (three times the rate in Korea), and 563 "fraggings" (attacks) against officers. Marine Corps historian Col. Robert Heinl wrote in the June 1971 *Armed Forces Journal* that "our army that now remains in Vietnam is in a state approaching collapse, with individual units avoiding or having refused combat, murdering their officers and noncommissioned officers, drug-ridden and dispirited where not near mutinous." Jonathan Neale, *A People's History of the Vietnam War* (New York: New Press, 2003), 149–184.

11. *Time*, May 5, 1975.

12. For a study of the antiwar movement, with sources, see Tom Hayden, *Ending the War in Iraq* (New York: Akashic, 2007).

13. Mark Leibovich, "In the 60's, a Future Candidate Poured Her Heart Out in Letters," *NY Times*, July 29, 2007.

14. Hillary Rodham commencement speech, May 31, 1969, http://www.wellesley.edu/public affairs/commencement/1969/053169Hillary.html.

15. *NY Times*, September 5, 2007.

16. Hillary Rodham, "Children under the Law," *Harvard Educational Review* 43 (1973): 487–514.

17. Clinton supported the 2002 authorization of the Iraq war and attacked Barack Obama for alleged associations with sixties radicals, when she herself had worked on the defense of revolutionary Black Panthers. Carl Bernstein, *A Woman in Charge* (New York: Knopf, 2008), writes that she interned at "the most radical law practice on the West Coast" (82), a firm that defended Panthers and union leaders accused of being communists. Two of the firm's partners were communists themselves.

NOTES TO CHAPTER THIRTEEN

1. Paul Chatt Smith and Robert Allen Warrior, *Like a Hurricane: The Indian Movement from Alcatraz to Wounded Knee* (New York: New Press, 1996), 115.

2. Ibid., 197; emphasis added.

3. Ibid., 213. See also "Army Tested Secret Civil Disturbance Plan at Wounded Knee, Memos Show," *NY Times*, December 3, 1976.

4. Dee Brown, *Bury My Heart at Wounded Knee* (New York: Holt, Rinehart, and Winston, 1970).

5. Vine Deloria, *Custer Died for Your Sins: An American Indian Manifesto* (New York: Macmillan, 1969).

6. Tom Hayden, *The Love of Possession Is a Disease with Them* (New York: Holt, Rinehart, and Winston, 1972).

7. See Vine Deloria, "The Application of the Constitution to American Indians," in Oren Lyons et al., *Exiled in the Land of the Free* (Santa Fe, NM: Clear Light, 1992), 281–316.

8. From an engineering and mining journal, cited in Peter Matthiessen, *In the Spirit of Crazy Horse* (New York: Viking, 1991), 626.

9. U.S. Bureau of Reclamation, *North Central Power Study,* 1971; Matthiessen, *In the Spirit of Crazy Horse,* 104.

10. According to the treaty, signed in 1868 by Gen. William T. Sherman, the United States agreed in Sec. 3 that the "territory [shall be] set apart for the absolute and undisturbed use and occupation of the Indians herein named, and for such other friendly tribes or individual Indians as from time to time they may be willing, with the consent of the United States, to admit amongst them; and the United States now solemnly agrees that no persons, except those herein designated and authorized so to do, and except such officers, agents, and employees of the government as may be authorized to enter upon Indian reservations in discharge of duties enjoined by law, shall ever be permitted to pass over, settle upon, or reside in the territory described in this article, or in such territory as may be added to this reservation for the use of said Indians, and henceforth they will and do hereby relinquish all claims or right in and to any portion of the United States or Territories, except such as is embraced within the limits aforesaid, and except as hereinafter provided." Furthermore, according to Article XVI, "the United States hereby agrees and stipulates that the country north of the North Platte river and east of the summits of the Big Horn mountains shall be held and considered to be unceded Indian territory, and also stipulates and agrees that no white person or persons shall be permitted to settle upon or occupy any portion of the same; or without the consent of the Indians, first had and obtained, to pass through the same; and it is further agreed by the United States, that within ninety days after the conclusion of peace with all the bands of the Sioux nation, the military posts now established in the territory in this article named shall be abandoned, and that the road leading to them and by them to the settlements in the Territory of Montana shall be closed." In exchange, the Indians agreed not to oppose the construction of railroads, attack wagon trains, capture white women or children, and never scalp or kill white men. PBS, Fort Laramie Treaty, *Archives of the West,* http://www.pbs.org/weta/thewest/resources/archives/four/ftlaram.htm.

11. Walt Whitman, "A Death-Sonnet for Custer," *New York Daily Tribune,* July 10, 1876.

12. Twenty-nine U.S. soldiers were killed, nearly all by friendly fire. Lori Liggett, Bowling Green State University, 1998, http://www.bgsu.edu/departments/acs/1890s/woundedknee/WEmscr.html.

13. At the height of the Wounded Knee showdown, on April 30, Nixon was firing John Dean and accepting the staged resignations of H. R. Haldeman and John Ehrlichman.

14. Senator William Fulbright, chairman of the Senate Foreign Relations Committee; Senator Edward Kennedy, chairman of the oversight committee for the BIA and Interior Department; and Senator James Abourezk, a Democrat from South Dakota and chairman of the Subcommittee on Indian Affairs, received the elders' letter, which was also sent to John Ehrlichman, Nixon's chief deputy for domestic policy.

15. When interviewed after their release, eighty-two-year-old Wilbur Reigert, the store proprietor, told reporters the hostages decided to stay in order to save AIM, because "had we not, those troops would have come down here and killed all of these people." Smith and Warrior, *Like a Hurricane,* 208.

16. *NY Times,* December 1, 1975.

17. On April 1, a Harris Poll showed 51 percent in favor of the Indians, with only 21 percent against. An incredible 93 percent said they were following news of the occupation. Matthiessen, *In the Spirit of Crazy Horse,* 69.

18. Buddy Lamont was killed by a sniper bullet at Wounded Knee. According to Matthiessen, his mother's grandparents had been with Crazy Horse at Little Big Horn and her great-aunt and great-uncle had died in the snow at Wounded Knee. Ibid., 78–87.

19. Ibid., 78. Matthiessen quotes McGovern as saying, "We cannot have one law for a handful of publicity-seeking militants and another law for ordinary citizens" (82). Perhaps catering to his constituents, McGovern's statement ignored the official neglect, and indeed complicity, of state and federal officials in the rampant lawlessness of the Pine Ridge Indian police under Wilson.

20. *NY Times,* December 1, 1975.

21. Smith and Warrior, *Like a Hurricane,* 236.

22. Ibid., 267; emphasis added.

23. Ibid.

24. Matthiessen, *In the Spirit of Crazy Horse. Incident at Oglala,* documentary by Robert Redford, Spanish Fork Motion Picture, 1992.

25. Ibid., 269. Dennis Banks, in his important autobiography, puts the number of AIM members arrested nationwide at twelve hundred, leading to at least four major trials on the scale of the Chicago conspiracy. "The idea was to tie up AIM and all its resources in never-ending court battles." Dennis Banks, with Richard Erdoes, *Ojibwa Warrior* (Norman: University of Oklahoma Press, 2004), 213.

26. Durham went on to testify before Congress and speak against AIM across the country, claiming it was a communist-inspired, violent conspiratorial movement.

27. Banks, *Ojibwa Warrior*, 353.

NOTES TO CHAPTER FOURTEEN

1. Roberto Fernandez Retamar, *Caliban and Other Essays* (Minneapolis: University of Minnesota Press, 1989), 18.

2. Jon Lee Anderson, *Che Guevara: A Revolutionary Life* (New York: Grove Press, 1997), 687.

3. Mary-Alice Waters, ed., *Pombo: A Man of Che's Guerrilla, with Che Guevara in Bolivia, 1966–68* (New York: Pathfinder Press, 1997), 148. Pombo was the guerrilla name of Harry Villegas. The guerrilla's diary quotes Che as saying, "This should provide us a lesson for the future: men who once gave their heart and soul for a cause have gotten used to life in an office; they have become bureaucrats, accustomed to giving orders, having everything solved in the office, having everything come to them already worked out" (148).

4. "Wherever a government has come to power through some form of popular consent, fraudulent or not, and maintains at least an appearance of constitutional legality, it is impossible to produce a guerrilla outbreak because all the possibilities of civic struggle have not been exhausted." Che Guevara, *Guerrilla Warfare* (Lincoln, NE: Bison Books, 1998), 27–28.

5. Che Guevara, *Guerrilla Warfare* (Lanham, MD: Rowman and Littlefield, 1997), 50.

6. Castro led an apparently suicidal attack on the dictatorship's Moncada barracks on July 26, 1953. More than 60 of 135 militants were killed. After a famous trial, Fidel was released to build the July Twenty-sixth Movement.

7. "Base communities" was the term describing thousands of small community-based groups that came together as neighbors to study the Bible and apply its radical implications to oppressive conditions in Latin America. This became a religious movement from below, often in opposition to the church as well as the military and state. It became so widespread that the Catholic bishops' meeting in Medellín, Colombia, in 1968 incorporated liberation theology's "special preference" for the poor into formal church doctrine, literature, and services. See Chapter 19.

8. Richard Goodwin, *Remembering America* (New York: Little, Brown, 1988), 201.

9. C. Wright Mills, *Listen, Yankee!* (New York: Ballantine Books, 1960).

10. A declassified 1973 CIA report on counterintelligence programs, named "Family Jewels," included a reference to 1968 "memos on Stokely Carmichael's travels abroad during a time when he had dropped from public view" and a memo "with special attention to links between black radicalism in the Caribbean and advocates of black power in the US." "Potentially Embarrassing Agency Activities," EYES ONLY memo to executive secretary, CIA Management Committee, May 8, 1973, http://www.gwu.edu/~nsarchiv/NSAEBB/NSAEBB222/index.htm.

11. Tom Hayden, *Rebellion in Newark: Official Violence and Ghetto Response* (New York: Vintage, 1967), 69, 71.

12. The "detonator" phrase is from Pablo Rivalta, the Cuban ambassador in Tanzania at the time. Richard Gott, "Introduction," in Che Guevara, *The African Dream: The Diaries of the Revolutionary War in the Congo* (New York: Grove Press, 1999), xxviii.

13. Ibid., xxxi.

14. Rodolfo Saldano, *Fertile Ground: Che Guevara and Bolivia* (New York: Pathfinder Press, 2001), 16.

15. Anderson, *Che Guevara*, 703.

16. Daniel James, ed., "Introduction," in *The Complete Bolivian Diaries of Che Guevara* (Lanham, MD: Cooper Square Press, 2000), 35. According to this introduction, by a retired U.S. Foreign Service officer, the James edition of the diary ignored any editor's discussion of the CIA's role in Bolivia, "adding fuel to the suggestion that the CIA had a hand in this edition" of Che's writings.

17. On April 20, 1967, Debray, Bustos, and a mysterious "journalist" named George Andrew Roth were captured by the Bolivian Army just after they left Che's group. Sixteen American Special Forces troops arrived in May to train a Bolivian battalion of six hundred to one thousand men. Ibid., 75.

18. Goodwin, *Remembering America*, 207.

19. Anderson, *Che Guevara*, 717.

20. Ibid., 726.
21. The SOA identified me as "one of the masters of terrorist planning" in documents divulged by Representative Joseph Kennedy. Lisa Haugaard, "Latin American Working Group," *In These Times*, October 14, 1996.
22. See Tom Hayden, ed., *The Zapatista Reader* (New York: Nation Books, 2002). I originally believed that the Zapatistas and Subcomandante Marcos evolved from a combination of indigenous militants and refugees from the 1968 student massacre in Mexico City. According to John Ross, a group from Monterrey (Linea Proletaria) under the leadership of Adolfo Orive, who had been in Paris during spring 1968, sent organizers into Chiapas in 1976, and a rival *foco* (Las Fuerzas de Liberación Nacional) followed next, making contact with indigenous fighters to form the first Zapatista cells. Marcos himself was a post-1968, post-Tlatelolco attendee at Mexico's National Autonomous University. Communication from researcher/writer John Ross, May 11, 2009.
23. Jeffrey Sachs, *The End of Poverty* (New York: Penguin, 2005), 90.
24. Ibid., 105, 90.
25. According to Sachs, he told the Bolivian Chamber of Commerce that "Germany's hyperinflation had ended in one day, November 20, 1923, and ... I predicted the same for Bolivia. The crowd was startled, and delighted, at the prospect." Ibid., 93.
26. Ibid., 99; emphasis added.
27. Amnesty International 2005 Annual Report for Bolivia.
28. Sachs, *The End of Poverty*, 107.
29. http://www.democracyctr.org/blog/2008/11/clinton-campaign-team-plots-return-to.html. In October 2008, the firm of Greenberg Quinlan Rosner Research posted a job opportunity for "a highly professional individual to work in-country as part of a political campaign in Bolivia."
30. Alvaro Garcia Linera and Jeffrey Webber, "Marxism and Indigenism in Bolivia: A Dialectic of Dialogue and Conflict," *ZNet*, April 25, 2005, http://www.zmag.org/znet/viewArticle/6397.
31. Che Guevara, *The Motorcycle Diaries* (New York: Ocean, 2004), 149; emphasis added.
32. The late Rodolfo Saldano, a Bolivian who fought with Che, offered the view that Bolivia was a "fertile ground" for guerrilla war but had no explanation for the defeat. Saldano, *Fertile Ground*. Another excellent account of the campaign is Waters, *Pombo*. These diaries describe the events from a tactical perspective, offering no general reasons for the failure.
33. Regis Debray, *Praised Be Our Lords* (London: Verso Books, 2007), 110.
34. Ibid., 106.
35. Regis Debray, *Revolution in the Revolution?* (New York: Grove Press, 1967), 84.
36. Greg Grandin, *Empire's Workshop* (New York: Owl Books, 2006), 198.
37. "Like Old Times: US Warns Latin Americans against Leftists," *NY Times*, August 19, 2005.
38. Grandin, *Empire's Workshop*, 44.
39. See the "independent conservative" Web site FreeRepublic.com, which was posting the Che scene as of December 2, 2008, when these words were written.
40. Jorge Castañeda, *The Life and Death of Che Guevara* (New York: Vintage, 1997), 408–410.
41. Korda quoted in Stephanie Holmes, "Che: The Icon and the Ad," *BBC News*, October 5, 2007.
42. Fitzgerald quoted in ibid.
43. Castañeda, *The Life and Death of Che Guevara*, 410.

NOTES TO CHAPTER FIFTEEN

1. Mary-Alice Waters, ed., *Pombo: A Man of Che's Guerrilla, with Che Guevara in Bolivia, 1966–68* (New York: Pathfinder Press, 1997), 41.
2. Ibid., 55.
3. Ibid.
4. Forty-two years later, new documents revealed that police officer Karl Heinz-Kurras was working undercover for the East Germans. Still alive in 2009, Kurras called the shooting an accident and denied that he had been paid by East Germany. It is possible that false records were planted in his files. But if true, the history of Germany would have developed in a different way. The "shot that changed the Republic" in a leftward direction would have been treated differently if the German public thought the killing was the work of an East German agent. See *NY Times*, international ed., May 27, 2009.
5. Ulrike Meinhof, *Everybody Talks about the Weather ... We Don't: The Writings of Ulrike Meinhof* (New York: Seven Stories Press, 2008), 239.

6. Ibid., 249.

7. Ibid., 190.

8. Ibid., 248. One of the arsonists was Andres Baader, who later formed the core of the Baader-Meinhof Gang with Ulrike Meinhof.

9. Ibid., 89.

10. I spent time in Los Angeles with Petra Kelly of the Green Party and on two occasions attended conferences on 1968 with activists such as K. D. Wolff, Eva Quistorp, Peter Schneider, and founders of the counterculture Kommune. We reflected on their direct experiences at the time. I am indebted to a younger generation of German scholars on the sixties led by Martin Klimke, an editor (along with Joachim Schareloth) of *1968 in Europe: A History of Protest and Activism, 1956–1977* (New York: Palgrave Macmillan, 2008). Discussions with the German writer Stefan Aust have been invaluable as well.

11. The German SDS was the Sozialistische Deutscher Studentenbund, the youth branch of the German Social Democratic Party.

12. There were other violent movements on the European continent, in Ireland, and in Quebec, but none with the self-destructive force of the German and Italian ones. Ireland and Quebec were propelled by national independence platforms. In France, the Gauche Prolétarienne and its armed wing, the Nouvelle Résistance Populaire, carried out many actions starting in 1969, but declined in 1973. French youth, of course, were raised in the shadow of Nazi collaboration. Japan, with its own history of militarism, gave rise to significant violence in the sixties as well. See Dorothea Hauser, "Terrorism," in Klimke and Schareloth, eds., *1968 in Europe,* 269.

13. Perversely, the same experience led many members of the RAF to adopt the Palestinian cause against Israel on the grounds that the Israelis were repeating what had been done to them and the Palestinians therefore were the new Jews.

14. James Gilligan, *Violence: Our Deadly Epidemic and Its Causes* (New York: Putnam Adult, 1996).

15. Frantz Fanon, *The Wretched of the Earth* (New York: Grove Press, 2004).

16. "No other white person, not even Lincoln, has been so widely admired among American blacks as has John Brown." David S. Reynolds, *John Brown, Abolitionist: The Man Who Killed Slavery, Sparked the Civil War, and Seeded Civil Rights* (New York: Knopf, 2005), 12.

17. Bill Ayers, *Fugitive Days* (Boston: Beacon Press, 2001), 121.

18. Che Guevara, *Guerrilla Warfare* (Lincoln: University of Nebraska Press, 1998), 4.

19. For Ayers's own description, see *Fugitive Days.* See also Kirkpatrick Sale, *SDS* (New York: Random House, 1973), 606.

20. Ayers, *Fugitive Days,* 169.

21. Jeremy Varon, *Bringing the War Home* (Berkeley and Los Angeles: University of California Press, 2004), 82.

22. Ayers, *Fugitive Days,* 177.

23. The Madison bombing took place on August 24, 1970. Karl Amstrong, who served seven years for the act, was a young activist who had been radicalized in the campus protests against the Dow Chemical corporation the year before.

24. Cathy Wilkerson, *Flying Close to the Sun* (New York: Seven Stories Press, 2007).

25. Ibid., 341.

26. Ibid., 343.

27. Ayers, *Fugitive Days,* 275.

28. Ibid., 227.

29. Jonathan Neale, *A People's History of the Vietnam War* (New York: Verso Books, 2001), 169.

30. Wilkerson, *Flying Close to the Sun,* 376.

31. Kevin Gillies, "The Last Radical," *Vancouver* (November 1998).

32. But not all did. Kathy Boudin was captured as an accomplice, a passenger, in a Brinks robbery that unexpectedly resulted in two police fatalities in 1981; she acknowledged responsibility, sought clemency, and served twenty-two years in prison before being paroled in 2004, a legal victory for her attorney, Leonard Weinglass. Her driving partner and lover, David Gilbert, adopted an unrepentant stance in court, leading to a life sentence that he still serves. Gilbert has written of "our sickening and inexcusable glorification of violence" in the 1969–1970 period and regularly visits with his son, Chesa. David Gilbert, *SDS/WUO: Students for a Democratic Society and the Weather Underground* (Oakland, CA: AK Press, 2002).

33. Varon, *Bringing the War Home,* 257, 359. Two FBI officials, Patrick Gray and Mark Felt, were convicted but ultimately pardoned by President Ronald Reagan.

34. *New York Times,* September 11, 2001.

35. In an April 6, 2008, blog, Bill tried to explain himself this way: "Life brings misgivings, doubts, uncertainty, loss, regret. I'm sometimes asked if I regret anything I did to oppose the war in Viet Nam, and I say 'no, I don't regret anything I did to try to stop the slaughter of millions of human beings by my own government.' Sometimes I add, 'I don't think I did enough.' This is then elided: he has "no regrets for setting bombs and thinks there should be more bombings."

NOTES TO CHAPTER SIXTEEN

1. Marshall L. Michel III, *The 11 Days of Christmas* (San Francisco: Encounter Books, 2002), 46, 239.

2. Dr. Stein Tonnesson, "A Successful State with Regional Security: The Case of 'the Vietnam Peace,'1989–2006," paper commissioned by the United Nations Development Programme, December 2006. Tonnesson is the Oslo-based director of the International Peace Research Institute.

3. Robert Templer, *Shadows and Wind: A View of Modern Vietnam* (New York: Penguin, 1999), 354.

4. Ibid., 326–327.

5. Bao Ninh, *The Sorrow of War: A Novel of North Vietnam* (New York: Pantheon, 1995).

6. Ibid., 193.

NOTES TO CHAPTER SEVENTEEN

1. Gerry Adams, *Before the Dawn: An Autobiography* (New York: Morrow, 1996), 93.

2. Tim Pat Coogan, *The Troubles: Ireland's Ordeal 1966–95 and the Search for Peace* (London: Hutchinson, 1995), 113.

3. Bob Purdie, *Politics in the Street: The Origins of the Civil Rights Movement in Northern Ireland* (Belfast, NIR: Blackstaff, 1990), 2.

4. Roddy Doyle, *The Commitments* (London: Minerva, 1988), 9.

5. In 1971, the university admitted only married African Americans and then only in tiny numbers. The university ended a ban on interracial dating in 2000, the same year George Bush campaigned in the South Carolina presidential primary. A Bob Jones faculty member that year spread the false rumor that another candidate, John McCain, had a black child out of wedlock. As of 2009, students are prohibited from listening to jazz, new age, rock, country music, or "contemporary" Christian music and from attending movies above a G-rating. They may use e-mail only through the school. Rooms are inspected daily (bju/prospective/expect/rhall.html).

6. Adams, *Before the Dawn,* 143; emphasis added.

7. Tom Herron and John Lynch, *After Bloody Sunday* (Cork, Ireland: Cork University Press, 2007).

8. From handwritten notes on an official memorandum of Lord Chief Justice Widgery, in Don Mullen, ed., *Eyewitness Bloody Sunday* (Dublin: Wolfhound Press, 1997), 63.

9. Prime Minister Edward Heath, February 1, 1972, confidential Downing Street minutes, in ibid., 43.

10. Herron and Lynch, *After Bloody Sunday,* 2. For an objective description of each of the thirty-six hundred deaths, see David McKittrick, Seamus Kelters, Brian Feeney, and Chris Thornton, *Lost Lives: The Stories of the Men and Women Who Died as a Result of the Troubles* (Edinburgh: Mainstream, 1999).

11. Peter Taylor, *Provos: The IRA and Sinn Fein* (London: Bloomsbury, 1997), 327.

12. BBC, March 4, 2001.

13. "Intelligence Quotas: Effect of Ceasefire in Northern Ireland on British Intelligence Service," *New Statesman,* October 7, 1994.

14. It is noteworthy that secret intelligence agencies, previously engaged in secret collaboration with Loyalist assassination teams, would continue their operations despite the shift to a peaceful political context. Ibid.; emphasis added.

15. The others were Michael Gaughan, Frank Stagg, Francis Hughes, Patsy O'Hara, Raymond McCreesh, Joe McDonnell, Martin Hurson, Kevin Lynch, Kieran Doherty, Thomas McElwee, and Mickey Define.

16. In 1986, the decision by Sinn Fein to end its policy of abstentionism (with regard to the north) was 429–161, only 11 votes over the required two-thirds, for example. A later split occurred, in 1996, over continuing armed struggle. The result was a disastrous bombing at Omagh, which the Adams leadership denounced. See Gerard Murray and Jonathan Tonge, *Sinn Fein and the SDLP: From Alienation to Participation* (Dublin: O'Brien, 2005), 161.

17. Clinton recalls how his roots in the civil rights crisis affected his perception of Northern

Ireland while at Oxford. He told Conor O'Clery that he "never dreamed when it all started and I was a young man living in England and just fascinated by it and heartbroken by it, that I'd ever have a chance to do something about it." He remembered following Bernadette Devlin around and reading everything about her, too. The account is in Conor O'Clery, *The Greening of the White House* (Dublin: Gill and Macmillan, 1996), 16–17.

18. Tom Hayden, *Irish on the Inside* (London: Verso Books, 1997).
19. Taylor, *Provos*, 316, 318.
20. Ibid., 315. Brooke came from a longtime Unionist family with roots in Ireland going back two centuries. One of his ancestors was the poet Charlotte Brooke, who first used the epithet "fenian" to disparage republicans.
21. Ibid., 318.
22. "Marches in Derry," a memo by Lt. Col. Harry Dalzell-Payne, January 27, 1972, three days before Bloody Sunday.
23. Taylor, *Provos*, 354.
24. Michael Oatley, *Sunday Times*, October 31, 1999.
25. Murray and Tonge, *Sinn Fein*, 209–210.
26. *NY Times*, March 8, 2009.

NOTES TO CHAPTER EIGHTEEN

1. For several decades I have been uncomfortable with the usual choices of "riot" and "rebellion" in describing these events. Labeling hundreds of similar and repeated spontaneous upheavals as "riots" turns their logic into an incomprehensible blur, which suits the advocates of law enforcement repression. However, the label "rebellion" for such brief upheavals implies more leadership, organization, and demands than existed in such profoundly spontaneous explosions. Taken together in that five-year period, one could say, they represented a prolonged pattern of rage on the part of the oppressed. In *Rebellion in Newark: Official Violence and Ghetto Response* (New York: Vintage, 1967), I wrote that the riot was an "awkward" form of history-making by people lacking other means.
2. SWAT stands for Special Weapons and Tactics. Chief Darryl Gates originally wished to name them Special Weapons Attack Teams, but the acronym was changed. CRASH means Community Resources Against Street Hoodlums. Originally the forty-four-member street team was named TRASH, or Total Resources Against Street Hoodlums.
3. U.S. Riot Commission, *Report of the National Advisory Commission on Civil Disorders* (New York: Dutton, 1968), 24.
4. Ibid., 16.
5. According to city officials, Newark had the nation's largest percentage of substandard housing, the most crime, the heaviest per capita tax burden, and the highest rates of venereal disease, maternal mortality, and new cases of tuberculosis. Hayden, *Rebellion in Newark*, 5.
6. Cover of July 28, 1967, issue of *Life*: "Newark: The Predictable Insurrection—Shooting War in the Streets."
7. Hayden, *Rebellion in Newark*, 71.
8. Ibid.
9. For the 1971 Attica prison riot, see Tom Wicker, *A Time to Die* (New York: Crown, 1975); and http://www.history.com/this-day-in-history.do?action=article&id=5342. For San Quentin, see Bettina Aptheker, *The Morning Breaks: The Trial of Angela Davis* (Ithaca, NY: Cornell University Press, 1976). See also George Jackson, *Blood in My Eye* (New York: Random House, 1972).
10. Louis Yablonsky, *Gangsters: Fifty Years of Madness, Drugs, and Death on the Streets of America* (New York: New York University Press, 1997), 29.
11. James Diego Vigil, *A Rainbow of Gangs: Street Cultures in the Mega-city* (Austin: University of Texas Press, 2002), 75.
12. Luis Rodriguez, *Always Running: La Vida Loca: Gang Days in LA* (New York: Touchstone Press, 1993), 154.
13. See Mike Royko, *Boss* (New York: Dutton, 1972): "Daley had seen the same thing happen before. He recalled Regan's Colts, the Irish thieves and street fighters who became the most potent political force in neighboring Canaryville, and his own neighborhood's Hamburgs, who got their start in the same brawling way before *turning to politics and eventually launching his career*" (206–207; emphasis added).
14. John Hagedorn, personal correspondence.
15. Report by the Special Advisor to the Board of Police Commissioners on the Civil Disorder in Los Angeles, October 21, 1992, 23.

16. *LA Times,* December 31, 1999.

17. *LA Times,* December 6, 2002.

18. *LA Times,* January 26, 1998.

19. LA County Sheriff's Department data, 2003.

20. Violence Prevention Coalition of Greater Los Angeles, based on sheriff's data, September 13, 1996.

21. The percentage was provided to me by the head of the California Department of Corrections.

22. Anthony Platt, "Social Insecurity: The Transformation of American Criminal Justice," *Social Science Journal* 28, no. 1 (2001). Adam Liptak, "Inmate Count in US Dwarfs Other Nations'," *NY Times,* April 23, 2008.

23. *LA Times,* October 18, 1998.

24. J. H. Mollenkopf and M. Castells, *Dual City: Restructuring New York* (New York: Russell Sage Foundation, 1991). Job losses cited in Ric Curtis, "The Negligible Role of Gangs in Drug Distribution in New York City in the 1990s" (New York: John Jay School of Criminal Justice, 1992). For Atlanta, see Atlanta *Journal Constitution,* April 9, 2000, and *Journal Constitution,* April 29, 1991.

25. Walter Miller, Office of Juvenile Justice and Delinquency Prevention, *The Growth of Youth Gang Problems in the United States, 1970–1998* (Washington, DC: U.S. Department of Justice, April 2001).

26. Ibid., 44; emphasis added.

27. Ibid.

28. James Q. Wilson, *Thinking about Crime* (New York: Vintage, 1975), xv.

29. James Q. Wilson, *The Moral Sense* (New York: Free Press, 1993), 10.

30. William Bennett, John Dilulio, and John P. Walters, *Body Count: Moral Poverty and How to Win America's War against Crime and Drugs* (New York: Simon and Schuster, 1996), 26.

31. *Weekly Standard,* November 27, 1995.

32. *LA Times,* July 23, 1996.

33. "Head of Religion-Based Initiative Resigns," *NY Times,* August 18, 2001.

34. Bennett et al., *Body Count,* jacket statement.

35. Cited in Andrew Karmen, *New York Murder Mystery: The True Story behind the Crime Crash of the 1990s* (New York: New York University Press, 2000), 194.

36. Robert Kaplan, *Warrior Politics* (New York: Random House, 2002), 119, 136.

37. Ibid., 121; emphasis added.

38. James Moore and Wade Slater, *Bush's Brain: How Karl Rove Made George Bush President* (New York: Wiley, 2003), 202.

39. Ibid., 202.

40. The finest book on this crisis is James Gilligan, *Preventing Violence* (New York: Thames and Hudson, 2001), 24.

41. *Atlantic Monthly* (July–August 2005): 118.

42. Private communication from advocates who met with Holder in 2009.

43. Cited in Frederick Thrasher, *The Gang* (Chicago: University of Chicago Press, 1927), 342.

44. Ibid., 356.

45. Ibid., 350.

NOTES TO CHAPTER NINETEEN

1. Ignazio Silone, *Bread and Wine* (New York: Signet, 1962), 88.

2. Karl Marx and Friedrich Engels, *The Communist Manifesto* (New York: Penguin, 2002), 223.

3. Albert Camus, *The Plague* (New York: Knopf, 1988), 229.

4. Christian Smith, *The Emergence of Liberation Theology: Radical Religion and Social Movement Theory* (Chicago: University of Chicago Press, 1991).

5. Ibid., 5. See also Harvey Cox, *The Silencing of Leonardo Boff: The Vatican and the Future of World Christianity* (London: Collins, 1989).

6. Smith, *The Emergence of Liberation Theology,* 26.

7. Ibid.

8. Peggy Lernoux, *People of God: The Struggle for World Catholicism* (New York: Viking, 1989), 466.

9. Smith, *The Emergence of Liberation Theology*, 20.

10. Ibid., 18.

11. Ibid., 19.

12. Ibid. According to Michael Dodson, "The [Sandinistas] found the work of organizing people in the insurrection to be much easier in areas where [BECs] were firmly rooted. These institutions of religious inspiration were, in short, effective vehicles of grassroots political action in the revolutionary setting of popular insurrection" (227).

13. The ad hoc Santa Fe Committee was formed by conservatives at the beginning of the Reagan administration, and issued a document titled "A New Inter-American Policy for the Eighties." A number of its authors took positions in Reagan's state department and national security agencies. See Greg Grandin, *Empire's Workshop: Latin America, the United States and the New Imperialism* (New York: Metropolitan, 2007), 70–71.

14. Smith, *The Emergence of Liberation Theology*, 216.

15. Interview with K. D. Wolff, Heidelberg, 2005. Wolff, now a reputable artist and entrepreneur, was a leading student revolutionary at the time.

16. Sidney Blumenthal, Salon.com, April 2005.

17. *NY Times*, April 21, 2008.

NOTES TO CHAPTER TWENTY

1. Hana R. Alberts, Forbes.com, March 24, 2008.

2. Barack Obama, *Dreams from My Father: A Story of Race and Inheritance* (New York: Three Rivers Press, 1995), 282.

3. Interview, *Bill Moyers Journal*, April 25, 2008, http://www.pbs.org/moyers/journal/04252008/transcript1.html.

4. NPR, *All Things Considered*, March 18, 2008.

5. Cone's account of the dispute with the Latin American theologians appears in James Cone and Gayraud Wilmore, *Black Theology: A Documentary History*, vol. 2: *1980–92* (Maryknoll, NY: Orbis Books, 2003), 371–387.

6. James Cone, *Black Theology and Black Power* (June 2008): 55.

7. James Cone, *God of the Oppressed* (New York: Seabury Books, 1975), 184.

8. Luke 4:18–19.

9. John 3:8.

10. Isaiah 53:3.

11. James Cone, *The Spirituals and the Blues* (New York: Seabury Books, 2008), 7.

12. Obama, *Dreams from My Father*, 288.

13. Ibid., 294.

14. Harvey Cox, *The Silencing of Leonardo Boff: The Vatican and the Future of World Christianity* (London: Collins, 1989), 48. See also Leonardo Boff, *Church: Charisma and Power*.

15. Interview, *Bill Moyers Journal*, 2008.

16. Barack Obama, "A More Perfect Union," speech, March 18, 2008, Philadelphia, in David Olive, ed., *An American Story: The Speeches of Barack Obama* (Toronto: ECW Press, 2008), 262.

17. Ibid., 265.

NOTES TO CHAPTER TWENTY-ONE

1. Jeffrey Kripal, *Esalen, America, and the Religion of No Religion* (Chicago: University of Chicago Press, 2007).

2. I should know. I was the state of California's first chair of the SolarCal Council, an agency commissioned to advance a plan for the maximum feasible development of solar energy's potential.

3. "There was a big high wall there / that tried to stop me / sign painted black said private property / but on the back side it didn't say nothing / that side was made for you and me."

4. Martin Lee and Bruce Shlain, *Acid Dreams, a Complete Social History of LSD: The CIA, the Sixties, and Beyond* (New York: Grove, 1992), 79.

5. Aldous Huxley, *The Doors of Perception and Heaven and Hell* (New York: First Perennial Classics, 2004), 67.

6. Jack Kerouac, *The Dharma Bums* (New York: Penguin, 2006), with an introduction by Ann Douglas.

7. Ibid., 9.

8. Historian Robert Ellwood, cited in Douglas's introduction, ibid., 9.

9. Jason Shinder, *The Poem That Changed America: Howl, Fifty Years Later* (New York: Farrar, Straus, and Giroux, 2006), xxv.

10. Kerouac, *The Dharma Bums,* 128.

11. Ibid., 73–74.

12. See Jack Kerouac, "Beatific: The Origins of the Beat Generation," *Playboy* (June 1959).

13. Jack Kerouac, "Beatific: The Origins of the Beat Generation," in Ann Chalmers, ed., *The Portable Jack Kerouac* (New York: Viking, 1995), 563.

14. Ibid., 571.

15. Kerouac, "About the Beat Generation," in ibid., 559.

16. Kerouac, "After Me, the Deluge," in ibid., 576.

17. Ibid.

18. Gary Snyder, *Earth House Hold* (New York: New Directions, 1969), summarized in "Buddhism and the Possibilities of a Planetary Culture," in *The Gary Snyder Reader* (Washington, DC: Counterpoint, 1999), 41–43.

NOTES TO CHAPTER TWENTY-THREE

1. Barack Obama, "A More Perfect Union," speech, March 28, 2008, Philadelphia, in David Olive, ed., *An American Story: The Speeches of Barack Obama* (Toronto: ECW Press, 2008), 255.

2. "Civil Rights Battlefields Enter World of Tourism," *NY Times,* August 10, 2004.

3. On November 3, 1979, hundreds of civil rights and worker rights demonstrators held a permitted march in Greensboro. A carload of Klan members and Nazis, including an undercover member of the police department, opened fire, killing five and wounding ten others. Police arrested protesters trying to help the wounded. In subsequent 1980 state and 1984 federal trials, the assailants were found not guilty. In a third 1985 federal civil rights trial, they were found liable for the wrongful death of one individual, with $350,000 awarded to the victim's widow. Amy Goodman interview, November 18, 2004; Sally Bermanzohn, *Through Survivors' Eyes: From the Sixties to the Greensboro Massacre* (Nashville, TN: Vanderbilt University Press, 2003).

4. Murray's words conclude an extraordinary work of social movement history by Glenda Elizabeth Gilmore, *Defying Dixie: The Radical Roots of Civil Rights, 1919–1950* (New York: Norton, 2008), 444; emphasis added.

NOTES TO CHAPTER TWENTY-FOUR

1. New York's Robert Kennedy Jr., however, supported Hillary Clinton in the primaries.

NOTES TO CHAPTER TWENTY-FIVE

1. *NY Times Magazine,* November 11, 2007; emphasis added.

2. Daniel Ellsberg, *Secrets: A Memoir of Vietnam and the Pentagon Papers* (New York: Viking, 2002).

3. *The Nation,* April 6, 2009.

4. *NY Times,* November 25, 2008.

Index

About the Author

After fifty years of activism, politics, and writing, no one is more qualified to write about the sixties era and its legacy than Tom Hayden.

From his days as a founding member of the Students for a Democratic Society (SDS), freedom rider in the deep South, and prominent Vietnam War protester to today, Hayden remains a leading voice for reforming politics through greater citizen participation.

The author of seventeen books and the original Port Huron Statement—long considered the founding document of the sixties movement—he has more recently authored *Voices of the Chicago 8: A Generation on Trial* (2008) and *Writings for a Democratic Society: The Tom Hayden Reader* (2008). He continues to write for *The Nation* and many other magazines.